NABI

THE PROTOTYPE

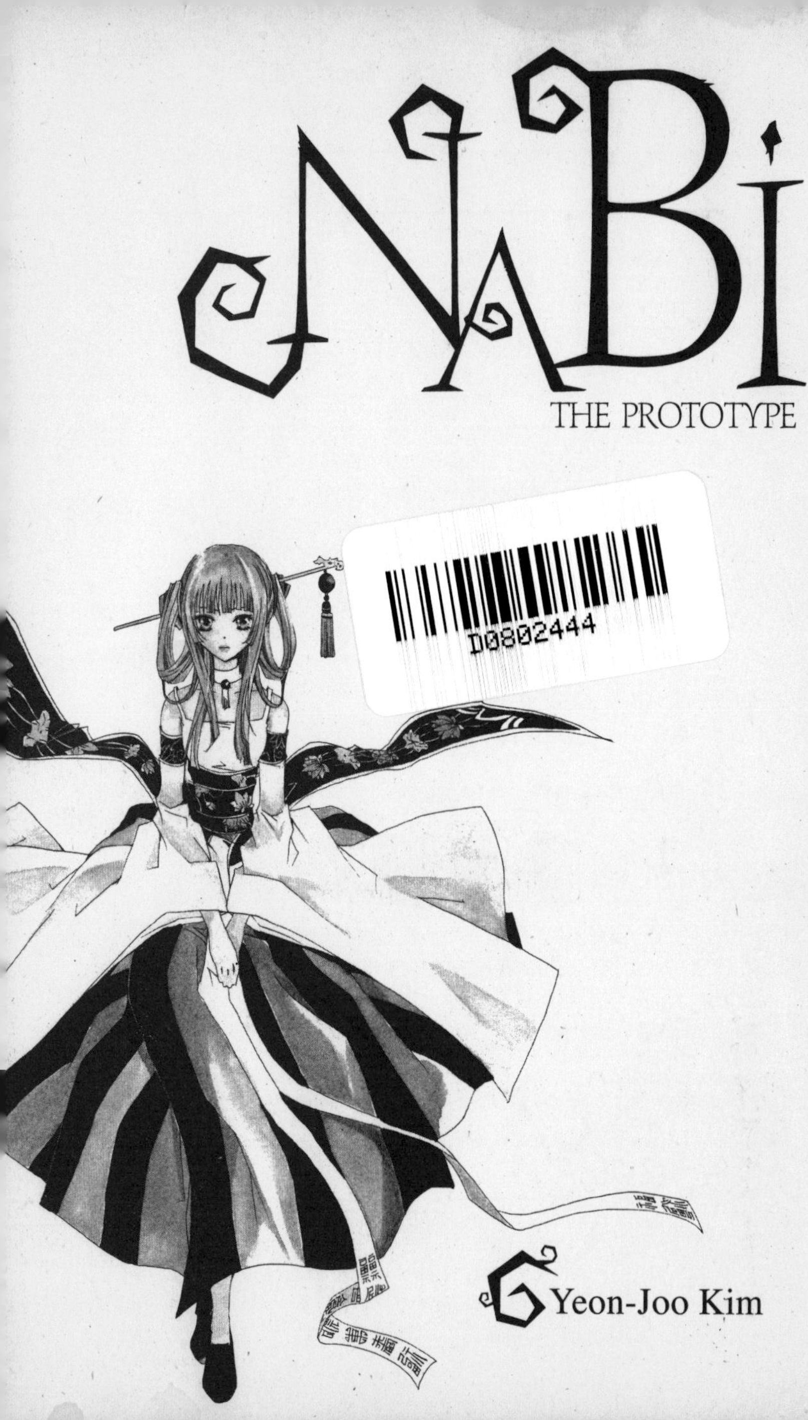

Yeon-Joo Kim

Nabi the Prototype
Created by Yeon-Joo Kim

Translation - Woo Sok Park
English Adaptation - Liz Forbes
Copy Editor - Sarah Mercurio
Retouch and Lettering - Star Print Brokers
Production Artist - Courtney Geter
Graphic Designer - Louis Csontos

Editor - Hyun Joo Kim
Digital Imaging Manager - Chris Buford
Pre-Production Supervisor - Erika Terriquez
Production Manager - Elisabeth Brizzi
Managing Editor - Vy Nguyen
Creative Director - Anne Marie Horne
Editor-in-Chief - Rob Tokar
Publisher - Mike Kiley
President and C.O.O. - John Parker
C.E.O. and Chief Creative Officer - Stuart Levy

A **TOKYOPOP** Manga

TOKYOPOP and ⊙ are trademarks or registered trademarks of TOKYOPOP Inc.

TOKYOPOP Inc.
5900 Wilshire Blvd. Suite 2000
Los Angeles, CA 90036

E-mail: info@TOKYOPOP.com
Come visit us online at www.TOKYOPOP.com

ISBN: 978-1-4278-0302-3

First TOKYOPOP printing: October 2007
10 9 8 7 6 5 4 3 2 1
Printed in the USA

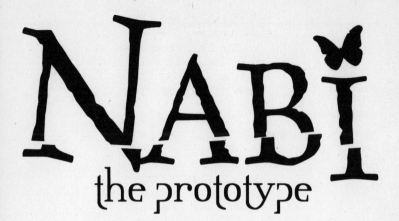

NABI
the prototype

BY
YEON-JOO KIM

HAMBURG // LONDON // LOS ANGELES // TOKYO

TABLE OF CONTENTS

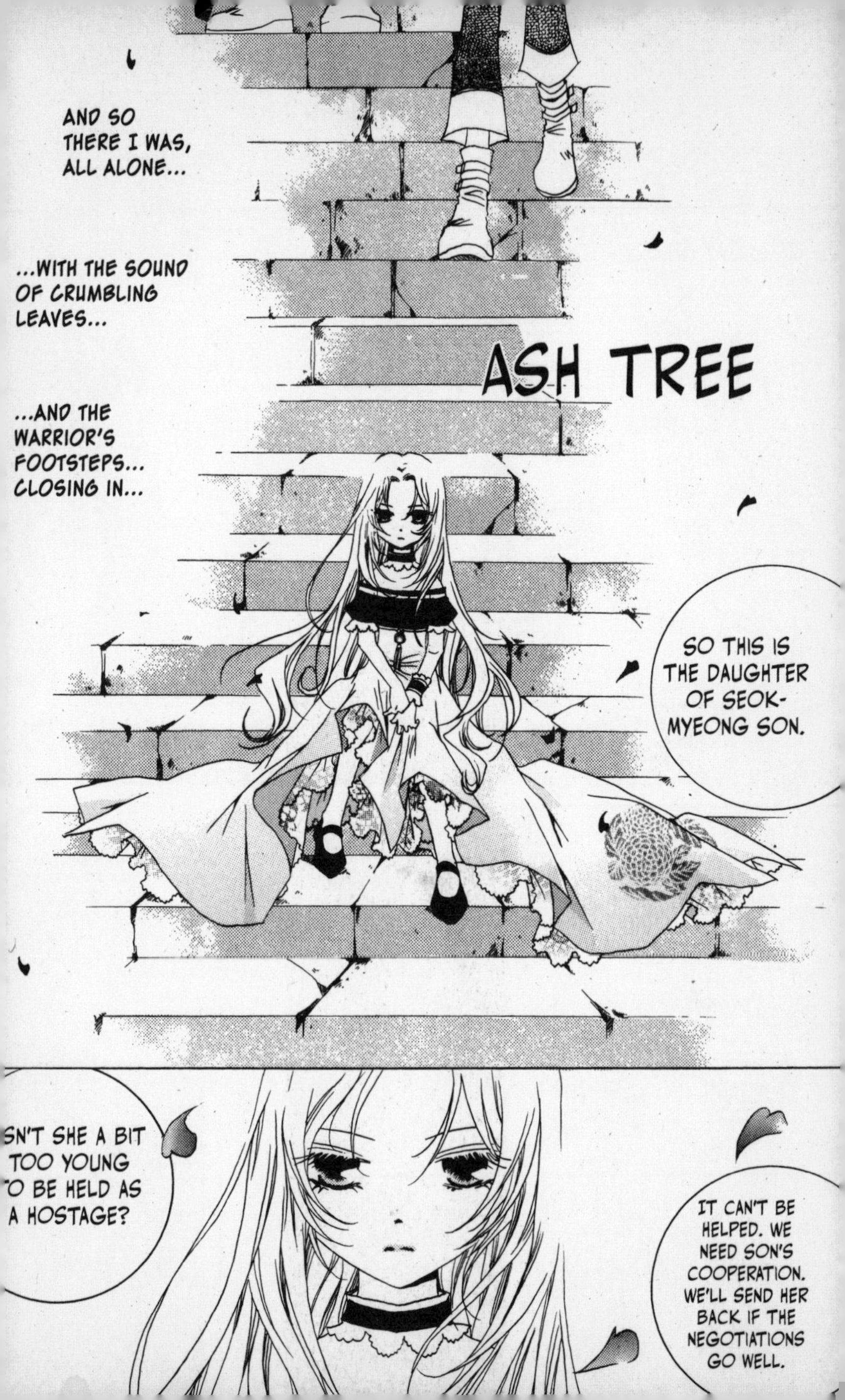
AND SO THERE I WAS, ALL ALONE...
...WITH THE SOUND OF CRUMBLING LEAVES...
...AND THE WARRIOR'S FOOTSTEPS... CLOSING IN...
ASH TREE
SO THIS IS THE DAUGHTER OF SEOK-MYEONG SON.
SN'T SHE A BIT TOO YOUNG O BE HELD AS A HOSTAGE?
IT CAN'T BE HELPED. WE NEED SON'S COOPERATION. WE'LL SEND HER BACK IF THE NEGOTIATIONS GO WELL.

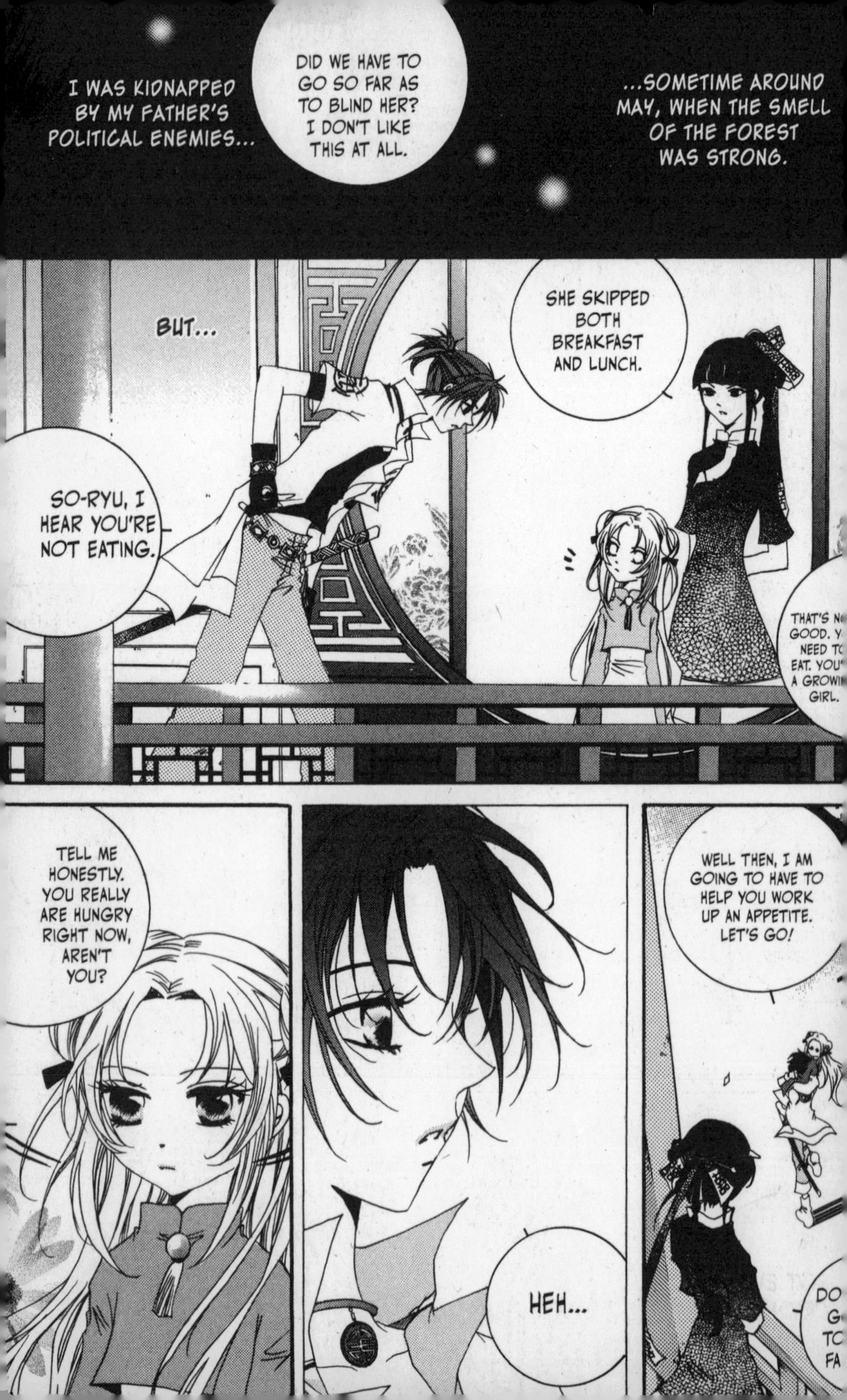
I WAS KIDNAPPED BY MY FATHER'S POLITICAL ENEMIES...
DID WE HAVE TO GO SO FAR AS TO BLIND HER? I DON'T LIKE THIS AT ALL.
...SOMETIME AROUND MAY, WHEN THE SMELL OF THE FOREST WAS STRONG.
BUT...
SO-RYU, I HEAR YOU'RE NOT EATING.
SHE SKIPPED BOTH BREAKFAST AND LUNCH.
THAT'S N GOOD. Y NEED TC EAT. YOU' A GROWI GIRL.
TELL ME HONESTLY. YOU REALLY ARE HUNGRY RIGHT NOW, AREN'T YOU?
HEH...
WELL THEN, I AM GOING TO HAVE TO HELP YOU WORK UP AN APPETITE. LET'S GO!
DO G TC FA

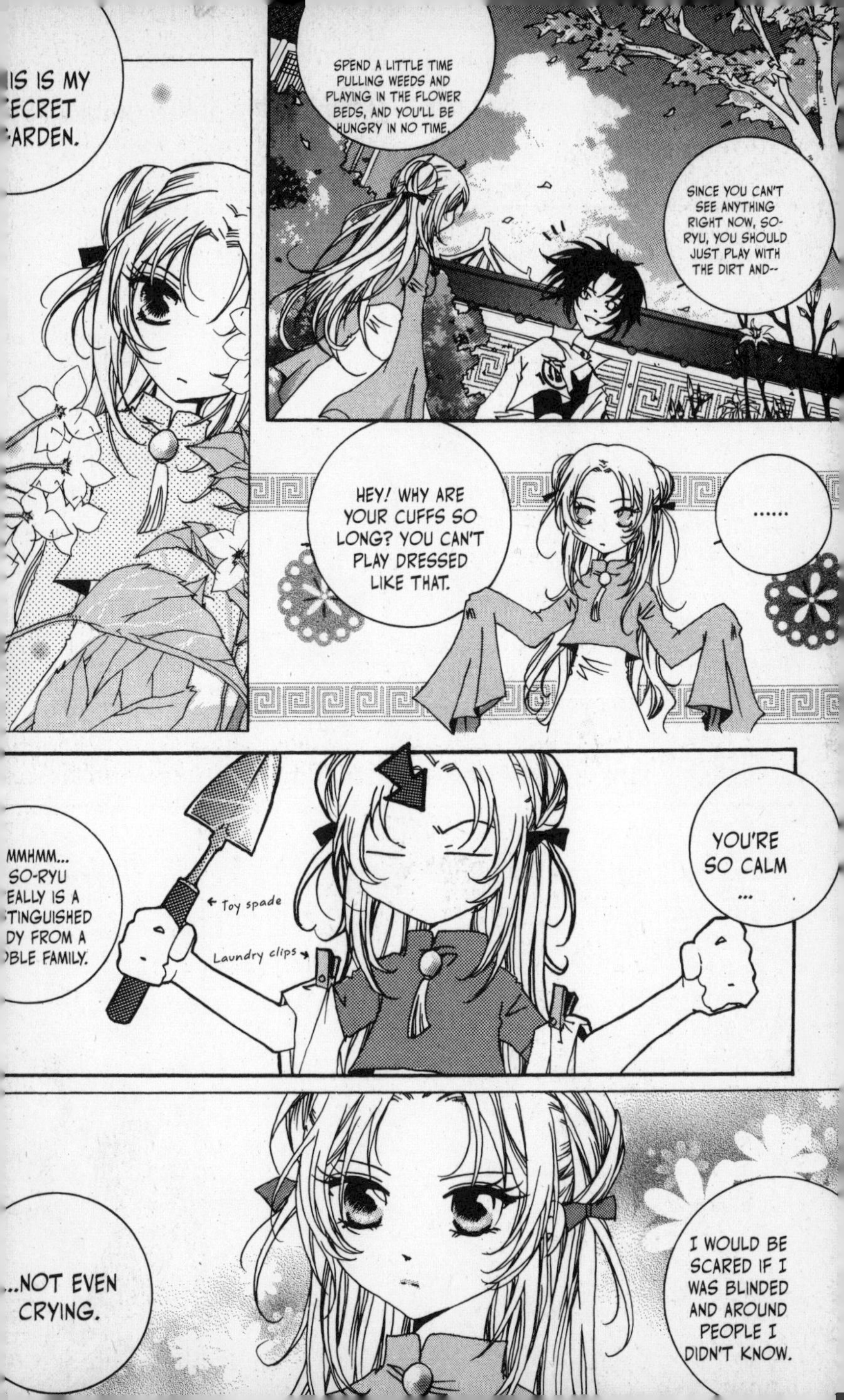
IS IS MY ECRET ARDEN.
SPEND A LITTLE TIME PULLING WEEDS AND PLAYING IN THE FLOWER BEDS, AND YOU'LL BE HUNGRY IN NO TIME.
SINCE YOU CAN'T SEE ANYTHING RIGHT NOW, SO-RYU, YOU SHOULD JUST PLAY WITH THE DIRT AND--
HEY! WHY ARE YOUR CUFFS SO LONG? YOU CAN'T PLAY DRESSED LIKE THAT.
......
MMHMM... SO-RYU EALLY IS A TINGUISHED DY FROM A OBLE FAMILY.
← Toy spade
Laundry clips →
YOU'RE SO CALM ...
...NOT EVEN CRYING.
I WOULD BE SCARED IF I WAS BLINDED AND AROUND PEOPLE I DIDN'T KNOW.

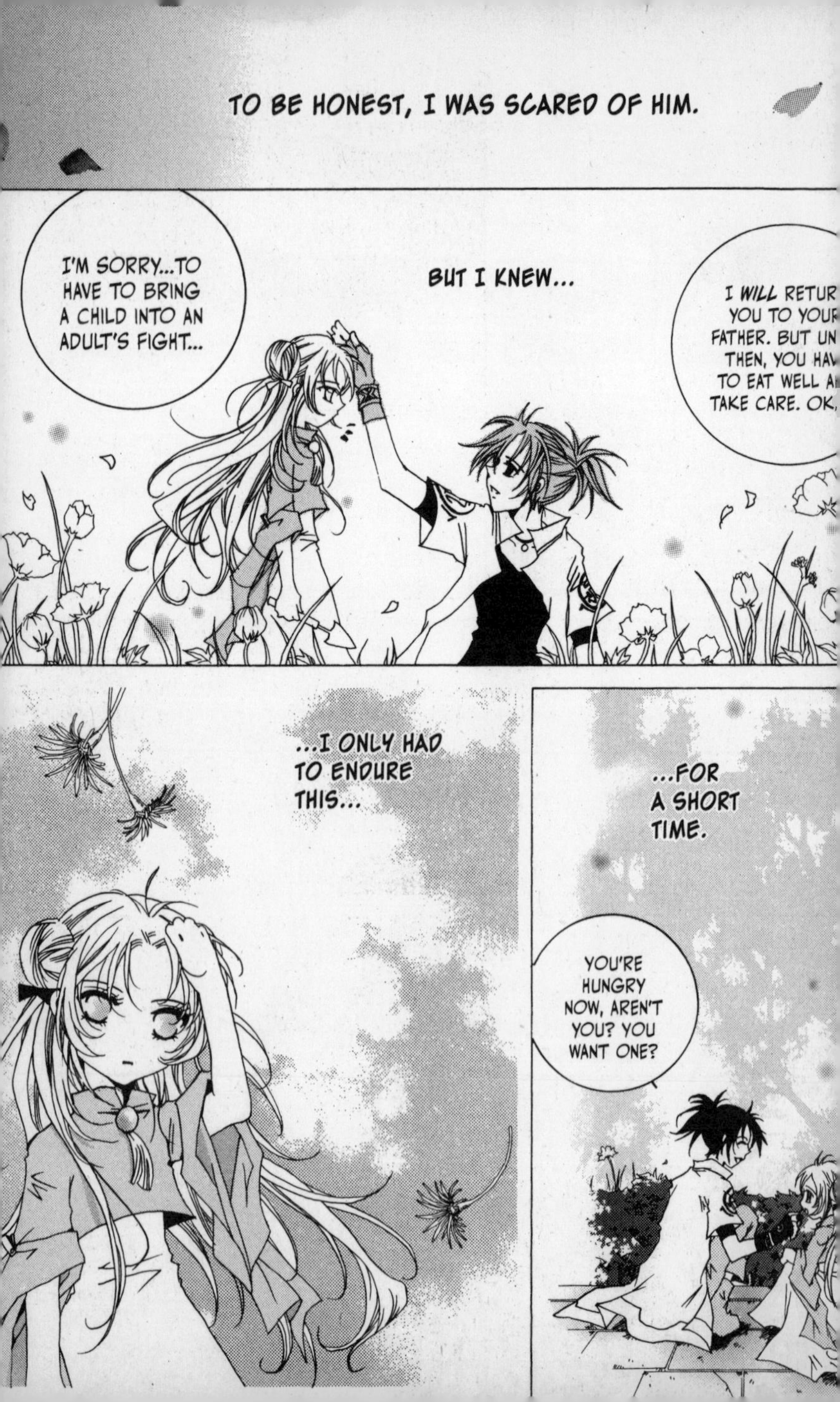
TO BE HONEST, I WAS SCARED OF HIM.
I'M SORRY...TO HAVE TO BRING A CHILD INTO AN ADULT'S FIGHT...
BUT I KNEW...
I *WILL* RETUR YOU TO YOUR FATHER. BUT UN THEN, YOU HAV TO EAT WELL A TAKE CARE. OK,
...I ONLY HAD TO ENDURE THIS...
...FOR A SHORT TIME.
YOU'RE HUNGRY NOW, AREN'T YOU? YOU WANT ONE?

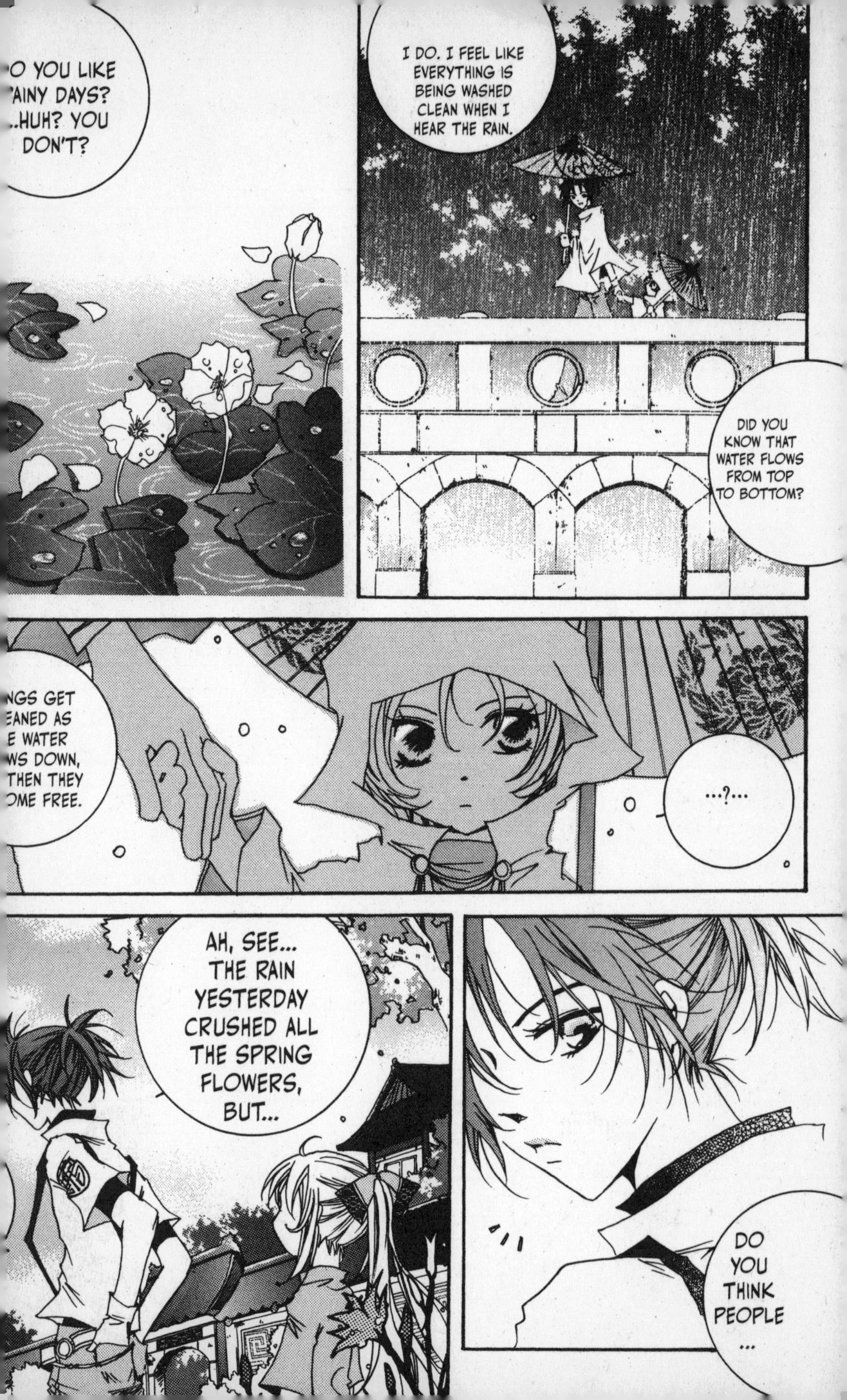
O YOU LIKE
AINY DAYS?
..HUH? YOU
DON'T?
I DO. I FEEL LIKE
EVERYTHING IS
BEING WASHED
CLEAN WHEN I
HEAR THE RAIN.
DID YOU
KNOW THAT
WATER FLOWS
FROM TOP
TO BOTTOM?
NGS GET
EANED AS
E WATER
WS DOWN,
THEN THEY
OME FREE.
...?...
AH, SEE...
THE RAIN
YESTERDAY
CRUSHED ALL
THE SPRING
FLOWERS,
BUT...
DO
YOU
THINK
PEOPLE
...

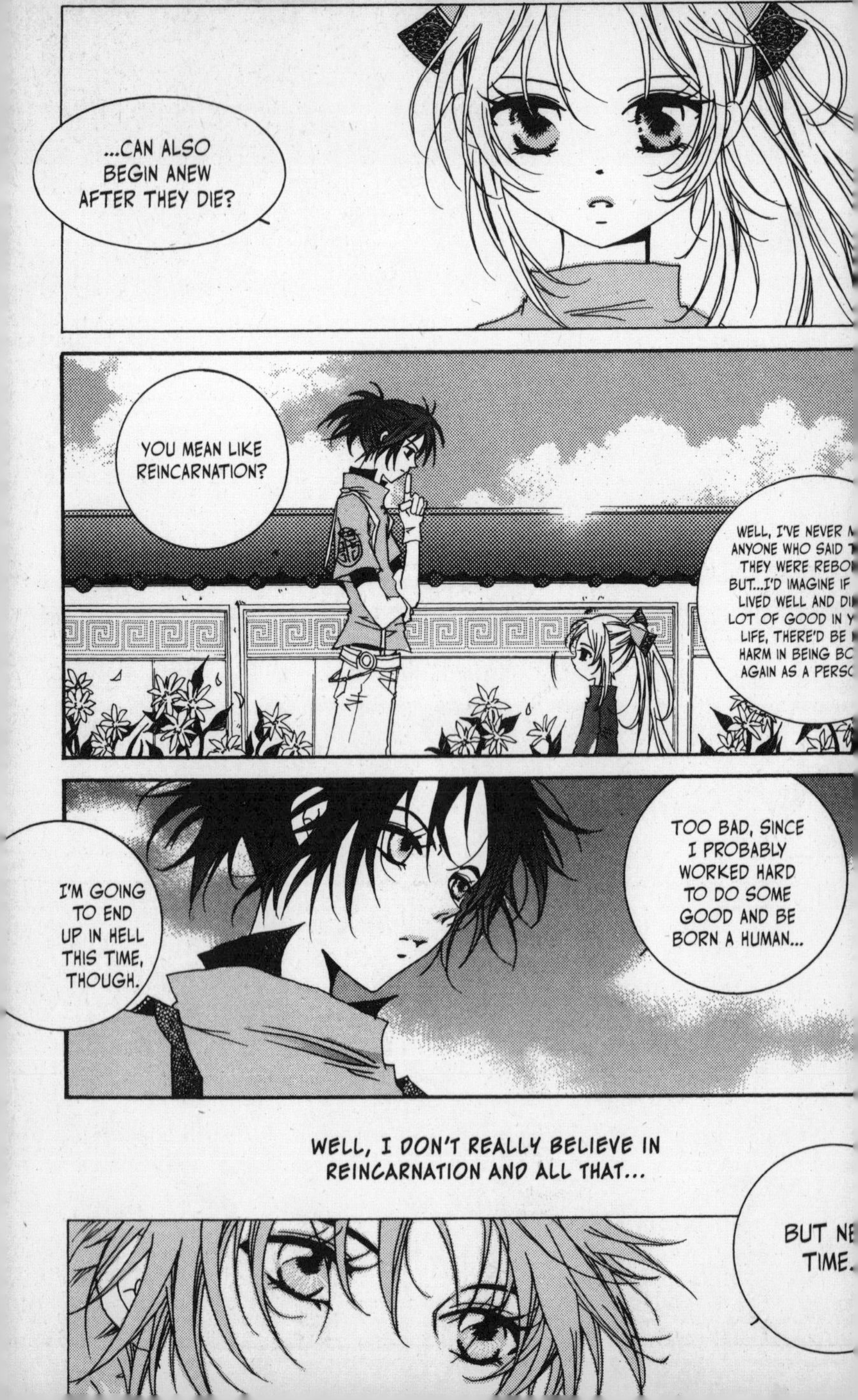
...CAN ALSO BEGIN ANEW AFTER THEY DIE?
YOU MEAN LIKE REINCARNATION?
WELL, I'VE NEVER M ANYONE WHO SAID T THEY WERE REBO BUT...I'D IMAGINE IF LIVED WELL AND DI LOT OF GOOD IN Y LIFE, THERE'D BE HARM IN BEING BO AGAIN AS A PERSO
I'M GOING TO END UP IN HELL THIS TIME, THOUGH.
TOO BAD, SINCE I PROBABLY WORKED HARD TO DO SOME GOOD AND BE BORN A HUMAN...
WELL, I DON'T REALLY BELIEVE IN REINCARNATION AND ALL THAT...
BUT NE TIME.

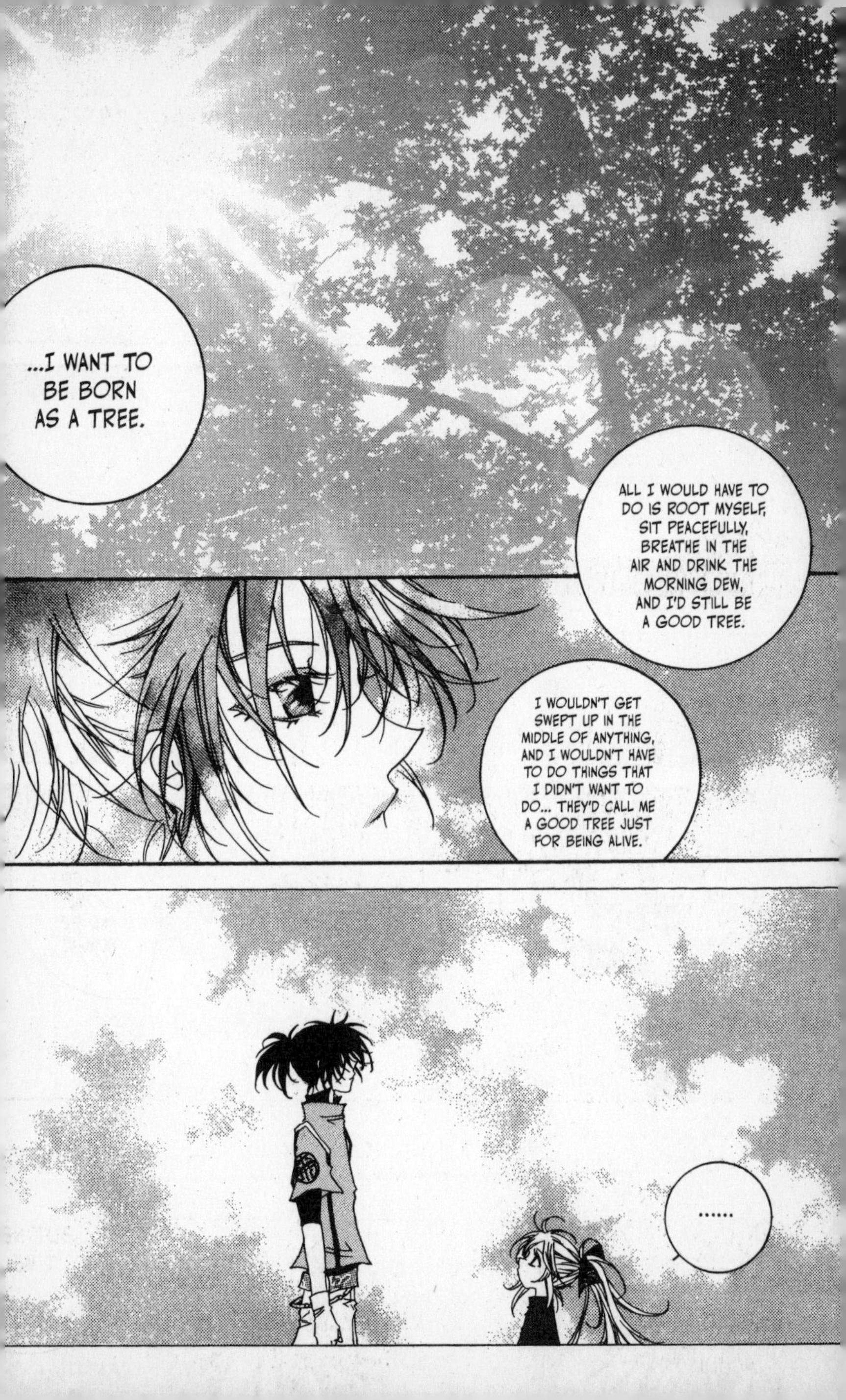
...I WANT TO BE BORN AS A TREE.
ALL I WOULD HAVE TO DO IS ROOT MYSELF, SIT PEACEFULLY, BREATHE IN THE AIR AND DRINK THE MORNING DEW, AND I'D STILL BE A GOOD TREE.
I WOULDN'T GET SWEPT UP IN THE MIDDLE OF ANYTHING, AND I WOULDN'T HAVE TO DO THINGS THAT I DIDN'T WANT TO DO... THEY'D CALL ME A GOOD TREE JUST FOR BEING ALIVE.
......

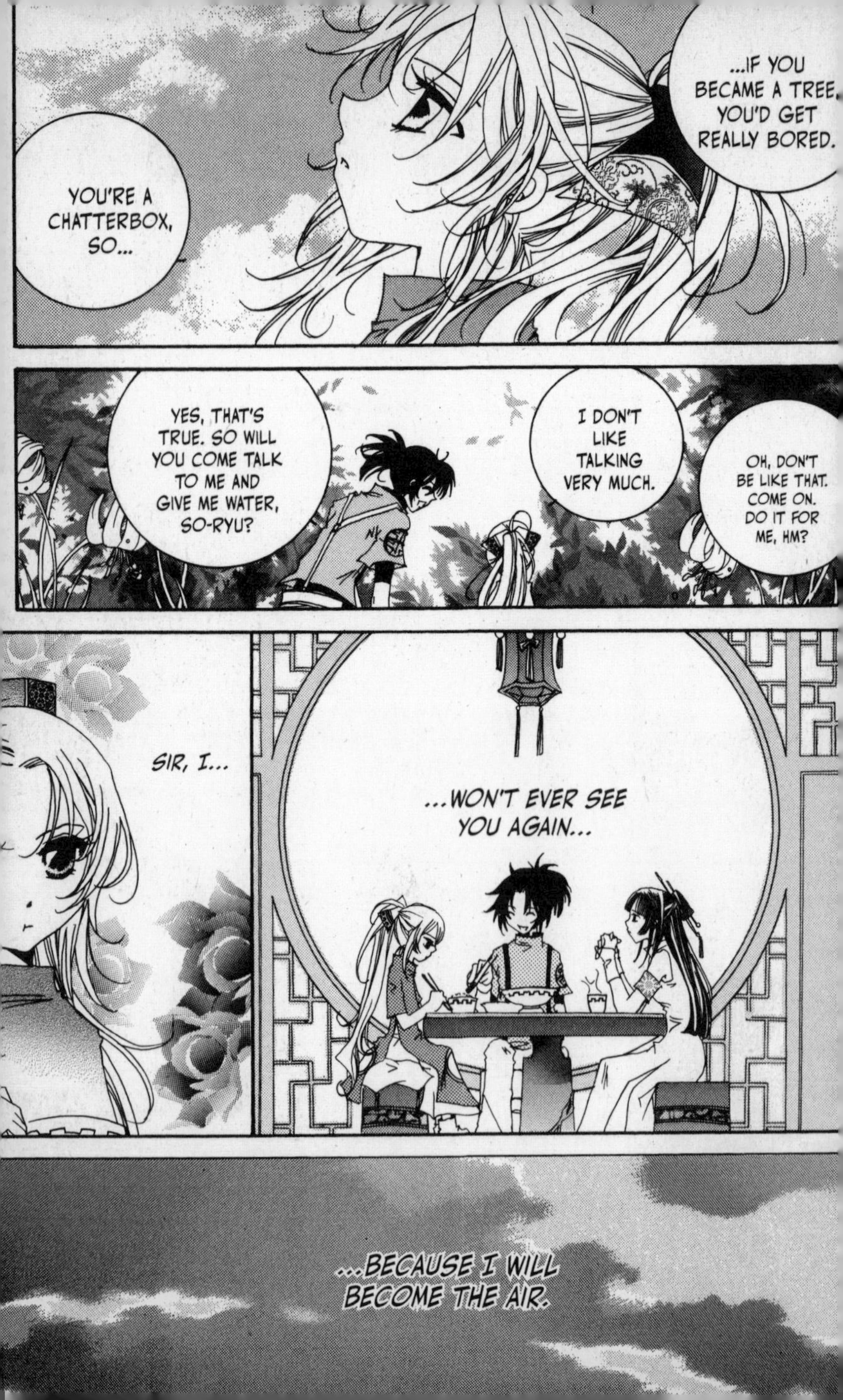
YOU'RE A CHATTERBOX, SO...
...IF YOU BECAME A TREE, YOU'D GET REALLY BORED.
YES, THAT'S TRUE. SO WILL YOU COME TALK TO ME AND GIVE ME WATER, SO-RYU?
I DON'T LIKE TALKING VERY MUCH.
OH, DON'T BE LIKE THAT. COME ON. DO IT FOR ME, HM?
SIR, I...
...WON'T EVER SEE YOU AGAIN...
...BECAUSE I WILL BECOME THE AIR.

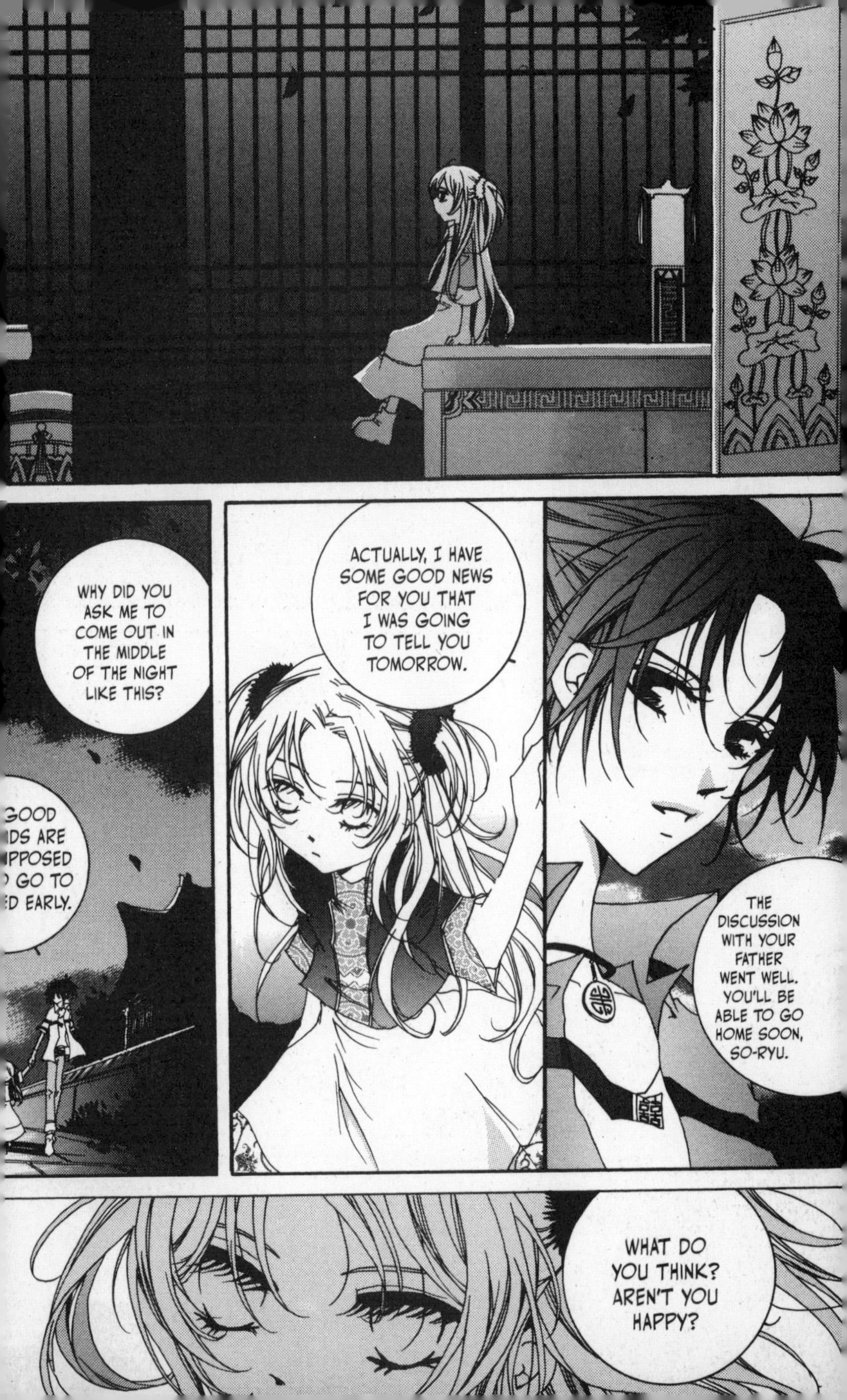
WHY DID YOU ASK ME TO COME OUT IN THE MIDDLE OF THE NIGHT LIKE THIS?
GOOD DS ARE PPOSED GO TO D EARLY.
ACTUALLY, I HAVE SOME GOOD NEWS FOR YOU THAT I WAS GOING TO TELL YOU TOMORROW.
THE DISCUSSION WITH YOUR FATHER WENT WELL. YOU'LL BE ABLE TO GO HOME SOON, SO-RYU.
WHAT DO YOU THINK? AREN'T YOU HAPPY?

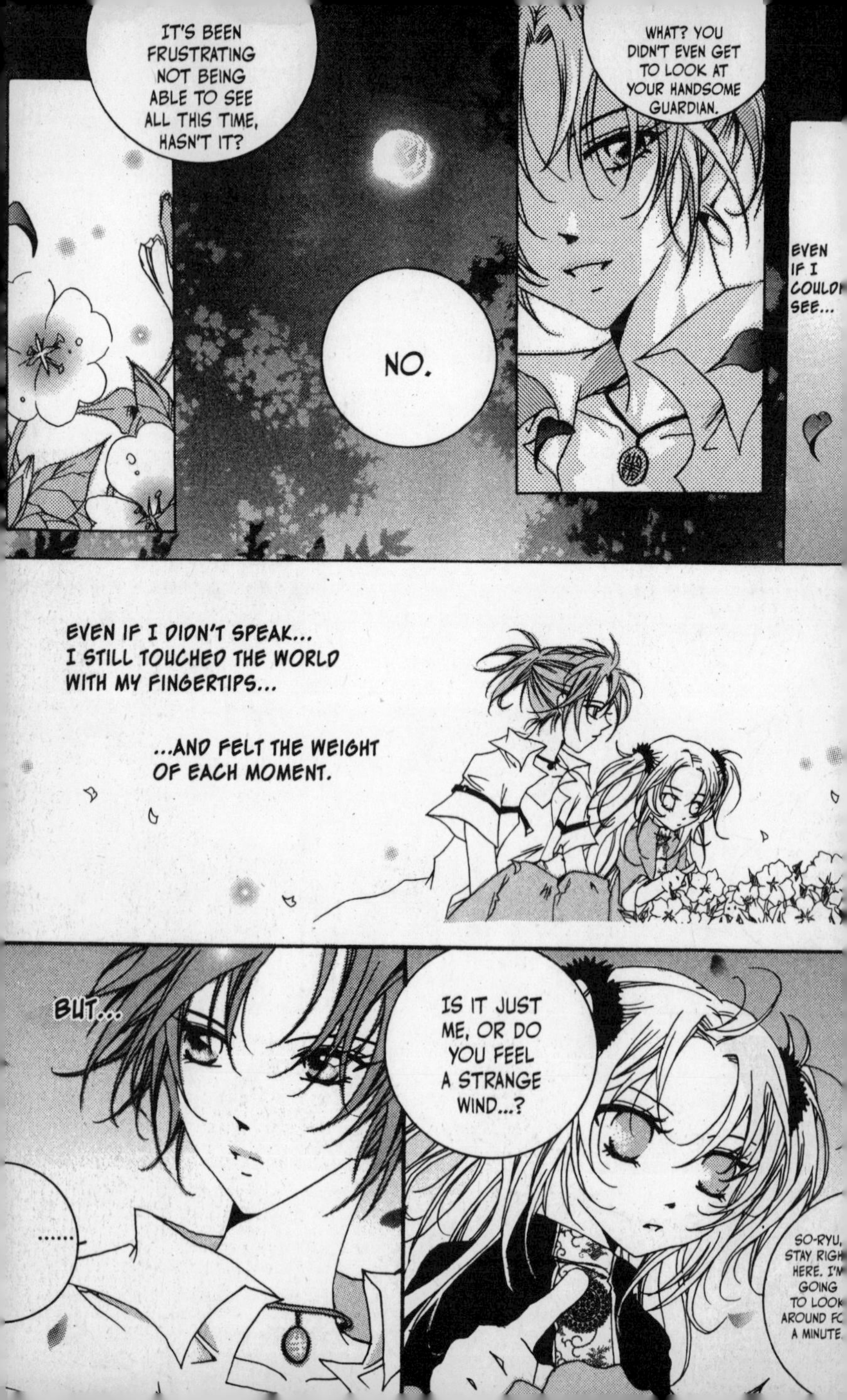
IT'S BEEN FRUSTRATING NOT BEING ABLE TO SEE ALL THIS TIME, HASN'T IT?
NO.
WHAT? YOU DIDN'T EVEN GET TO LOOK AT YOUR HANDSOME GUARDIAN.
EVEN IF I COULD SEE...
EVEN IF I DIDN'T SPEAK... I STILL TOUCHED THE WORLD WITH MY FINGERTIPS...
...AND FELT THE WEIGHT OF EACH MOMENT.
BUT...
......
IS IT JUST ME, OR DO YOU FEEL A STRANGE WIND...?
SO-RYU, STAY RIGH HERE. I'M GOING TO LOOK AROUND FO A MINUTE.

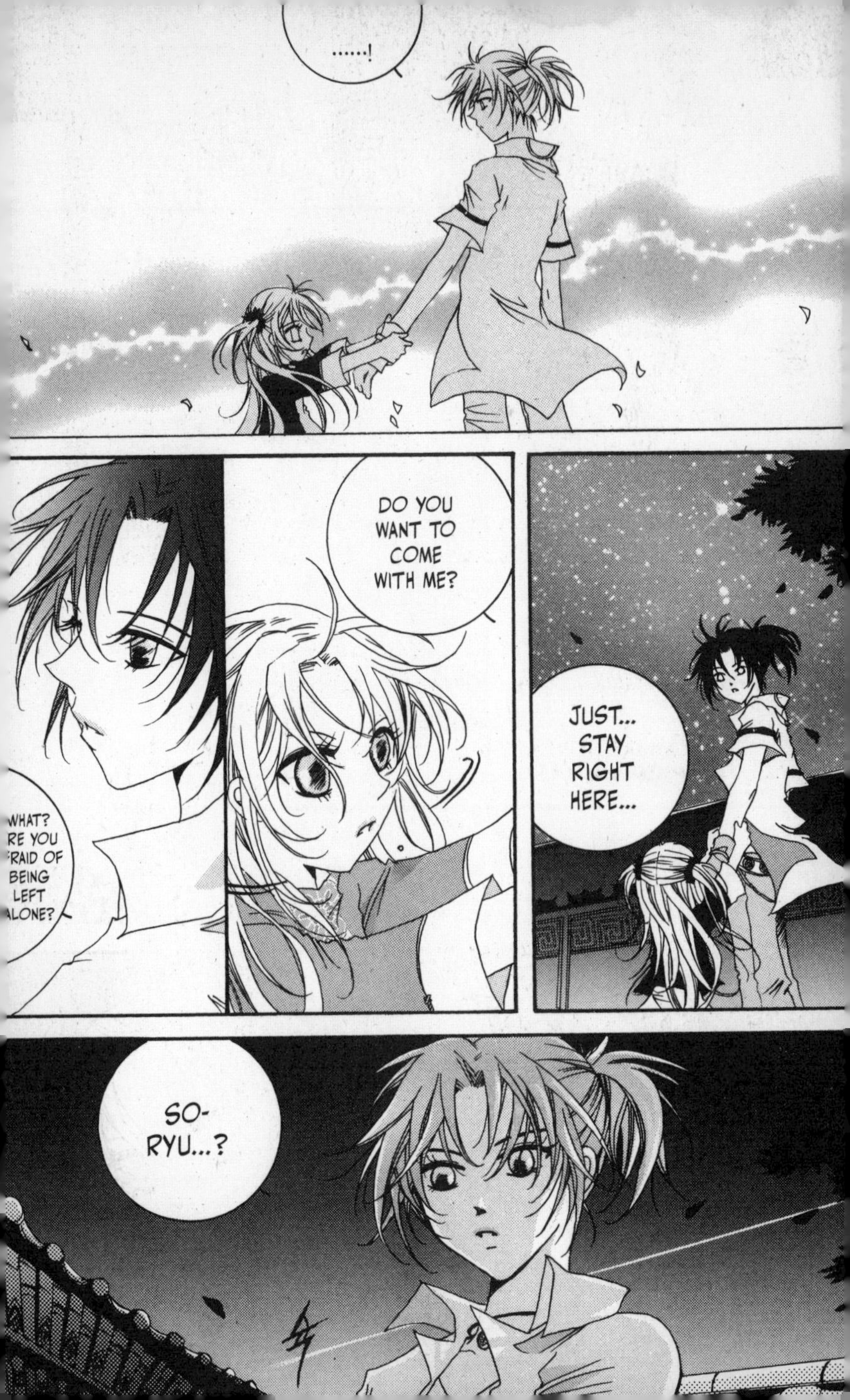
......!
WHAT? ARE YOU AFRAID OF BEING LEFT ALONE?
DO YOU WANT TO COME WITH ME?
JUST... STAY RIGHT HERE...
SO-RYU...?

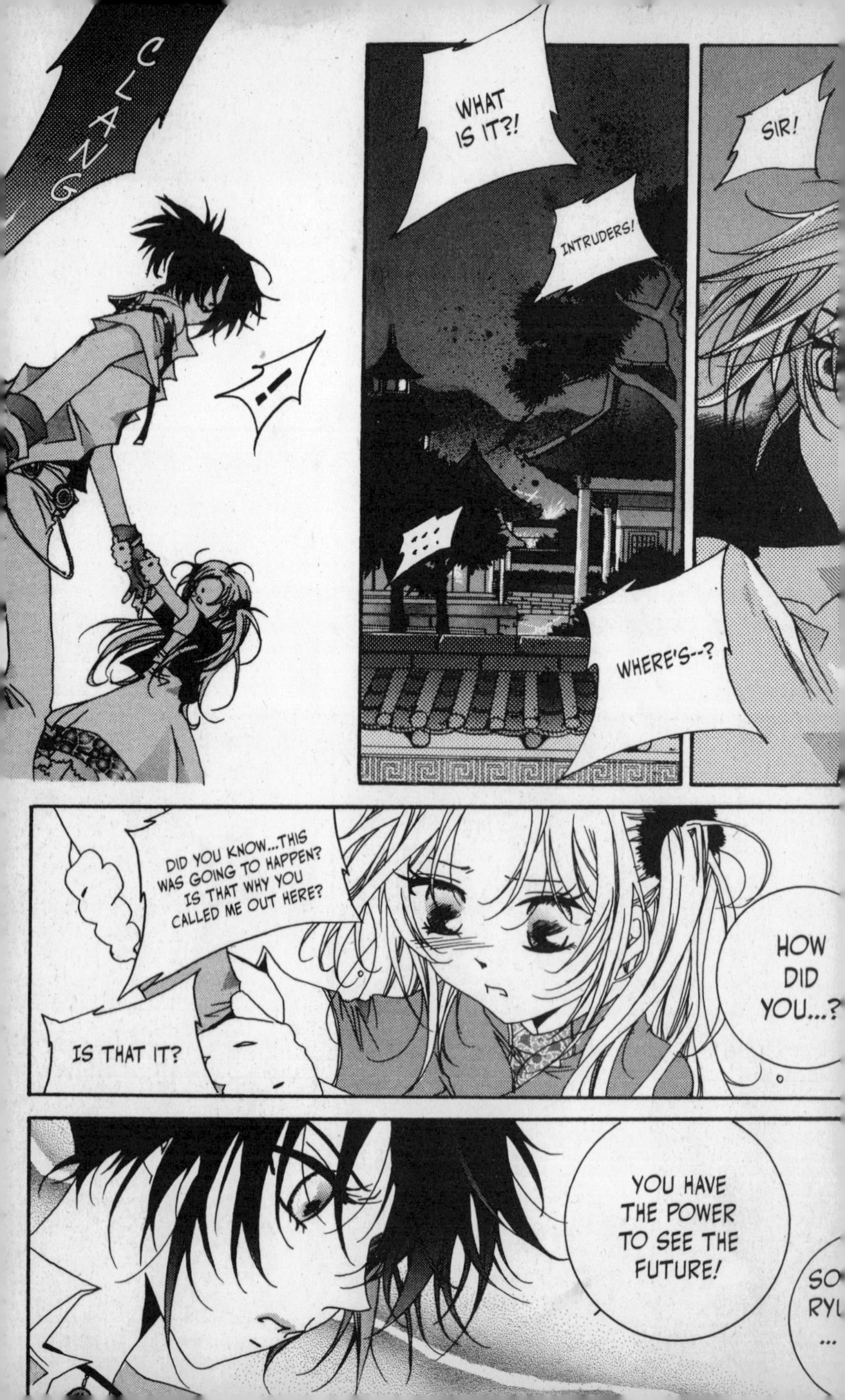
CLANG
..!
WHAT IS IT?!
INTRUDERS!
SIR!
WHERE'S--?
DID YOU KNOW...THIS WAS GOING TO HAPPEN? IS THAT WHY YOU CALLED ME OUT HERE?
IS THAT IT?
HOW DID YOU...?
YOU HAVE THE POWER TO SEE THE FUTURE!

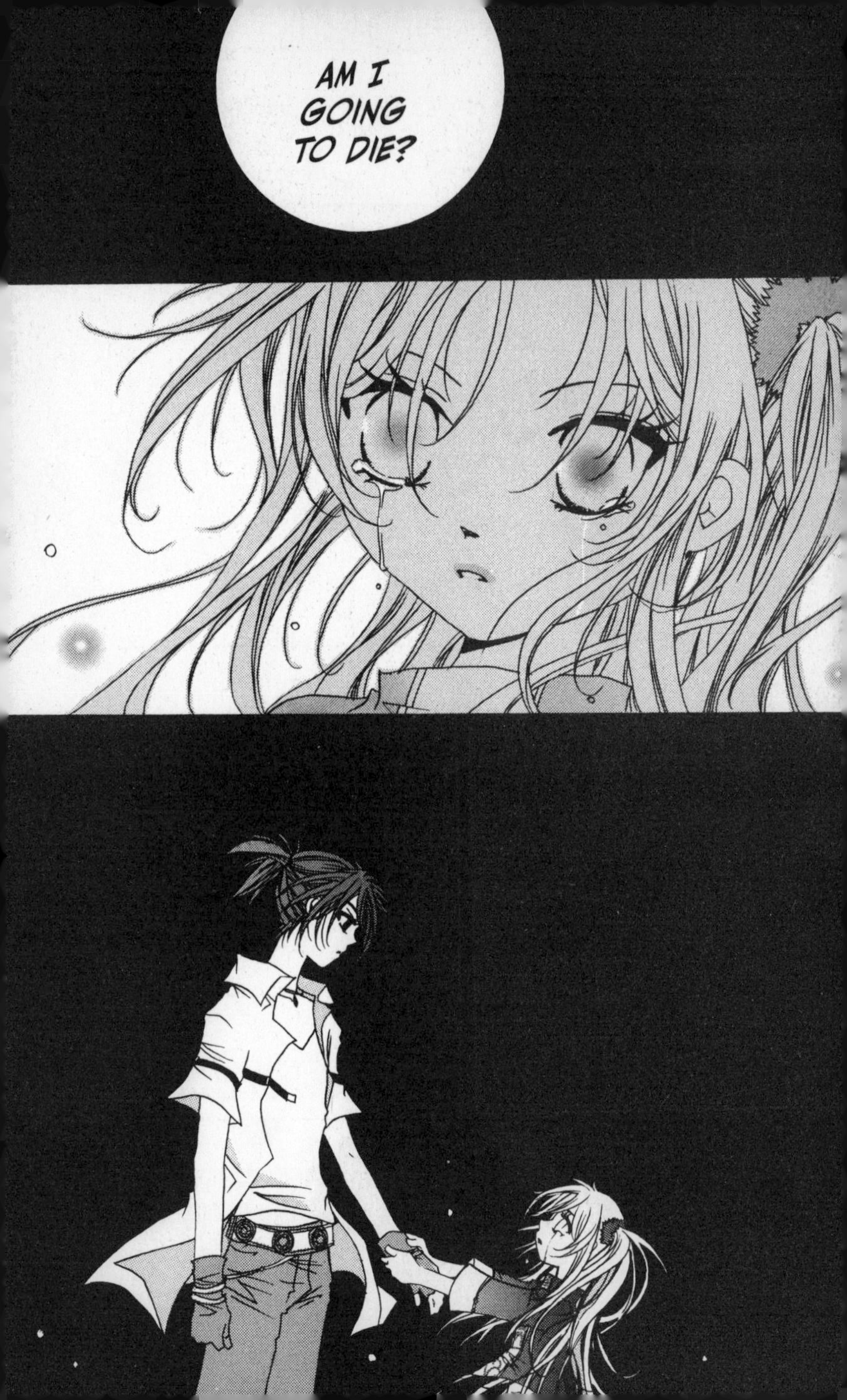
AM I GOING TO DIE?

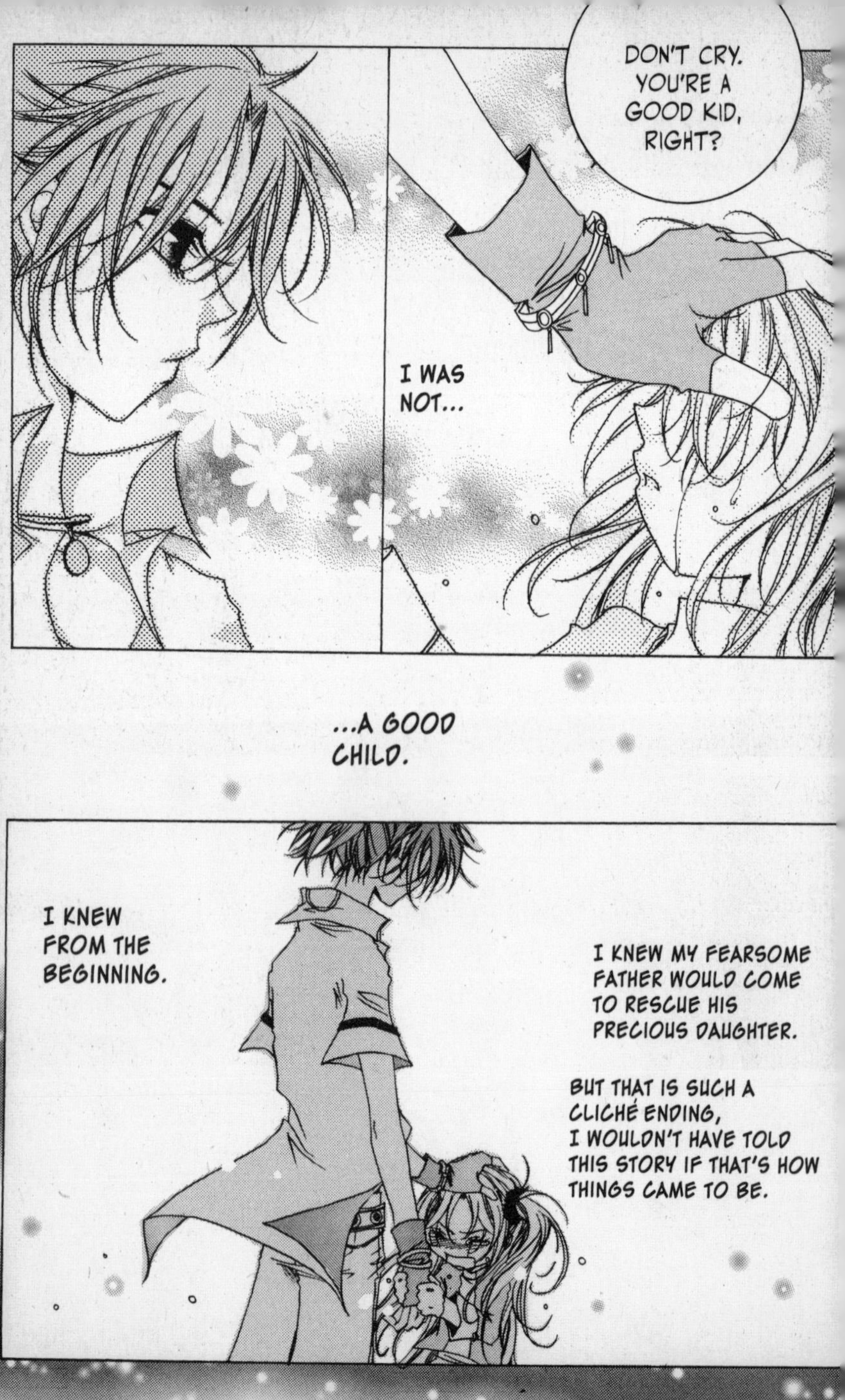
DON'T CRY. YOU'RE A GOOD KID, RIGHT?
I WAS NOT...
...A GOOD CHILD.
I KNEW FROM THE BEGINNING.
I KNEW MY FEARSOME FATHER WOULD COME TO RESCUE HIS PRECIOUS DAUGHTER.
BUT THAT IS SUCH A CLICHÉ ENDING, I WOULDN'T HAVE TOLD THIS STORY IF THAT'S HOW THINGS CAME TO BE.

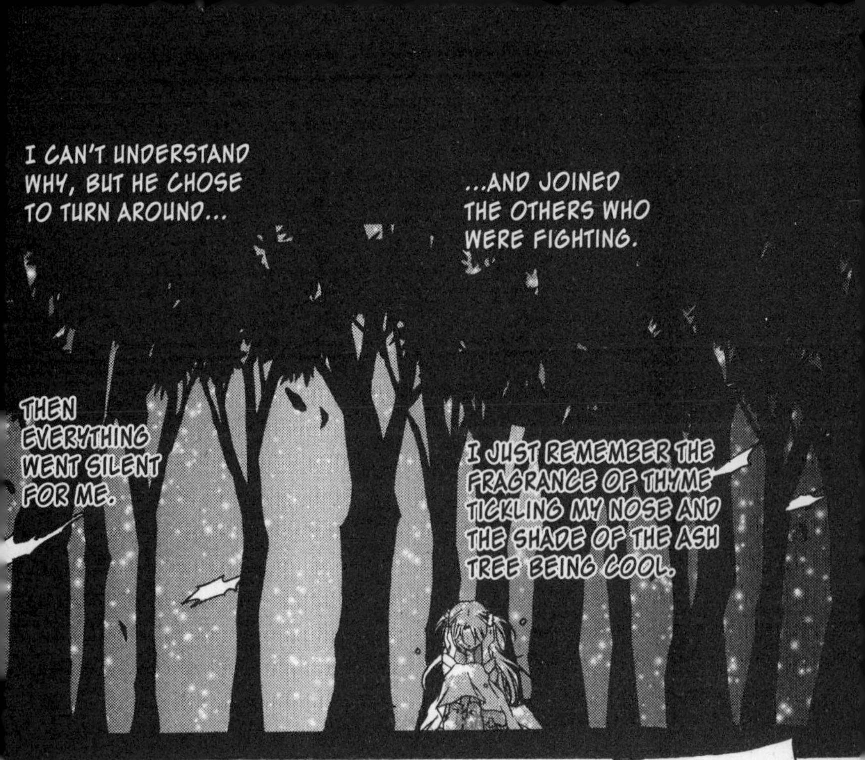
I CAN'T UNDERSTAND WHY, BUT HE CHOSE TO TURN AROUND...
...AND JOINED THE OTHERS WHO WERE FIGHTING.
THEN EVERYTHING WENT SILENT FOR ME.
I JUST REMEMBER THE FRAGRANCE OF THYME TICKLING MY NOSE AND THE SHADE OF THE ASH TREE BEING COOL.

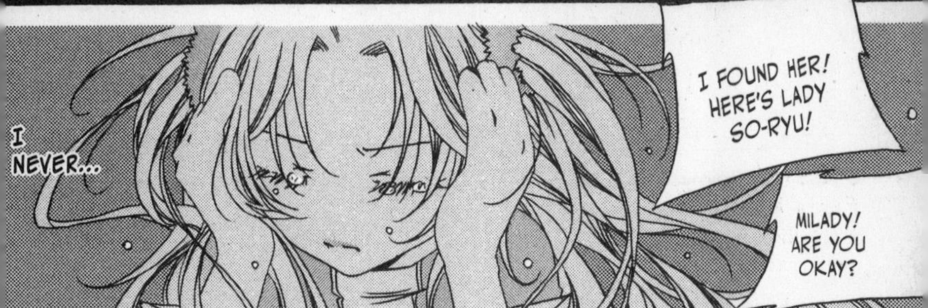
I NEVER...
I FOUND HER! HERE'S LADY SO-RYU!
MILADY! ARE YOU OKAY?

...GOT TO SEE THE WARRIOR WITH THE GENTLE HAND.

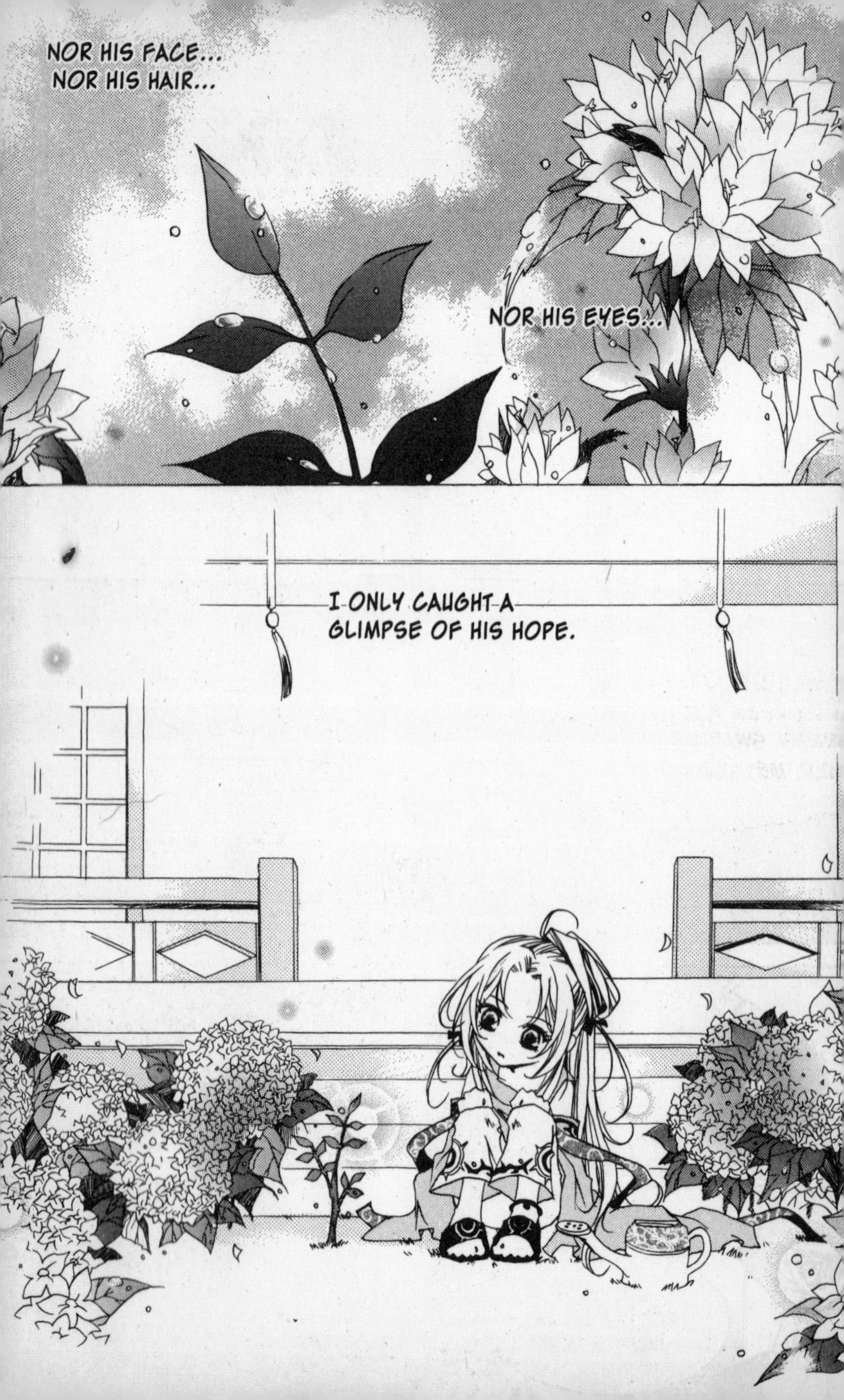
NOR HIS FACE...
NOR HIS HAIR...
NOR HIS EYES...
I ONLY CAUGHT A
GLIMPSE OF HIS HOPE.

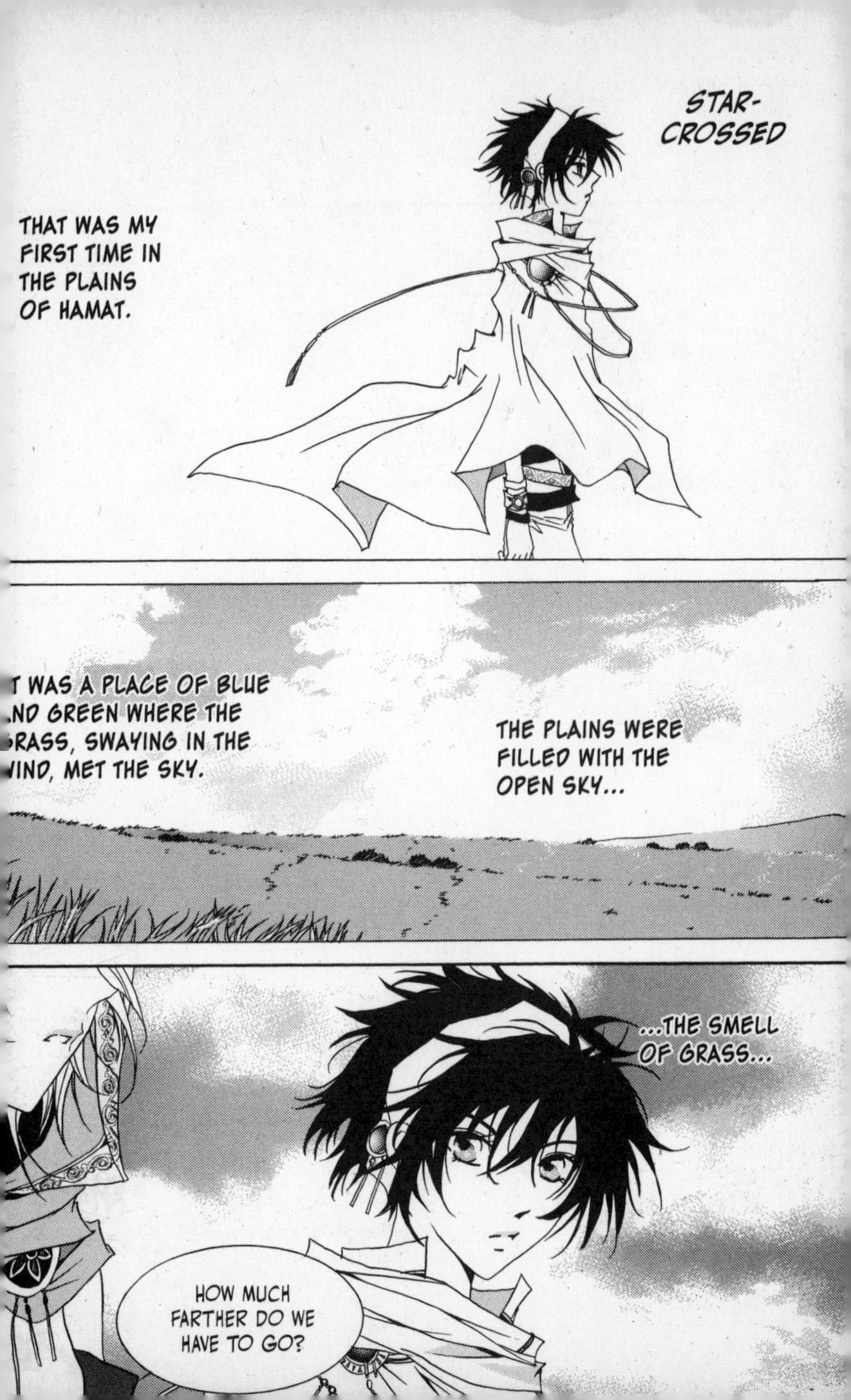
STAR-CROSSED
THAT WAS MY FIRST TIME IN THE PLAINS OF HAMAT.
T WAS A PLACE OF BLUE ND GREEN WHERE THE RASS, SWAYING IN THE IND, MET THE SKY.
THE PLAINS WERE FILLED WITH THE OPEN SKY...
...THE SMELL OF GRASS...
HOW MUCH FARTHER DO WE HAVE TO GO?

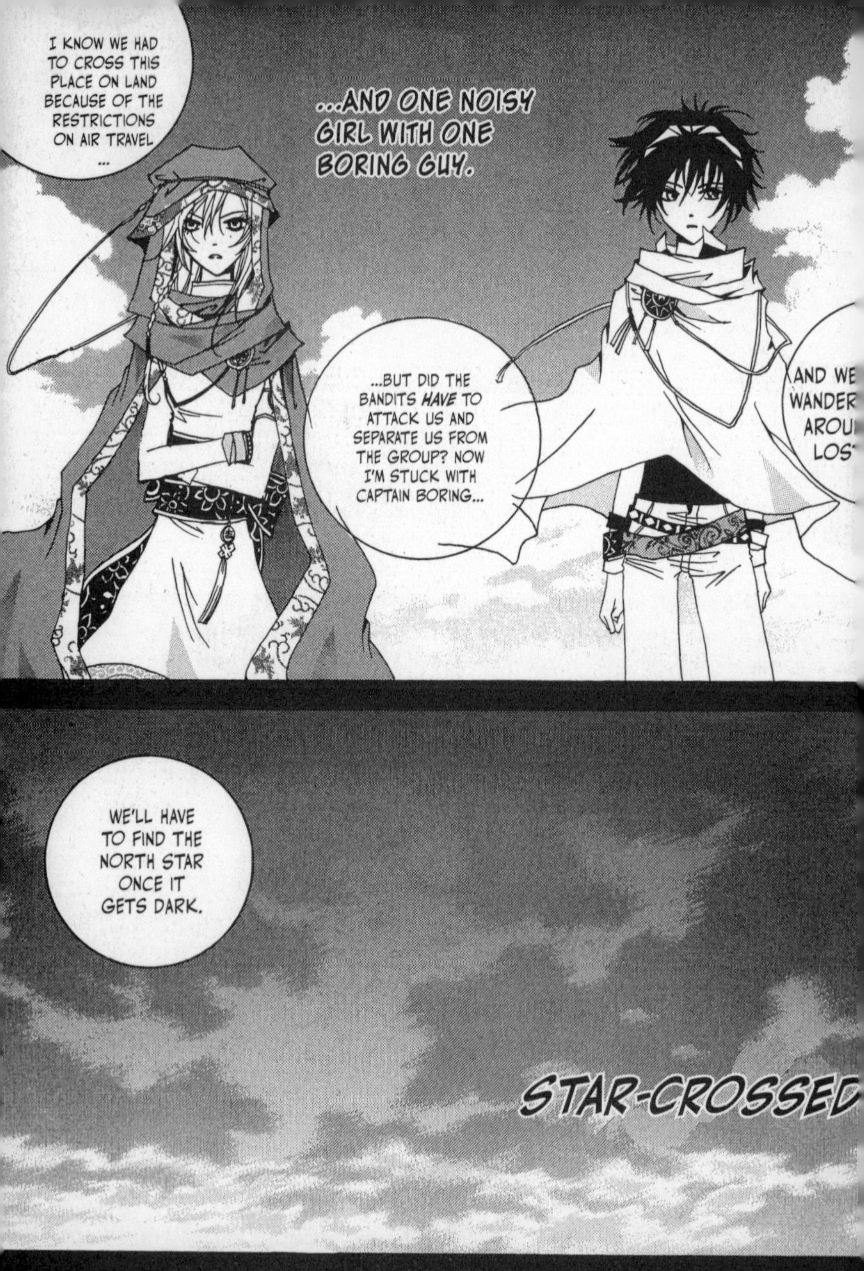
I KNOW WE HAD TO CROSS THIS PLACE ON LAND BECAUSE OF THE RESTRICTIONS ON AIR TRAVEL ...
...AND ONE NOISY GIRL WITH ONE BORING GUY.
...BUT DID THE BANDITS *HAVE* TO ATTACK US AND SEPARATE US FROM THE GROUP? NOW I'M STUCK WITH CAPTAIN BORING...
AND WE WANDER AROU LOS
WE'LL HAVE TO FIND THE NORTH STAR ONCE IT GETS DARK.
STAR-CROSSED

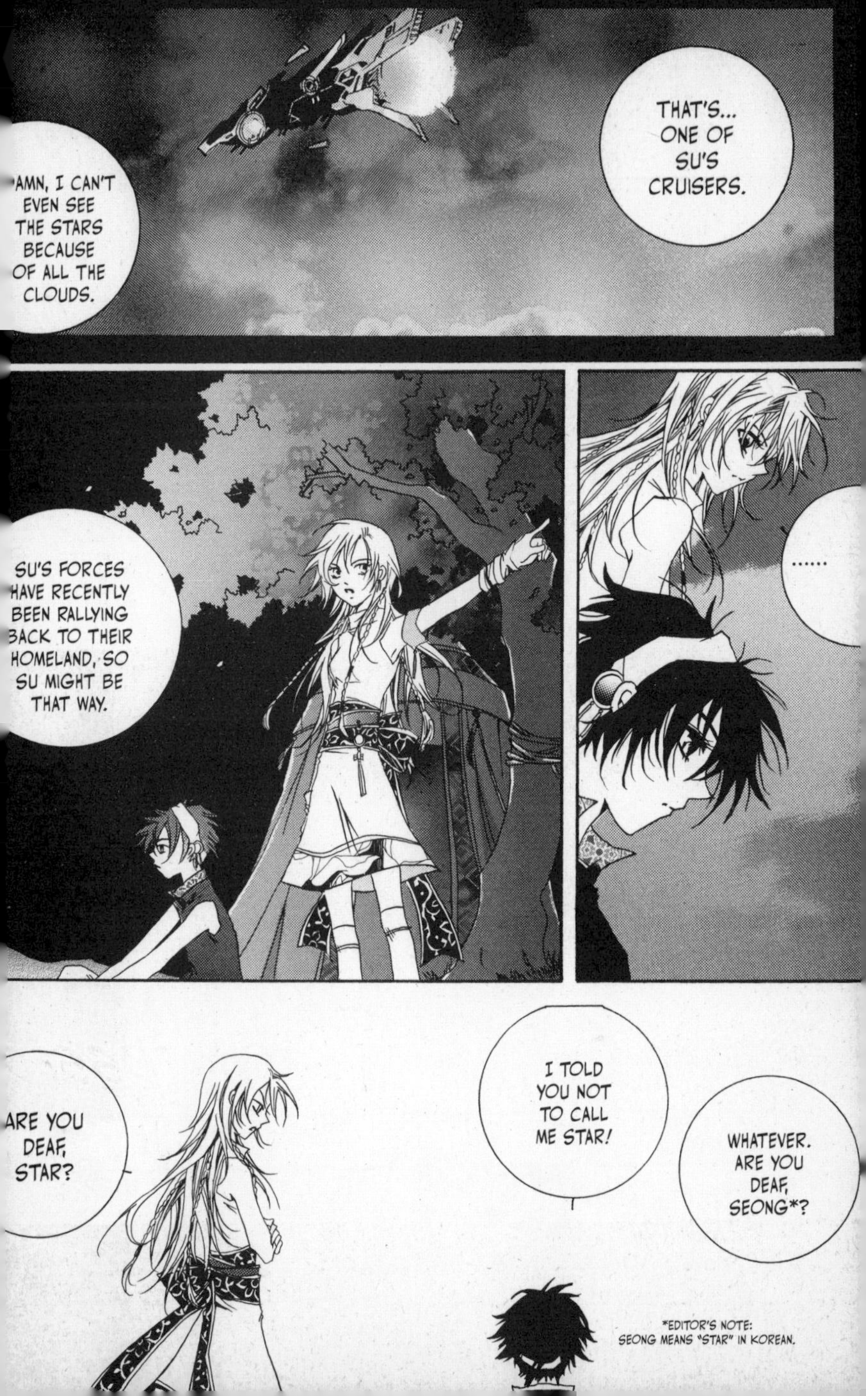

DAMN, I CAN'T EVEN SEE THE STARS BECAUSE OF ALL THE CLOUDS.
THAT'S... ONE OF SU'S CRUISERS.
SU'S FORCES HAVE RECENTLY BEEN RALLYING BACK TO THEIR HOMELAND, SO SU MIGHT BE THAT WAY.
......
ARE YOU DEAF, STAR?
I TOLD YOU NOT TO CALL ME STAR!
WHATEVER. ARE YOU DEAF, SEONG*?
*EDITOR'S NOTE: SEONG MEANS "STAR" IN KOREAN.

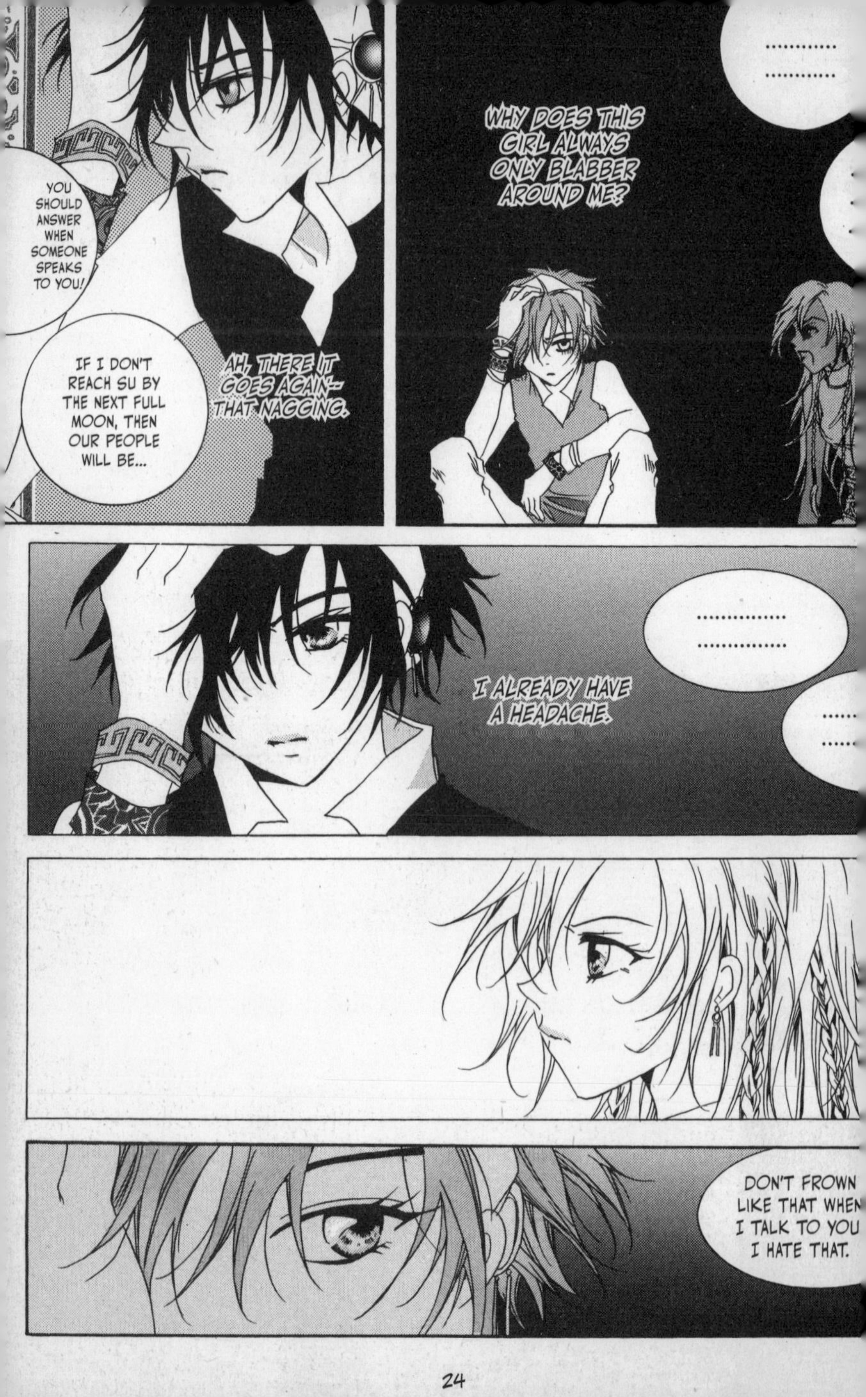
YOU SHOULD ANSWER WHEN SOMEONE SPEAKS TO YOU!
IF I DON'T REACH SU BY THE NEXT FULL MOON, THEN OUR PEOPLE WILL BE...
AH, THERE IT GOES AGAIN--THAT NAGGING.
WHY DOES THIS GIRL ALWAYS ONLY BLABBER AROUND ME?
....
I ALREADY HAVE A HEADACHE.
....
DON'T FROWN LIKE THAT WHEN I TALK TO YOU I HATE THAT.

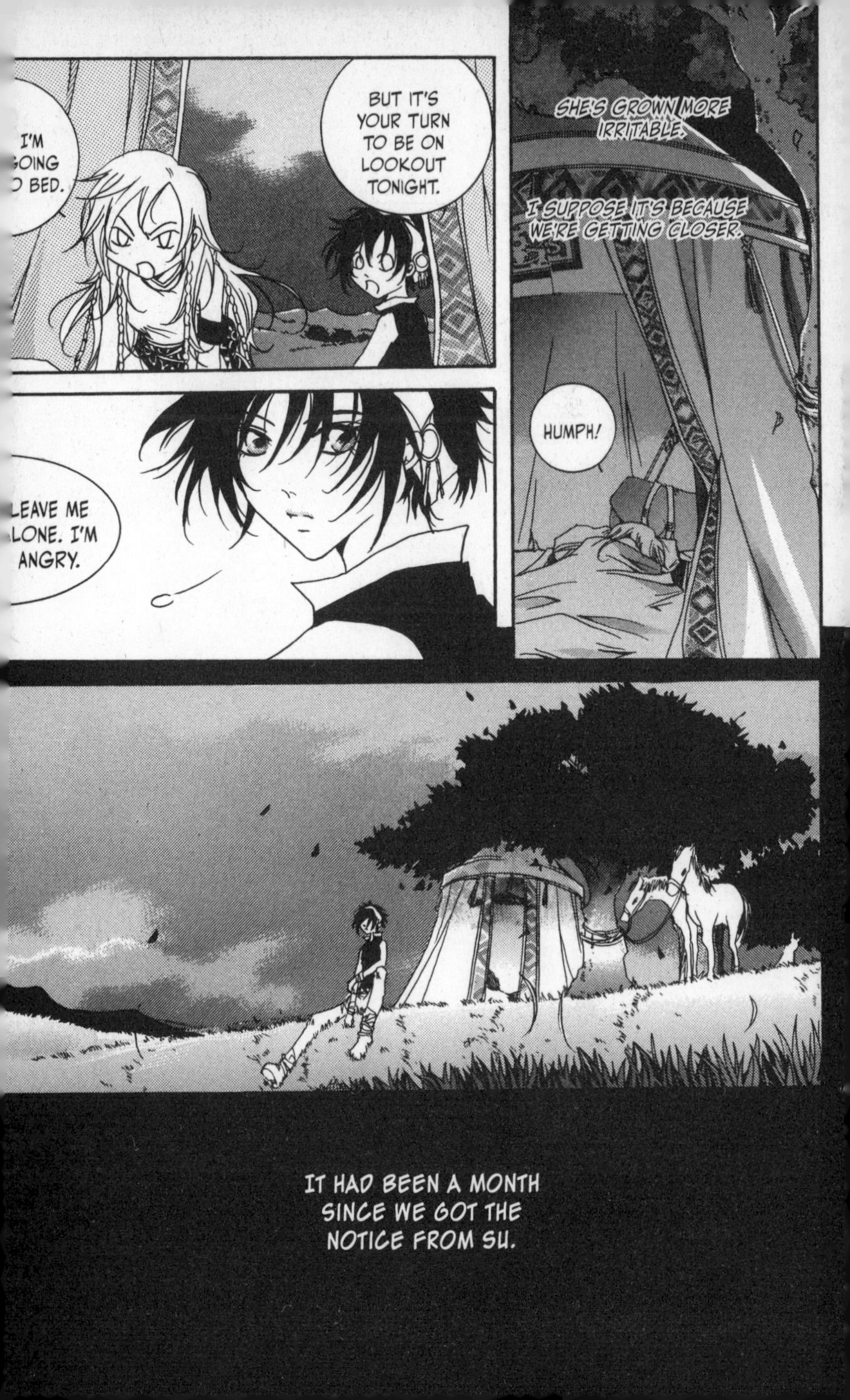
I'M GOING O BED.
BUT IT'S YOUR TURN TO BE ON LOOKOUT TONIGHT.
LEAVE ME LONE. I'M ANGRY.
SHE'S GROWN MORE IRRITABLE.
I SUPPOSE IT'S BECAUSE WE'RE GETTING CLOSER.
HUMPH!
IT HAD BEEN A MONTH SINCE WE GOT THE NOTICE FROM SU.

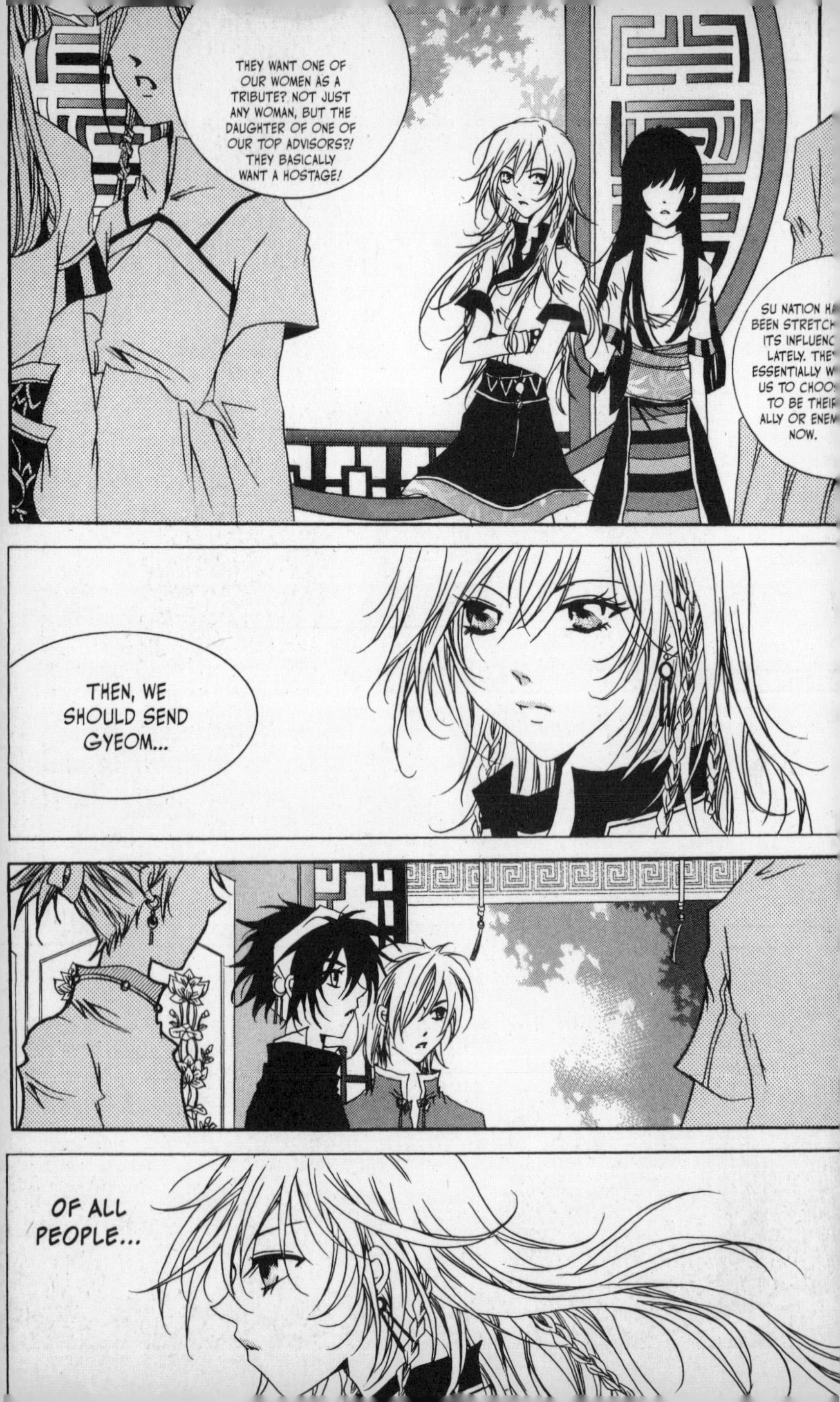
THEY WANT ONE OF OUR WOMEN AS A TRIBUTE? NOT JUST ANY WOMAN, BUT THE DAUGHTER OF ONE OF OUR TOP ADVISORS?! THEY BASICALLY WANT A HOSTAGE!
SU NATION HA BEEN STRETCH ITS INFLUENC LATELY. THE ESSENTIALLY W US TO CHOOS TO BE THEIR ALLY OR ENEM NOW.
THEN, WE SHOULD SEND GYEOM...
OF ALL PEOPLE...

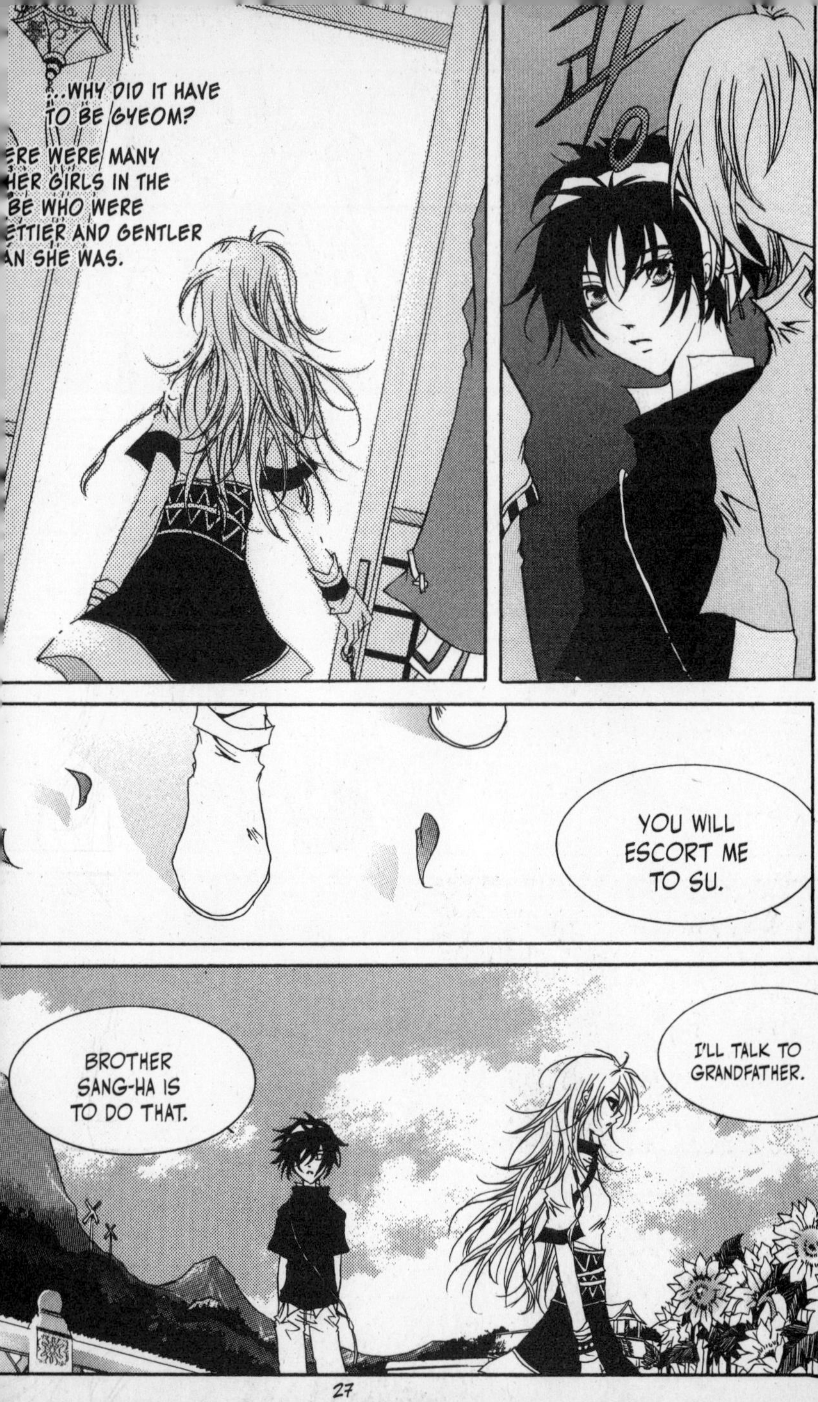
...WHY DID IT HAVE TO BE GYEOM?
ERE WERE MANY HER GIRLS IN THE BE WHO WERE ETTIER AND GENTLER AN SHE WAS.
YOU WILL ESCORT ME TO SU.
BROTHER SANG-HA IS TO DO THAT.
I'LL TALK TO GRANDFATHER.

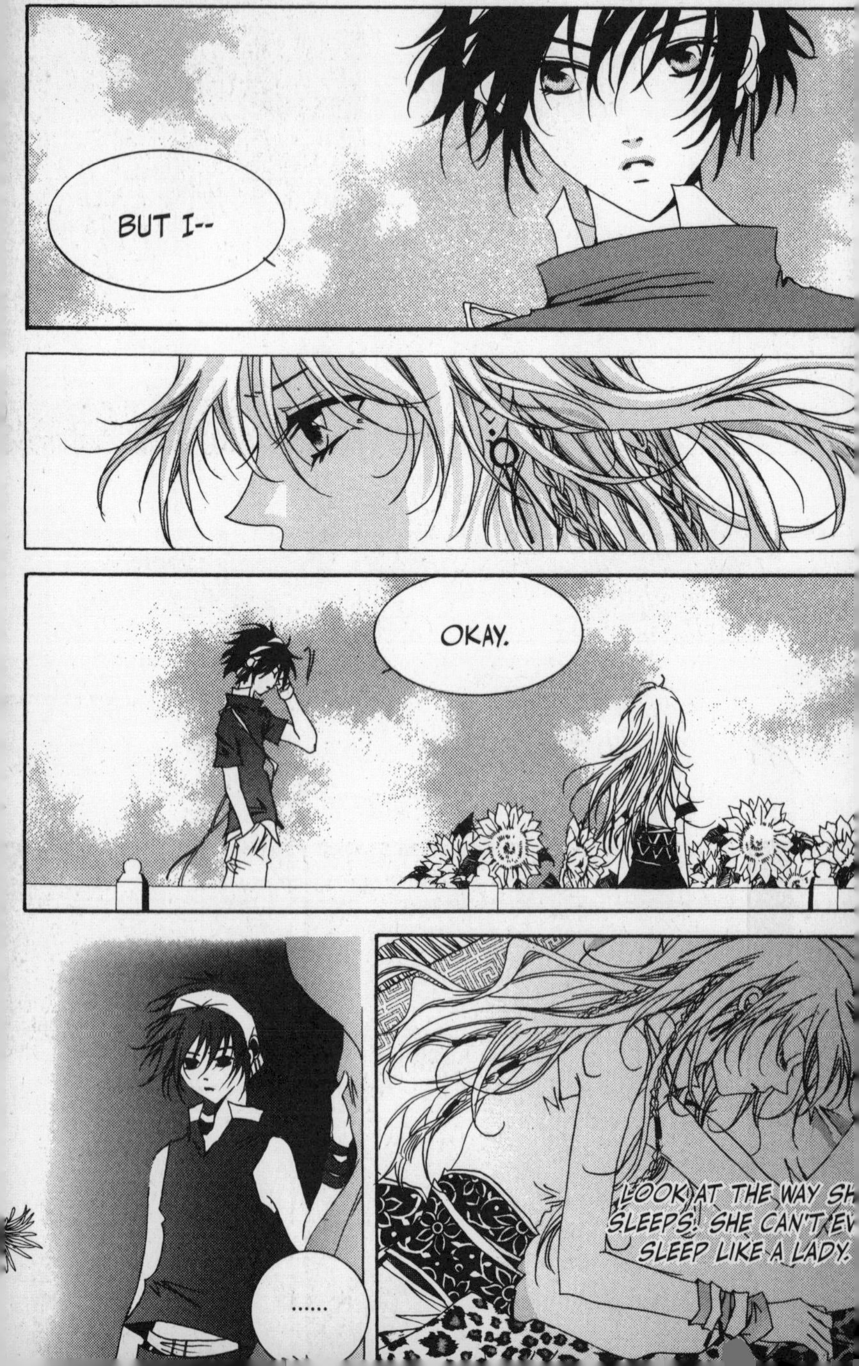
BUT I--
OKAY.
......
LOOK AT THE WAY SH
SLEEPS! SHE CAN'T EV
SLEEP LIKE A LADY.

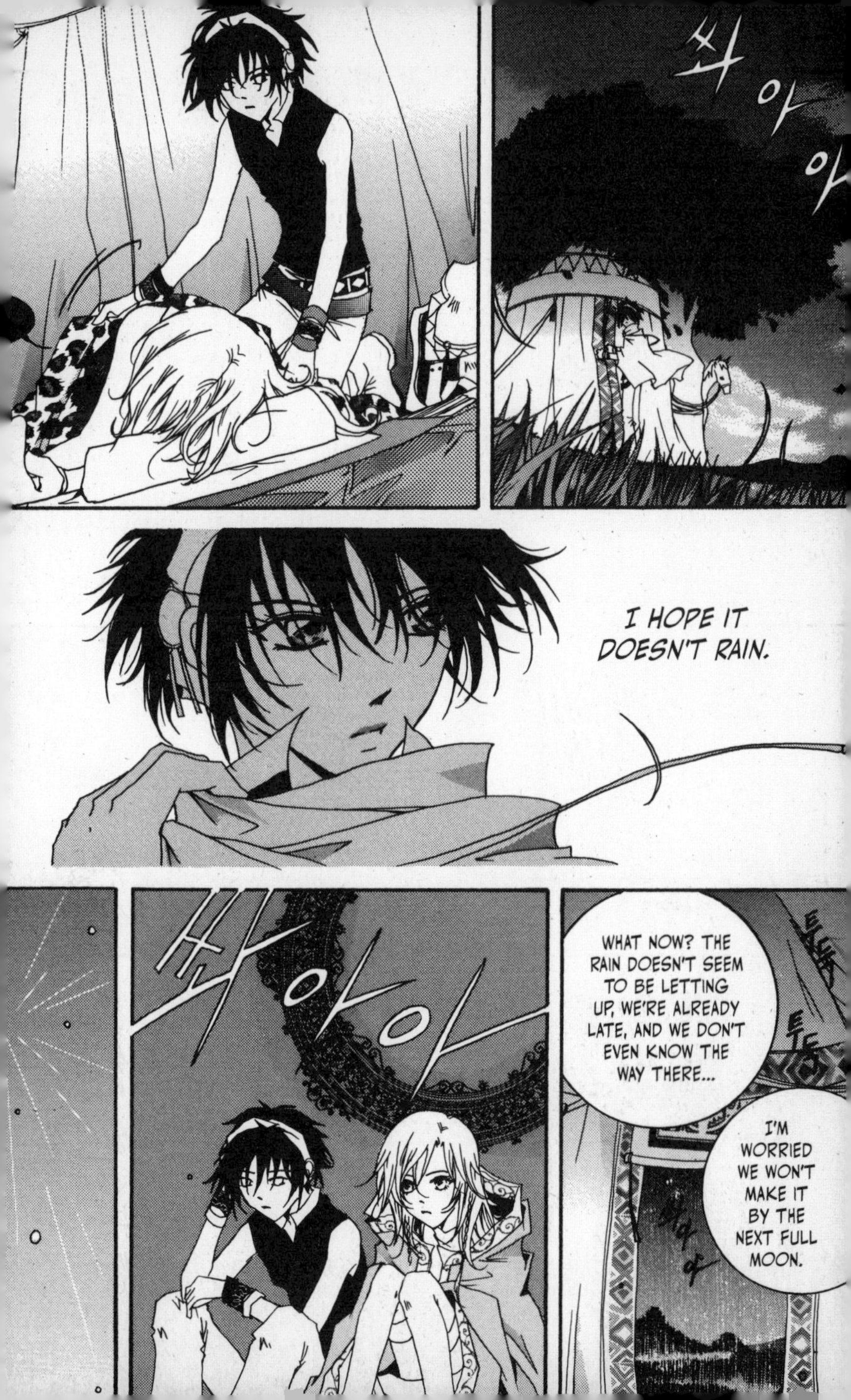
쏴아아
I HOPE IT DOESN'T RAIN.
WHAT NOW? THE RAIN DOESN'T SEEM TO BE LETTING UP, WE'RE ALREADY LATE, AND WE DON'T EVEN KNOW THE WAY THERE...
I'M WORRIED WE WON'T MAKE IT BY THE NEXT FULL MOON.

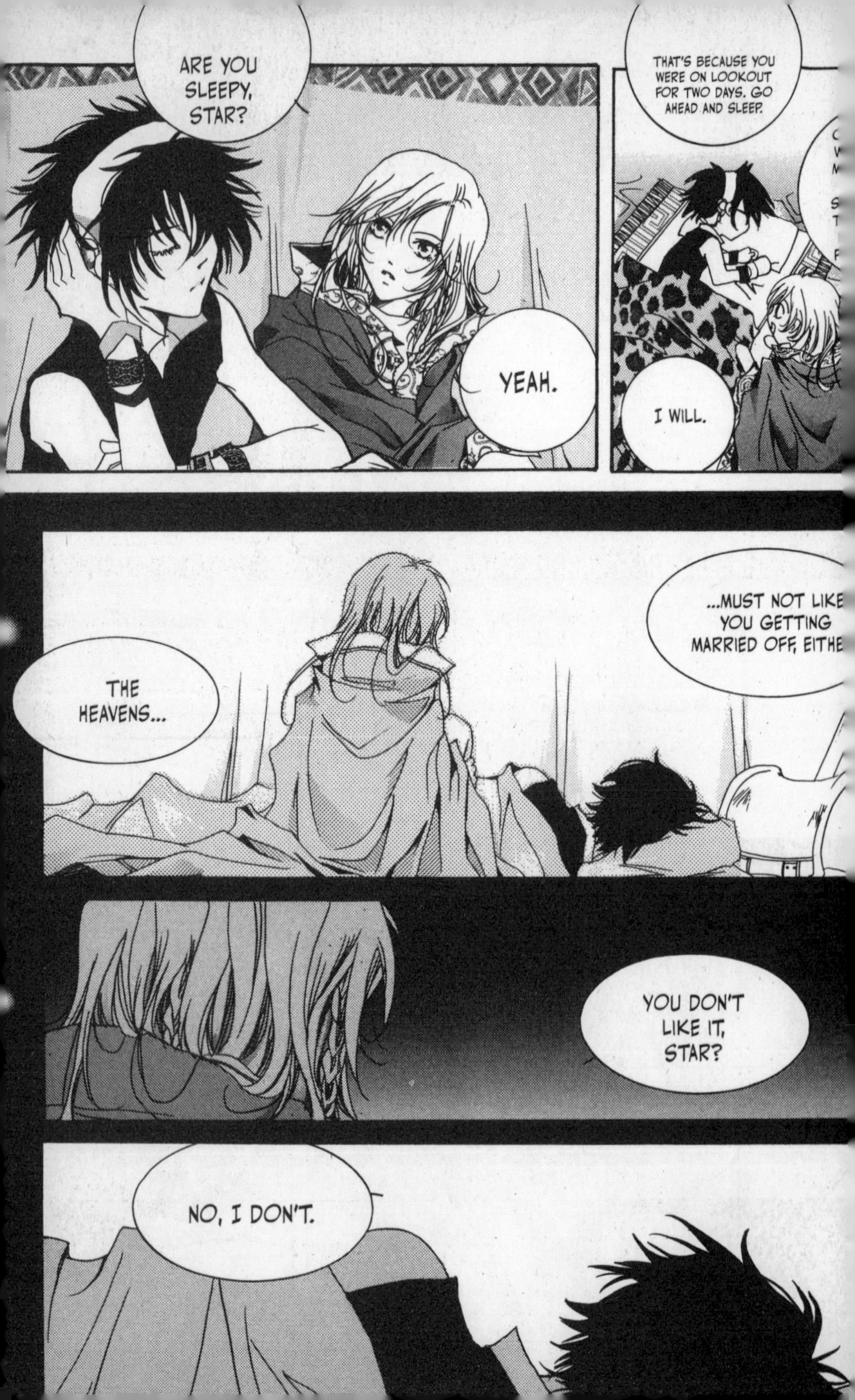
ARE YOU SLEEPY, STAR?
YEAH.
THAT'S BECAUSE YOU WERE ON LOOKOUT FOR TWO DAYS. GO AHEAD AND SLEEP.
I WILL.
THE HEAVENS...
...MUST NOT LIKE YOU GETTING MARRIED OFF, EITHE
YOU DON'T LIKE IT, STAR?
NO, I DON'T.

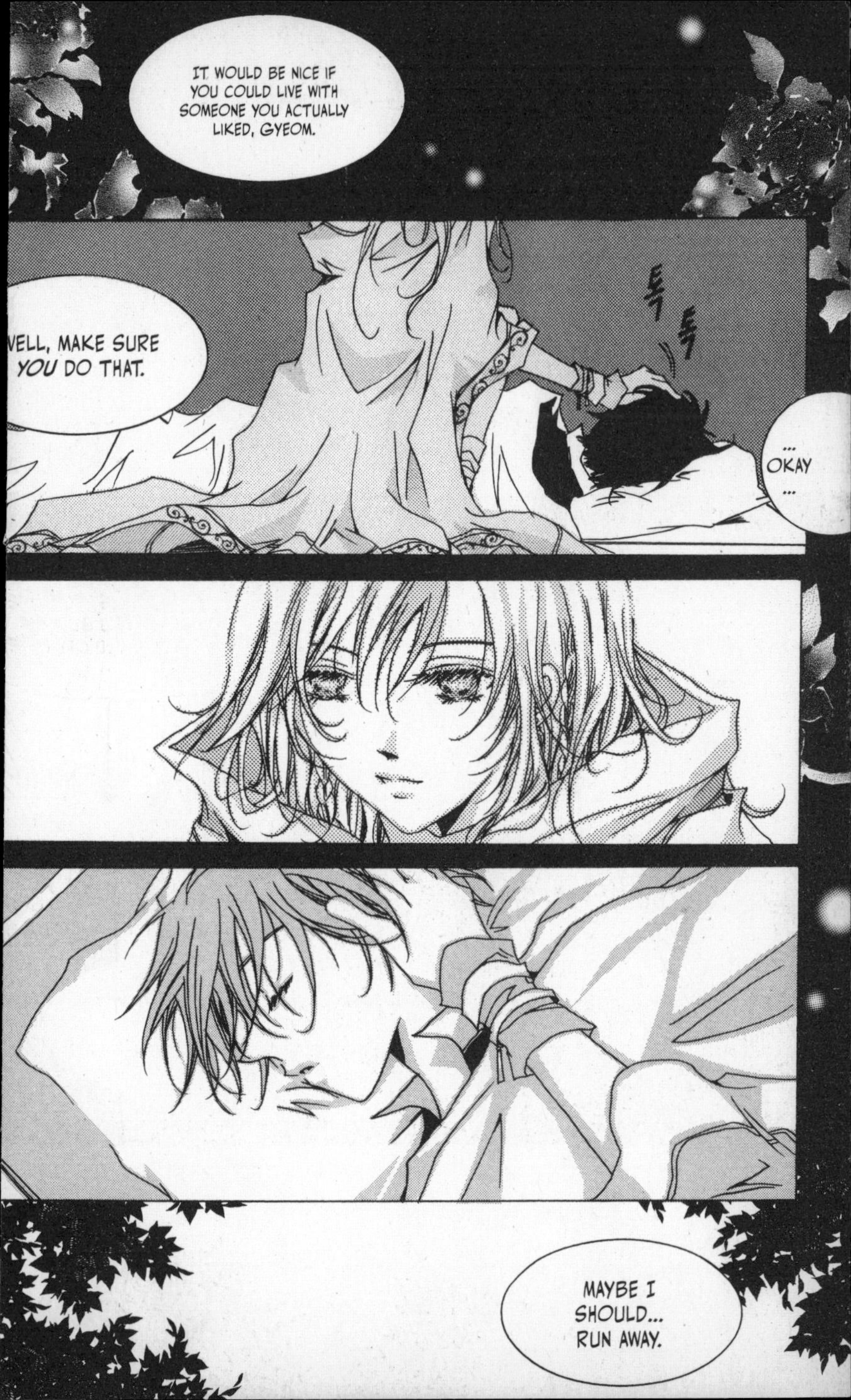
IT WOULD BE NICE IF YOU COULD LIVE WITH SOMEONE YOU ACTUALLY LIKED, GYEOM.
WELL, MAKE SURE *YOU* DO THAT.
톡 톡
...OKAY...
MAYBE I SHOULD... RUN AWAY.

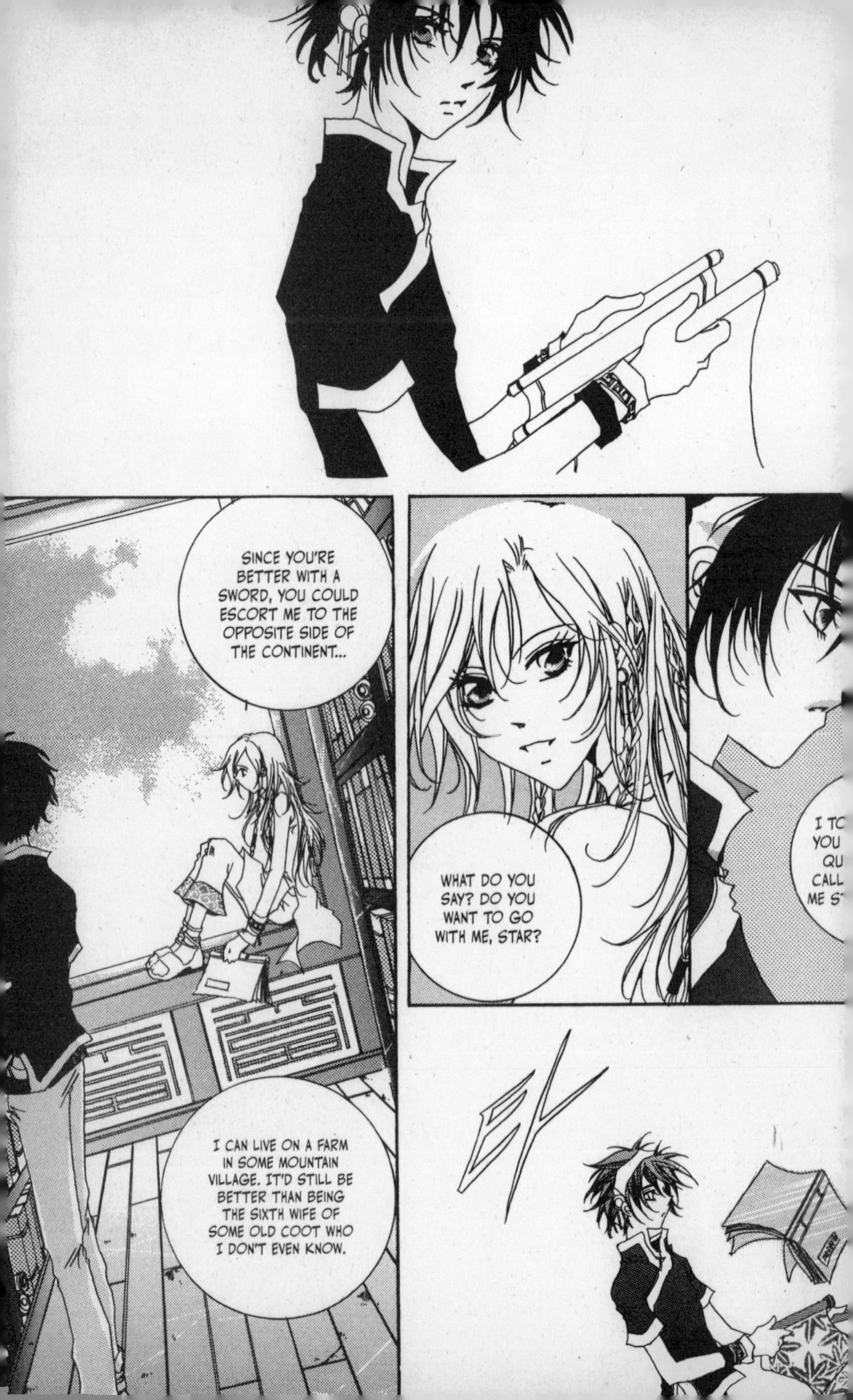
SINCE YOU'RE BETTER WITH A SWORD, YOU COULD ESCORT ME TO THE OPPOSITE SIDE OF THE CONTINENT...
I CAN LIVE ON A FARM IN SOME MOUNTAIN VILLAGE. IT'D STILL BE BETTER THAN BEING THE SIXTH WIFE OF SOME OLD COOT WHO I DON'T EVEN KNOW.
WHAT DO YOU SAY? DO YOU WANT TO GO WITH ME, STAR?

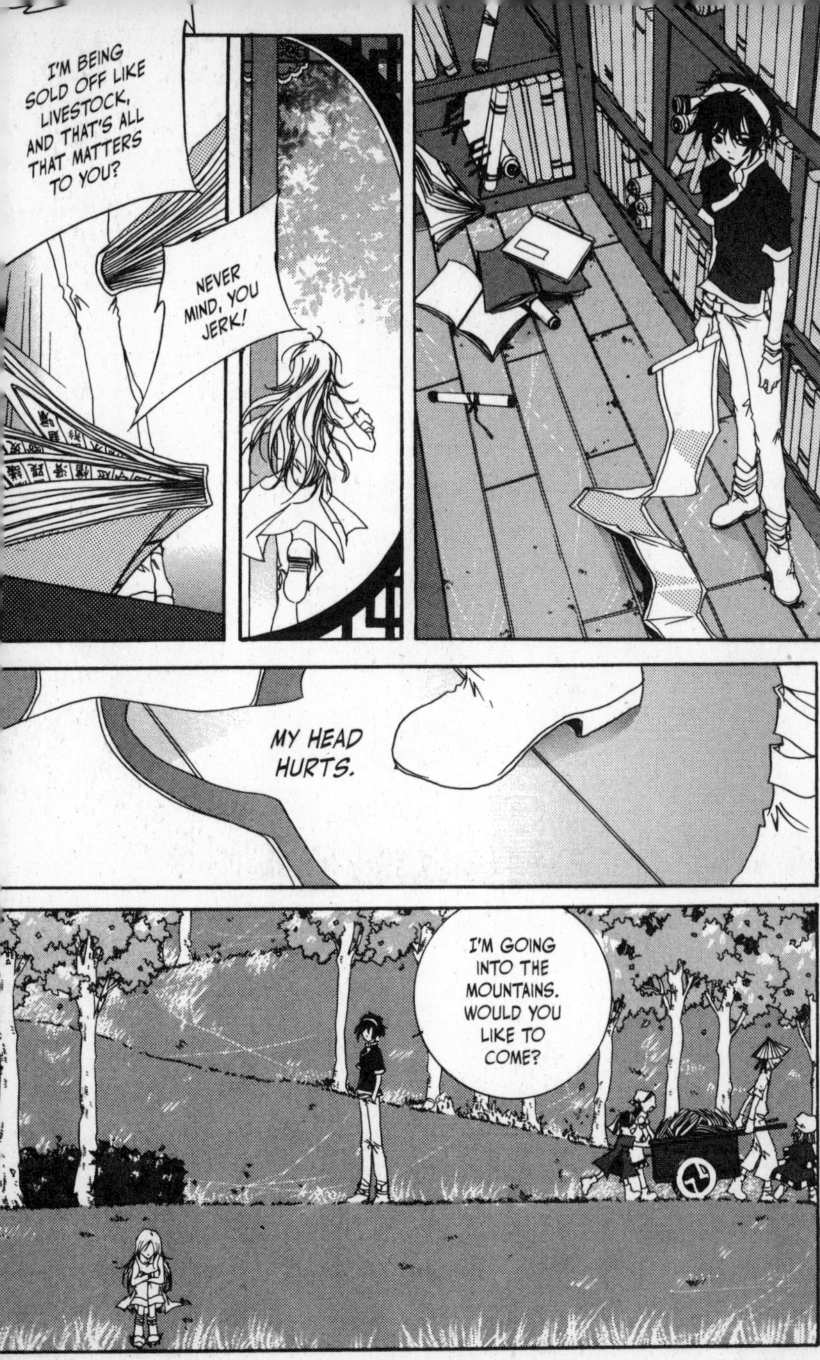
I'M BEING SOLD OFF LIKE LIVESTOCK, AND THAT'S ALL THAT MATTERS TO YOU?
NEVER MIND, YOU JERK!
MY HEAD HURTS.
I'M GOING INTO THE MOUNTAINS. WOULD YOU LIKE TO COME?

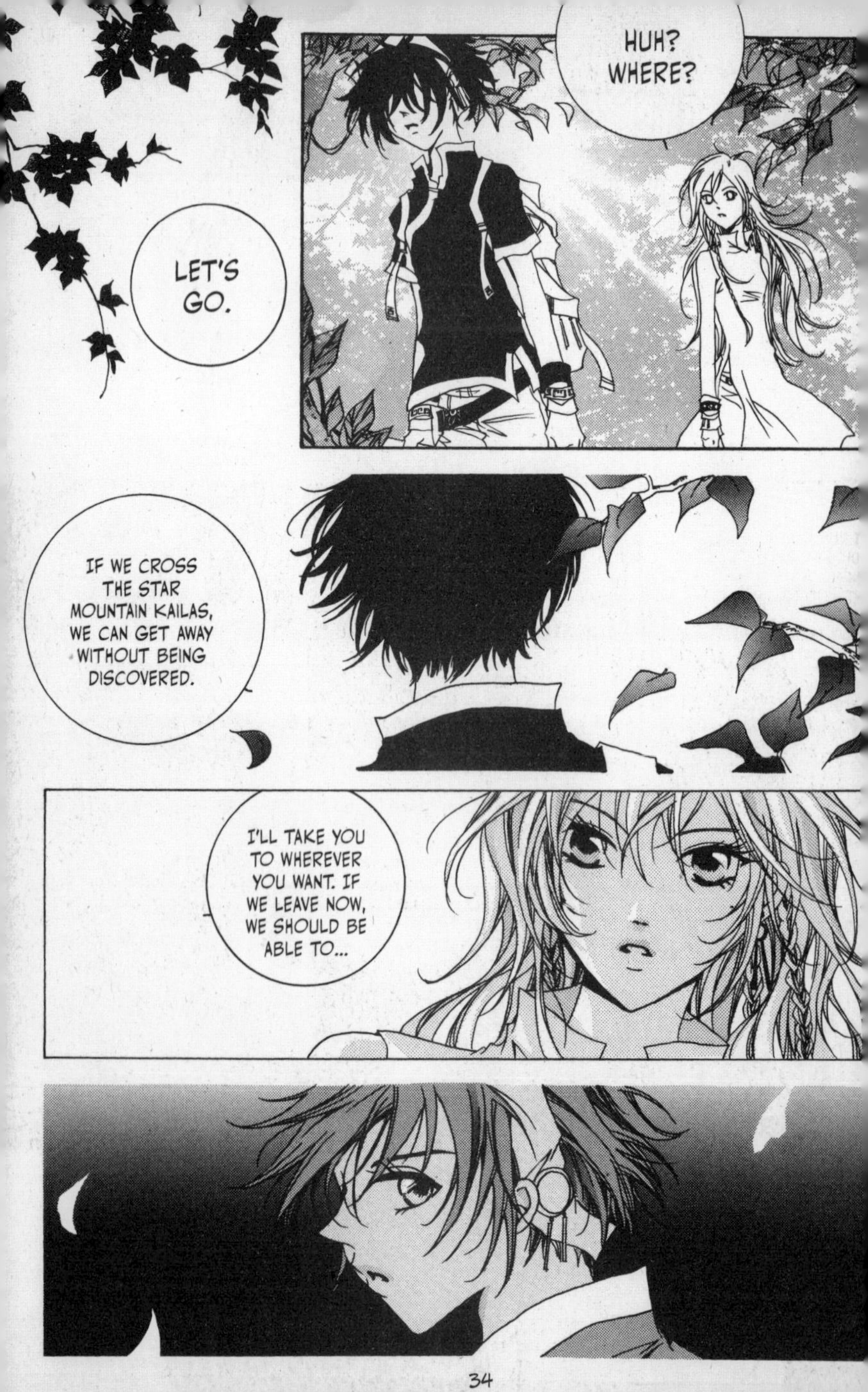
LET'S GO.
HUH? WHERE?
IF WE CROSS THE STAR MOUNTAIN KAILAS, WE CAN GET AWAY WITHOUT BEING DISCOVERED.
I'LL TAKE YOU TO WHEREVER YOU WANT. IF WE LEAVE NOW, WE SHOULD BE ABLE TO...

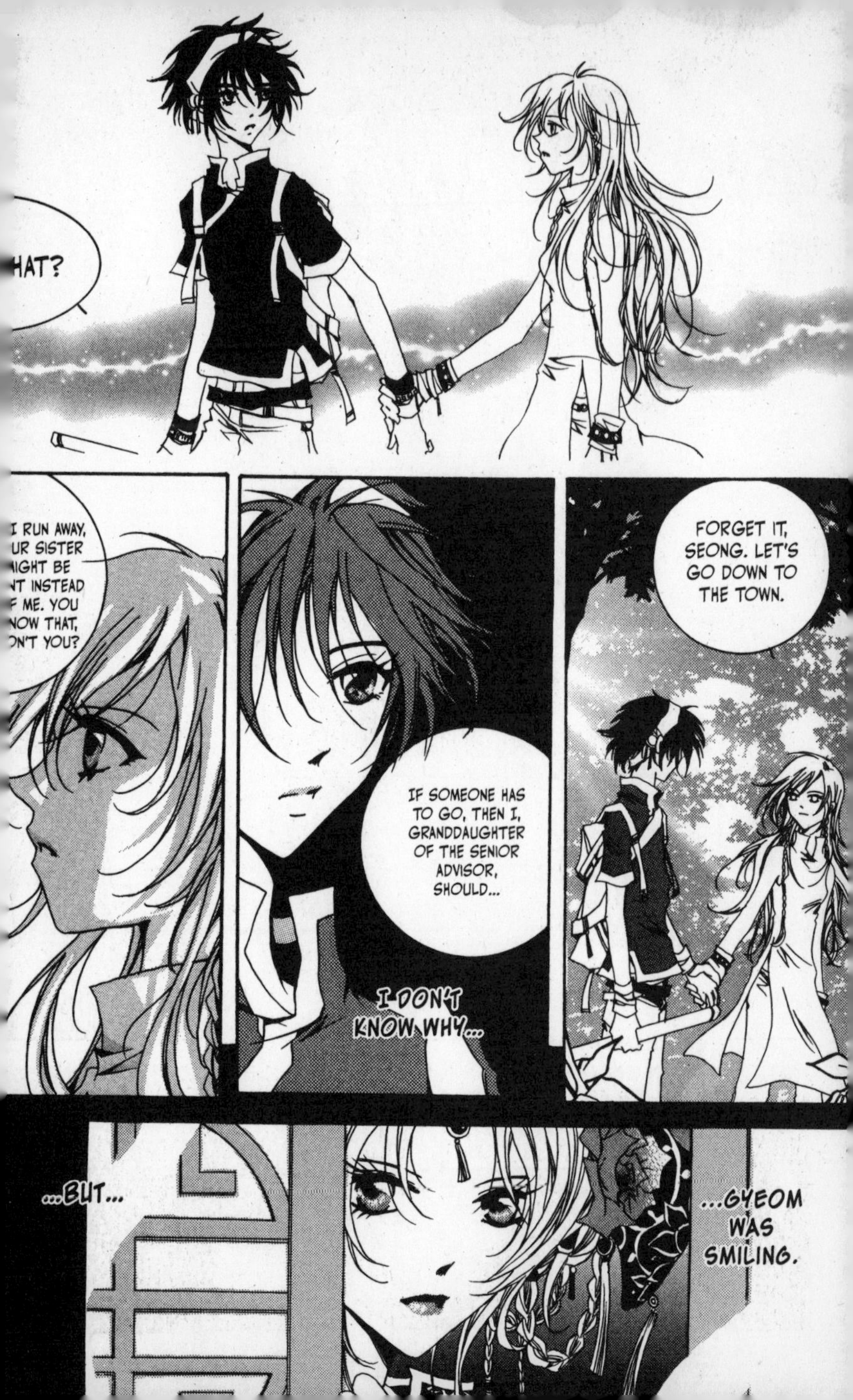
HAT?
I RUN AWAY, UR SISTER MIGHT BE NT INSTEAD F ME. YOU NOW THAT, ON'T YOU?
IF SOMEONE HAS TO GO, THEN I, GRANDDAUGHTER OF THE SENIOR ADVISOR, SHOULD...
I DON'T KNOW WHY...
FORGET IT, SEONG. LET'S GO DOWN TO THE TOWN.
...BUT...
...GYEOM WAS SMILING.

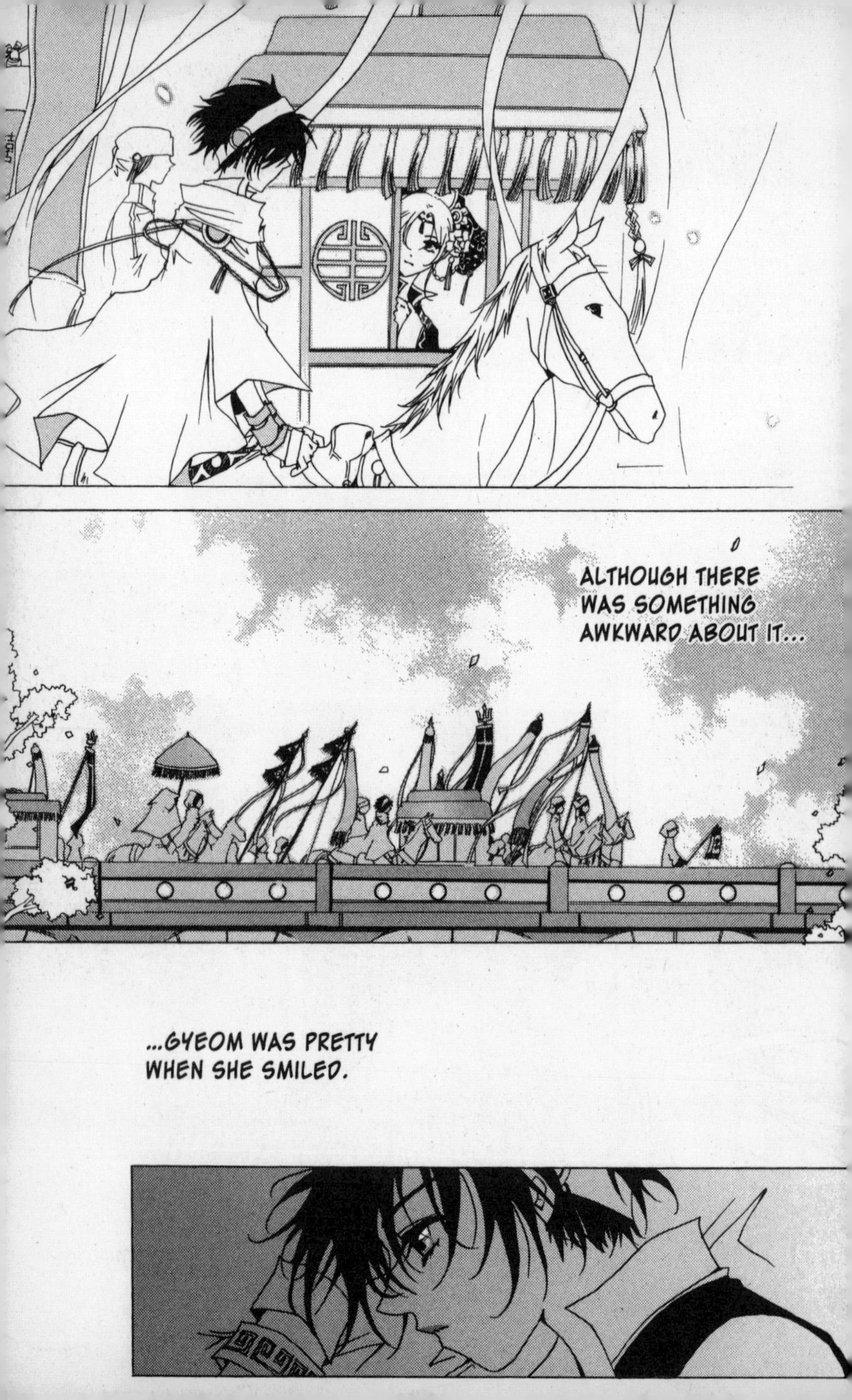
ALTHOUGH THERE WAS SOMETHING AWKWARD ABOUT IT...
...GYEOM WAS PRETTY WHEN SHE SMILED.

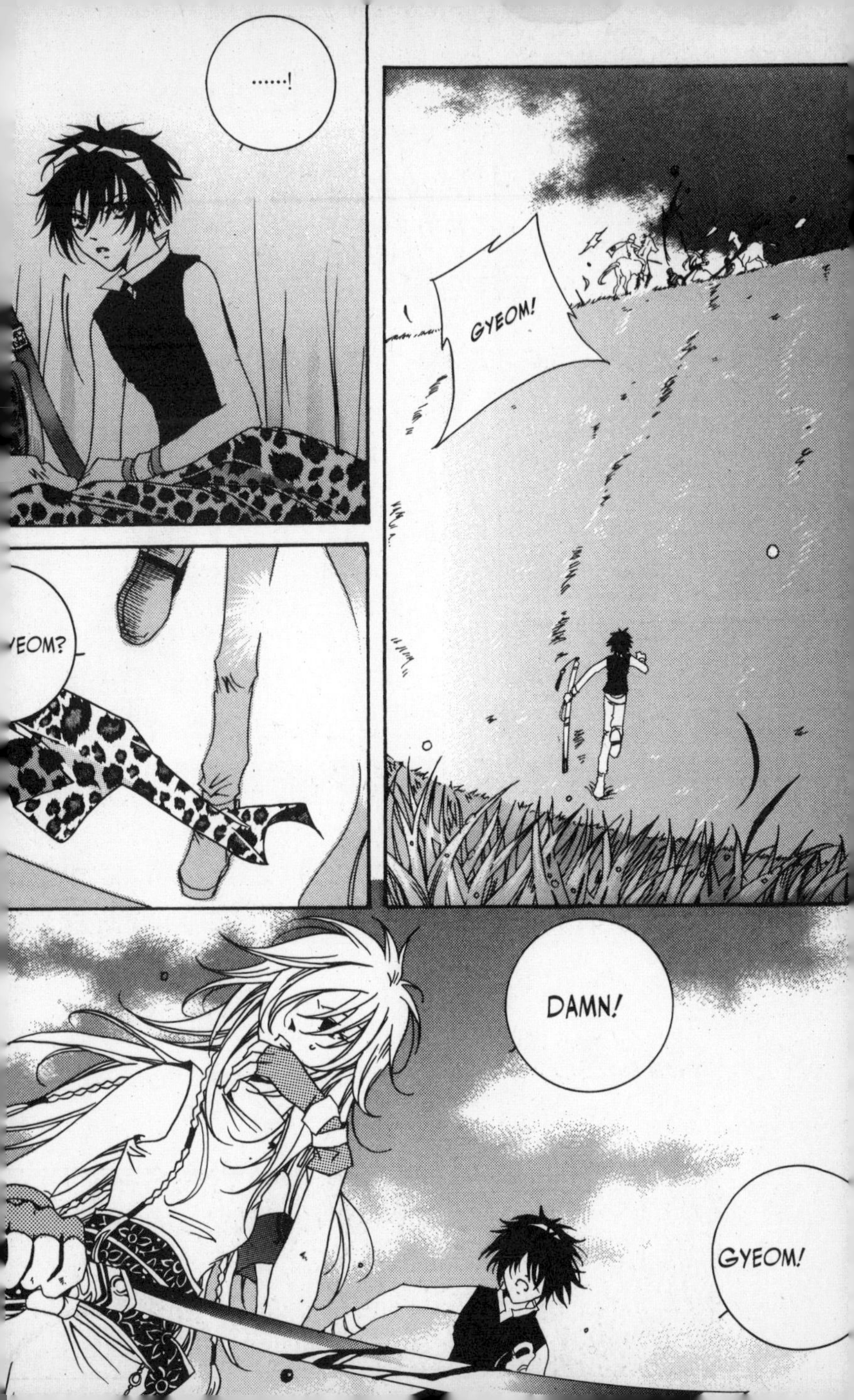

......!
YEOM?
GYEOM!
DAMN!
GYEOM!

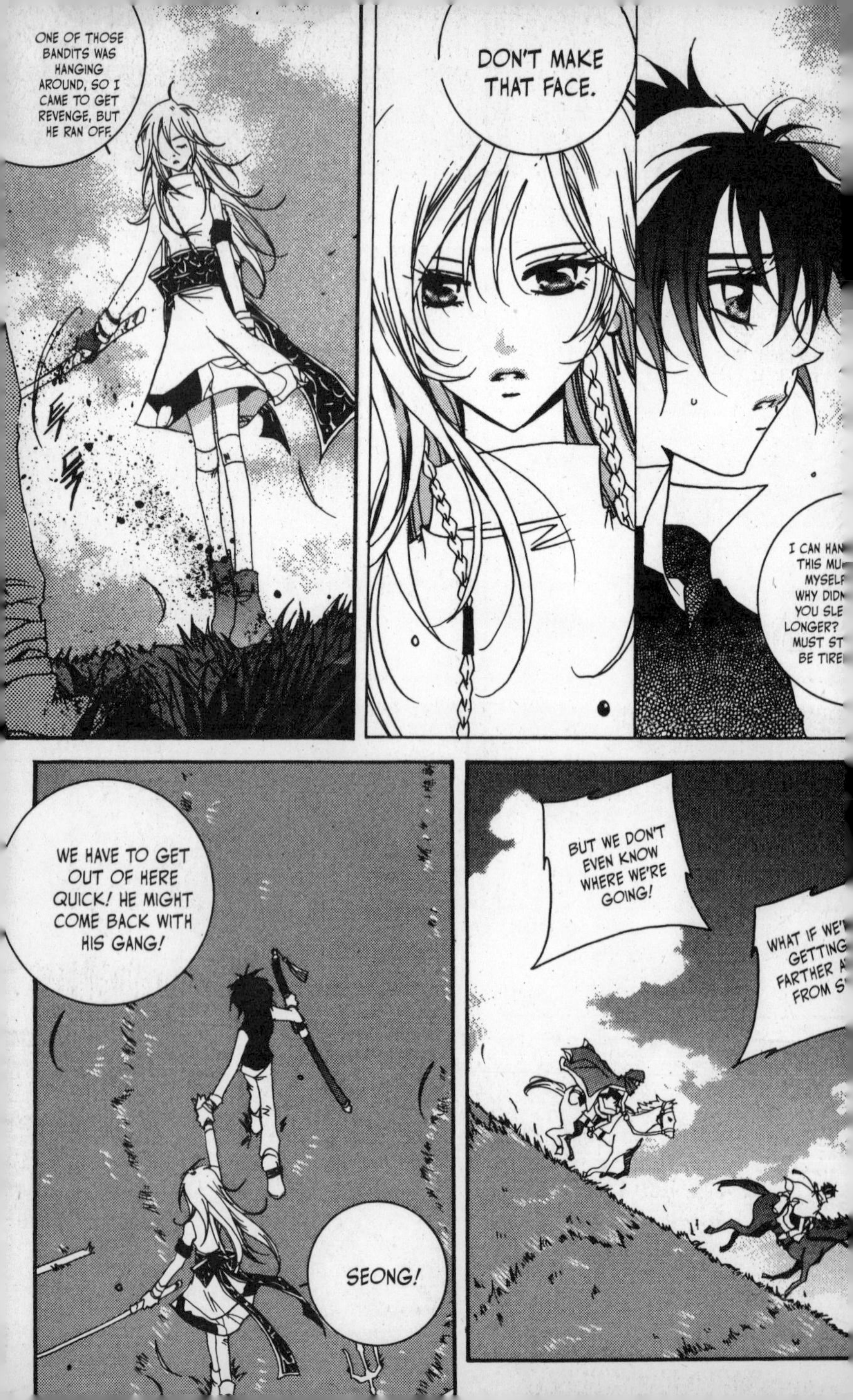
ONE OF THOSE BANDITS WAS HANGING AROUND, SO I CAME TO GET REVENGE, BUT HE RAN OFF.
DON'T MAKE THAT FACE.
I CAN HAN THIS MU MYSELF WHY DIDN YOU SLE LONGER? MUST ST BE TIRE
WE HAVE TO GET OUT OF HERE QUICK! HE MIGHT COME BACK WITH HIS GANG!
SEONG!
BUT WE DON'T EVEN KNOW WHERE WE'RE GOING!
WHAT IF WE' GETTING FARTHER A FROM S

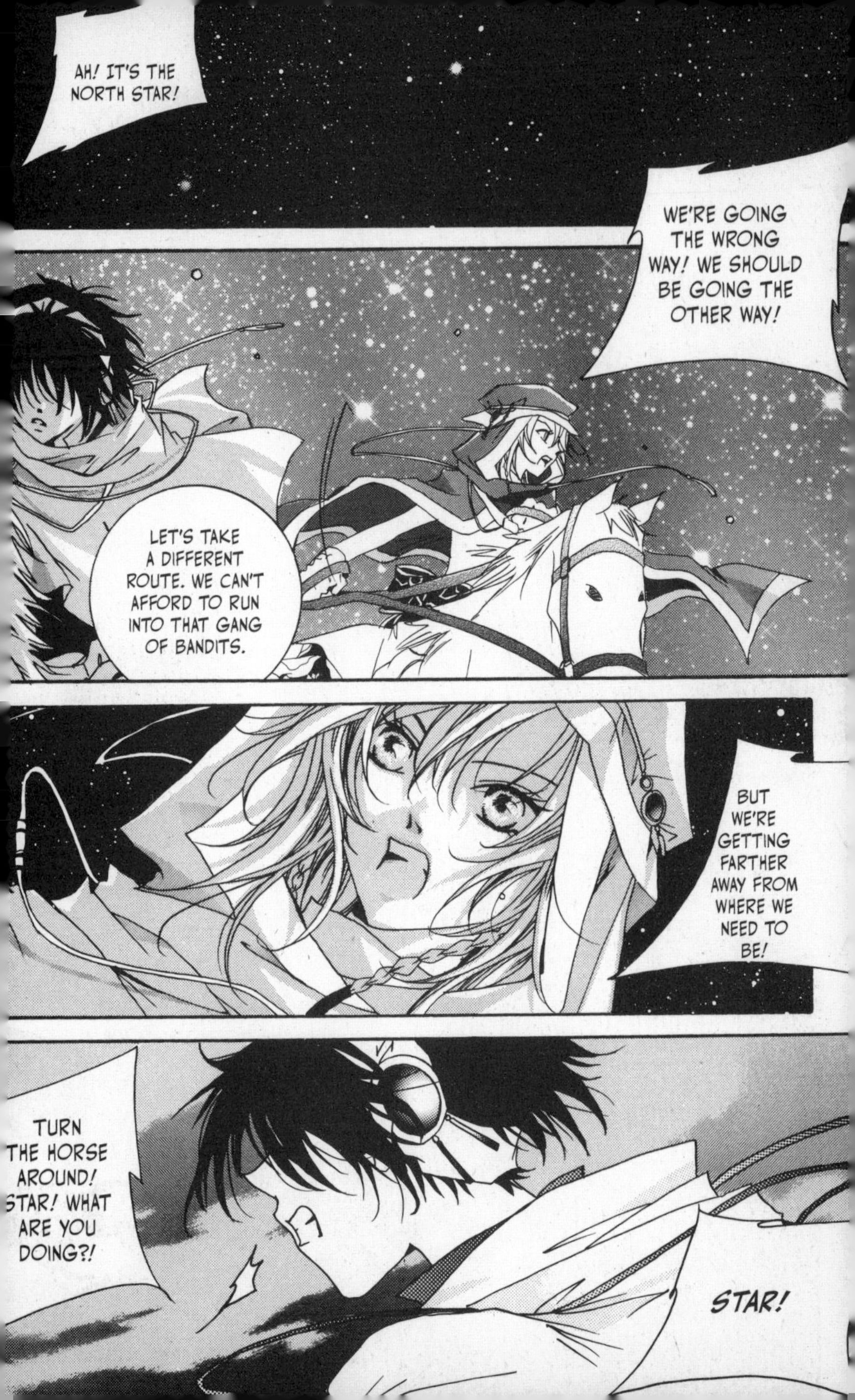
AH! IT'S THE NORTH STAR!
WE'RE GOING THE WRONG WAY! WE SHOULD BE GOING THE OTHER WAY!
LET'S TAKE A DIFFERENT ROUTE. WE CAN'T AFFORD TO RUN INTO THAT GANG OF BANDITS.
BUT WE'RE GETTING FARTHER AWAY FROM WHERE WE NEED TO BE!
TURN THE HORSE AROUND! STAR! WHAT ARE YOU DOING?!
STAR!

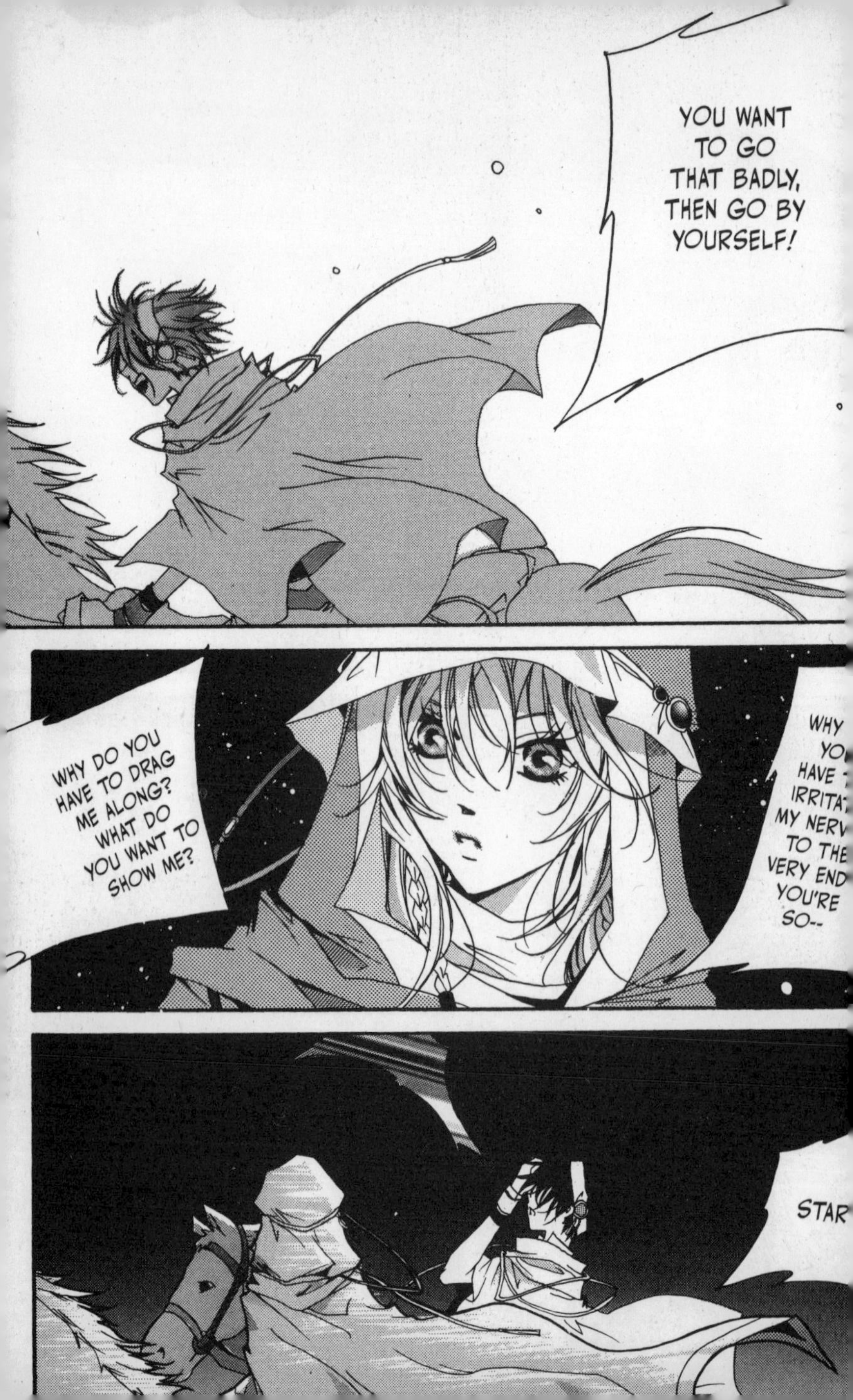
YOU WANT TO GO THAT BADLY, THEN GO BY YOURSELF!
WHY DO YOU HAVE TO DRAG ME ALONG? WHAT DO YOU WANT TO SHOW ME?
WHY YO HAVE IRRITAT MY NERV TO THE VERY END YOU'RE SO--
STAR

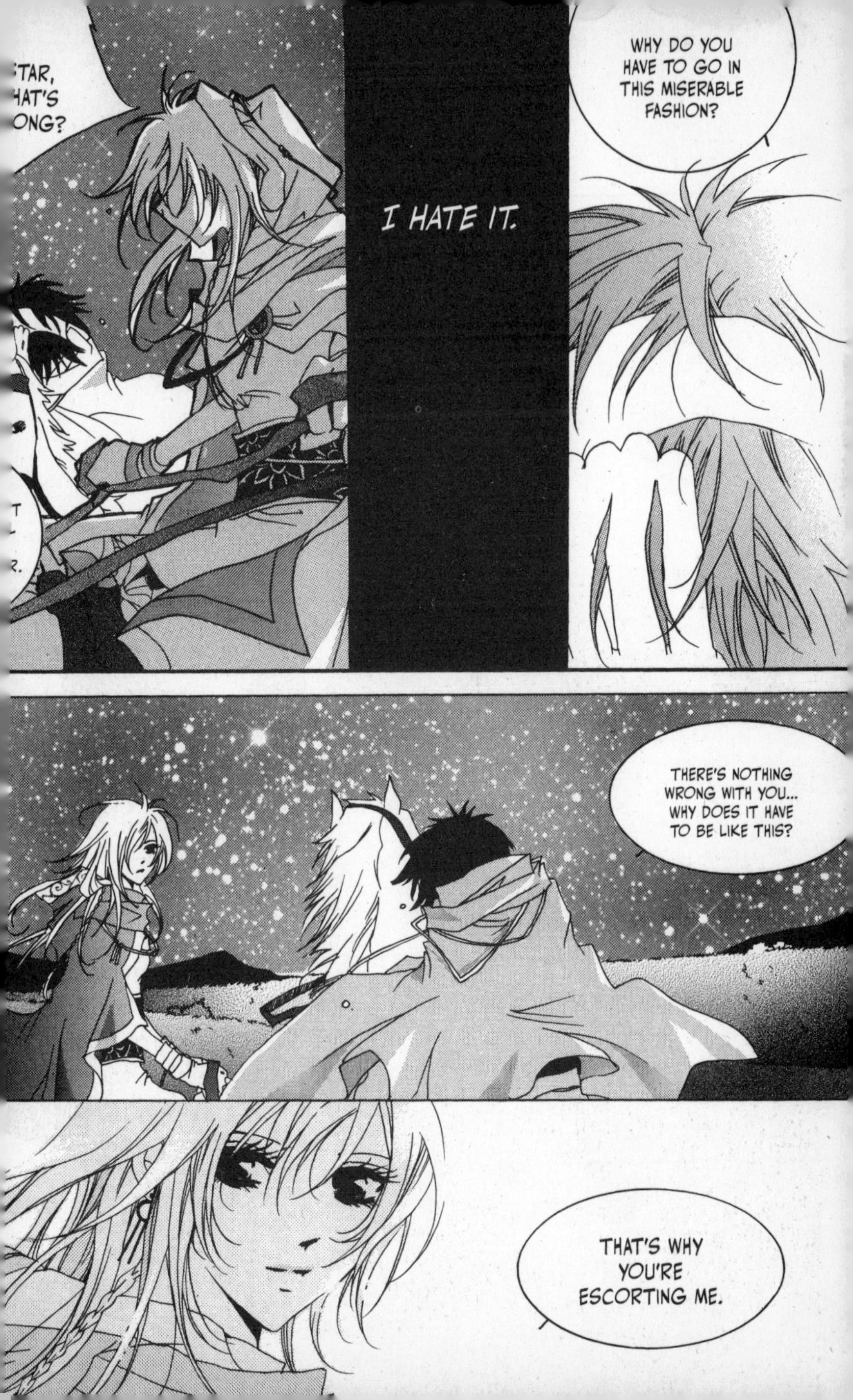
I HATE IT.
WHY DO YOU HAVE TO GO IN THIS MISERABLE FASHION?
THERE'S NOTHING WRONG WITH YOU... WHY DOES IT HAVE TO BE LIKE THIS?
THAT'S WHY YOU'RE ESCORTING ME.

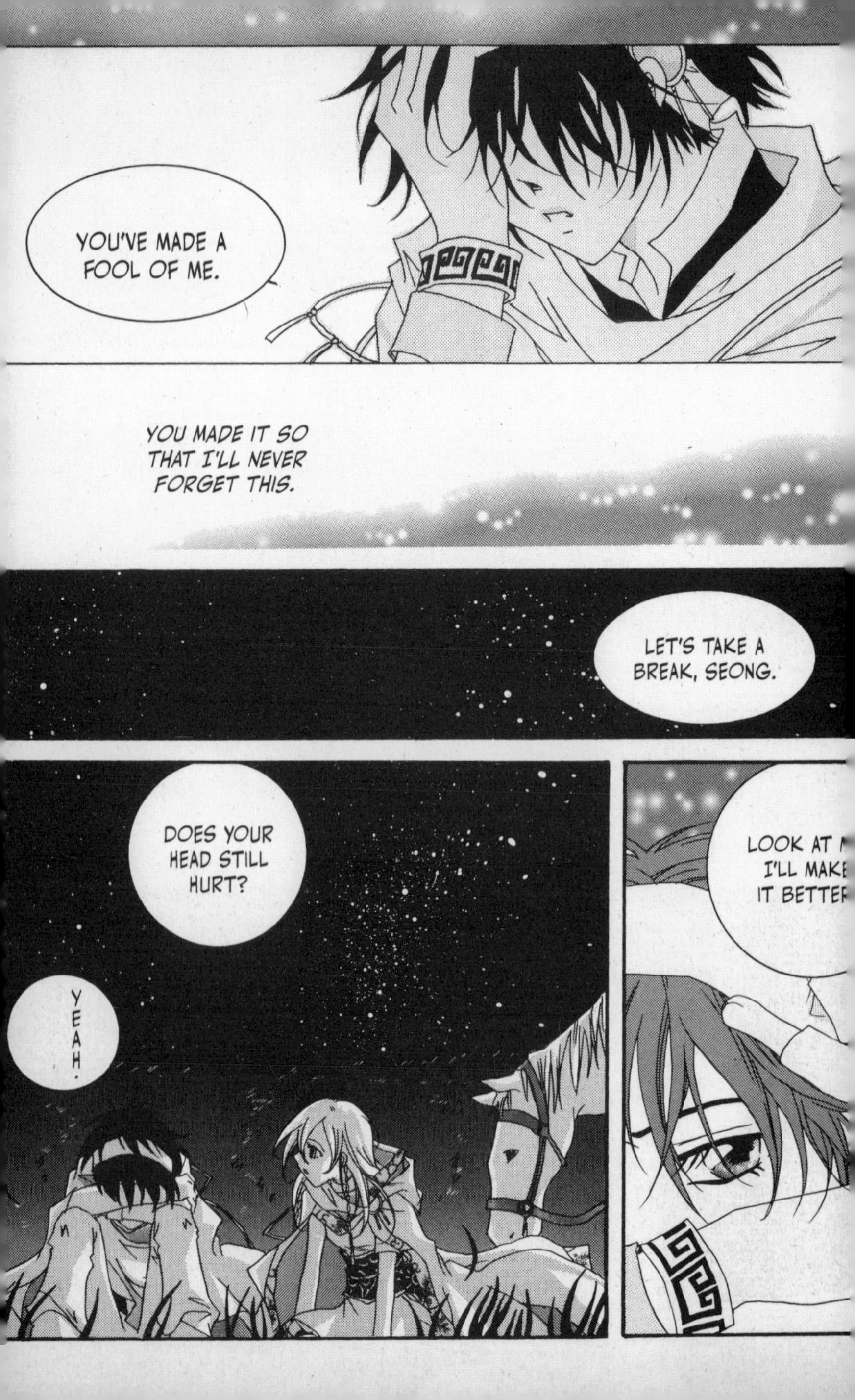
YOU'VE MADE A FOOL OF ME.
YOU MADE IT SO THAT I'LL NEVER FORGET THIS.
LET'S TAKE A BREAK, SEONG.
DOES YOUR HEAD STILL HURT?
YEAH.
LOOK AT I'LL MAKE IT BETTER

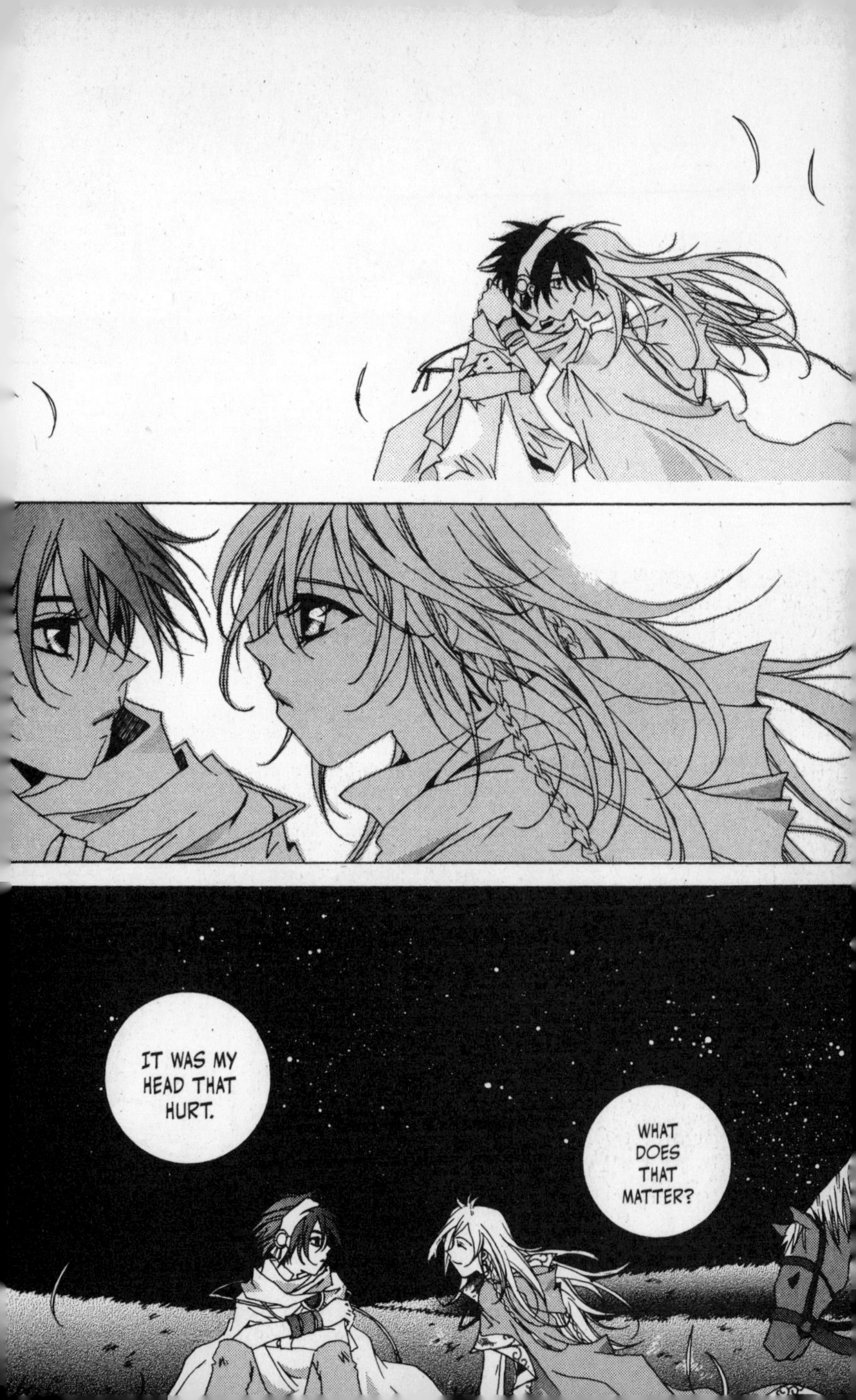
IT WAS MY HEAD THAT HURT.
WHAT DOES THAT MATTER?

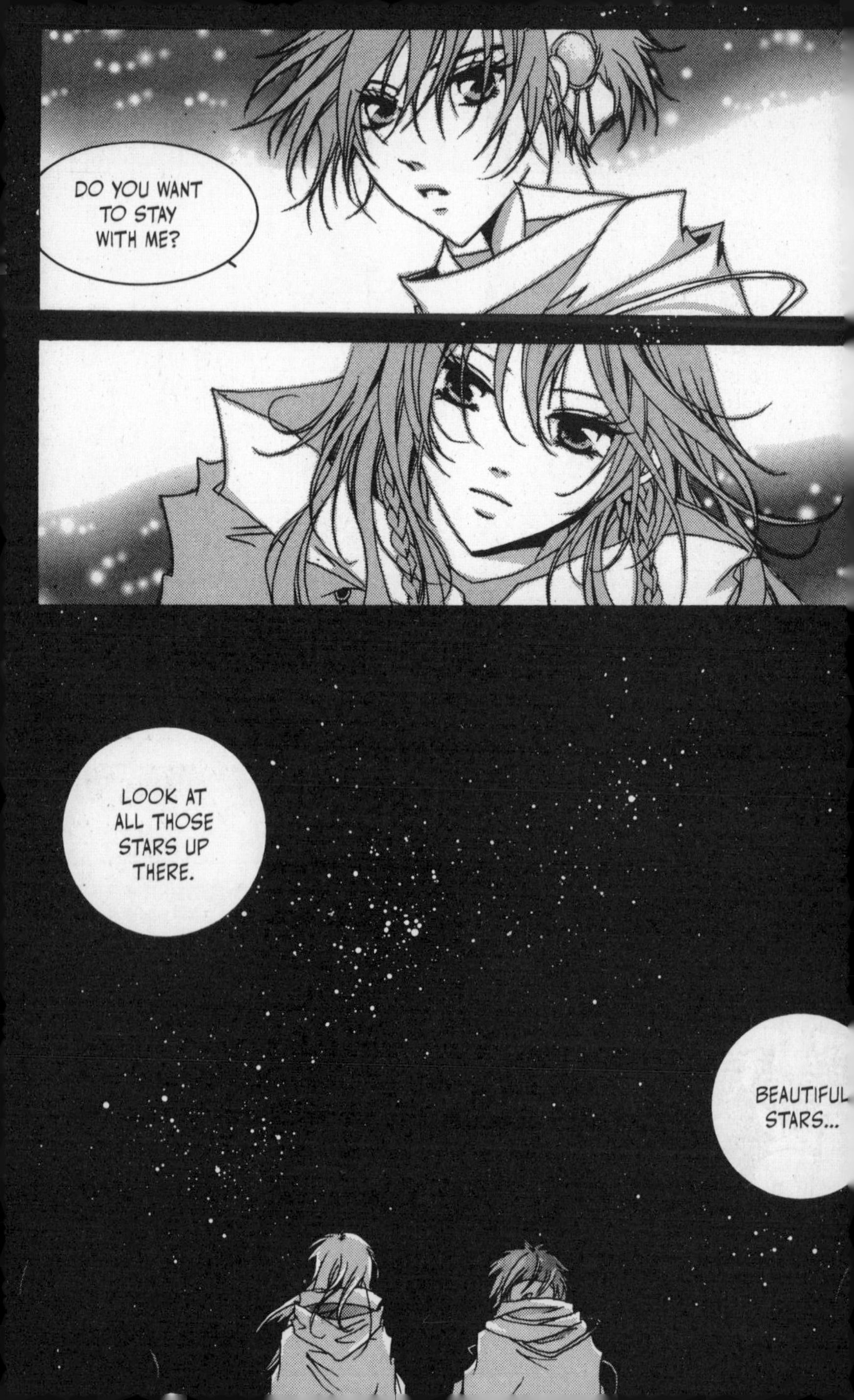
DO YOU WANT TO STAY WITH ME?
LOOK AT ALL THOSE STARS UP THERE.
BEAUTIFUL STARS...

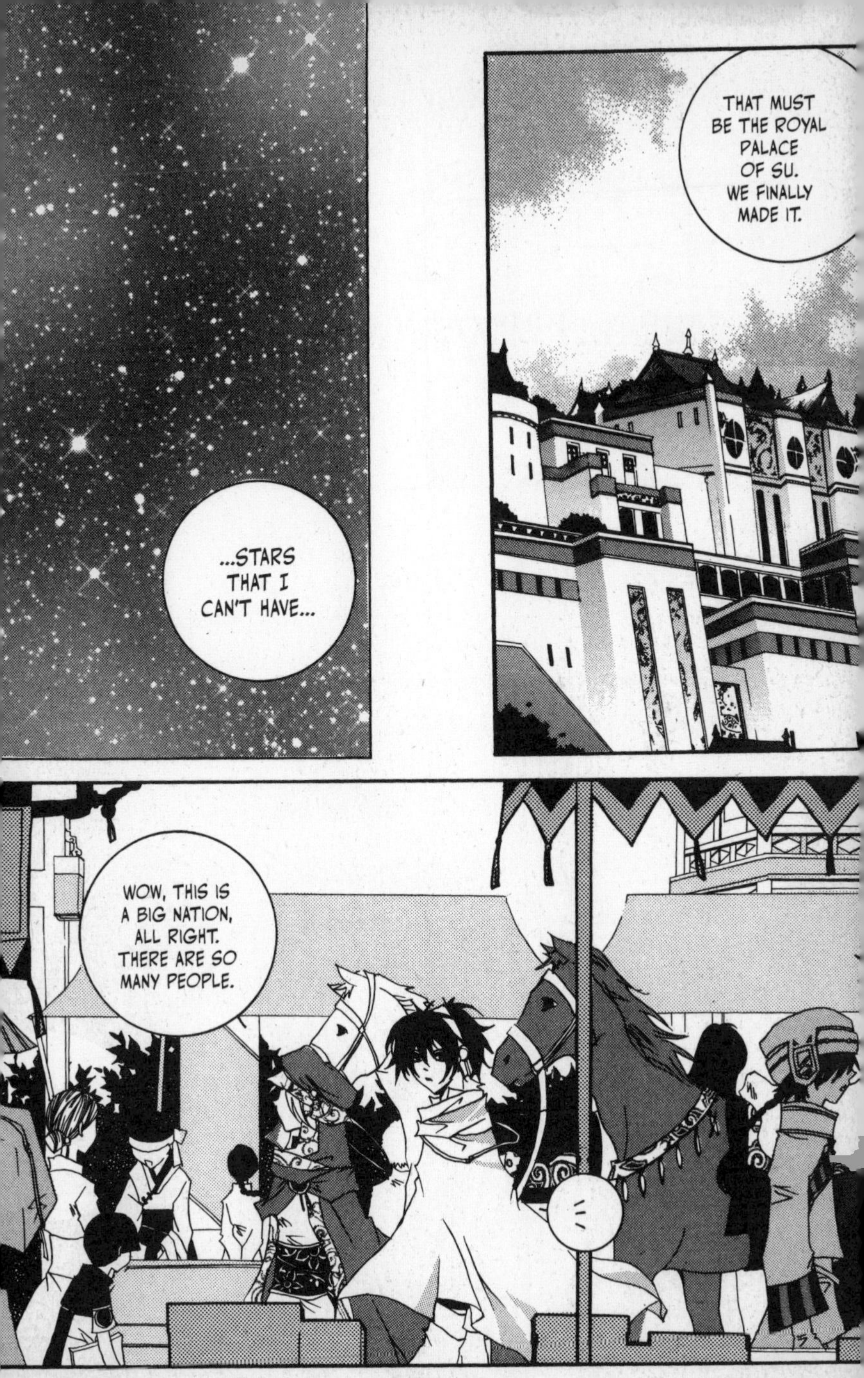
...STARS THAT I CAN'T HAVE...
THAT MUST BE THE ROYAL PALACE OF SU. WE FINALLY MADE IT.
WOW, THIS IS A BIG NATION, ALL RIGHT. THERE ARE SO MANY PEOPLE.

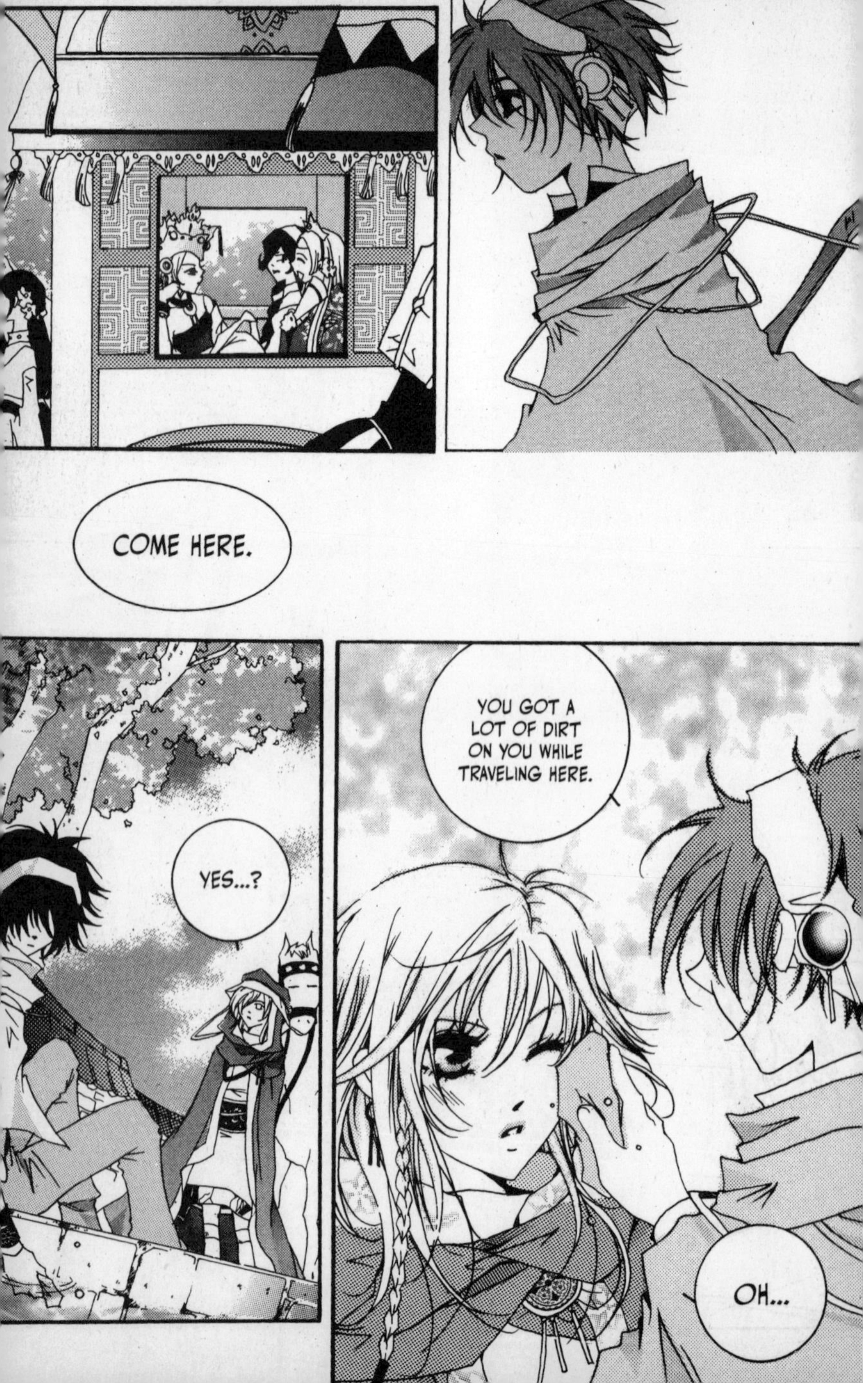
COME HERE.
YES...?
YOU GOT A LOT OF DIRT ON YOU WHILE TRAVELING HERE.
OH...

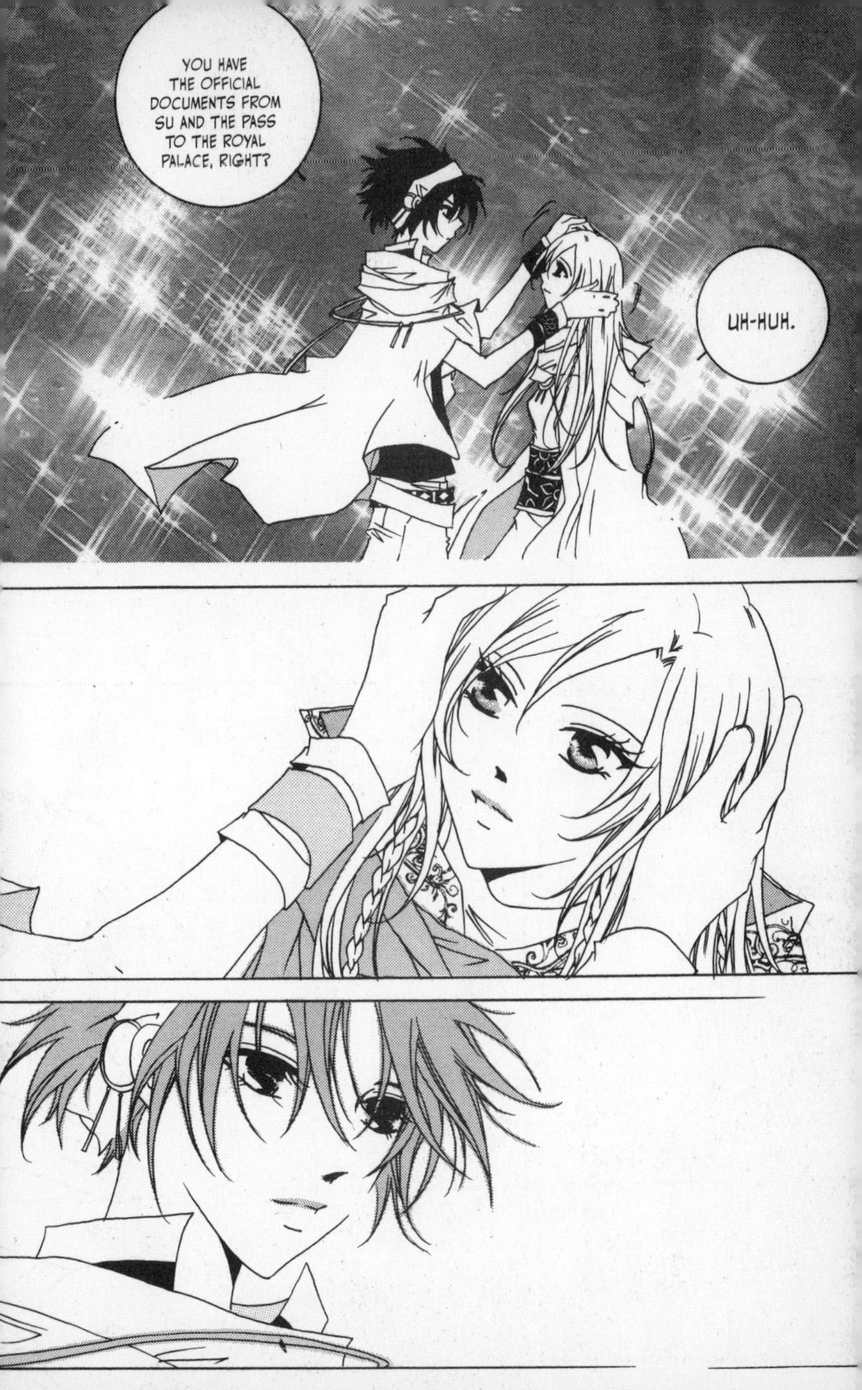
YOU HAVE THE OFFICIAL DOCUMENTS FROM SU AND THE PASS TO THE ROYAL PALACE, RIGHT?
UH-HUH.

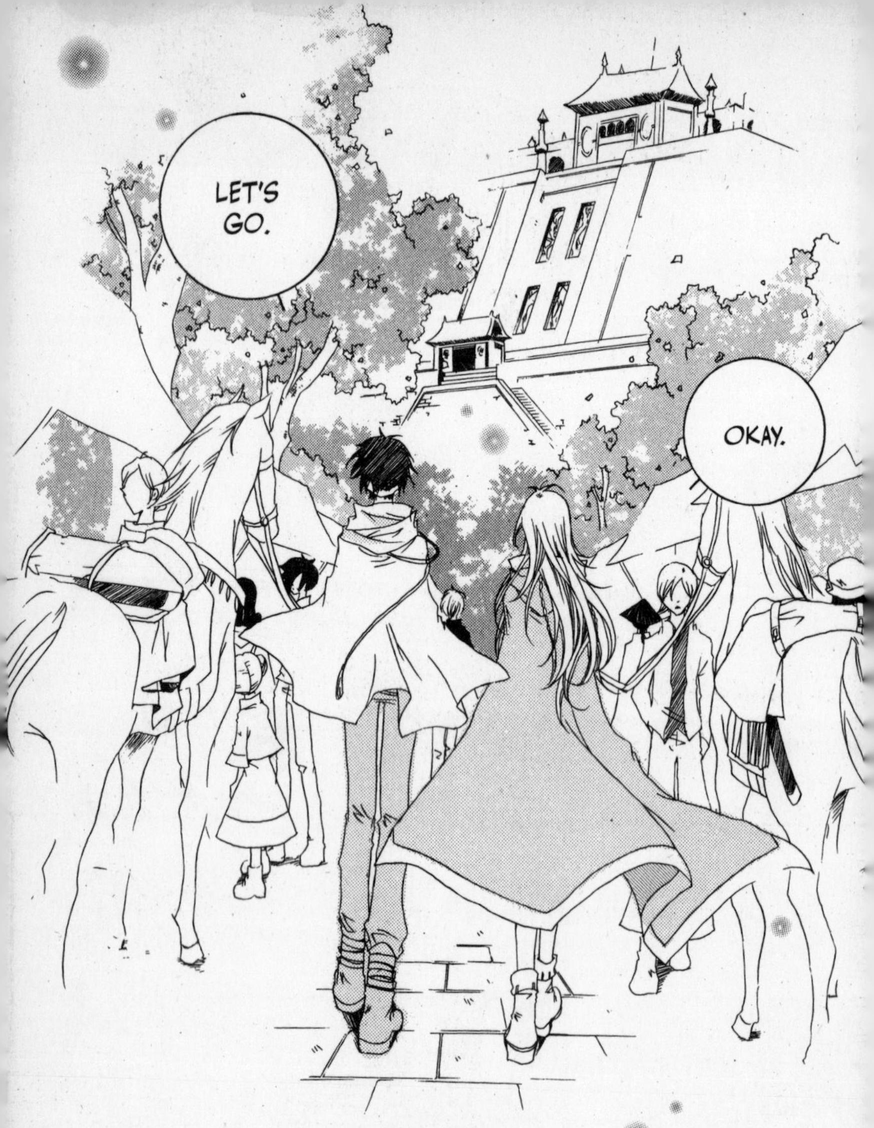
LET'S GO.
OKAY.

AND SO, I PARTED WITH HER
WHERE THE ROAD ENDED.

GYEOM WAS STILL SMILING.

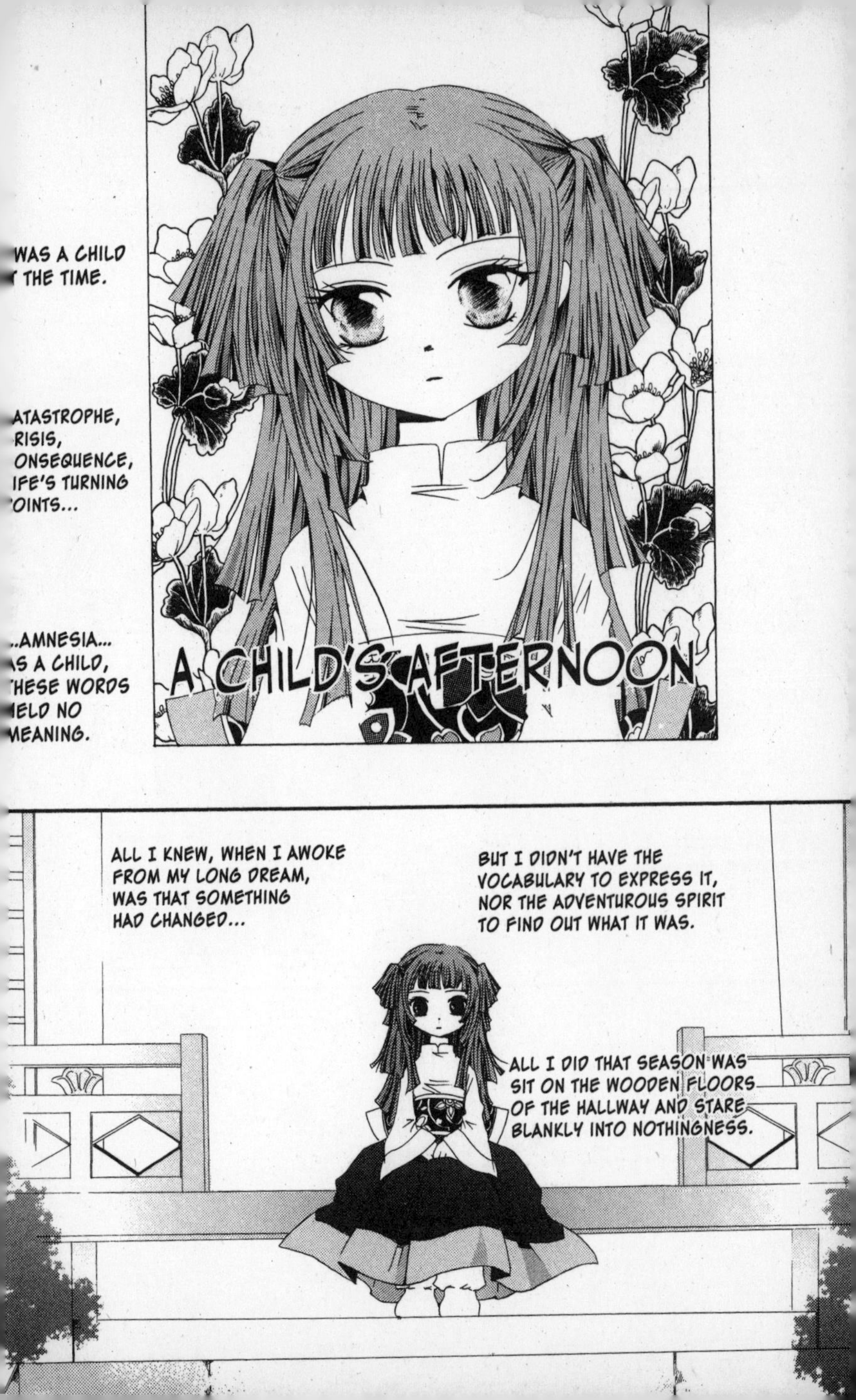
WAS A CHILD
THE TIME.
ATASTROPHE,
RISIS,
ONSEQUENCE,
IFE'S TURNING
OINTS...
..AMNESIA...
S A CHILD,
THESE WORDS
IELD NO
MEANING.
A CHILD'S AFTERNOON
ALL I KNEW, WHEN I AWOKE FROM MY LONG DREAM, WAS THAT SOMETHING HAD CHANGED...
BUT I DIDN'T HAVE THE VOCABULARY TO EXPRESS IT, NOR THE ADVENTUROUS SPIRIT TO FIND OUT WHAT IT WAS.
ALL I DID THAT SEASON WAS SIT ON THE WOODEN FLOORS OF THE HALLWAY AND STARE BLANKLY INTO NOTHINGNESS.

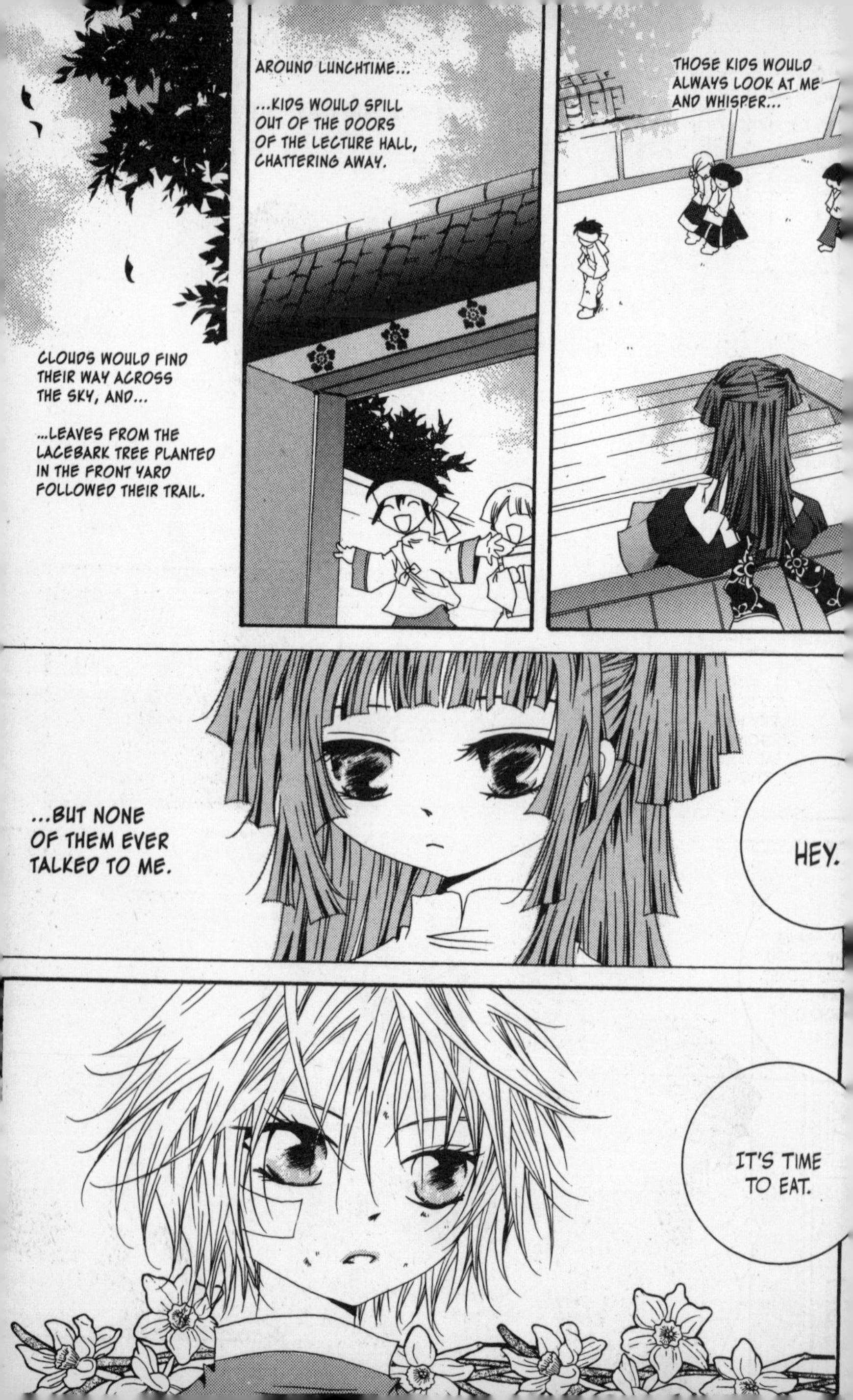
CLOUDS WOULD FIND THEIR WAY ACROSS THE SKY, AND...
...LEAVES FROM THE LACEBARK TREE PLANTED IN THE FRONT YARD FOLLOWED THEIR TRAIL.
AROUND LUNCHTIME...
...KIDS WOULD SPILL OUT OF THE DOORS OF THE LECTURE HALL, CHATTERING AWAY.
THOSE KIDS WOULD ALWAYS LOOK AT ME AND WHISPER...
...BUT NONE OF THEM EVER TALKED TO ME.
HEY.
IT'S TIME TO EAT.

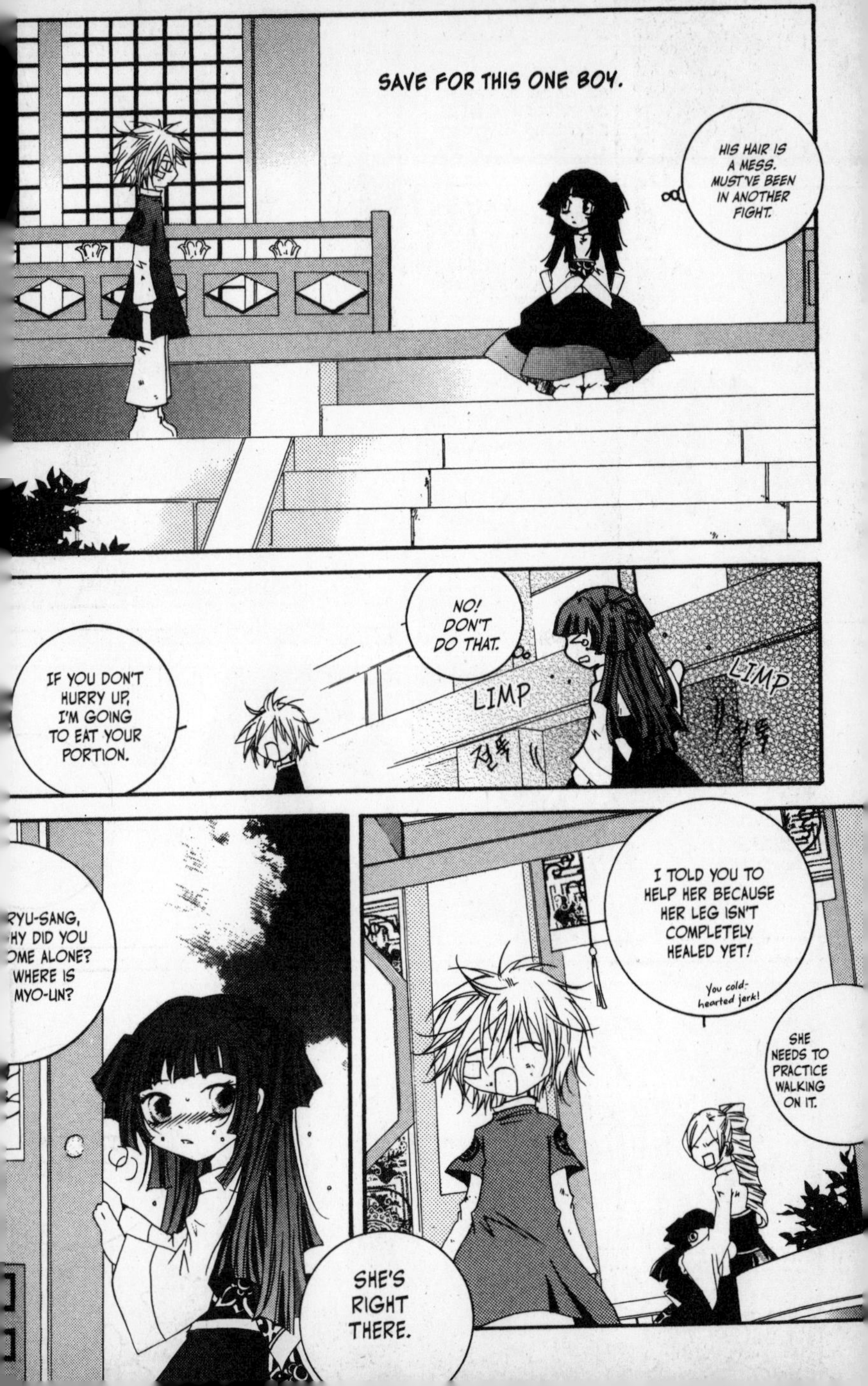
SAVE FOR THIS ONE BOY.
HIS HAIR IS A MESS. MUST'VE BEEN IN ANOTHER FIGHT.
IF YOU DON'T HURRY UP, I'M GOING TO EAT YOUR PORTION.
LIMP
절뚝
NO! DON'T DO THAT.
LIMP
절뚝
RYU-SANG, HY DID YOU OME ALONE? WHERE IS MYO-UN?
I TOLD YOU TO HELP HER BECAUSE HER LEG ISN'T COMPLETELY HEALED YET!
You cold-hearted jerk!
SHE NEEDS TO PRACTICE WALKING ON IT.
SHE'S RIGHT THERE.

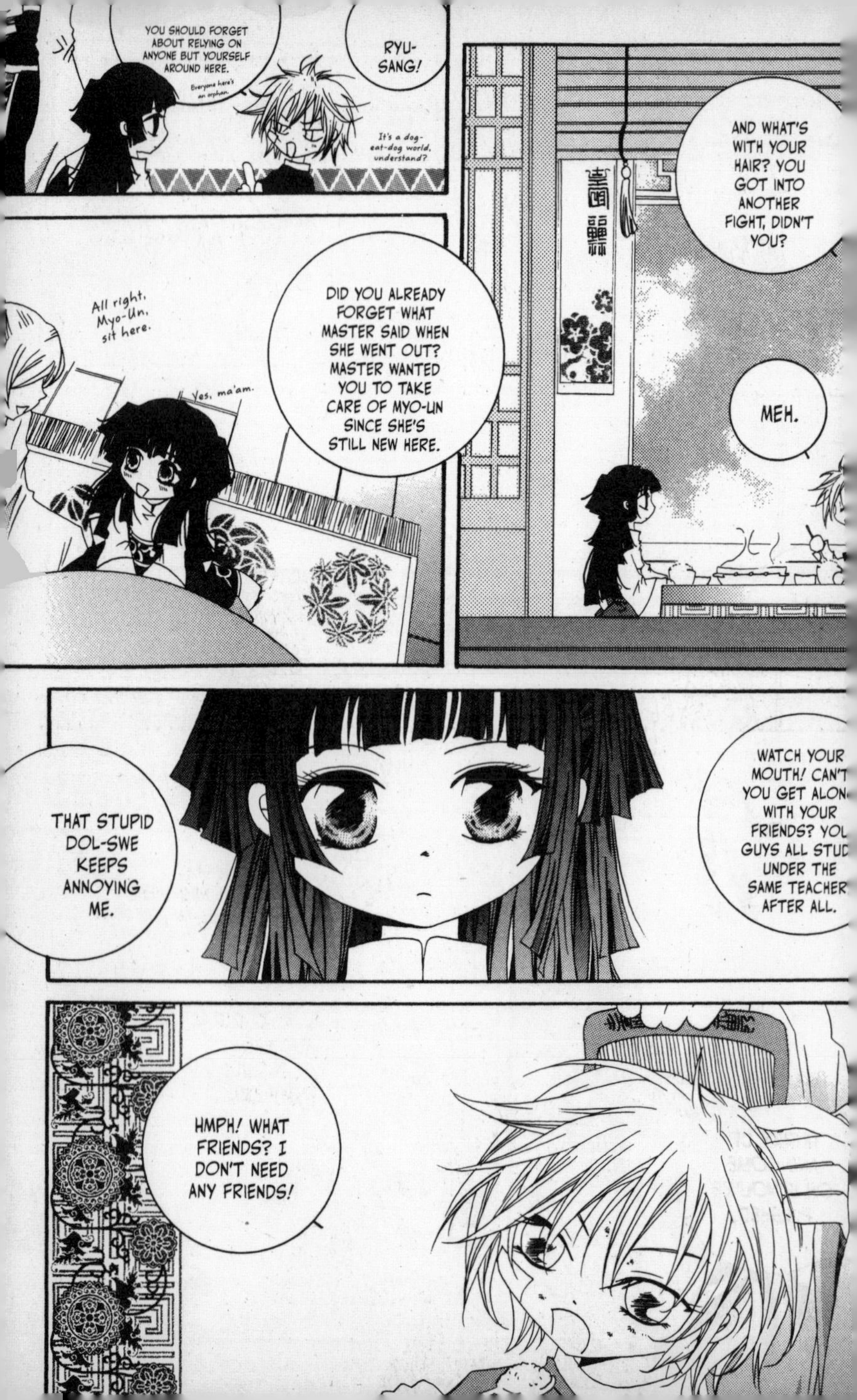
YOU SHOULD FORGET ABOUT RELYING ON ANYONE BUT YOURSELF AROUND HERE.
Everyone here's an orphan.
It's a dog-eat-dog world, understand?
RYU-SANG!
All right, Myo-Un, sit here.
Yes, ma'am.
DID YOU ALREADY FORGET WHAT MASTER SAID WHEN SHE WENT OUT? MASTER WANTED YOU TO TAKE CARE OF MYO-UN SINCE SHE'S STILL NEW HERE.
AND WHAT'S WITH YOUR HAIR? YOU GOT INTO ANOTHER FIGHT, DIDN'T YOU?
MEH.
THAT STUPID DOL-SWE KEEPS ANNOYING ME.
WATCH YOUR MOUTH! CAN'T YOU GET ALONG WITH YOUR FRIENDS? YOU GUYS ALL STUDY UNDER THE SAME TEACHER AFTER ALL.
HMPH! WHAT FRIENDS? I DON'T NEED ANY FRIENDS!

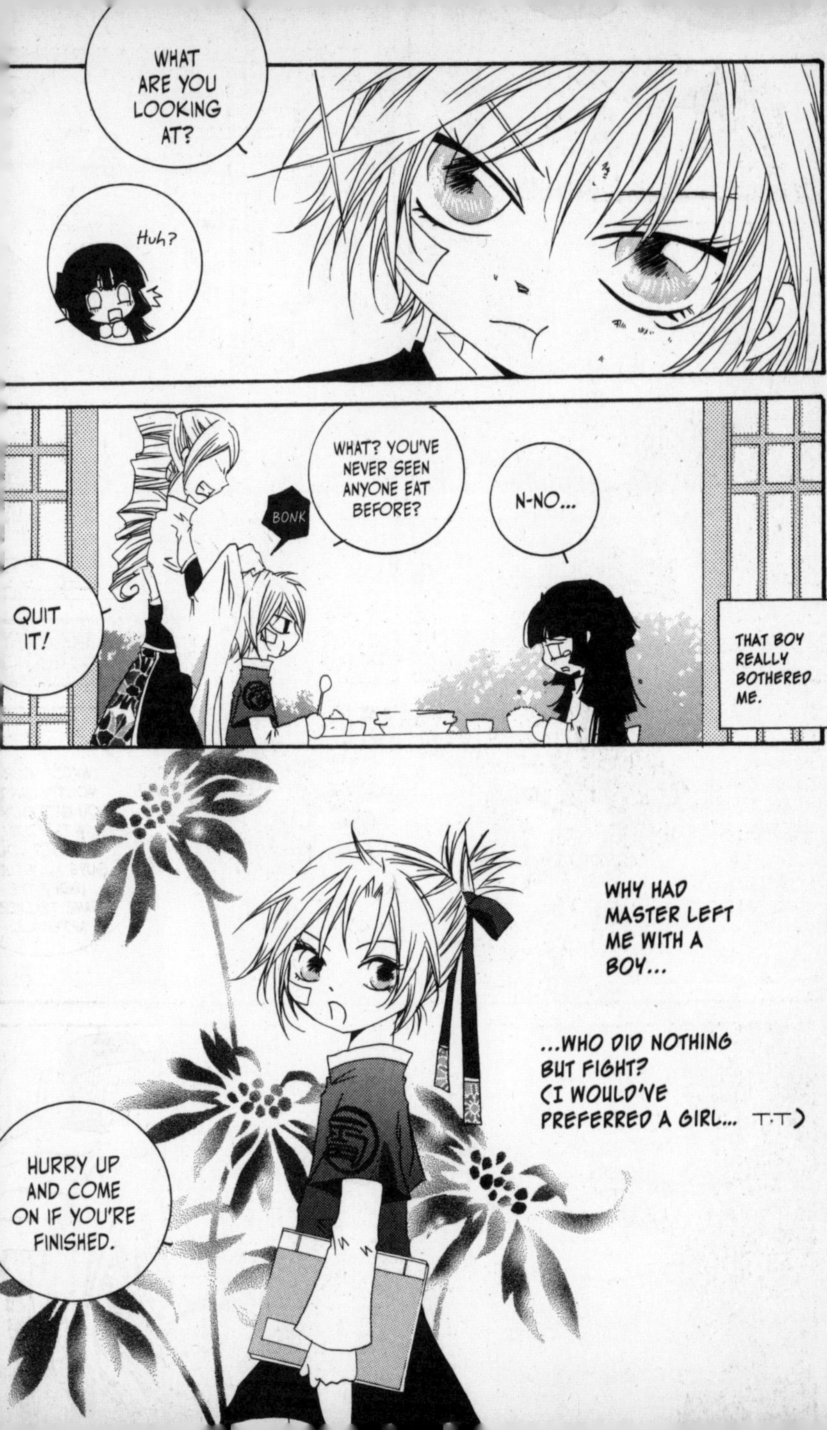
WHAT ARE YOU LOOKING AT?
Huh?
QUIT IT!
BONK
WHAT? YOU'VE NEVER SEEN ANYONE EAT BEFORE?
N-NO...
THAT BOY REALLY BOTHERED ME.
WHY HAD MASTER LEFT ME WITH A BOY...
...WHO DID NOTHING BUT FIGHT? (I WOULD'VE PREFERRED A GIRL... T.T)
HURRY UP AND COME ON IF YOU'RE FINISHED.

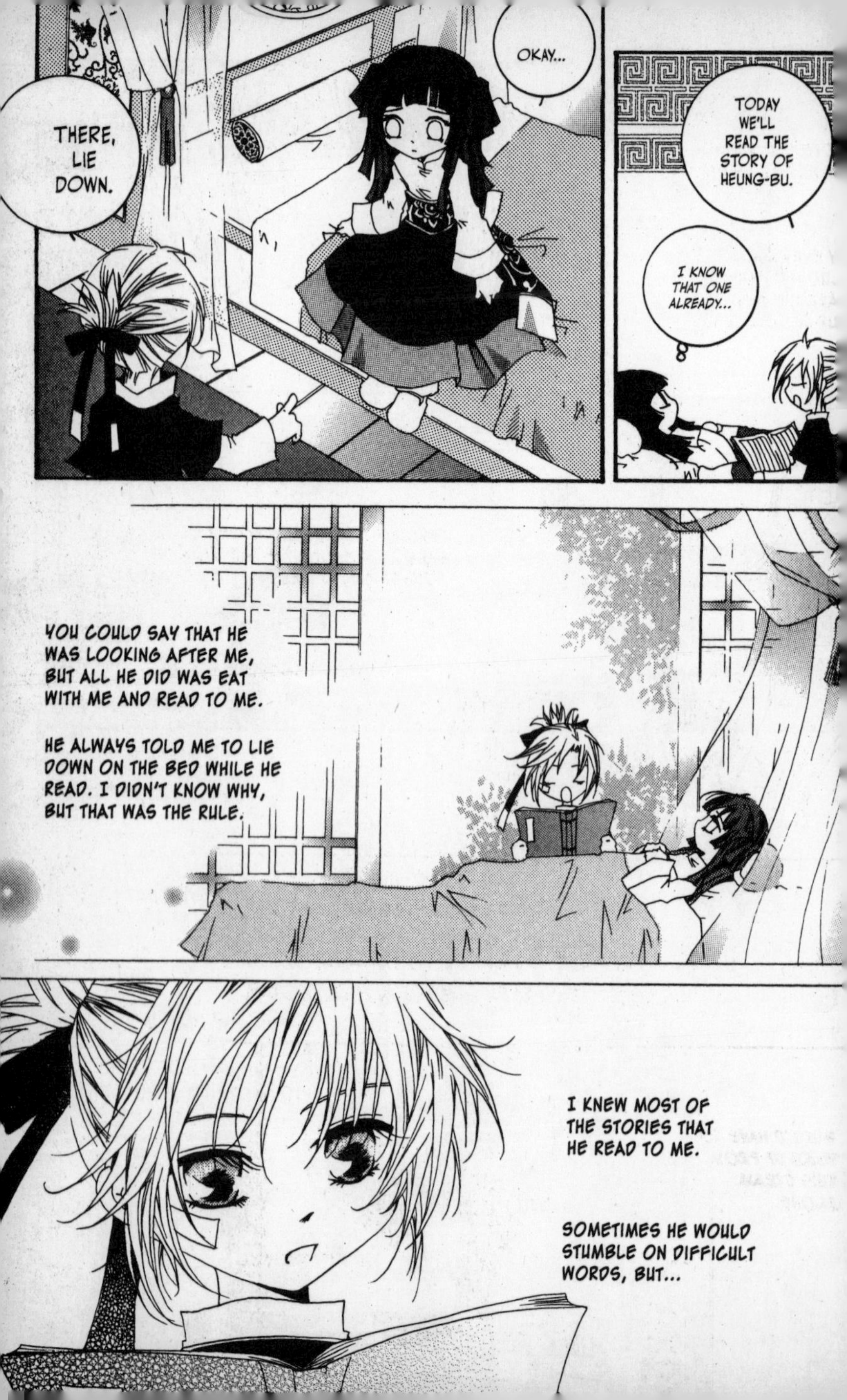
THERE, LIE DOWN.
OKAY...
TODAY WE'LL READ THE STORY OF HEUNG-BU.
I KNOW THAT ONE ALREADY...
YOU COULD SAY THAT HE WAS LOOKING AFTER ME, BUT ALL HE DID WAS EAT WITH ME AND READ TO ME.
HE ALWAYS TOLD ME TO LIE DOWN ON THE BED WHILE HE READ. I DIDN'T KNOW WHY, BUT THAT WAS THE RULE.
I KNEW MOST OF THE STORIES THAT HE READ TO ME.
SOMETIMES HE WOULD STUMBLE ON DIFFICULT WORDS, BUT...

I WOULD ALWAYS FALL ASLEEP AS HE READ TO ME.

MY EVENTUAL SLUMBER WOULD MARK THE END OF OUR LITTLE RITUAL.

THROUGH THE FADING SOUND OF HIS VOICE, SMELL OF THE BAMBOO FOREST WOULD ARISE.

WHEN I CLOSED MY EYES...

...I'D DREAM OF A TILED-ROOF HOUSE FILLED WITH WARMTH AND HAPPINESS IN ALL ITS 99 ROOMS.

WITH ITS GARDEN ALWAYS IN FULL BLOOM.

BUT I'D HAVE TO WAKE UP FROM THIS DREAM. ALONE.

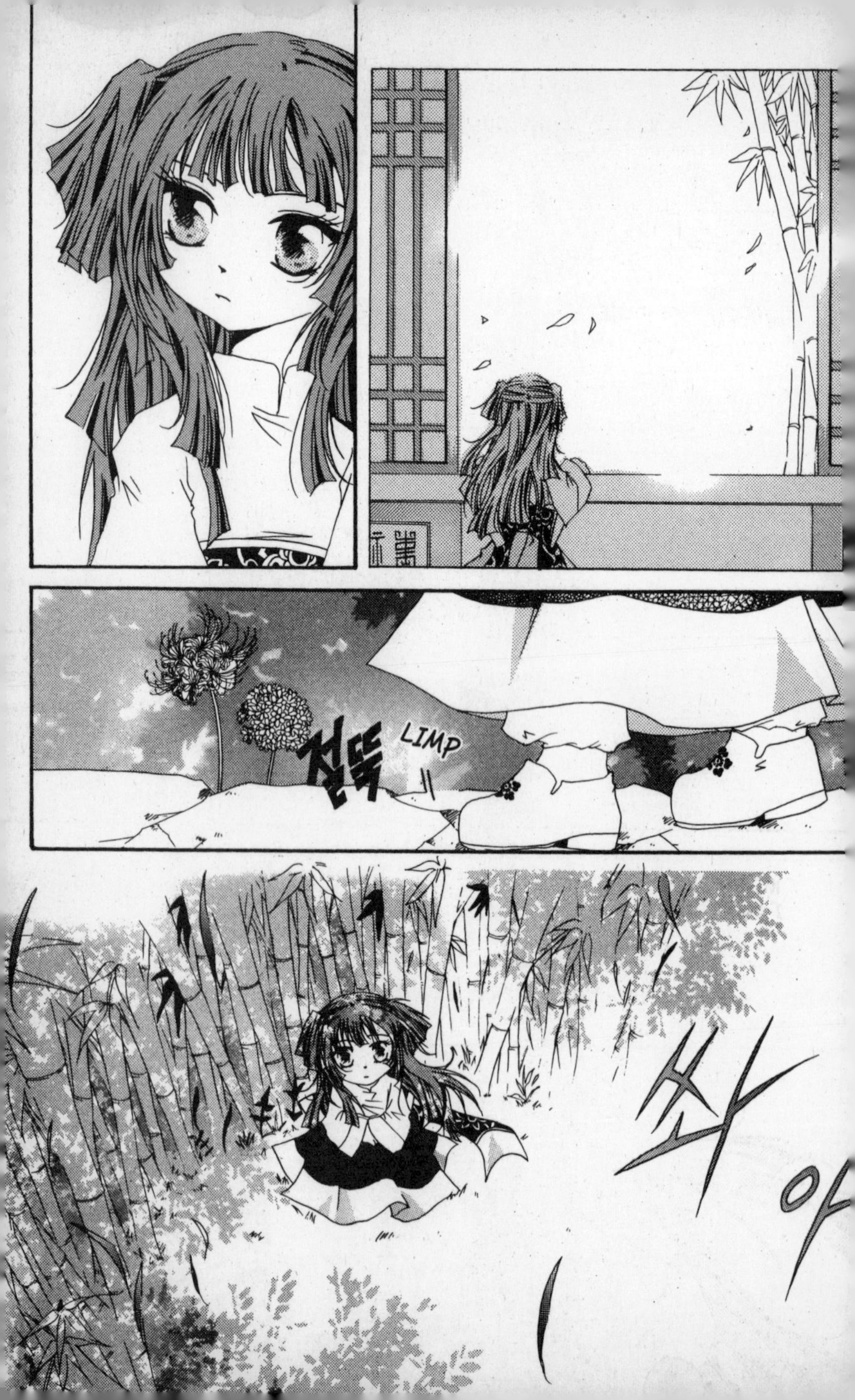

절뚝
LIMP
쏴아

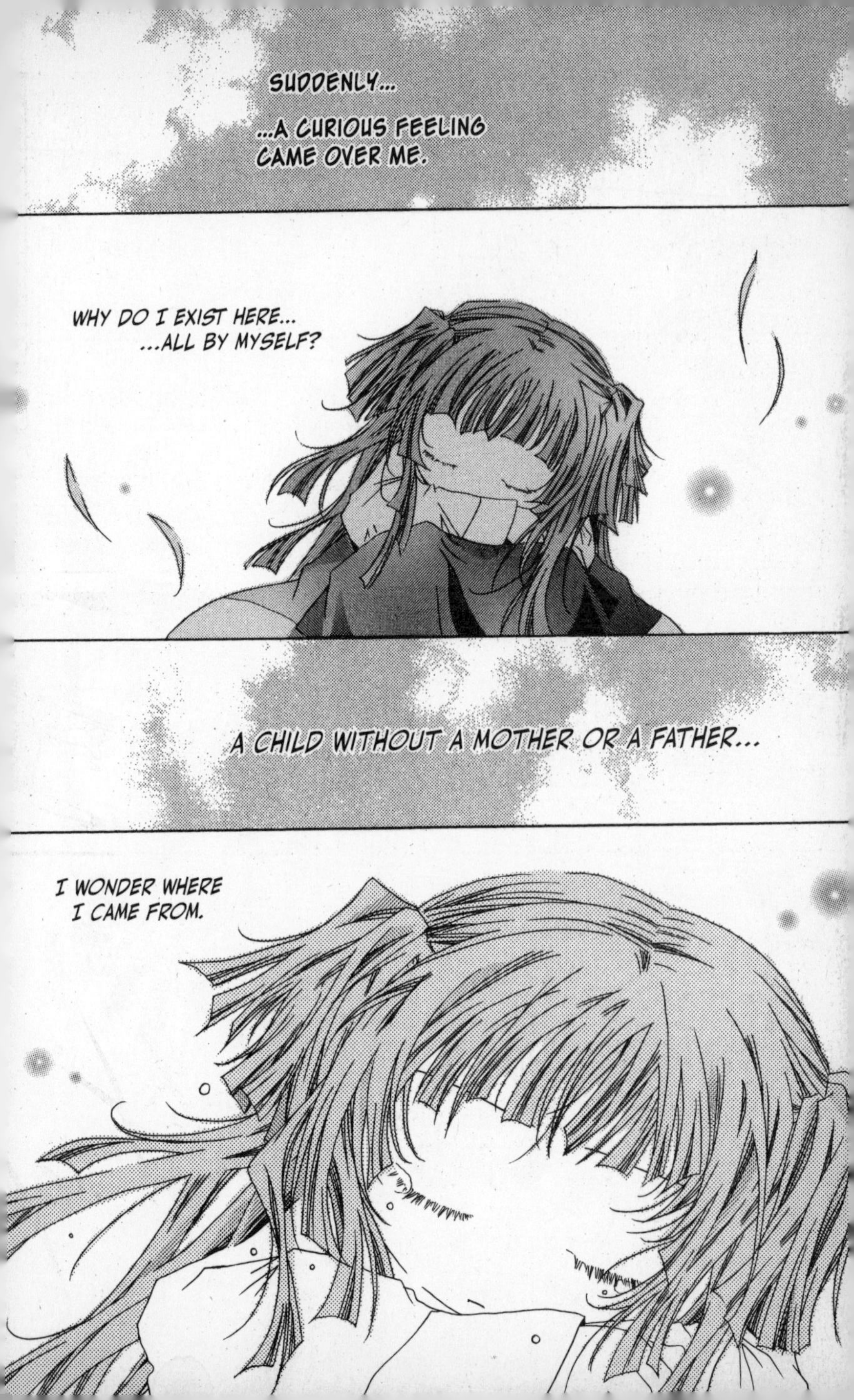
SUDDENLY...
...A CURIOUS FEELING CAME OVER ME.
WHY DO I EXIST HERE... ...ALL BY MYSELF?
A CHILD WITHOUT A MOTHER OR A FATHER...
I WONDER WHERE I CAME FROM.

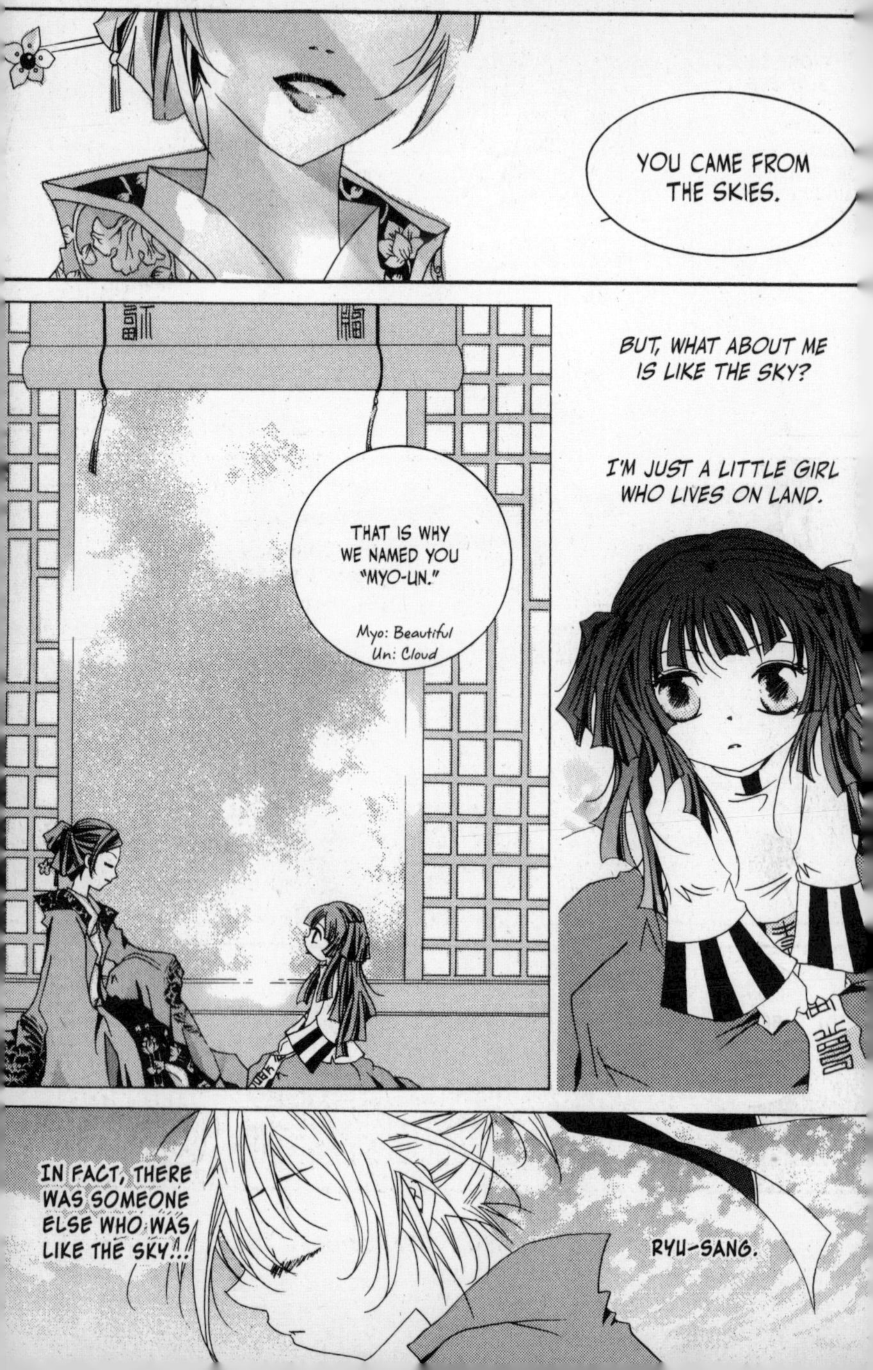
YOU CAME FROM THE SKIES.
THAT IS WHY WE NAMED YOU "MYO-UN."
Myo: Beautiful
Un: Cloud
BUT, WHAT ABOUT ME IS LIKE THE SKY?
I'M JUST A LITTLE GIRL WHO LIVES ON LAND.
IN FACT, THERE WAS SOMEONE ELSE WHO WAS LIKE THE SKY...
RYU-SANG.

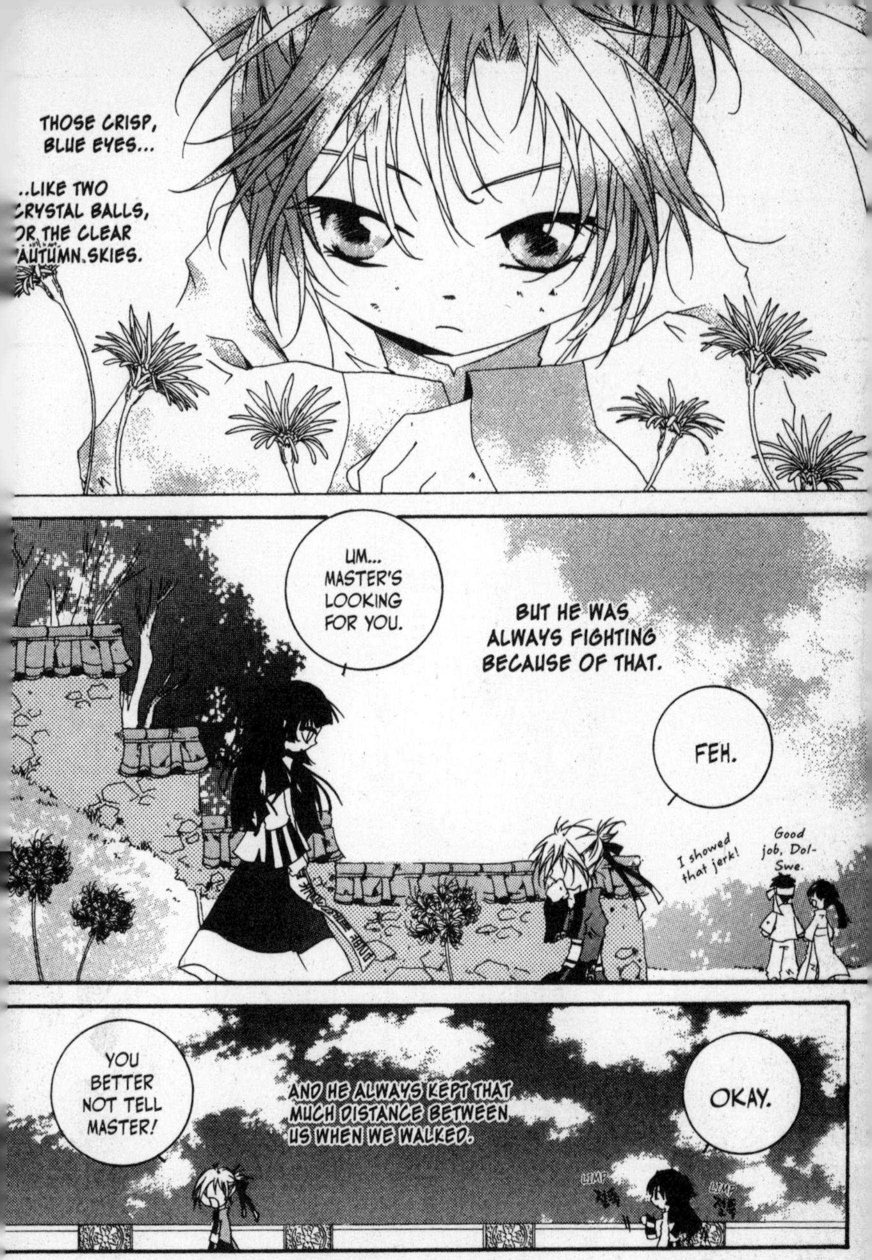
THOSE CRISP, BLUE EYES...
...LIKE TWO CRYSTAL BALLS, OR THE CLEAR AUTUMN SKIES.
UM... MASTER'S LOOKING FOR YOU.
BUT HE WAS ALWAYS FIGHTING BECAUSE OF THAT.
FEH.
I showed that jerk!
Good job, Dol-Swe.
YOU BETTER NOT TELL MASTER!
AND HE ALWAYS KEPT THAT MUCH DISTANCE BETWEEN US WHEN WE WALKED.
OKAY.
LIMP
LIMP

HE WAS AN UNTOUCHABLE SKY.

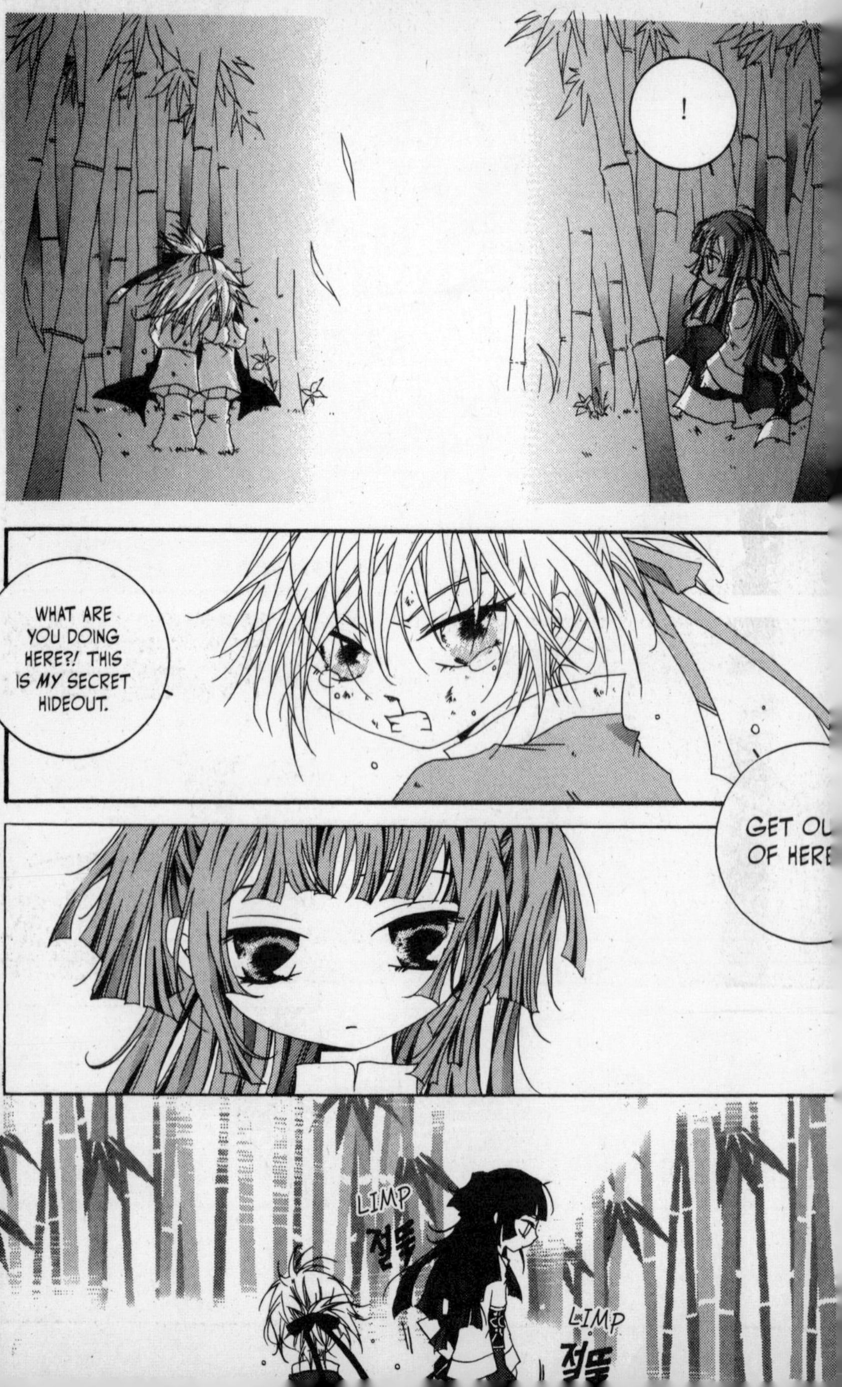
!
WHAT ARE YOU DOING HERE?! THIS IS MY SECRET HIDEOUT.
GET OU OF HERE
LIMP
절뚝
LIMP
절뚝

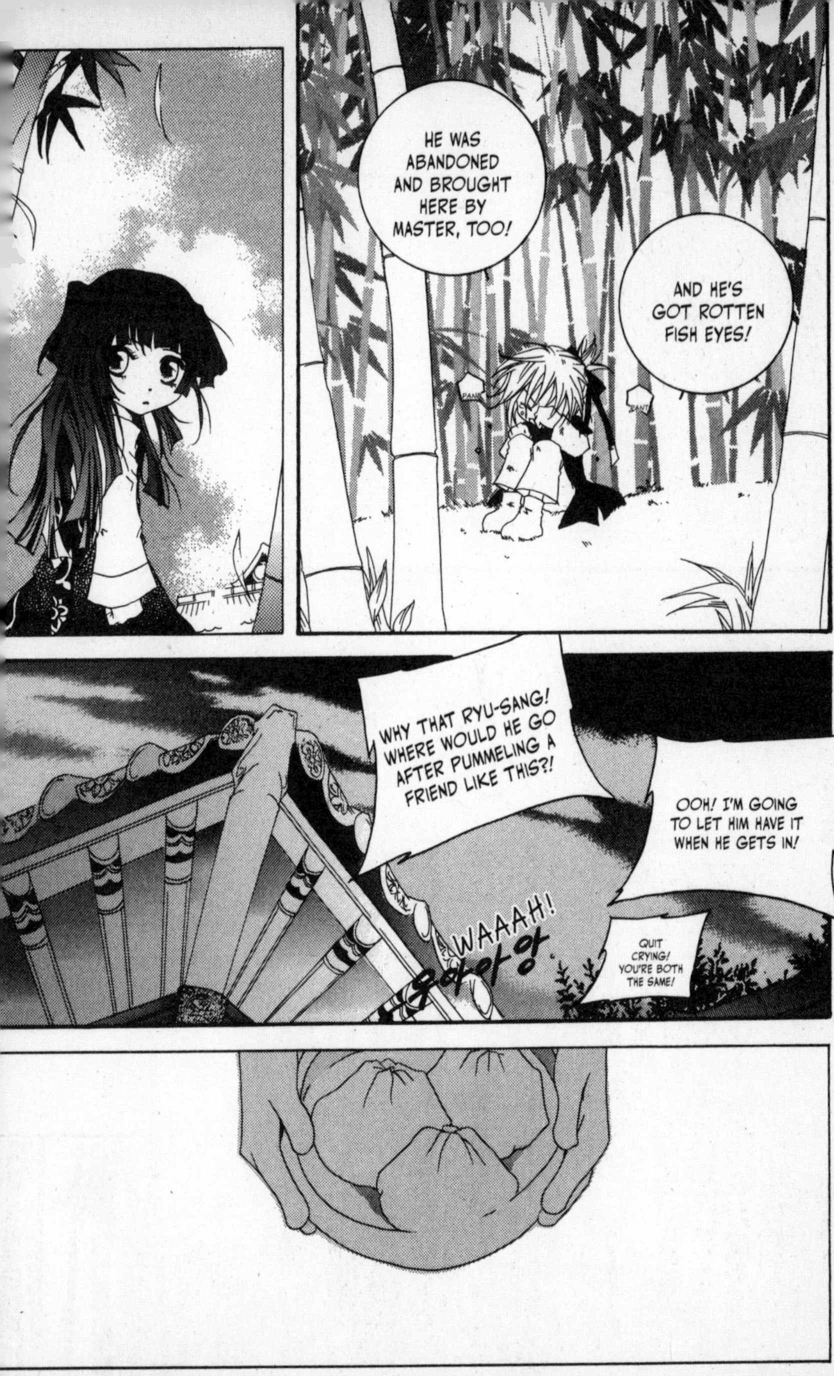
HE WAS ABANDONED AND BROUGHT HERE BY MASTER, TOO!
AND HE'S GOT ROTTEN FISH EYES!
PANT
PANT
WHY THAT RYU-SANG! WHERE WOULD HE GO AFTER PUMMELING A FRIEND LIKE THIS?!
OOH! I'M GOING TO LET HIM HAVE IT WHEN HE GETS IN!
WAAAH!
QUIT CRYING! YOU'RE BOTH THE SAME!

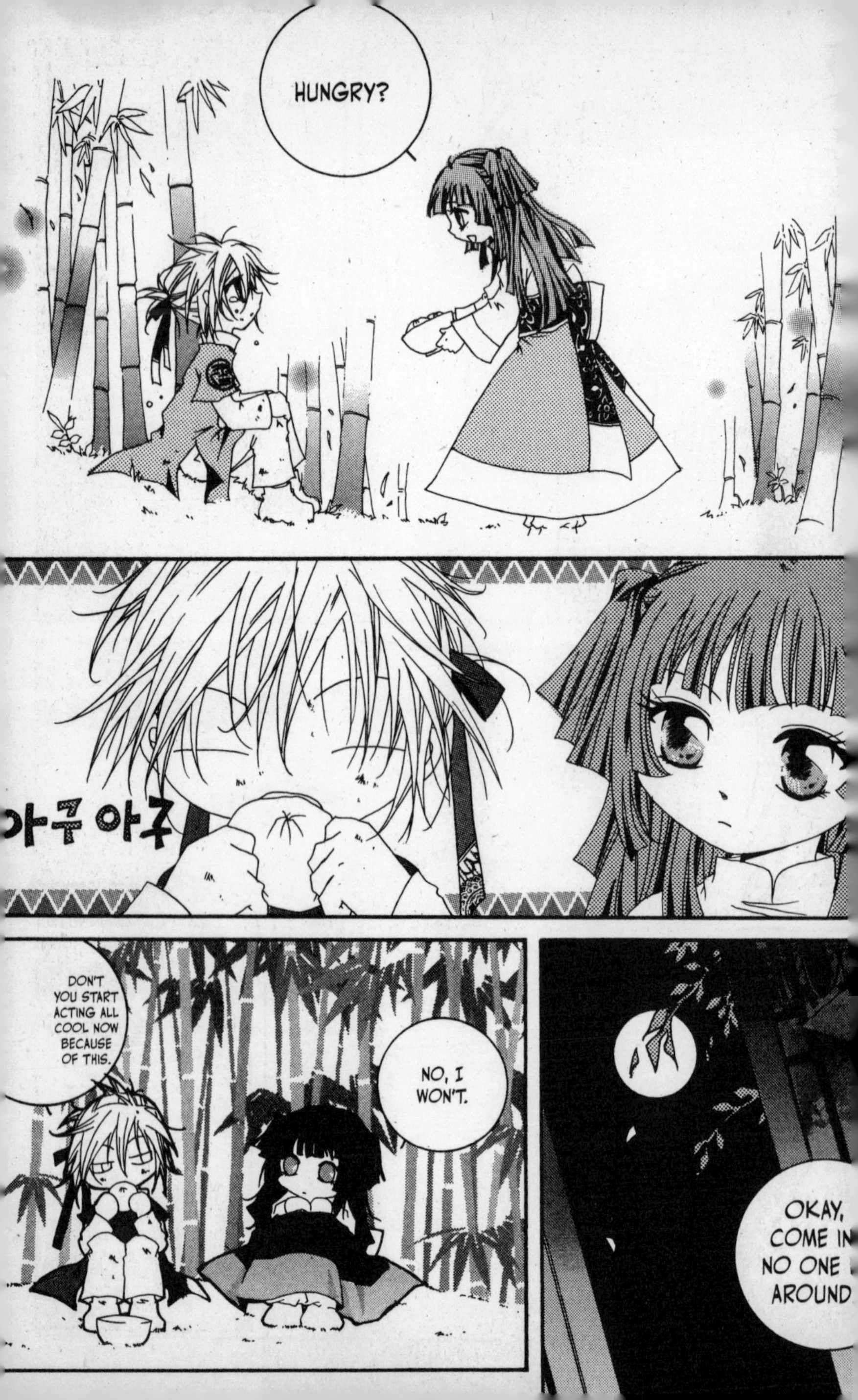
HUNGRY?
아구 아구
DON'T YOU START ACTING ALL COOL NOW BECAUSE OF THIS.
NO, I WON'T.
OKAY, COME IN NO ONE AROUND

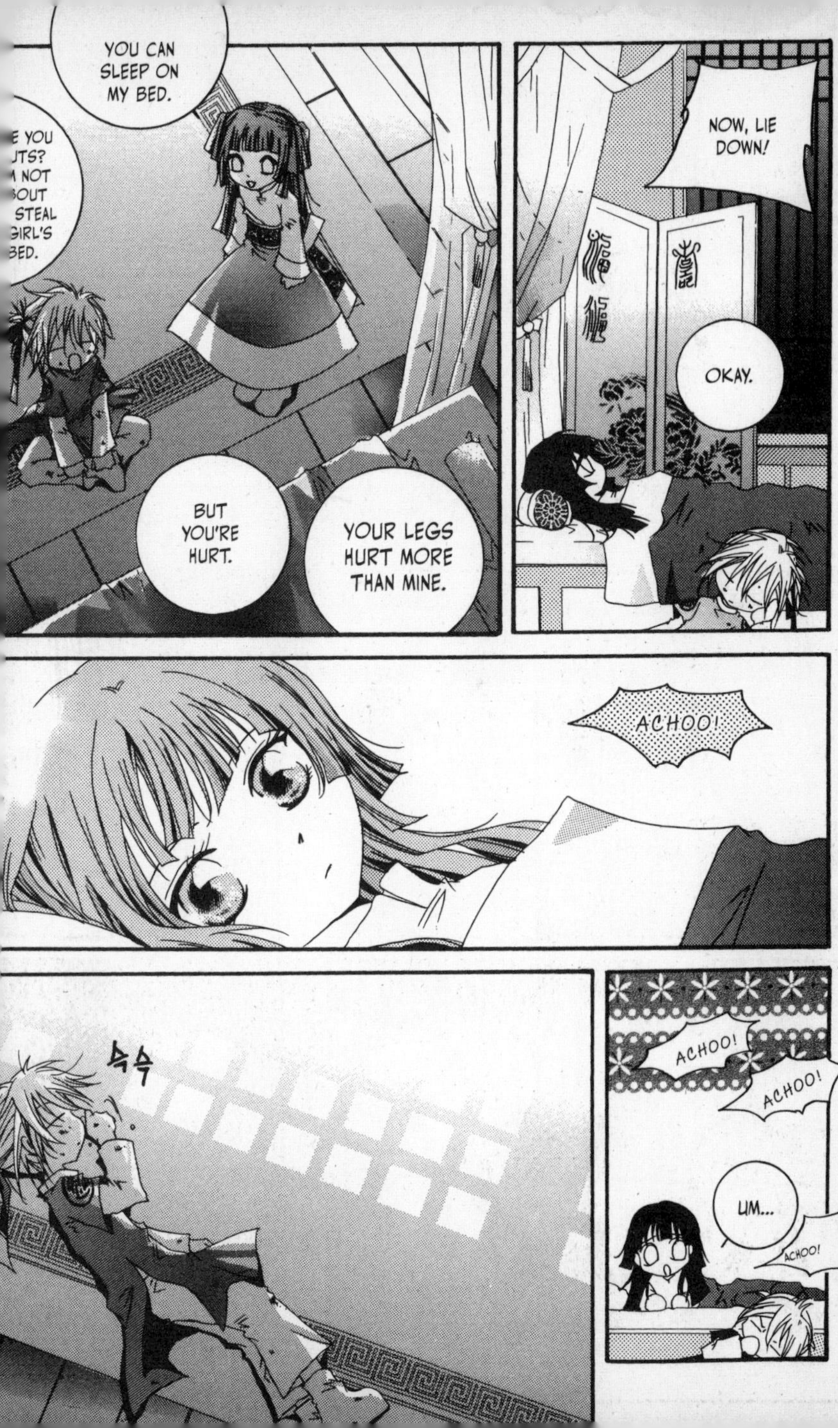
YOU CAN SLEEP ON MY BED.
E YOU UTS? M NOT BOUT STEAL GIRL'S BED.
BUT YOU'RE HURT.
YOUR LEGS HURT MORE THAN MINE.
NOW, LIE DOWN!
OKAY.
ACHOO!
슥슥
ACHOO!
ACHOO!
UM...
ACHOO!

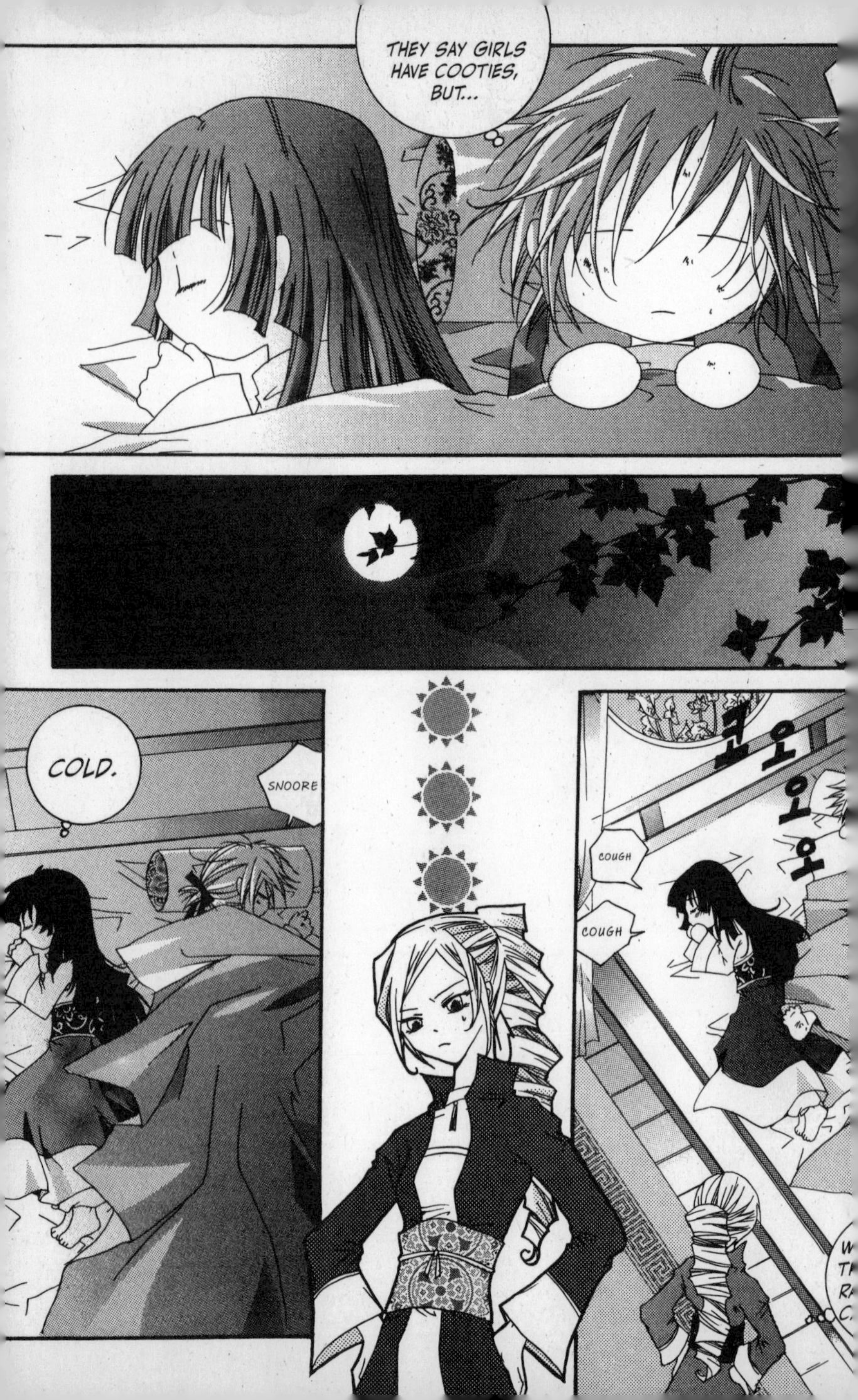
THEY SAY GIRLS HAVE COOTIES, BUT...
COLD.
SNOORE
코오오우
COUGH
COUGH

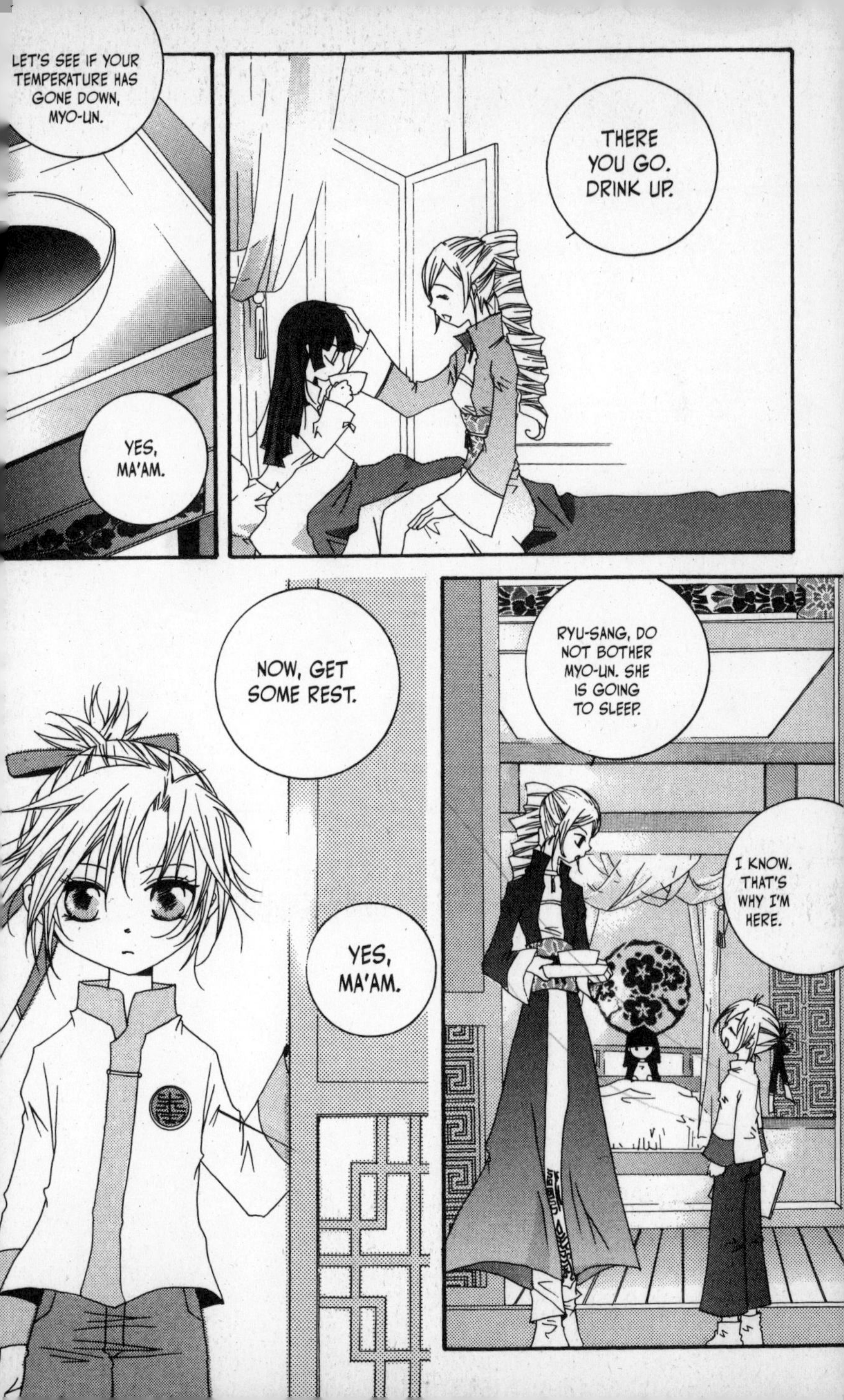
LET'S SEE IF YOUR TEMPERATURE HAS GONE DOWN, MYO-UN.
YES, MA'AM.
THERE YOU GO. DRINK UP.
NOW, GET SOME REST.
YES, MA'AM.
RYU-SANG, DO NOT BOTHER MYO-UN. SHE IS GOING TO SLEEP.
I KNOW. THAT'S WHY I'M HERE.

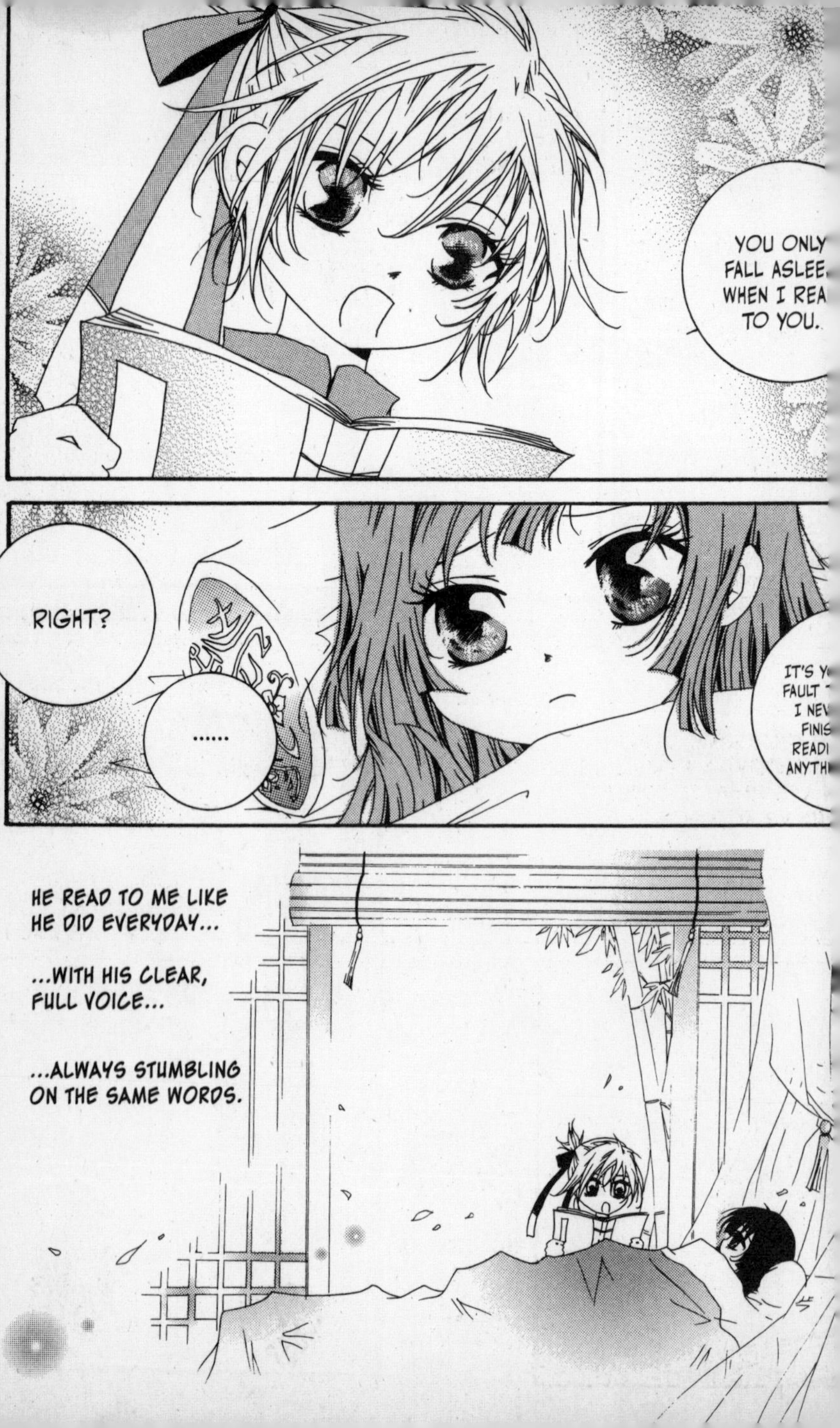
YOU ONLY FALL ASLEE WHEN I REA TO YOU.
RIGHT?
......
IT'S Y FAULT T I NEV FINIS READI ANYTH
HE READ TO ME LIKE HE DID EVERYDAY...
...WITH HIS CLEAR, FULL VOICE...
...ALWAYS STUMBLING ON THE SAME WORDS.

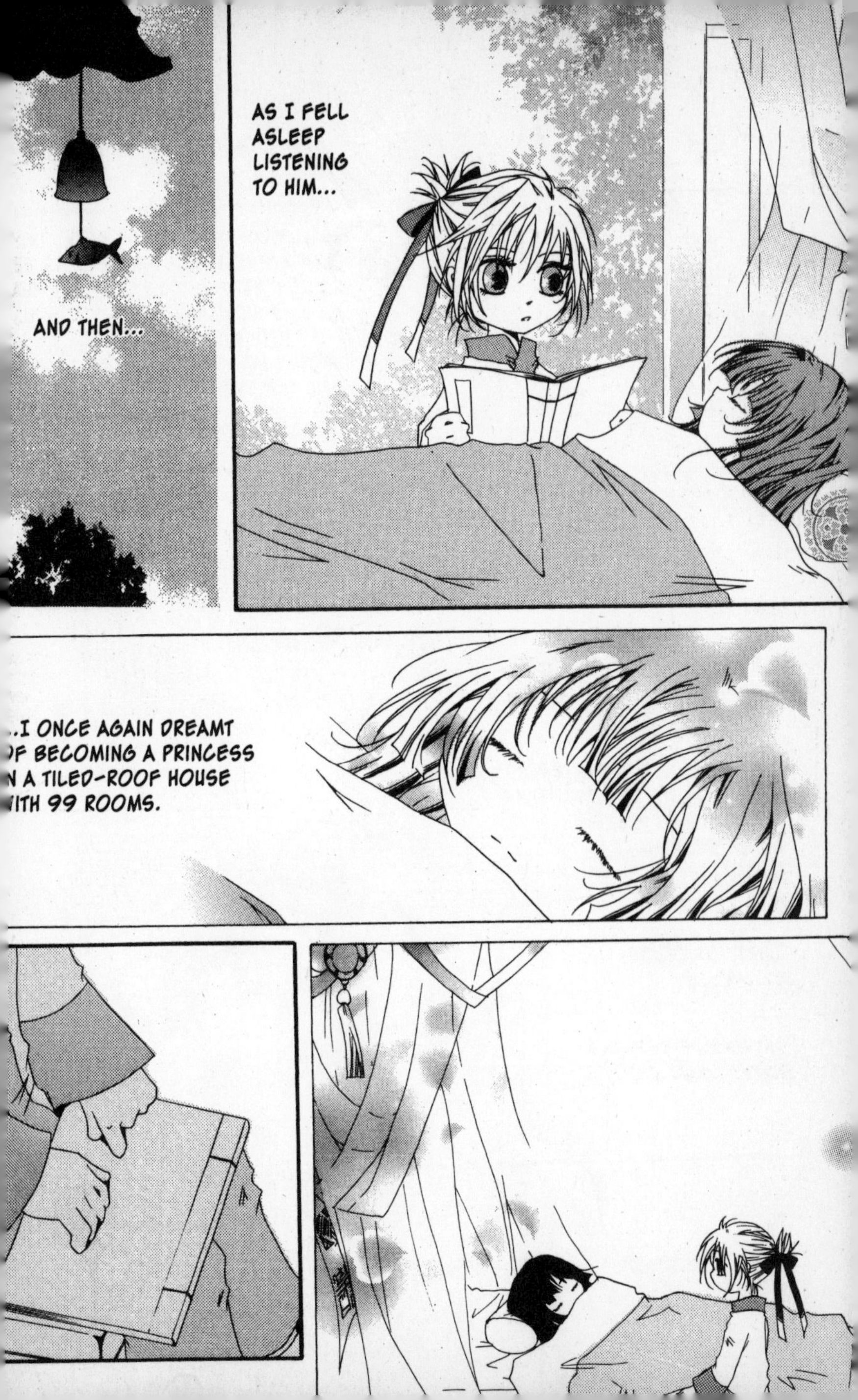
AND THEN...
AS I FELL ASLEEP LISTENING TO HIM...
..I ONCE AGAIN DREAMT
F BECOMING A PRINCESS
N A TILED-ROOF HOUSE
ITH 99 ROOMS.

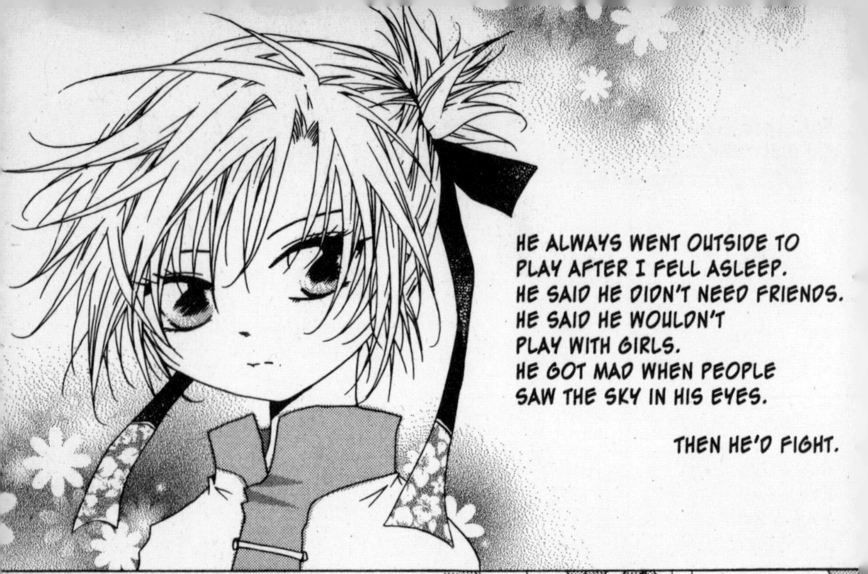
HE ALWAYS WENT OUTSIDE TO
PLAY AFTER I FELL ASLEEP.
HE SAID HE DIDN'T NEED FRIENDS.
HE SAID HE WOULDN'T
PLAY WITH GIRLS.
HE GOT MAD WHEN PEOPLE
SAW THE SKY IN HIS EYES.
THEN HE'D FIGHT.

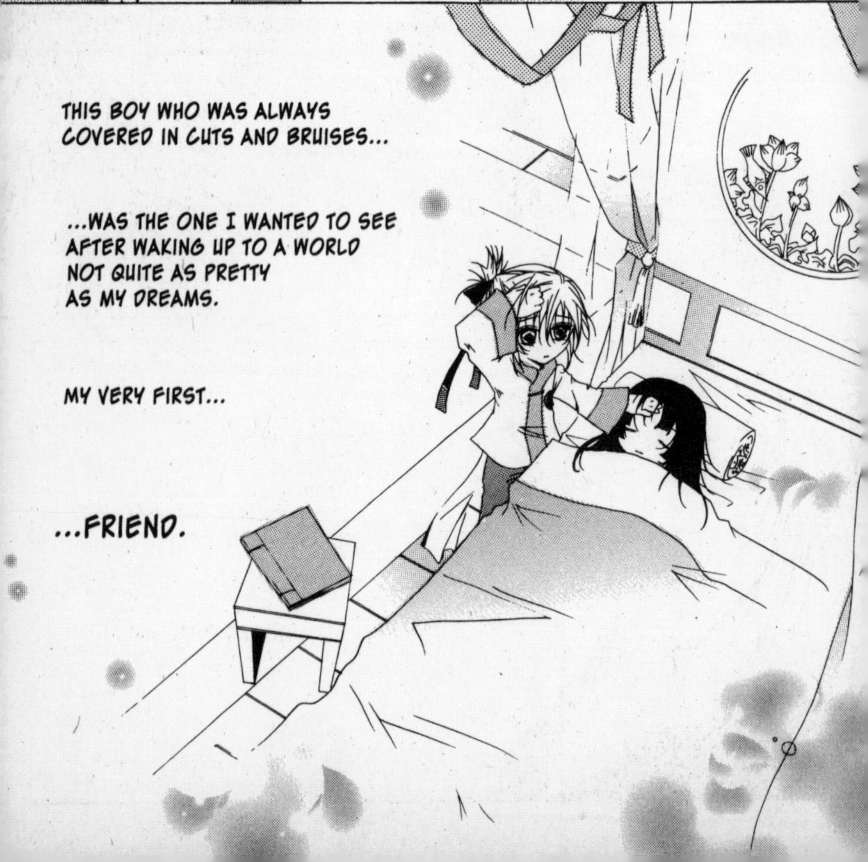
THIS BOY WHO WAS ALWAYS
COVERED IN CUTS AND BRUISES...
...WAS THE ONE I WANTED TO SEE
AFTER WAKING UP TO A WORLD
NOT QUITE AS PRETTY
AS MY DREAMS.
MY VERY FIRST...
...FRIEND.

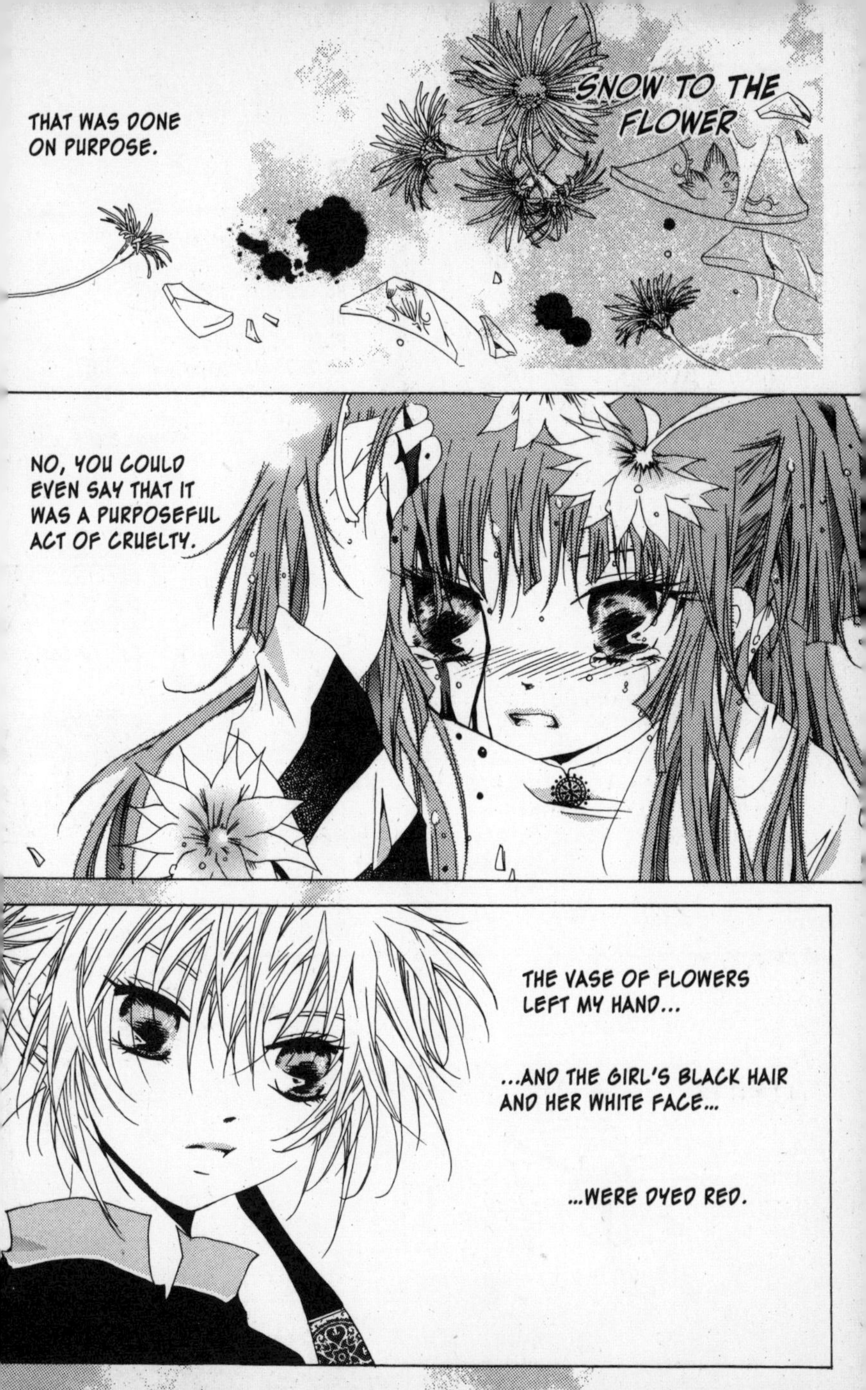

THAT WAS DONE ON PURPOSE.
SNOW TO THE FLOWER
NO, YOU COULD EVEN SAY THAT IT WAS A PURPOSEFUL ACT OF CRUELTY.
THE VASE OF FLOWERS LEFT MY HAND...
...AND THE GIRL'S BLACK HAIR AND HER WHITE FACE...
...WERE DYED RED.

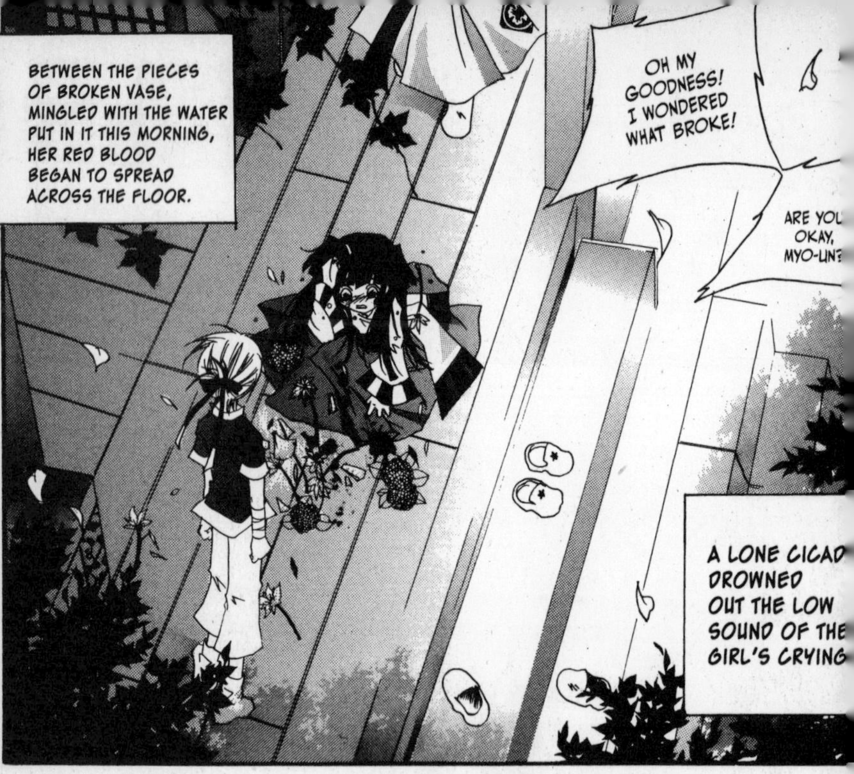
BETWEEN THE PIECES OF BROKEN VASE, MINGLED WITH THE WATER PUT IN IT THIS MORNING, HER RED BLOOD BEGAN TO SPREAD ACROSS THE FLOOR.
OH MY GOODNESS! I WONDERED WHAT BROKE!
ARE YOU OKAY, MYO-LIN?
A LONE CICAD DROWNED OUT THE LOW SOUND OF THE GIRL'S CRYING

THAT DAY, A FEW SUMMERS AGO,
I WAS ANGRY AT THIS ONE GIRL.
I WAS VERY ANGRY.

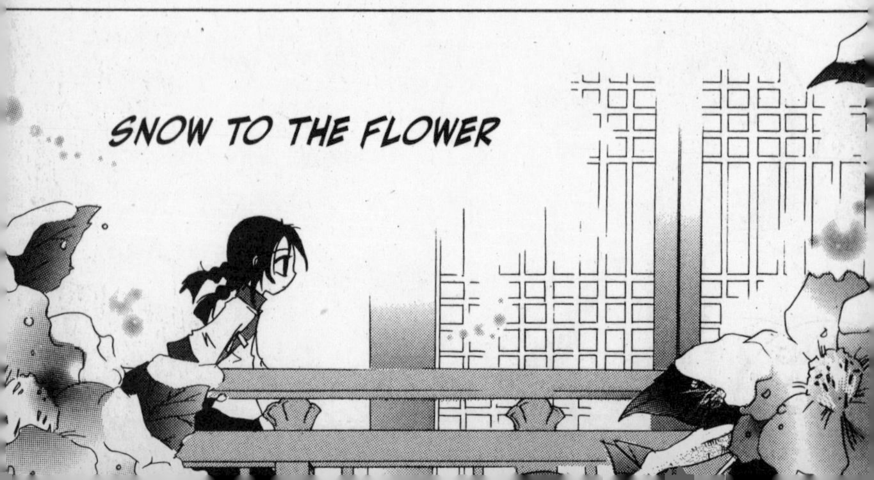
SNOW TO THE FLOWER

HOW IS
RYU-SANG?

I THOUGHT
WE'D HAVE A
FUNERAL.

IT'S THE START
OF A NEW YEAR,
AND ALREADY HE
COMES IN WITH
A STAB WOUND.
HE'S GOING
TO GIVE ME
GRAY HAIRS.

......

ARE YOU
GOING TO
STAY OUTSIDE?
IT'S COLD
OUT HERE.

RYU-SANG
WON'T LIKE
IT IF I GO
INSIDE.

THIS HAS
BEEN GOING
ON FOREVER
BETWEEN
YOU TWO.

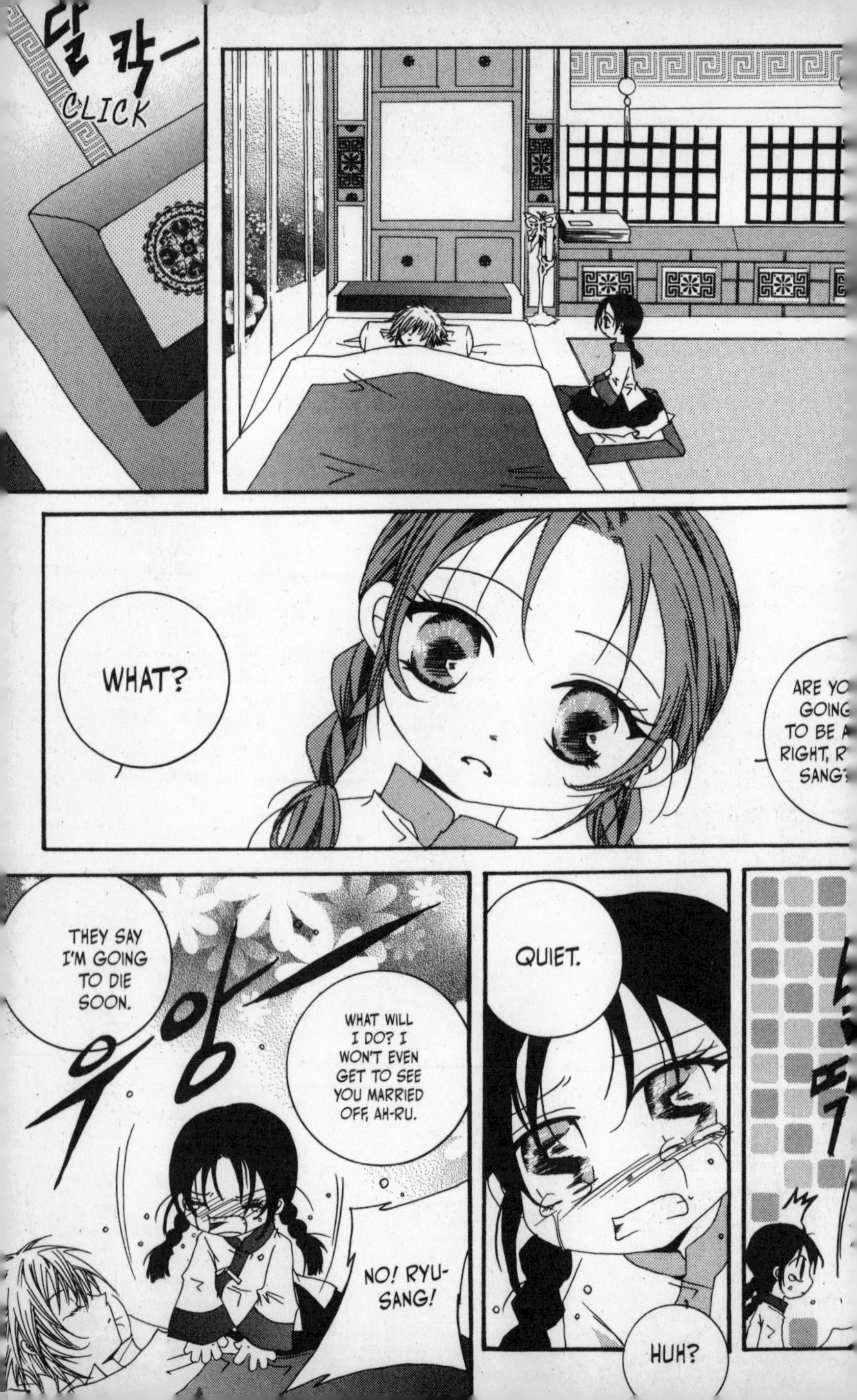
달칵—
CLICK
WHAT?
ARE YO GOING TO BE A RIGHT, R SANG?
THEY SAY I'M GOING TO DIE SOON.
WHAT WILL I DO? I WON'T EVEN GET TO SEE YOU MARRIED OFF, AH-RU.
NO! RYU-SANG!
QUIET.
HUH?

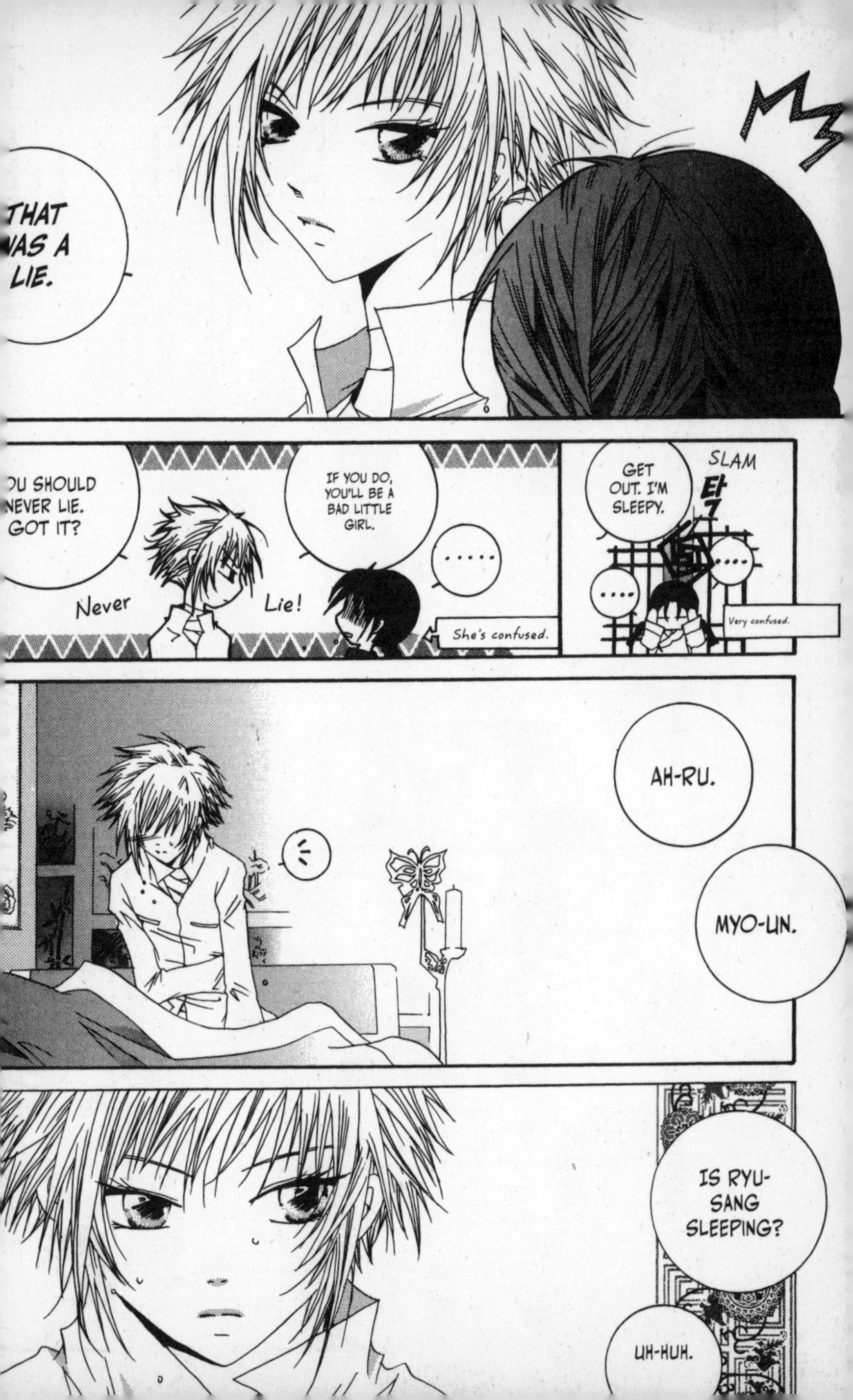
THAT WAS A LIE.
OU SHOULD NEVER LIE. GOT IT?
Never
Lie!
IF YOU DO, YOU'LL BE A BAD LITTLE GIRL.
.....
She's confused.
GET OUT. I'M SLEEPY.
SLAM
타
....
....
Very confused.
AH-RU.
MYO-UN.
IS RYU-SANG SLEEPING?
UH-HUH.

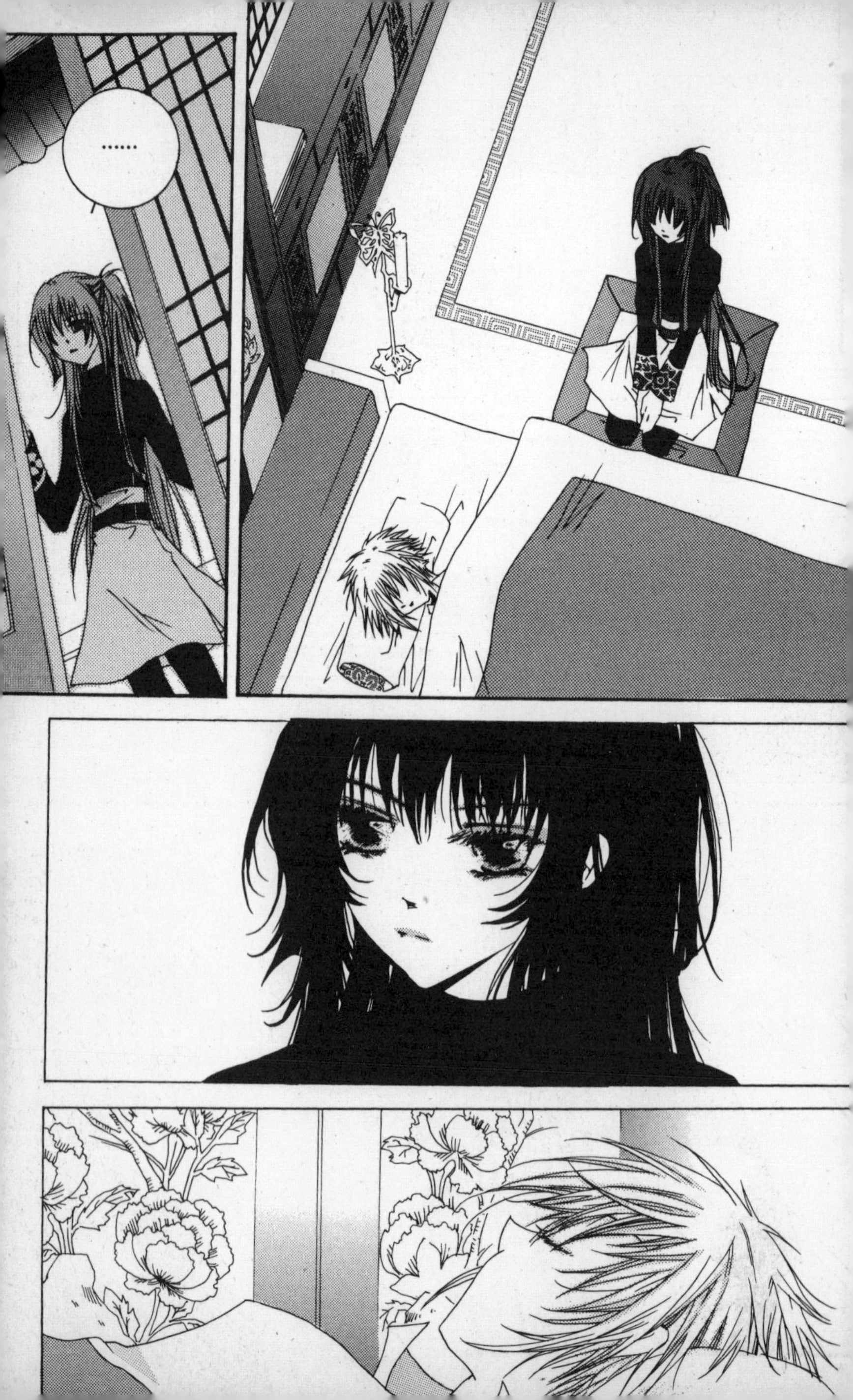
......

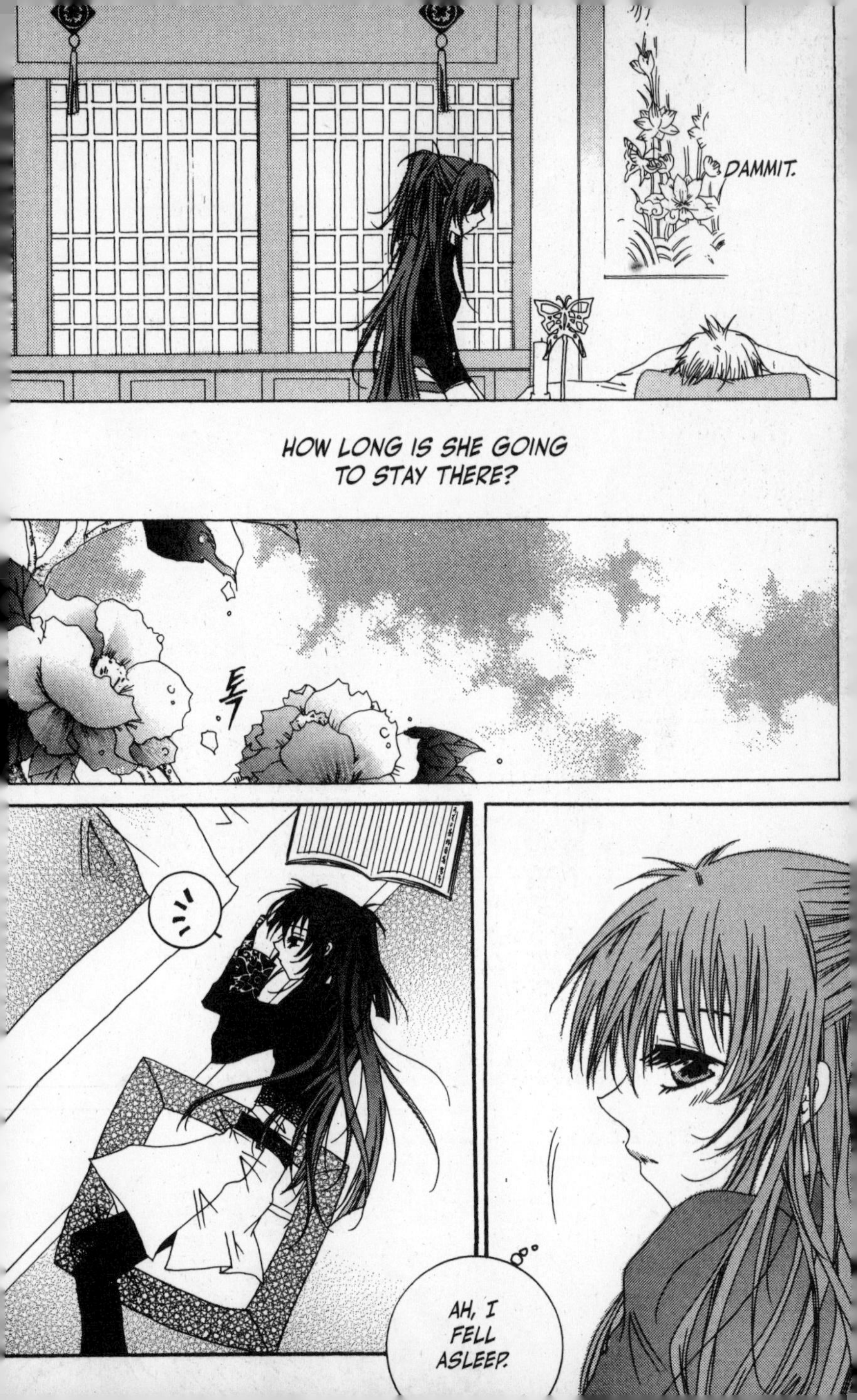
DAMMIT.
HOW LONG IS SHE GOING TO STAY THERE?
AH, I FELL ASLEEP.

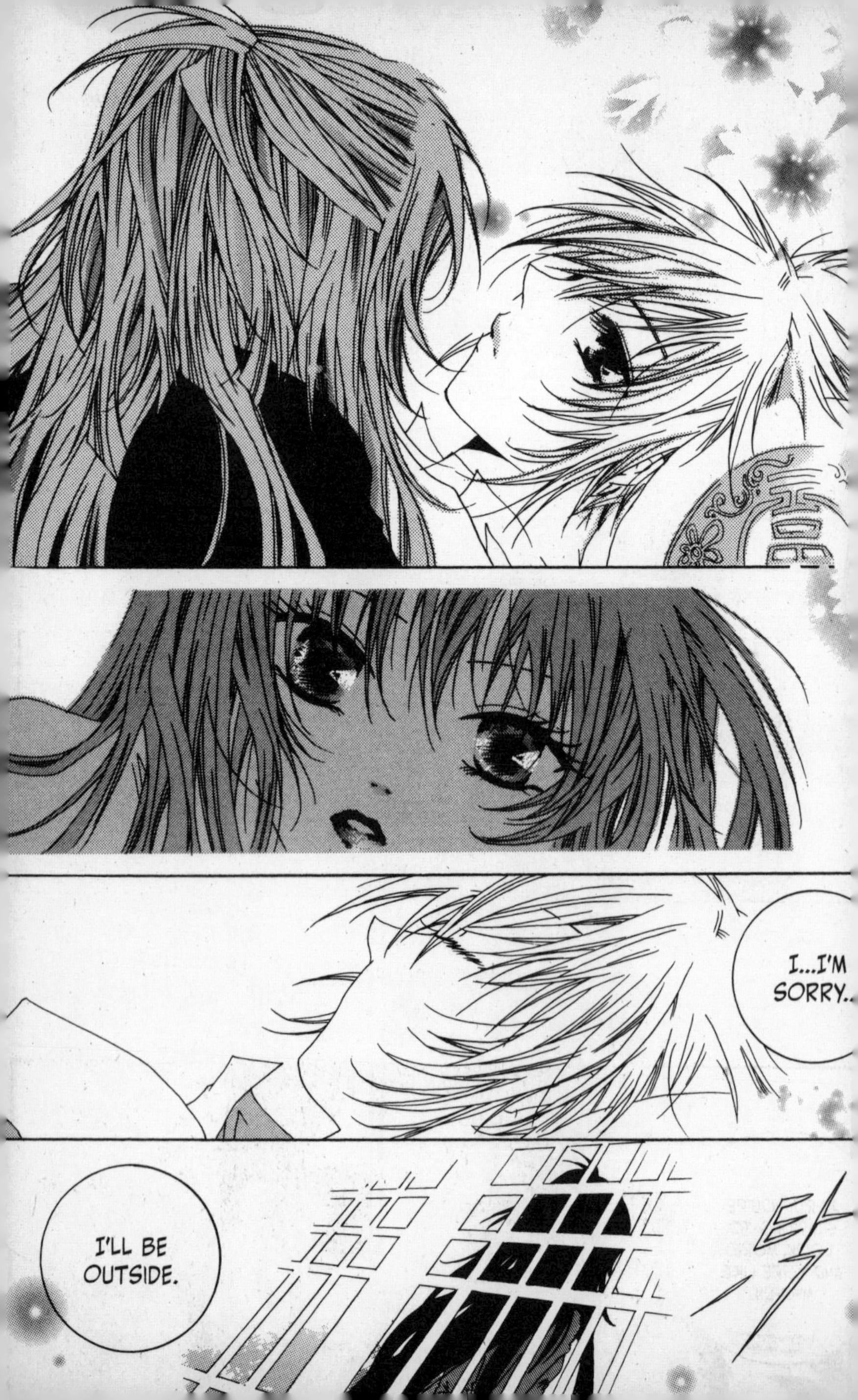
I...I'M SORRY...
I'LL BE OUTSIDE.
탁

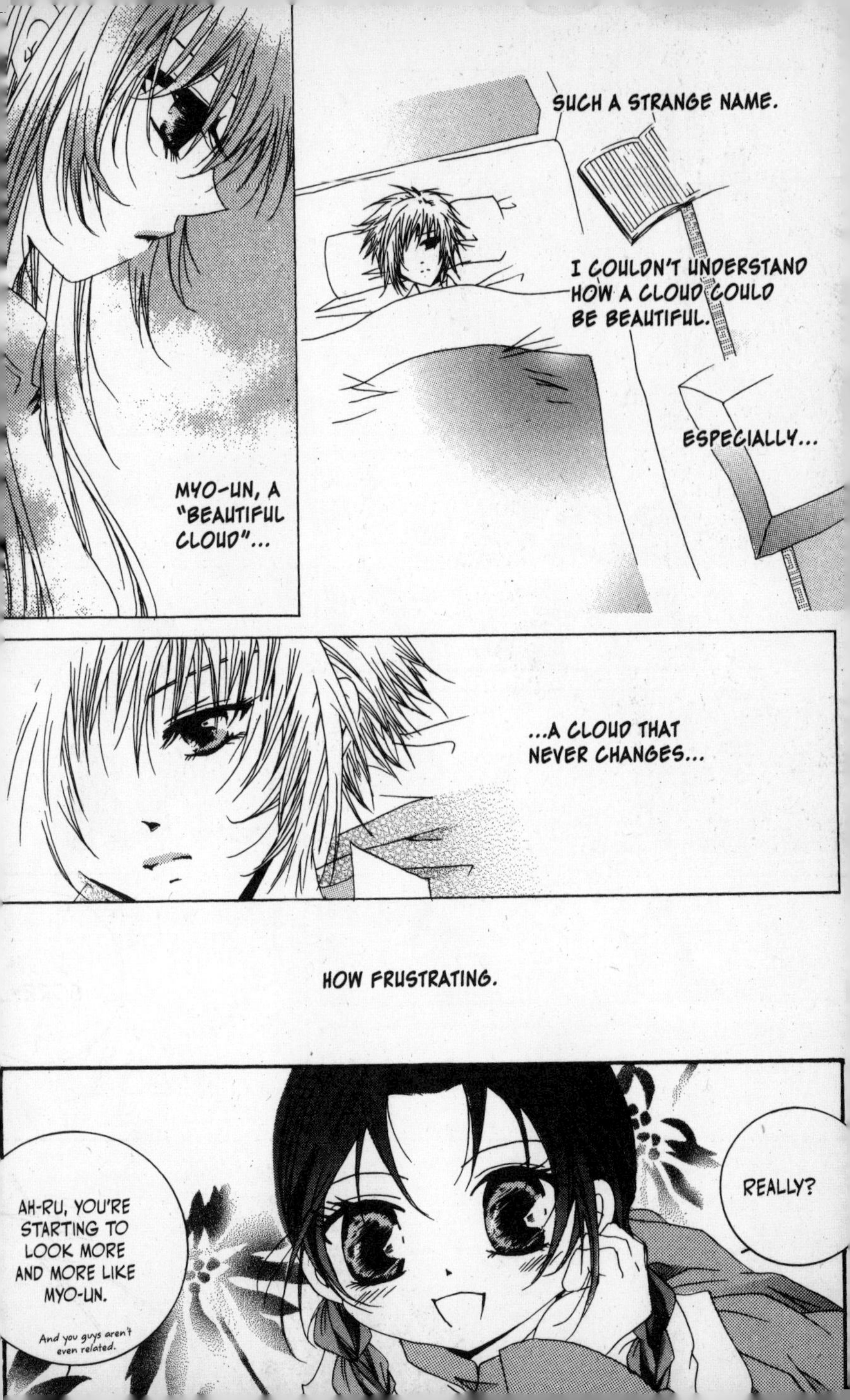
MYO-UN, A "BEAUTIFUL CLOUD"...
SUCH A STRANGE NAME.
I COULDN'T UNDERSTAND HOW A CLOUD COULD BE BEAUTIFUL.
ESPECIALLY...
...A CLOUD THAT NEVER CHANGES...
HOW FRUSTRATING.
AH-RU, YOU'RE STARTING TO LOOK MORE AND MORE LIKE MYO-UN.
And you guys aren't even related.
REALLY?

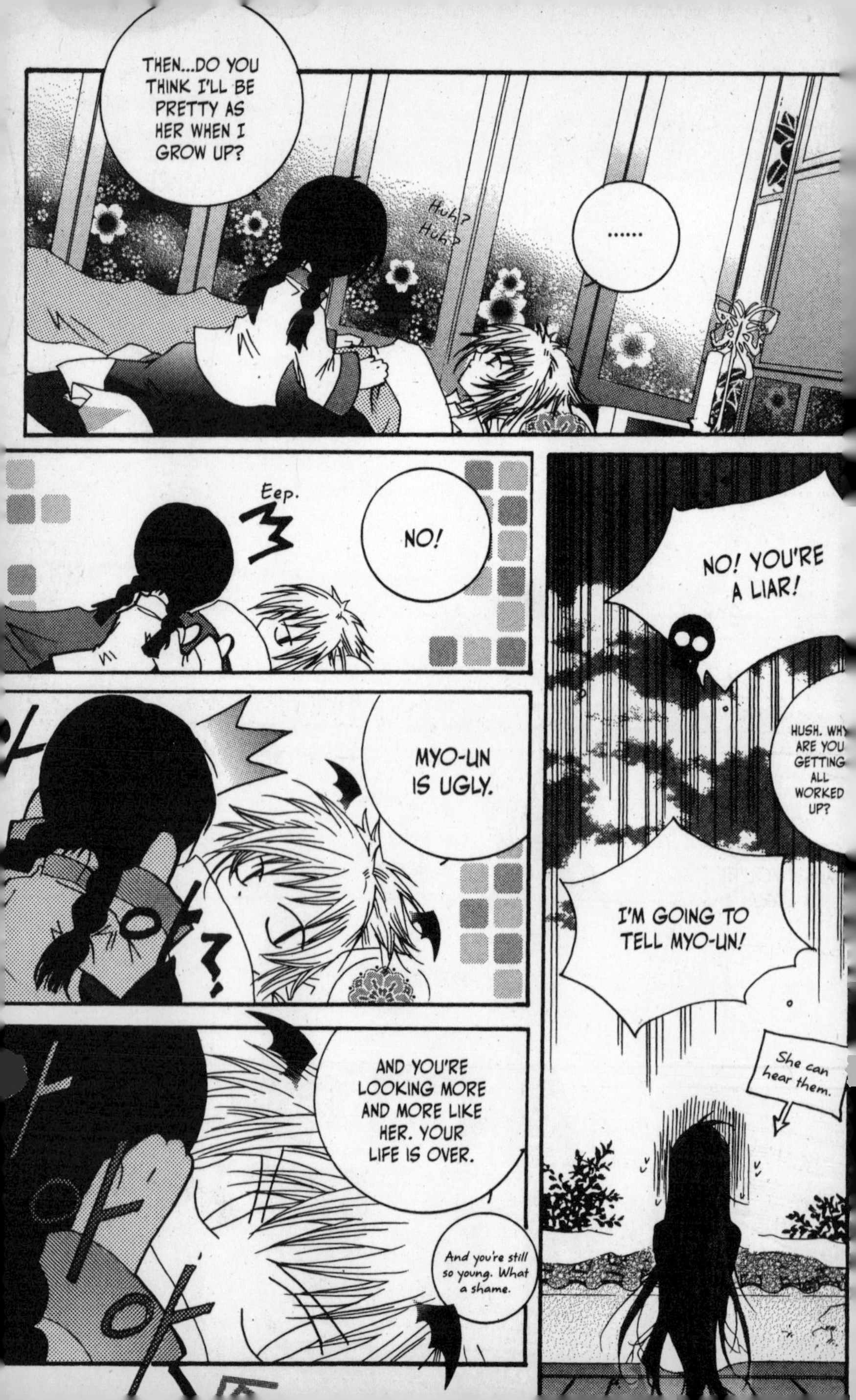
THEN...DO YOU THINK I'LL BE PRETTY AS HER WHEN I GROW UP?
Huh? Huh?
......
Eep.
NO!
MYO-UN IS UGLY.
AND YOU'RE LOOKING MORE AND MORE LIKE HER. YOUR LIFE IS OVER.
And you're still so young. What a shame.
NO! YOU'RE A LIAR!
HUSH. WHY ARE YOU GETTING ALL WORKED UP?
I'M GOING TO TELL MYO-UN!
She can hear them.

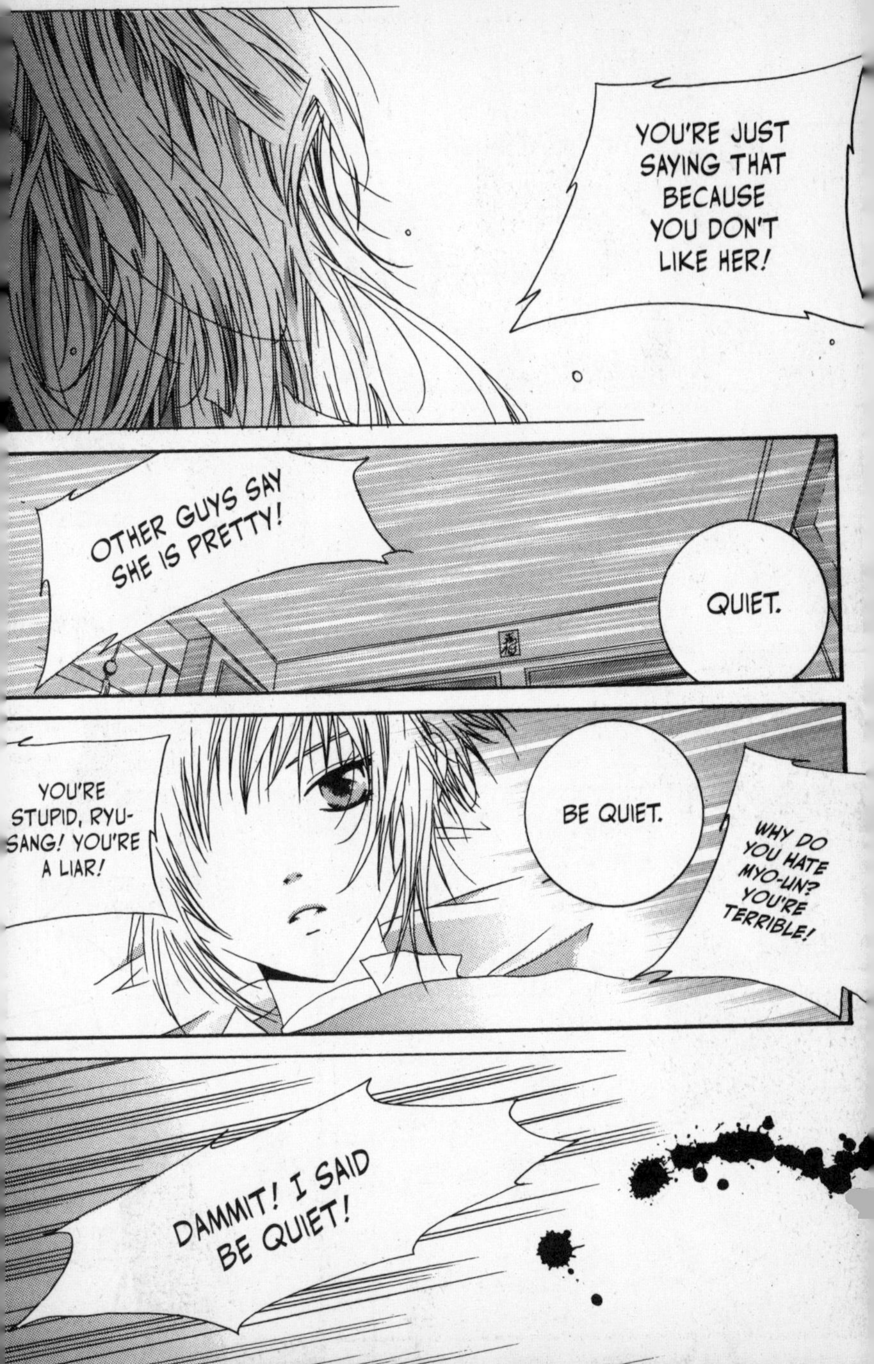
YOU'RE JUST SAYING THAT BECAUSE YOU DON'T LIKE HER!
OTHER GUYS SAY SHE IS PRETTY!
QUIET.
YOU'RE STUPID, RYU-SANG! YOU'RE A LIAR!
BE QUIET.
WHY DO YOU HATE MYO-UN? YOU'RE TERRIBLE!
DAMMIT! I SAID BE QUIET!

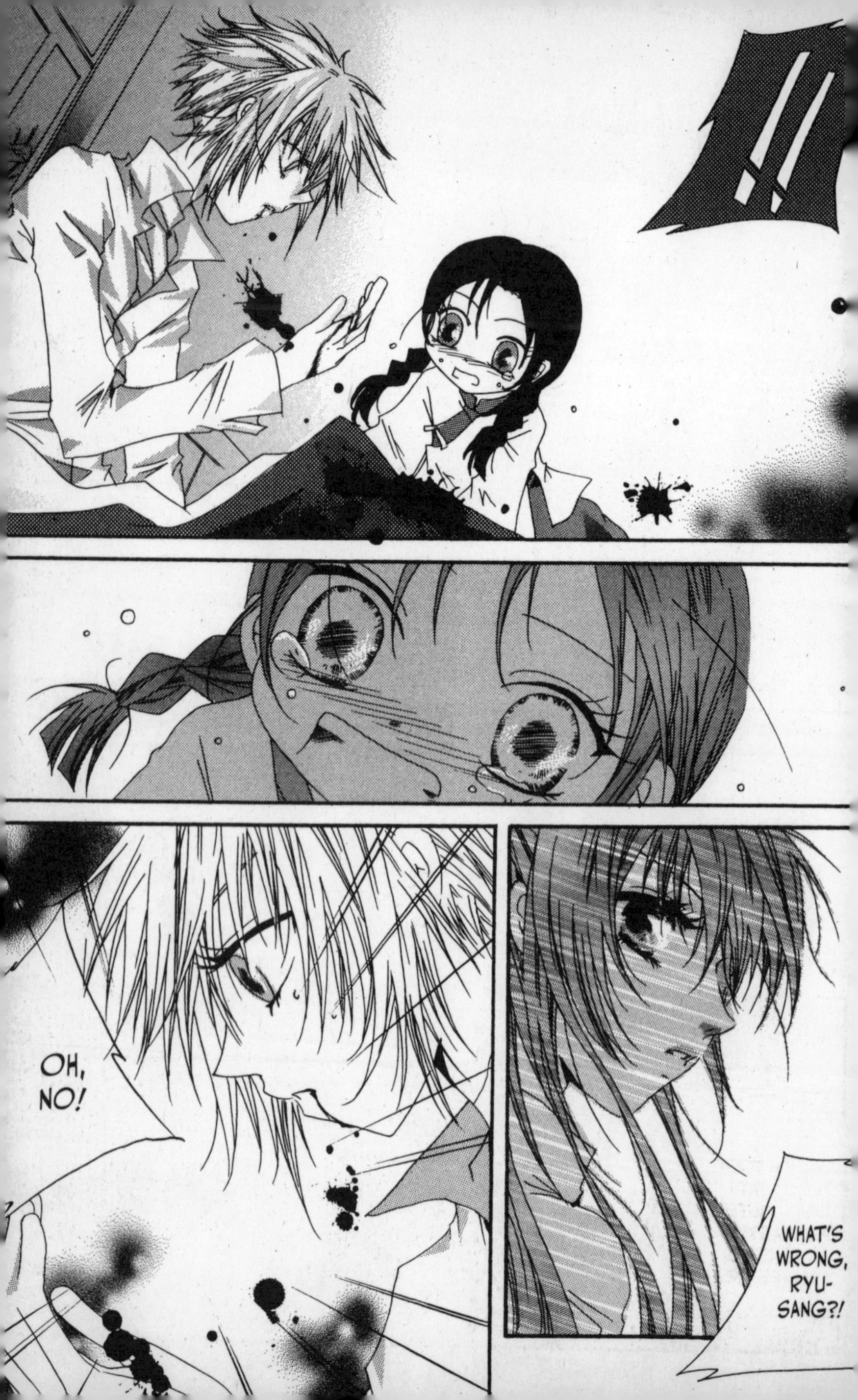
!!
OH, NO!
WHAT'S WRONG, RYU-SANG?!

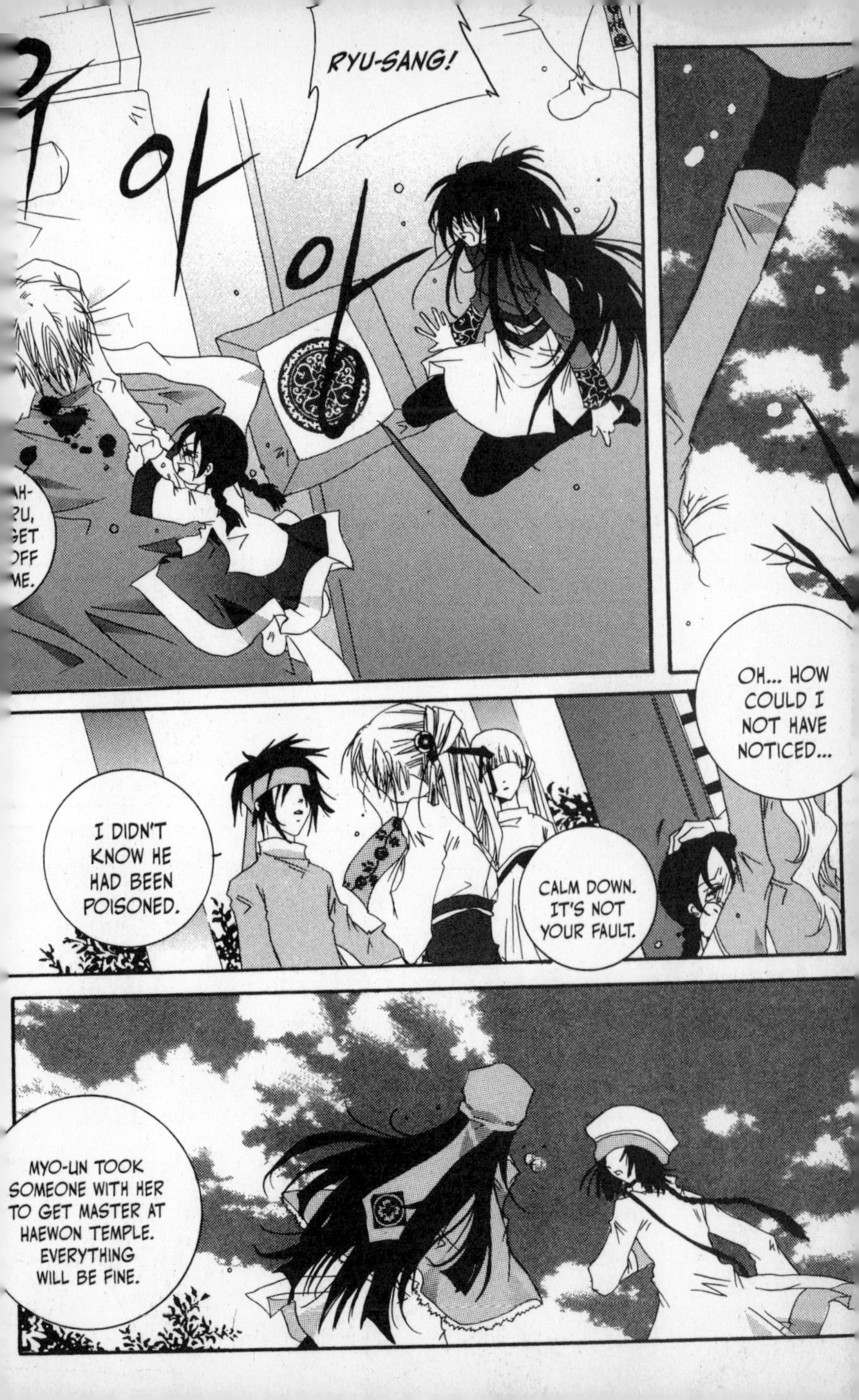
RYU-SANG!
GET OFF ME.
OH... HOW COULD I NOT HAVE NOTICED...
I DIDN'T KNOW HE HAD BEEN POISONED.
CALM DOWN. IT'S NOT YOUR FAULT.
MYO-UN TOOK SOMEONE WITH HER TO GET MASTER AT HAEWON TEMPLE. EVERYTHING WILL BE FINE.

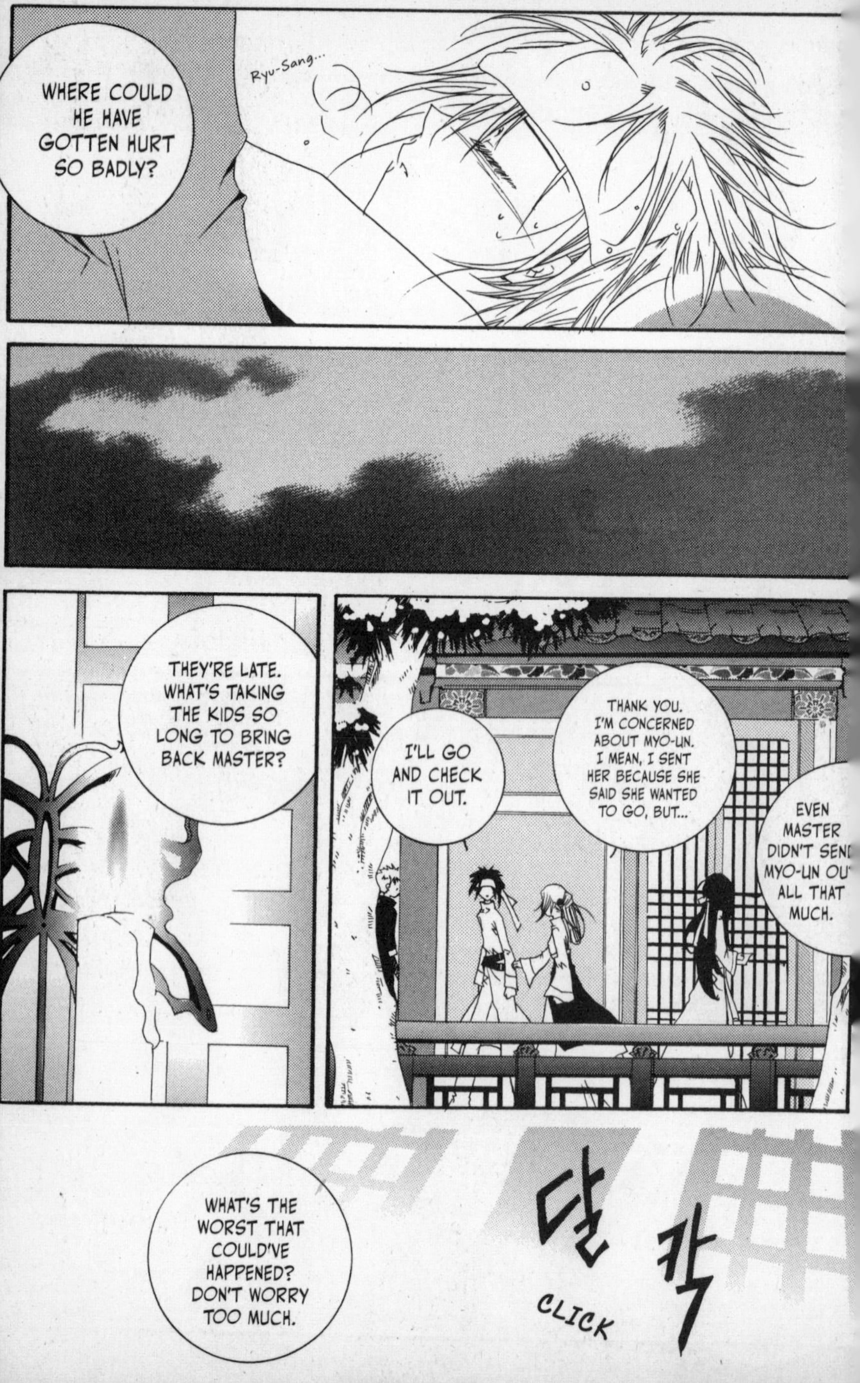
WHERE COULD HE HAVE GOTTEN HURT SO BADLY?
Ryu-Sang...
THEY'RE LATE. WHAT'S TAKING THE KIDS SO LONG TO BRING BACK MASTER?
I'LL GO AND CHECK IT OUT.
THANK YOU. I'M CONCERNED ABOUT MYO-UN. I MEAN, I SENT HER BECAUSE SHE SAID SHE WANTED TO GO, BUT...
EVEN MASTER DIDN'T SEND MYO-UN OUT ALL THAT MUCH.
WHAT'S THE WORST THAT COULD'VE HAPPENED? DON'T WORRY TOO MUCH.
달칵
CLICK

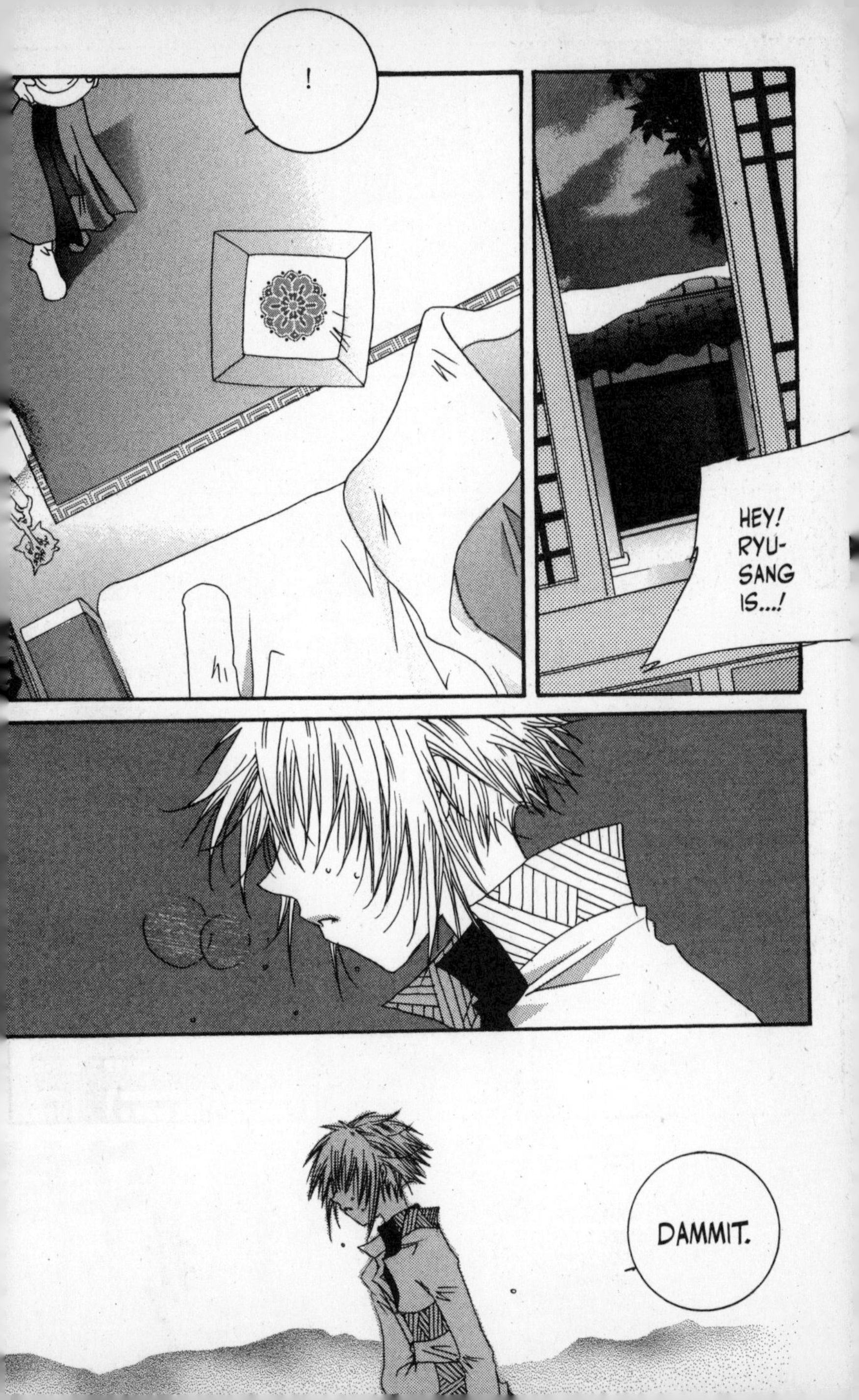
!
HEY! RYU-SANG IS...!
DAMMIT.

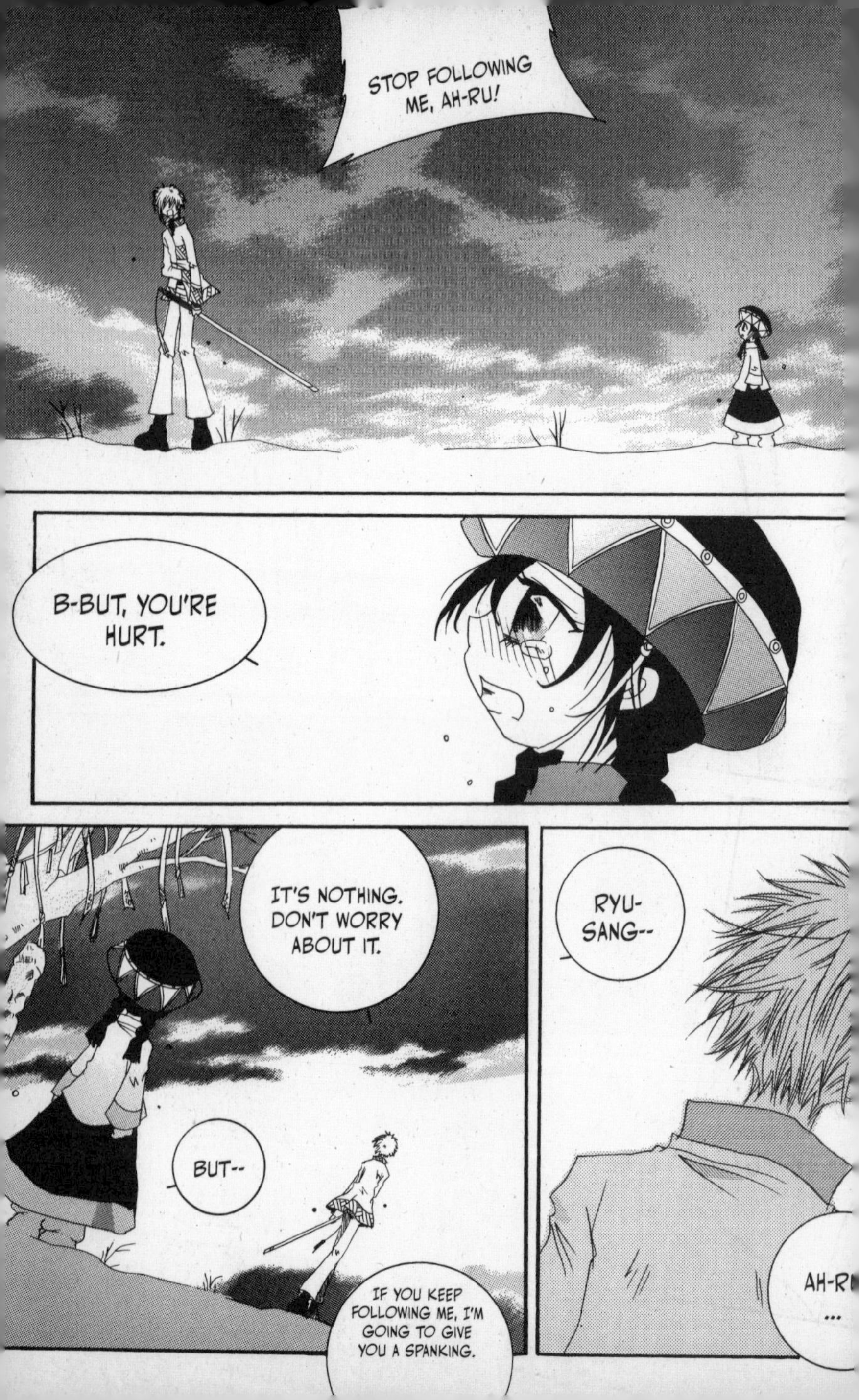
STOP FOLLOWING ME, AH-RU!
B-BUT, YOU'RE HURT.
IT'S NOTHING. DON'T WORRY ABOUT IT.
BUT--
IF YOU KEEP FOLLOWING ME, I'M GOING TO GIVE YOU A SPANKING.
RYU-SANG--
AH-R...

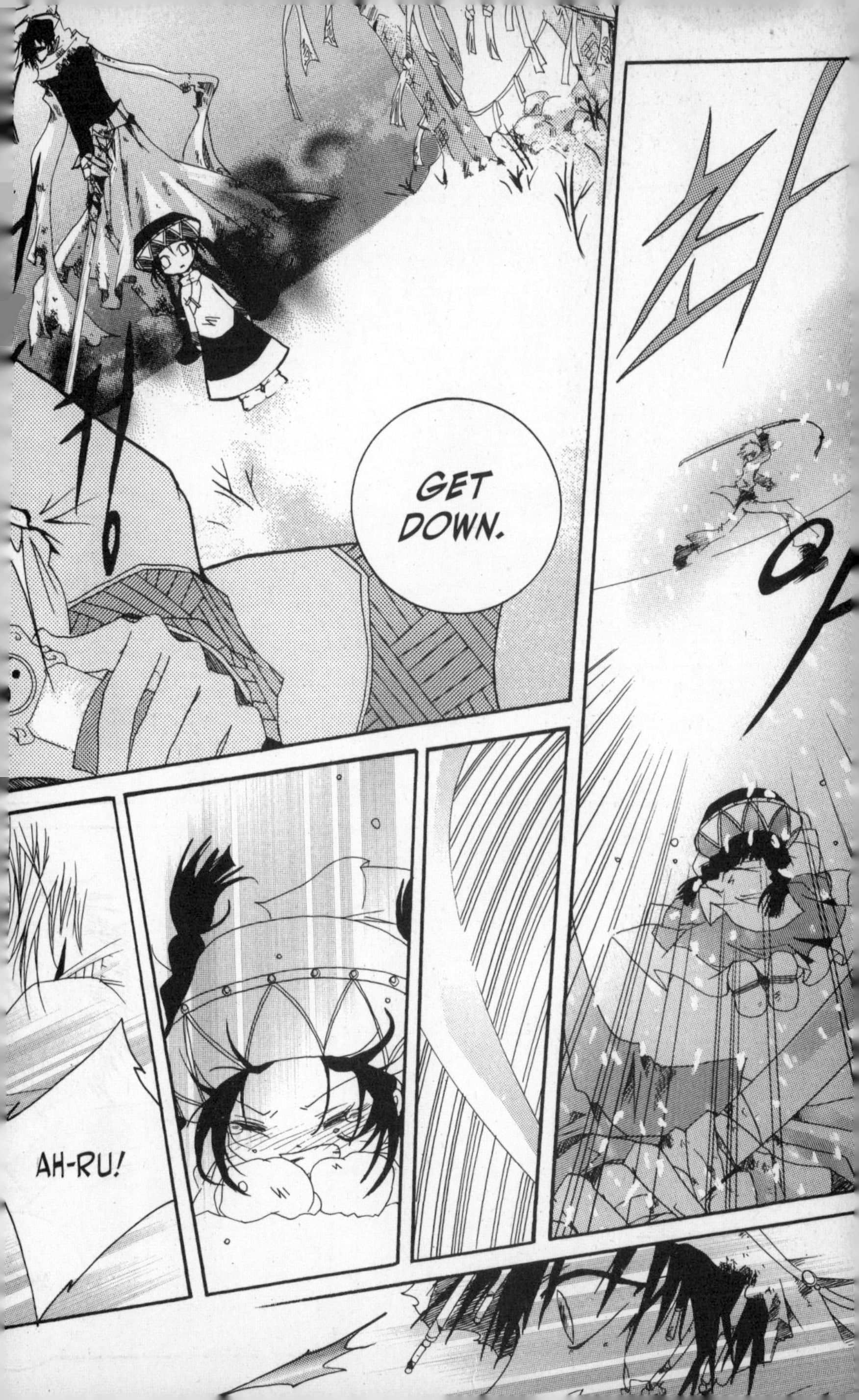
GET DOWN.
AH-RU!

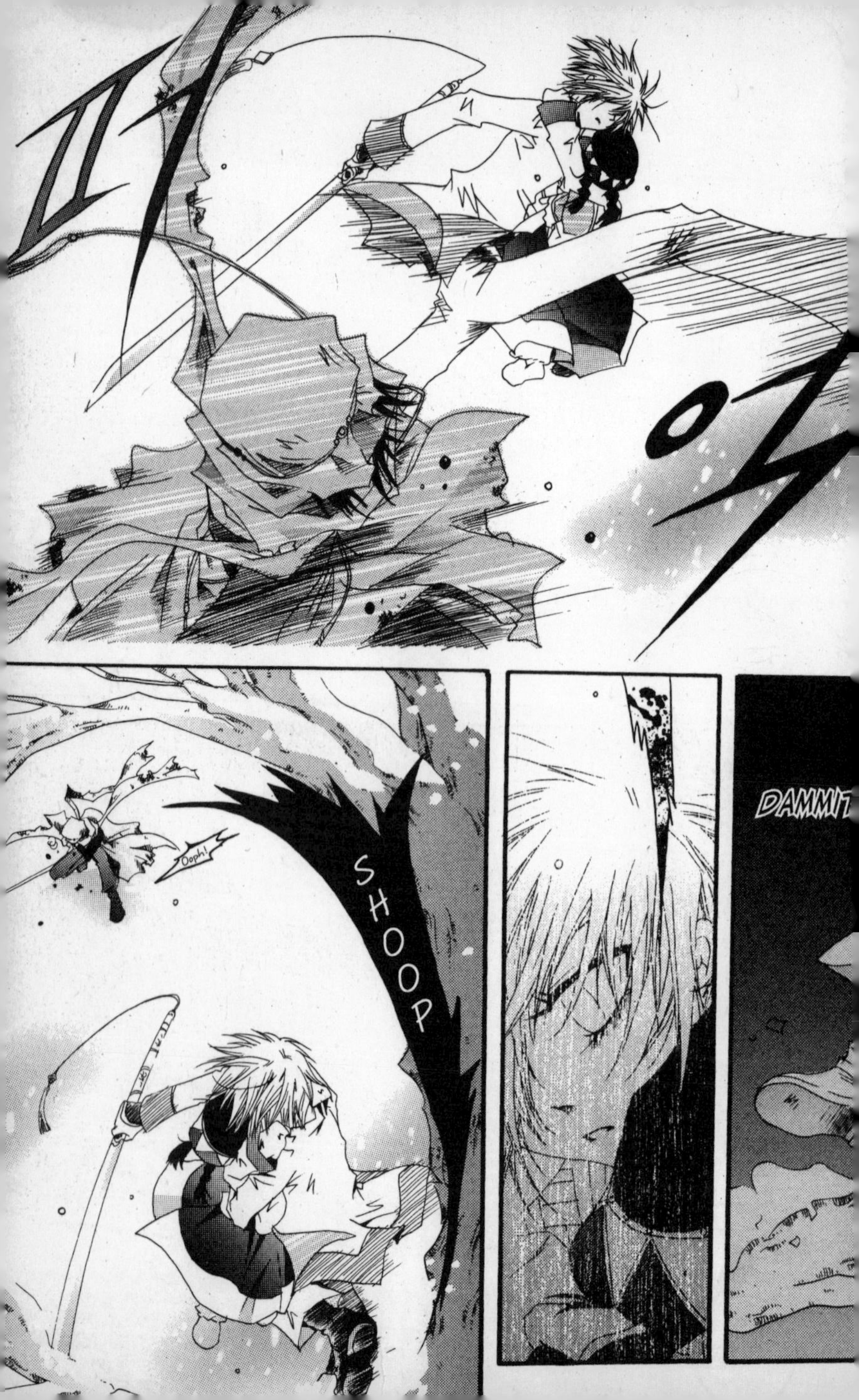
Ooph!
SHOOP
DAMMIT

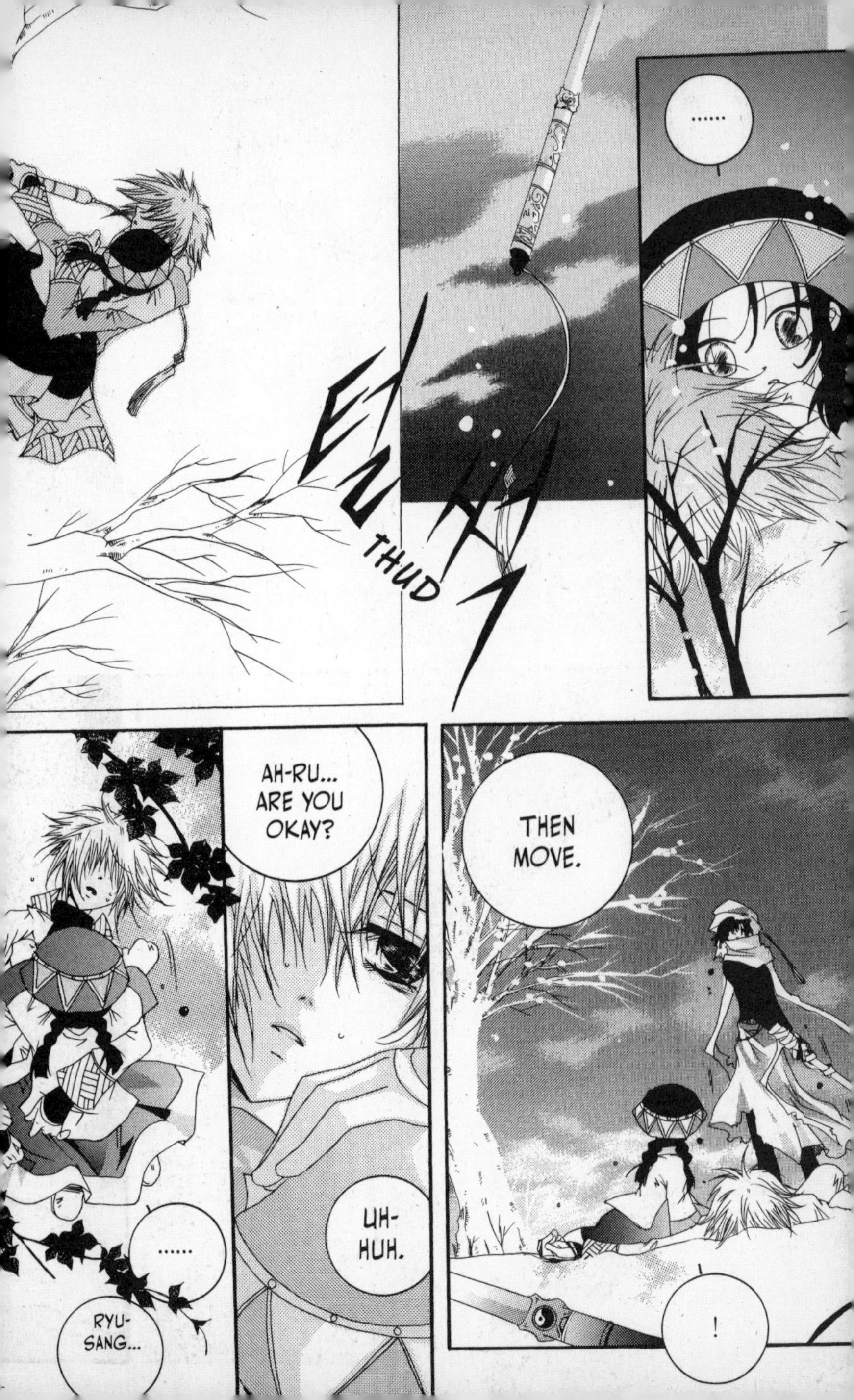
THUD
......
......
RYU-SANG...
AH-RU... ARE YOU OKAY?
UH-HUH.
THEN MOVE.
!

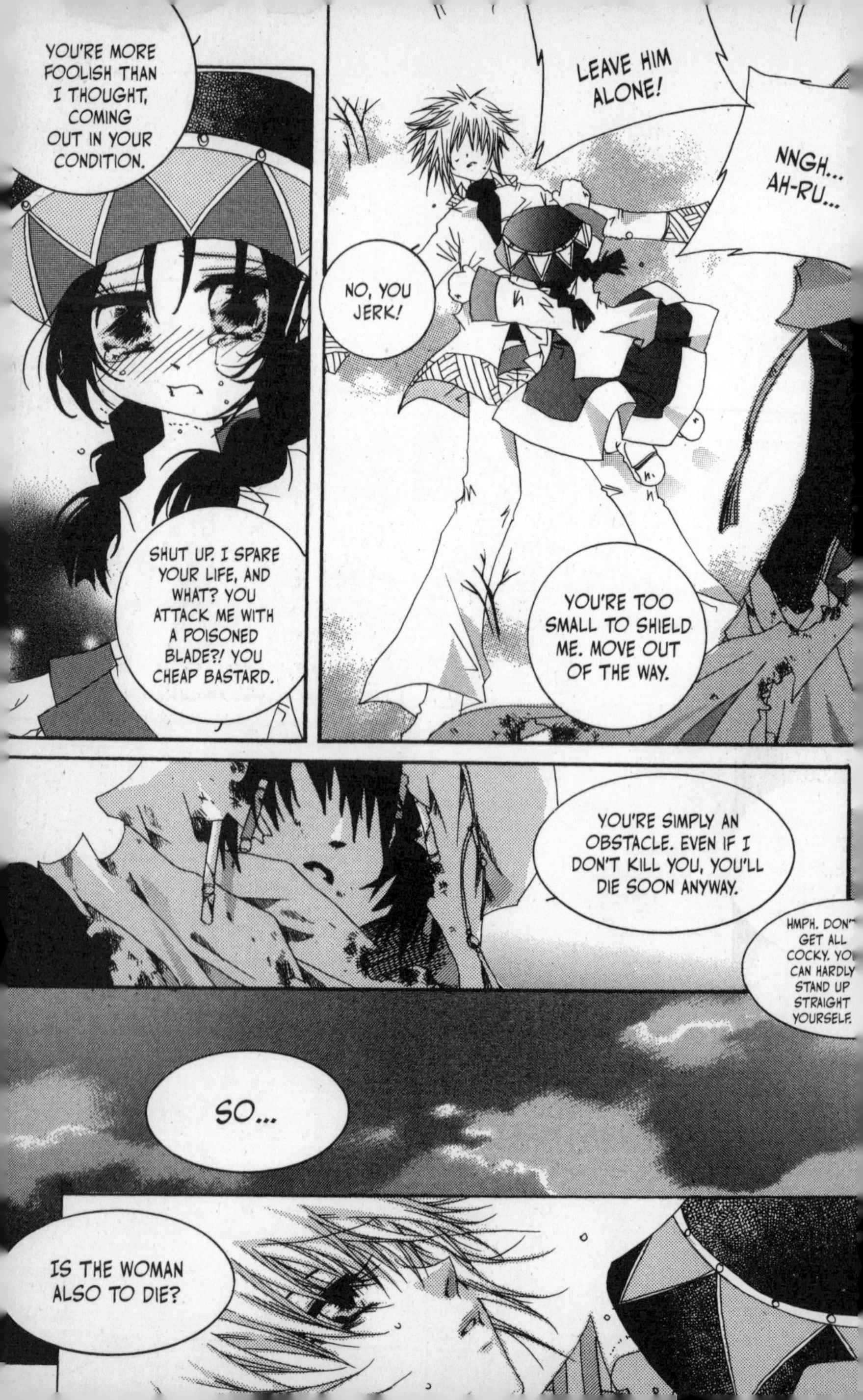
YOU'RE MORE FOOLISH THAN I THOUGHT, COMING OUT IN YOUR CONDITION.
SHUT UP. I SPARE YOUR LIFE, AND WHAT? YOU ATTACK ME WITH A POISONED BLADE?! YOU CHEAP BASTARD.
LEAVE HIM ALONE!
NNGH... AH-RU...
NO, YOU JERK!
YOU'RE TOO SMALL TO SHIELD ME. MOVE OUT OF THE WAY.
YOU'RE SIMPLY AN OBSTACLE. EVEN IF I DON'T KILL YOU, YOU'LL DIE SOON ANYWAY.
HMPH. DON'T GET ALL COCKY. YO CAN HARDLY STAND UP STRAIGHT YOURSELF.
SO...
IS THE WOMAN ALSO TO DIE?

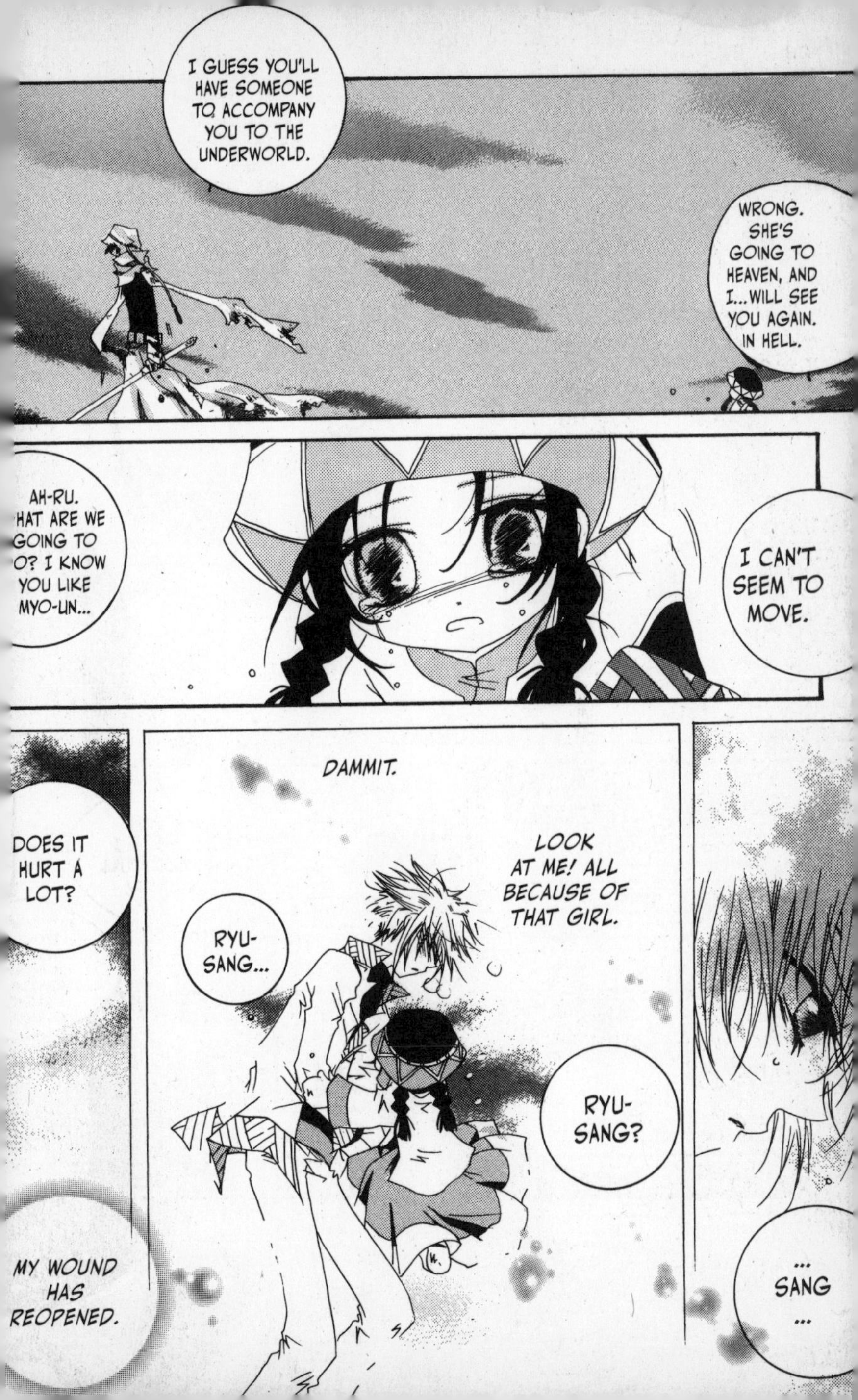
I GUESS YOU'LL HAVE SOMEONE TO ACCOMPANY YOU TO THE UNDERWORLD.
WRONG. SHE'S GOING TO HEAVEN, AND I...WILL SEE YOU AGAIN. IN HELL.
AH-RU. HAT ARE WE GOING TO O? I KNOW YOU LIKE MYO-UN...
I CAN'T SEEM TO MOVE.
DOES IT HURT A LOT?
MY WOUND HAS REOPENED.
DAMMIT.
LOOK AT ME! ALL BECAUSE OF THAT GIRL.
RYU-SANG...
RYU-SANG?
... SANG ...

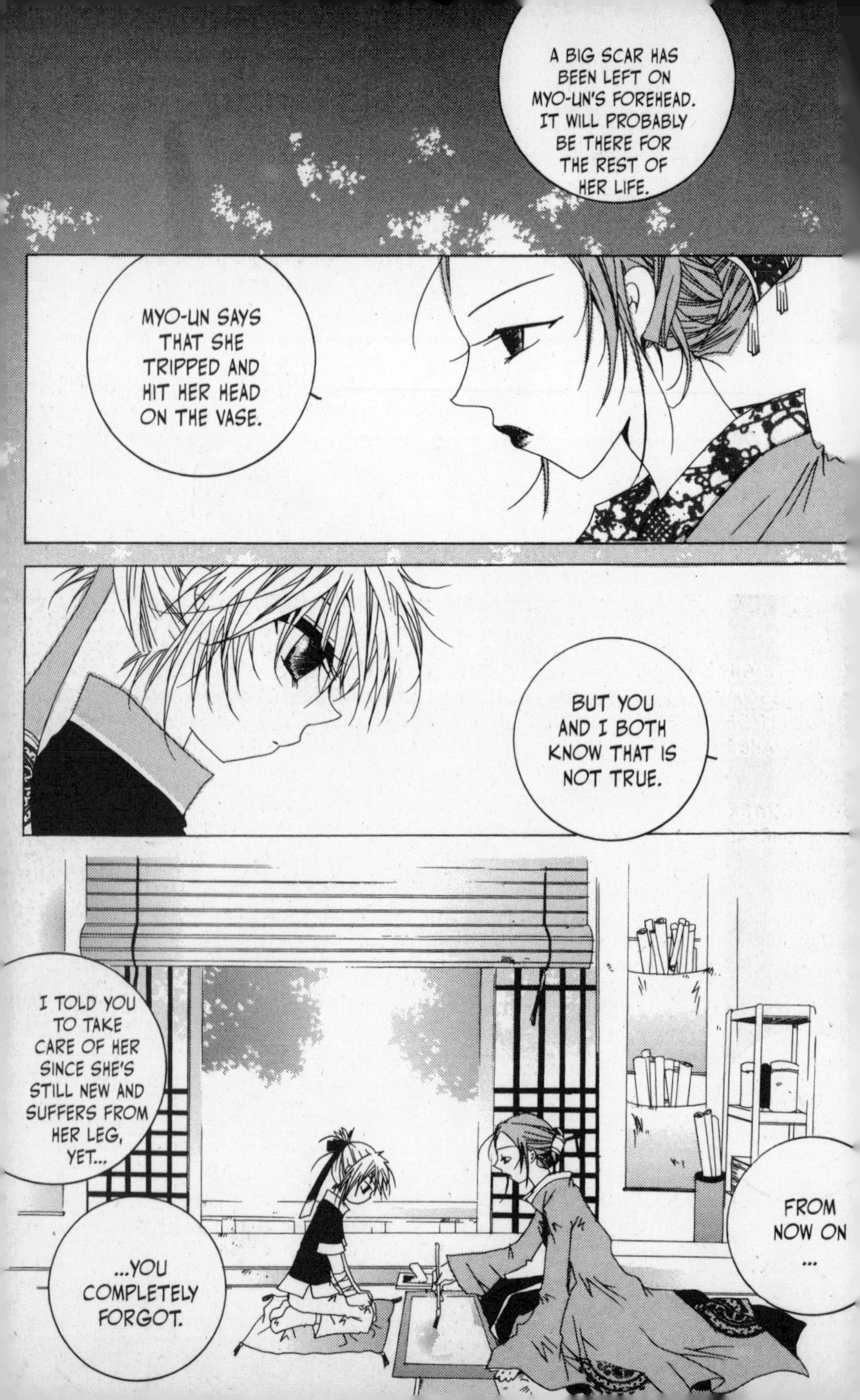
A BIG SCAR HAS BEEN LEFT ON MYO-UN'S FOREHEAD. IT WILL PROBABLY BE THERE FOR THE REST OF HER LIFE.
MYO-UN SAYS THAT SHE TRIPPED AND HIT HER HEAD ON THE VASE.
BUT YOU AND I BOTH KNOW THAT IS NOT TRUE.
I TOLD YOU TO TAKE CARE OF HER SINCE SHE'S STILL NEW AND SUFFERS FROM HER LEG, YET...
...YOU COMPLETELY FORGOT.
FROM NOW ON ...

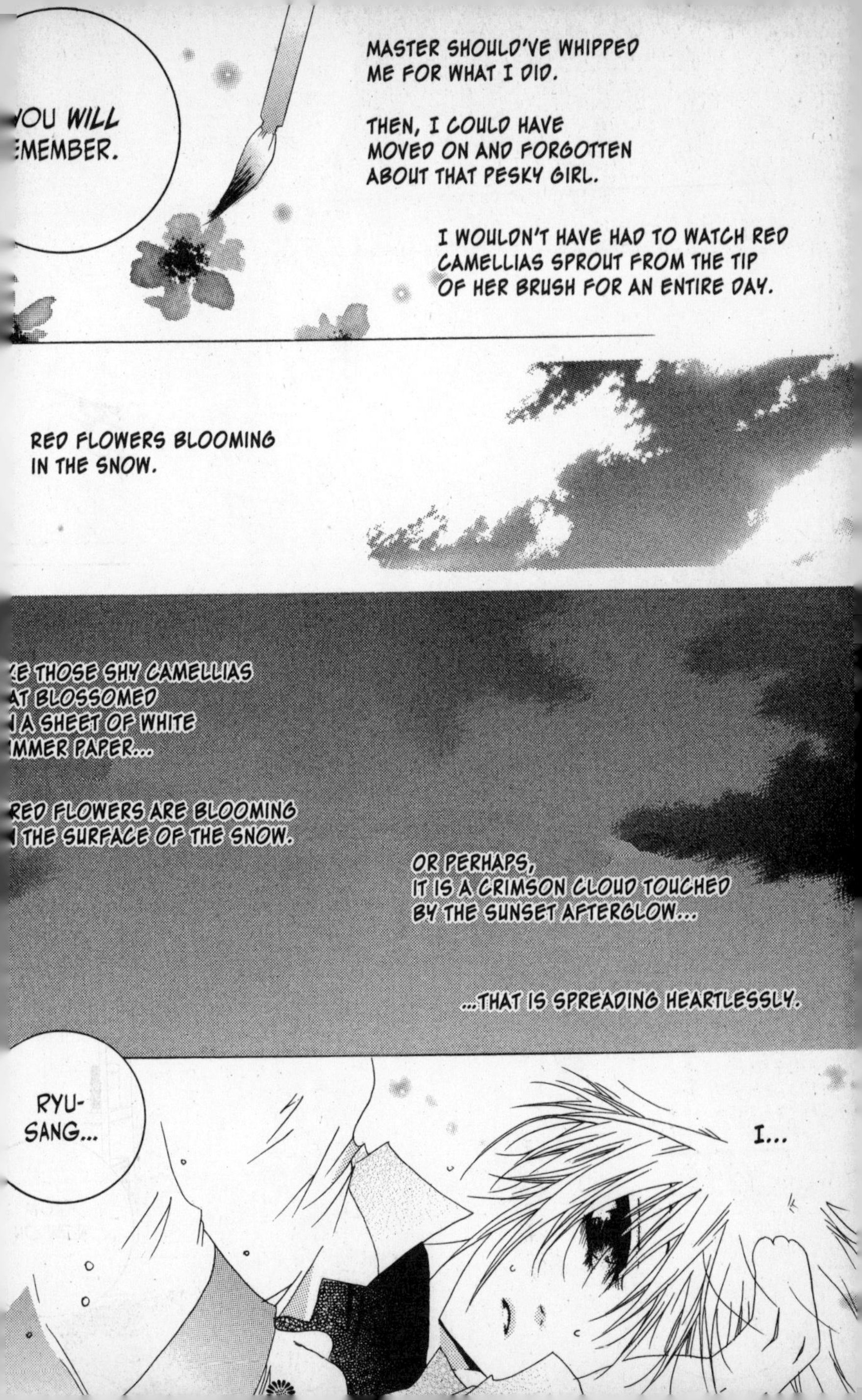

OU WILL EMEMBER.
MASTER SHOULD'VE WHIPPED ME FOR WHAT I DID.
THEN, I COULD HAVE MOVED ON AND FORGOTTEN ABOUT THAT PESKY GIRL.
I WOULDN'T HAVE HAD TO WATCH RED CAMELLIAS SPROUT FROM THE TIP OF HER BRUSH FOR AN ENTIRE DAY.
RED FLOWERS BLOOMING IN THE SNOW.
E THOSE SHY CAMELLIAS AT BLOSSOMED A SHEET OF WHITE IMMER PAPER...
RED FLOWERS ARE BLOOMING THE SURFACE OF THE SNOW.
OR PERHAPS, IT IS A CRIMSON CLOUD TOUCHED BY THE SUNSET AFTERGLOW...
...THAT IS SPREADING HEARTLESSLY.
RYU-SANG...
I...

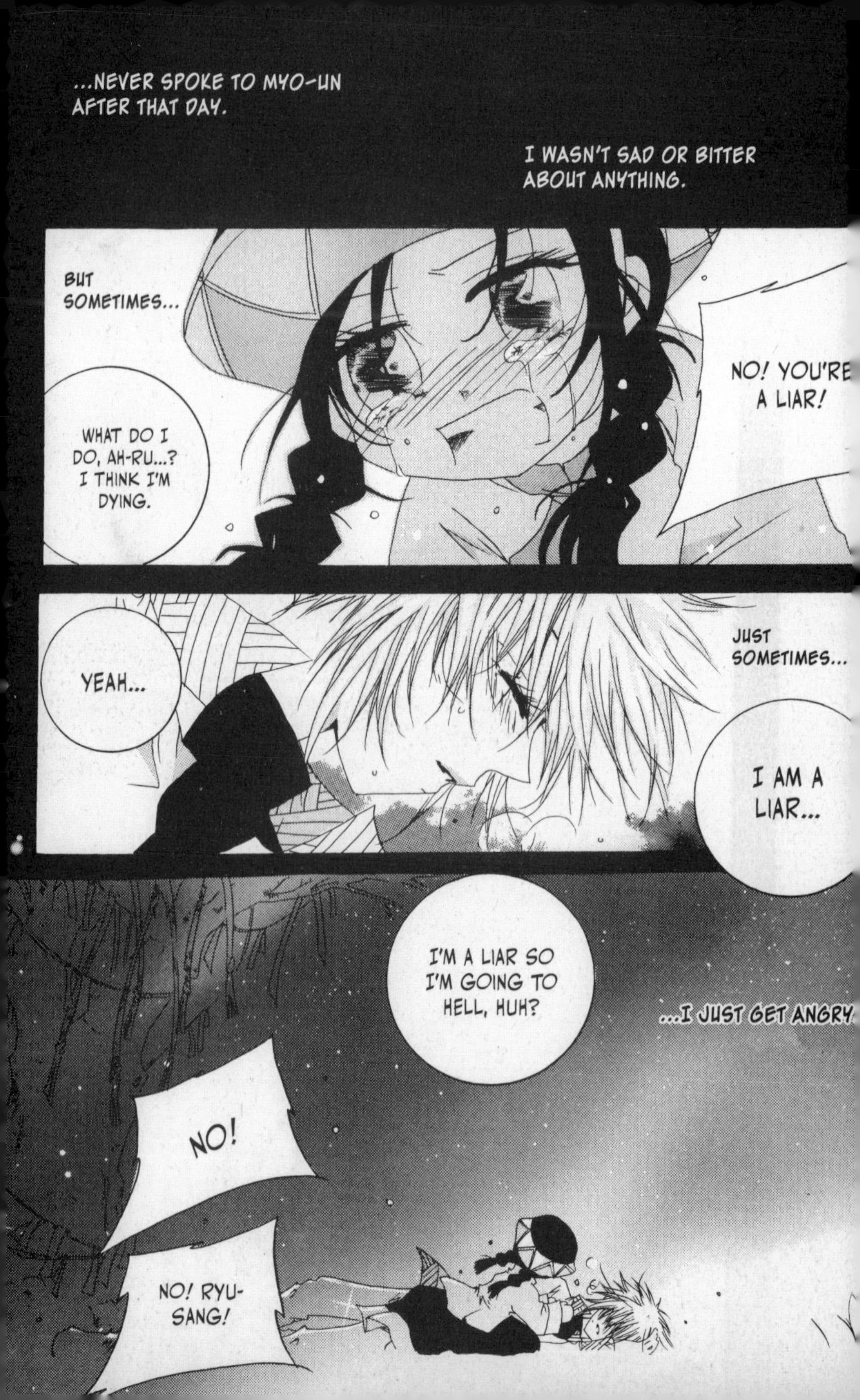
...NEVER SPOKE TO MYO-UN AFTER THAT DAY.
I WASN'T SAD OR BITTER ABOUT ANYTHING.
BUT SOMETIMES...
WHAT DO I DO, AH-RU...? I THINK I'M DYING.
NO! YOU'RE A LIAR!
YEAH...
JUST SOMETIMES...
I AM A LIAR...
I'M A LIAR SO I'M GOING TO HELL, HUH?
...I JUST GET ANGRY.
NO!
NO! RYU-SANG!

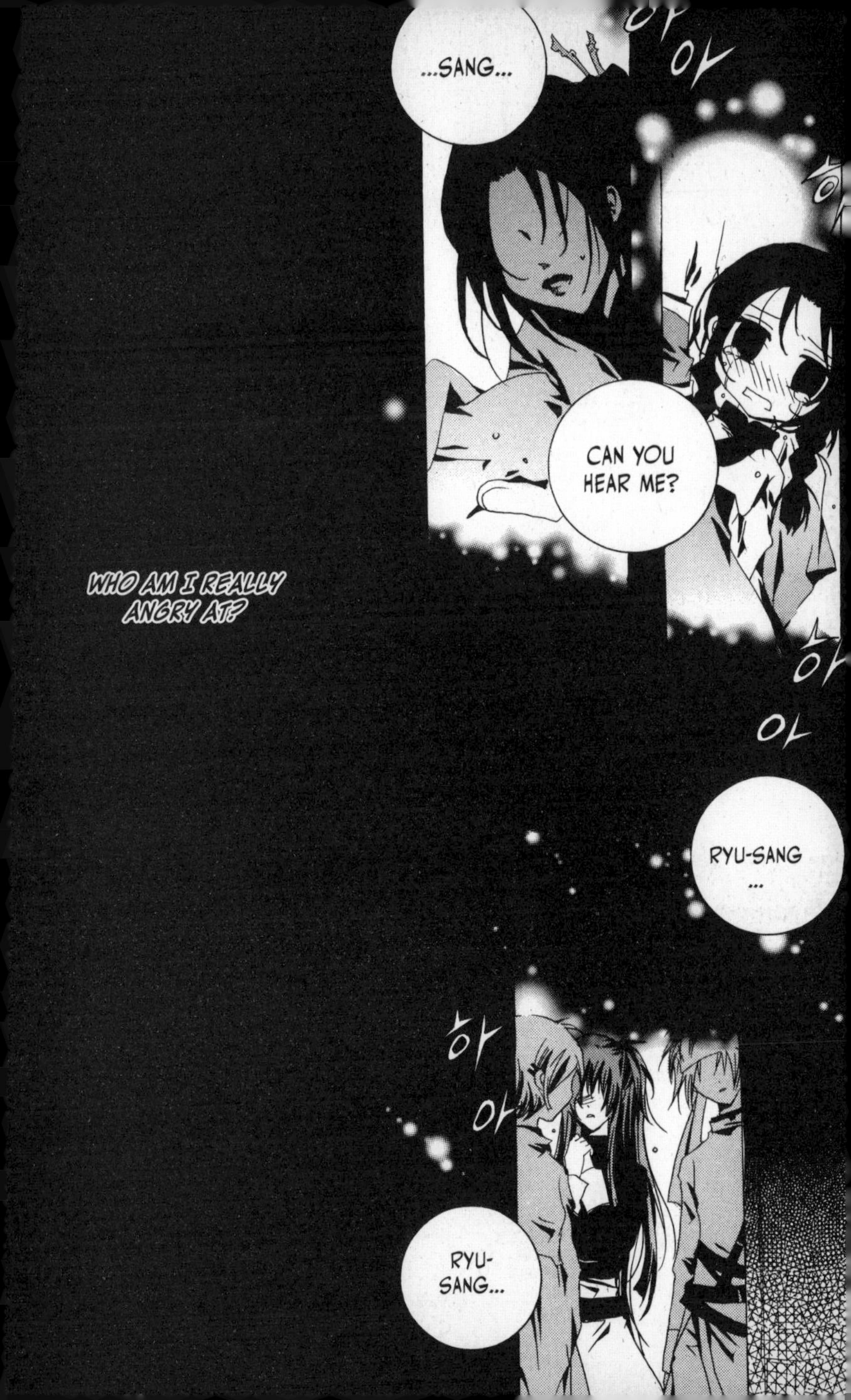

WHO AM I REALLY ANGRY AT?
...SANG...
CAN YOU HEAR ME?
하아
RYU-SANG ...
하아
RYU-SANG...

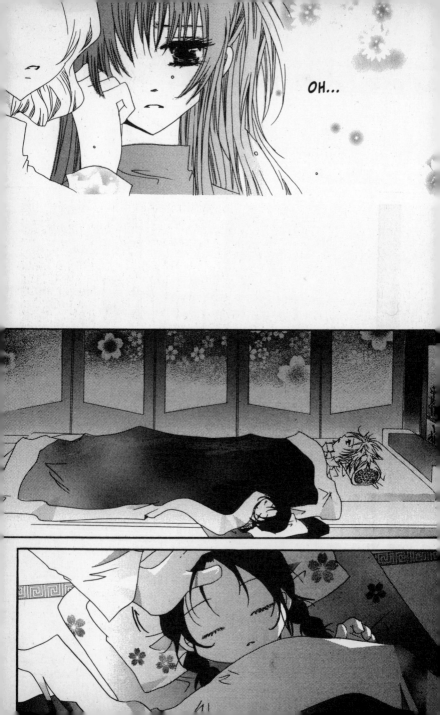

OH...

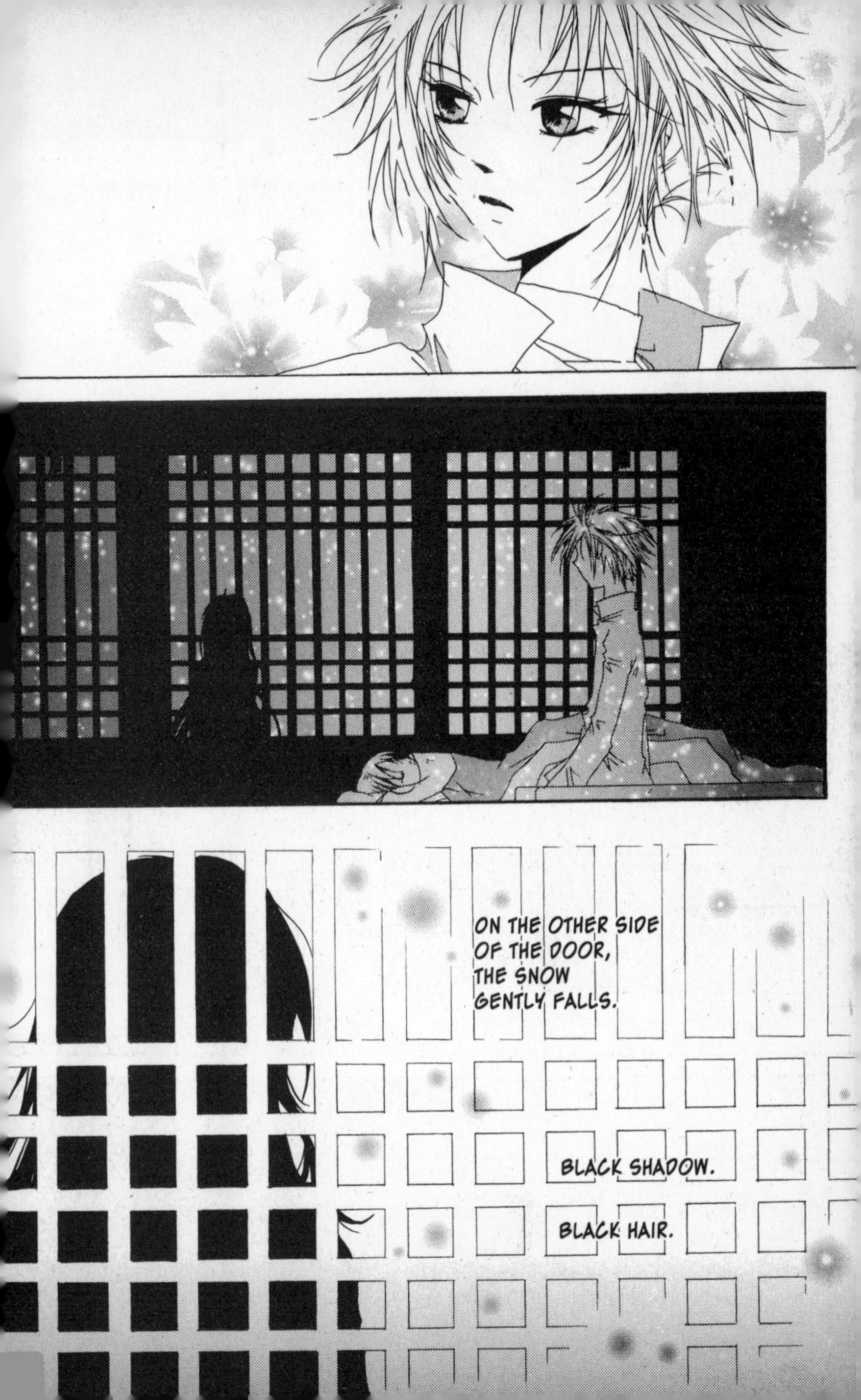
ON THE OTHER SIDE
OF THE DOOR,
THE SNOW
GENTLY FALLS.
BLACK SHADOW.
BLACK HAIR.

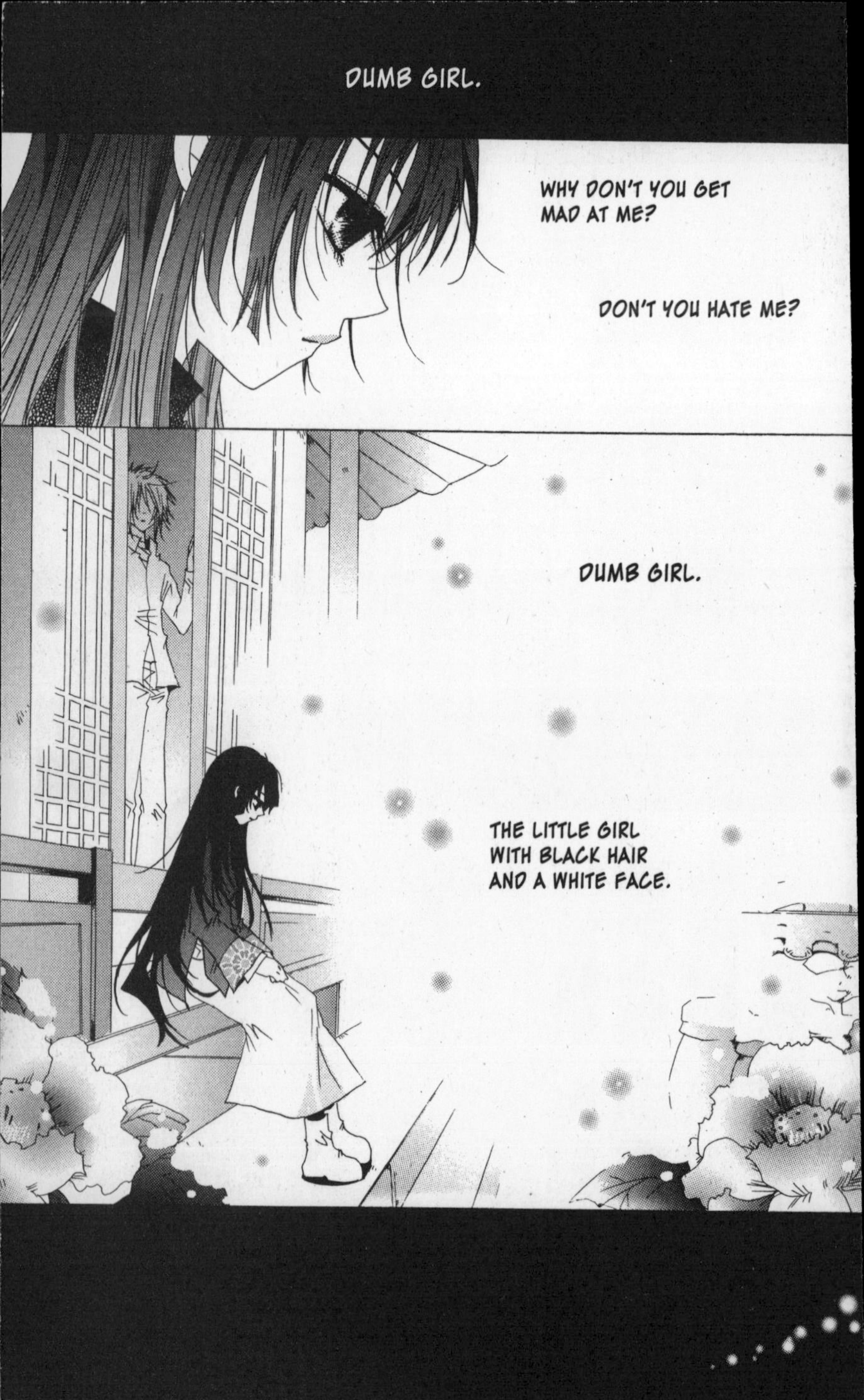
DUMB GIRL.
WHY DON'T YOU GET MAD AT ME?
DON'T YOU HATE ME?
DUMB GIRL.
THE LITTLE GIRL WITH BLACK HAIR AND A WHITE FACE.

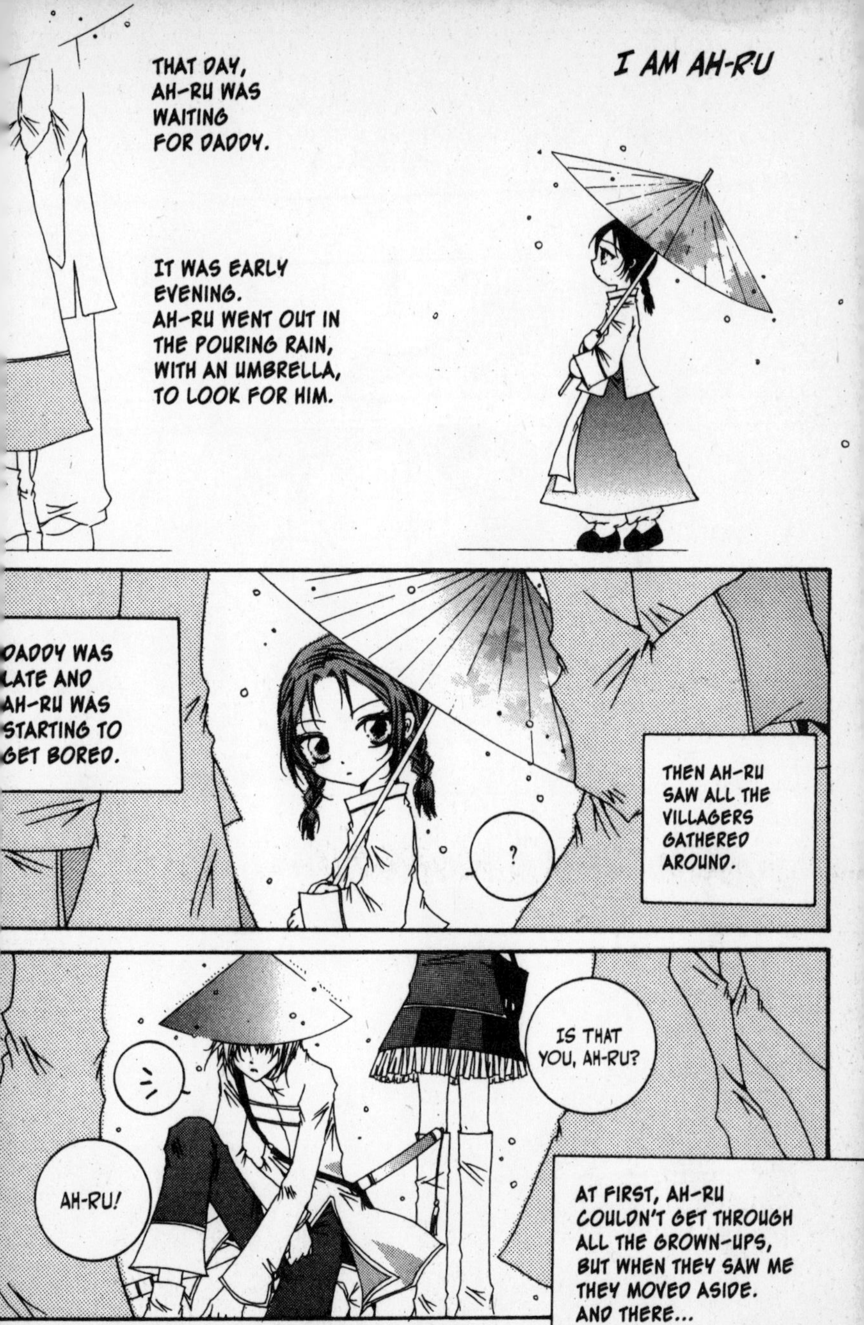
I AM AH-RU
THAT DAY, AH-RU WAS WAITING FOR DADDY.
IT WAS EARLY EVENING. AH-RU WENT OUT IN THE POURING RAIN, WITH AN UMBRELLA, TO LOOK FOR HIM.
DADDY WAS LATE AND AH-RU WAS STARTING TO GET BORED.
?
THEN AH-RU SAW ALL THE VILLAGERS GATHERED AROUND.
AH-RU!
IS THAT YOU, AH-RU?
AT FIRST, AH-RU COULDN'T GET THROUGH ALL THE GROWN-UPS, BUT WHEN THEY SAW ME THEY MOVED ASIDE. AND THERE...

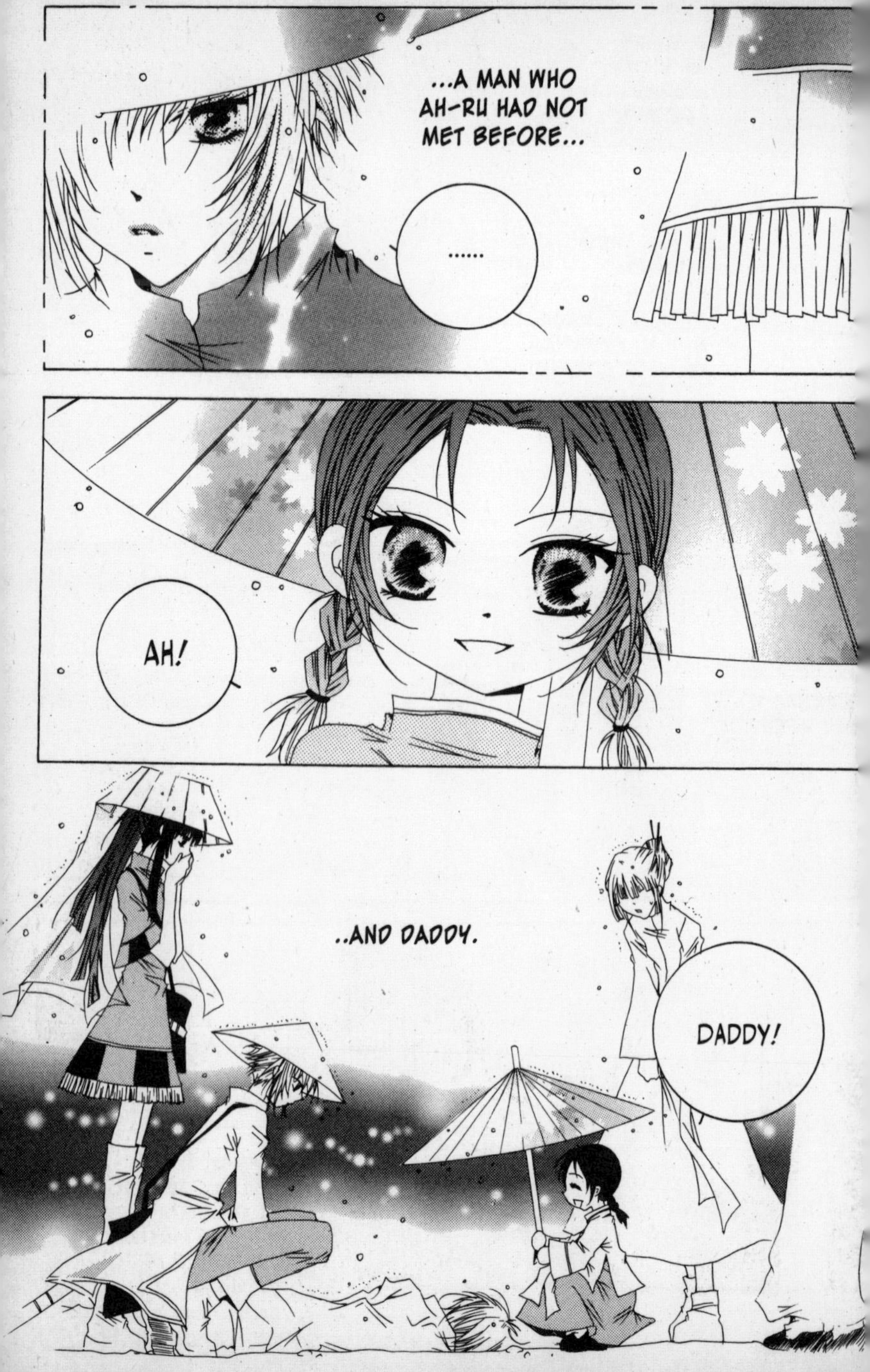
...A MAN WHO AH-RU HAD NOT MET BEFORE...
......
AH!
..AND DADDY.
DADDY!

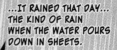

...IT RAINED THAT DAY...
THE KIND OF RAIN
WHEN THE WATER POURS
DOWN IN SHEETS.

DADDY...?

I AM AH-RU

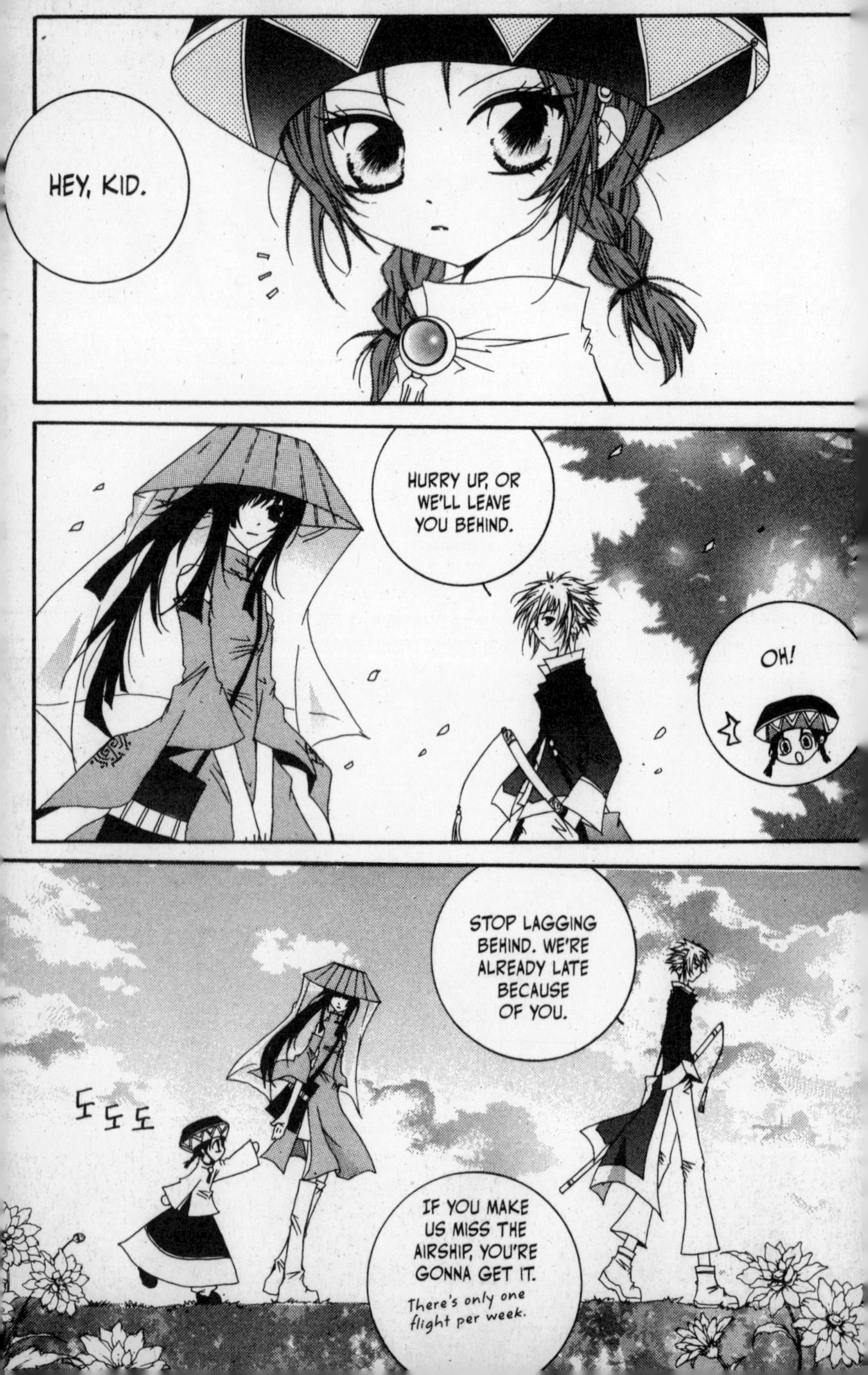
HEY, KID.
HURRY UP, OR WE'LL LEAVE YOU BEHIND.
OH!
STOP LAGGING BEHIND. WE'RE ALREADY LATE BECAUSE OF YOU.
도도도
IF YOU MAKE US MISS THE AIRSHIP, YOU'RE GONNA GET IT.
There's only one flight per week.

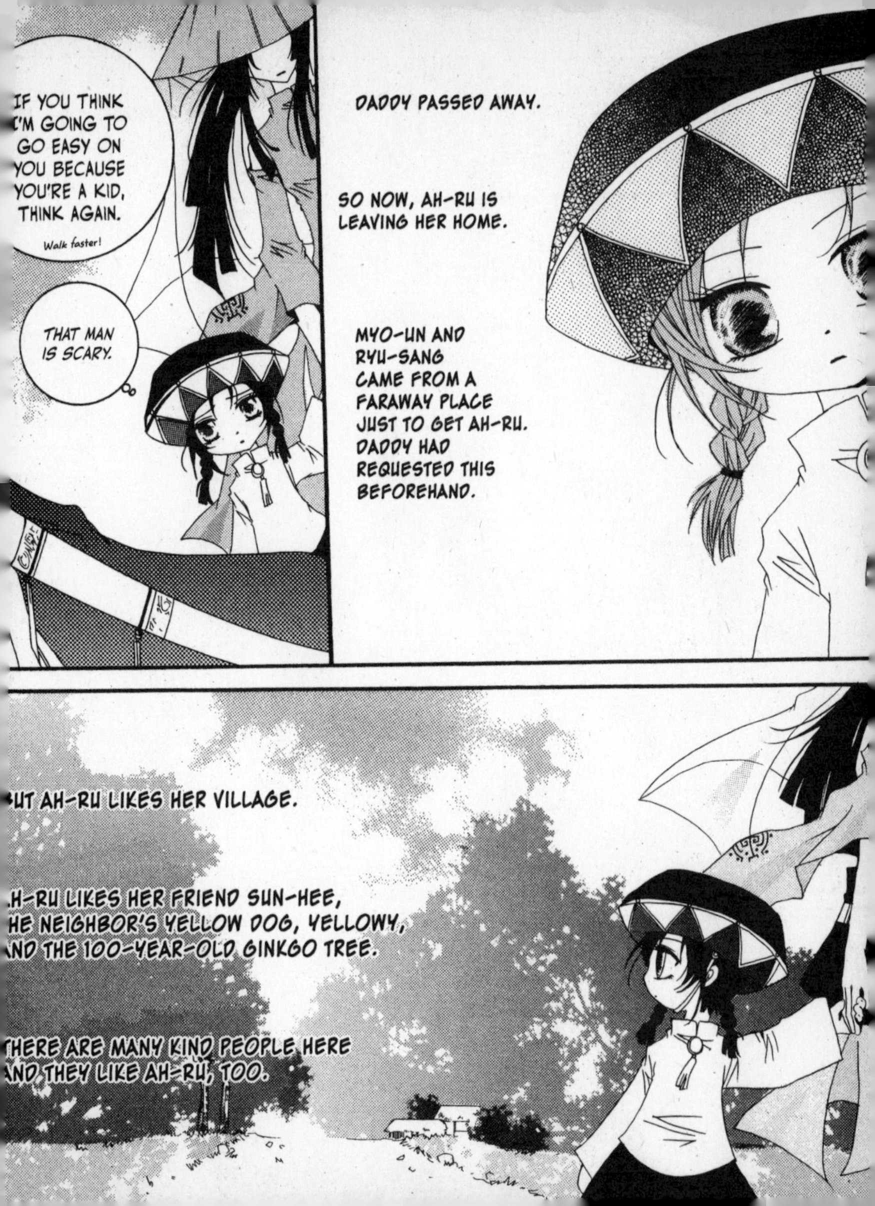
IF YOU THINK I'M GOING TO GO EASY ON YOU BECAUSE YOU'RE A KID, THINK AGAIN.
Walk faster!
THAT MAN IS SCARY.
DADDY PASSED AWAY.
SO NOW, AH-RU IS LEAVING HER HOME.
MYO-UN AND RYU-SANG CAME FROM A FARAWAY PLACE JUST TO GET AH-RU. DADDY HAD REQUESTED THIS BEFOREHAND.
UT AH-RU LIKES HER VILLAGE.
H-RU LIKES HER FRIEND SUN-HEE,
HE NEIGHBOR'S YELLOW DOG, YELLOWY,
ND THE 100-YEAR-OLD GINKGO TREE.
HERE ARE MANY KIND PEOPLE HERE
ND THEY LIKE AH-RU, TOO.

THAT MEANS HE BECAME A STAR.

AMONGST THE MILLIONS OF STARS-- THERE'S DADDY, THERE'S MOMMY.

SO...

AH-RU DOESN'T CRY.

AH-RU IS NOT AFRAID.

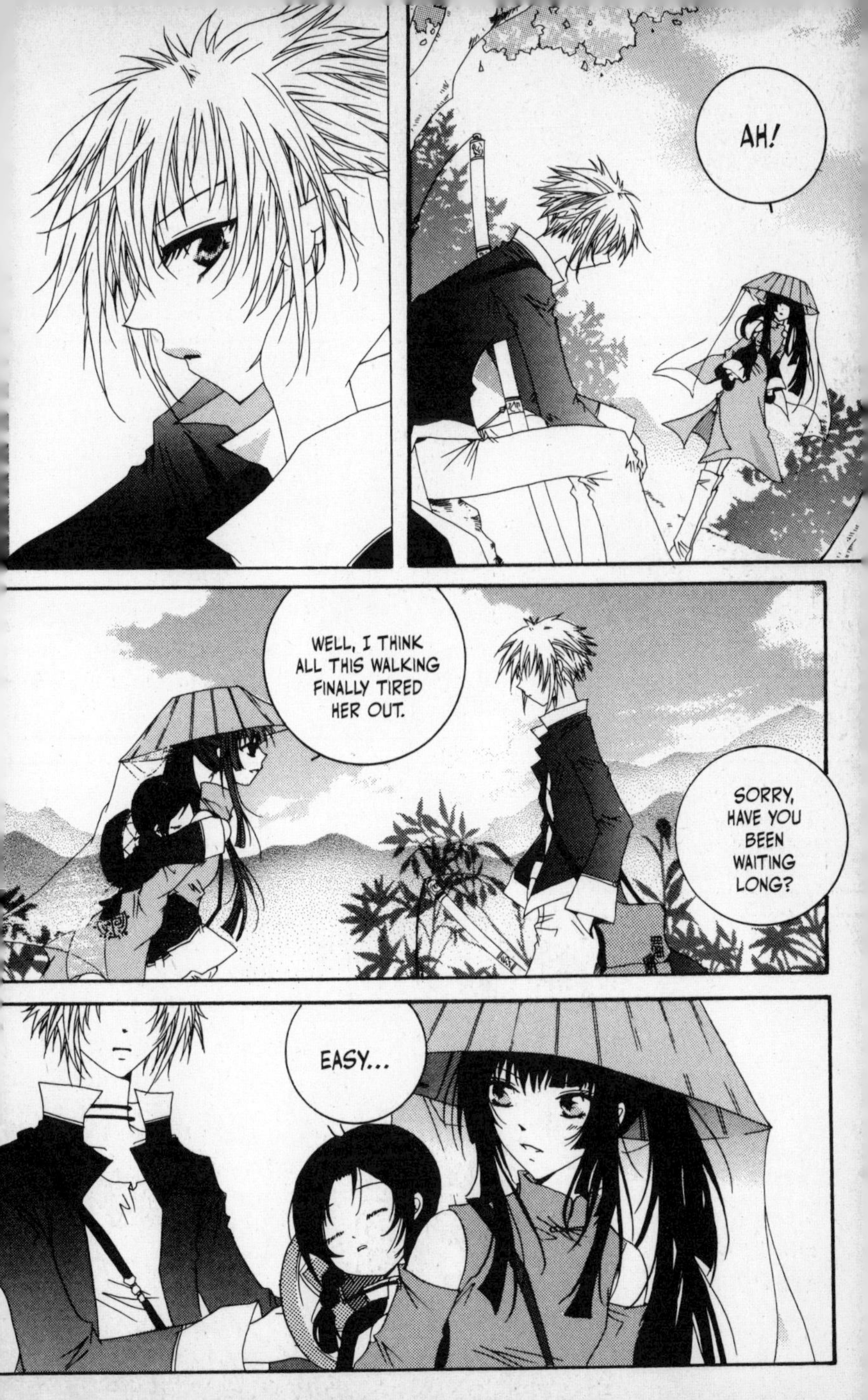
AH!
WELL, I THINK ALL THIS WALKING FINALLY TIRED HER OUT.
SORRY, HAVE YOU BEEN WAITING LONG?
EASY...

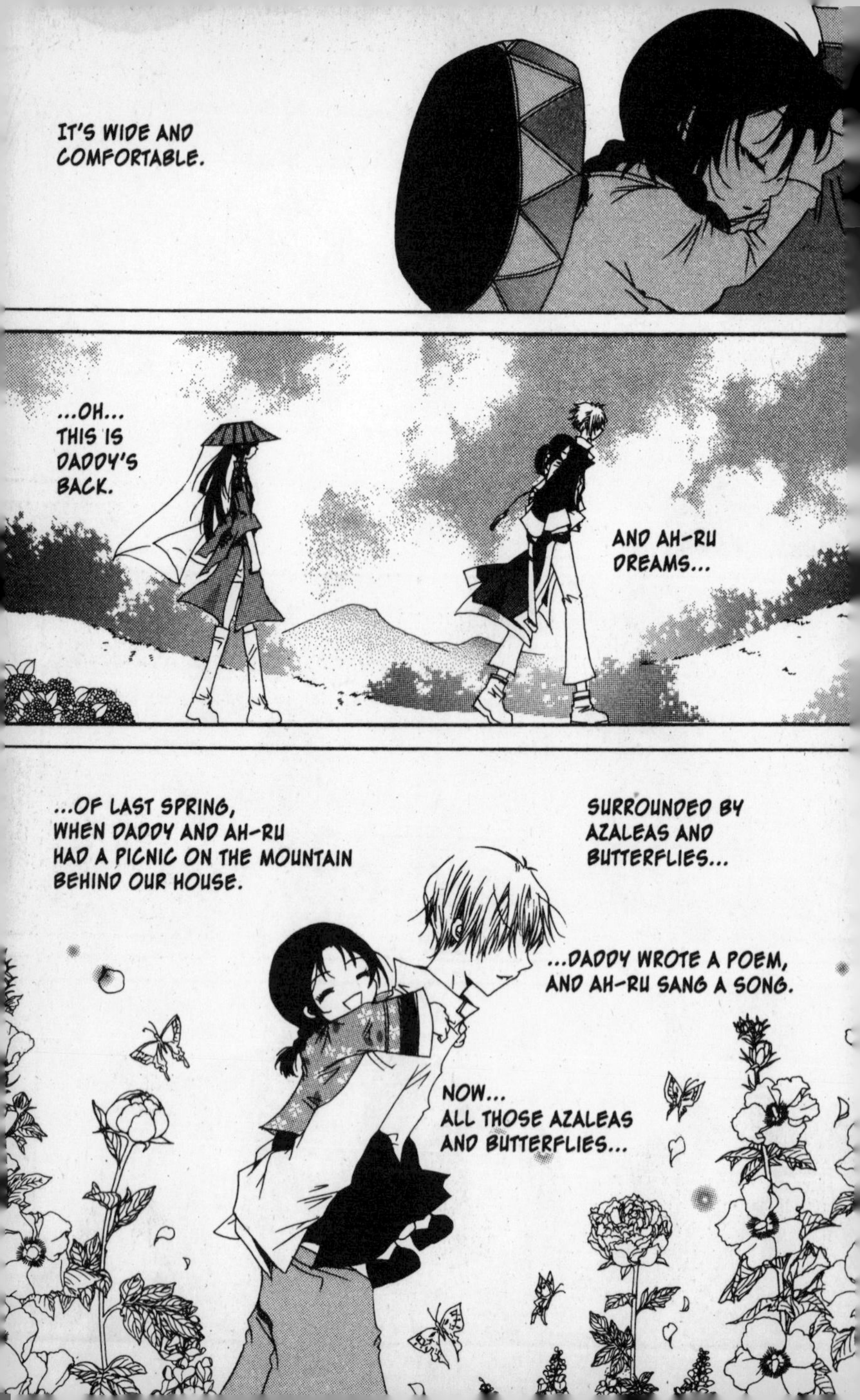
IT'S WIDE AND COMFORTABLE.
...OH... THIS IS DADDY'S BACK.
AND AH-RU DREAMS...
...OF LAST SPRING, WHEN DADDY AND AH-RU HAD A PICNIC ON THE MOUNTAIN BEHIND OUR HOUSE.
SURROUNDED BY AZALEAS AND BUTTERFLIES...
...DADDY WROTE A POEM, AND AH-RU SANG A SONG.
NOW... ALL THOSE AZALEAS AND BUTTERFLIES...

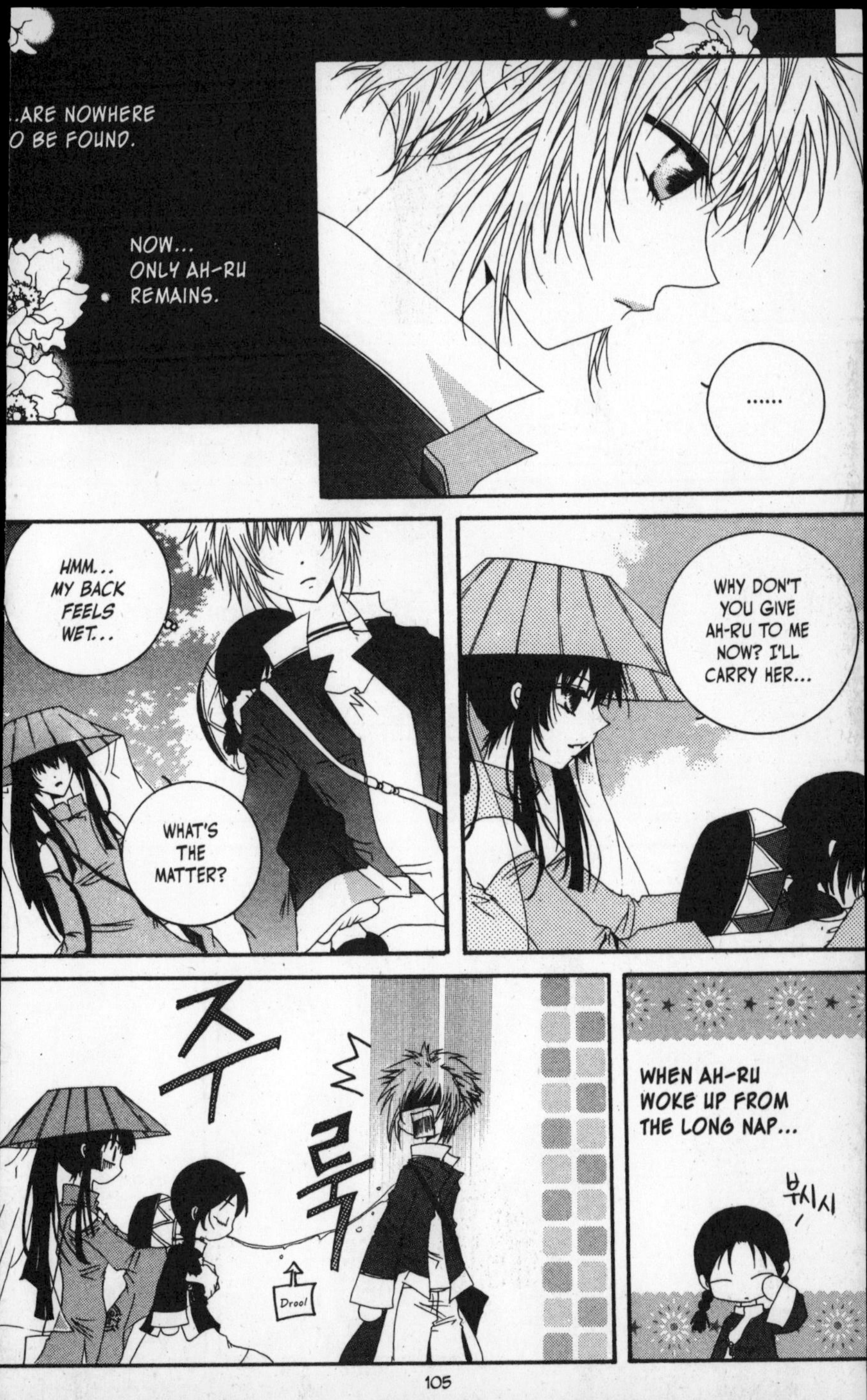

...ARE NOWHERE
TO BE FOUND.
NOW... ONLY AH-RU REMAINS.
......
HMM... MY BACK FEELS WET...
WHAT'S THE MATTER?
WHY DON'T YOU GIVE AH-RU TO ME NOW? I'LL CARRY HER...
Drool
WHEN AH-RU WOKE UP FROM THE LONG NAP...
부시시

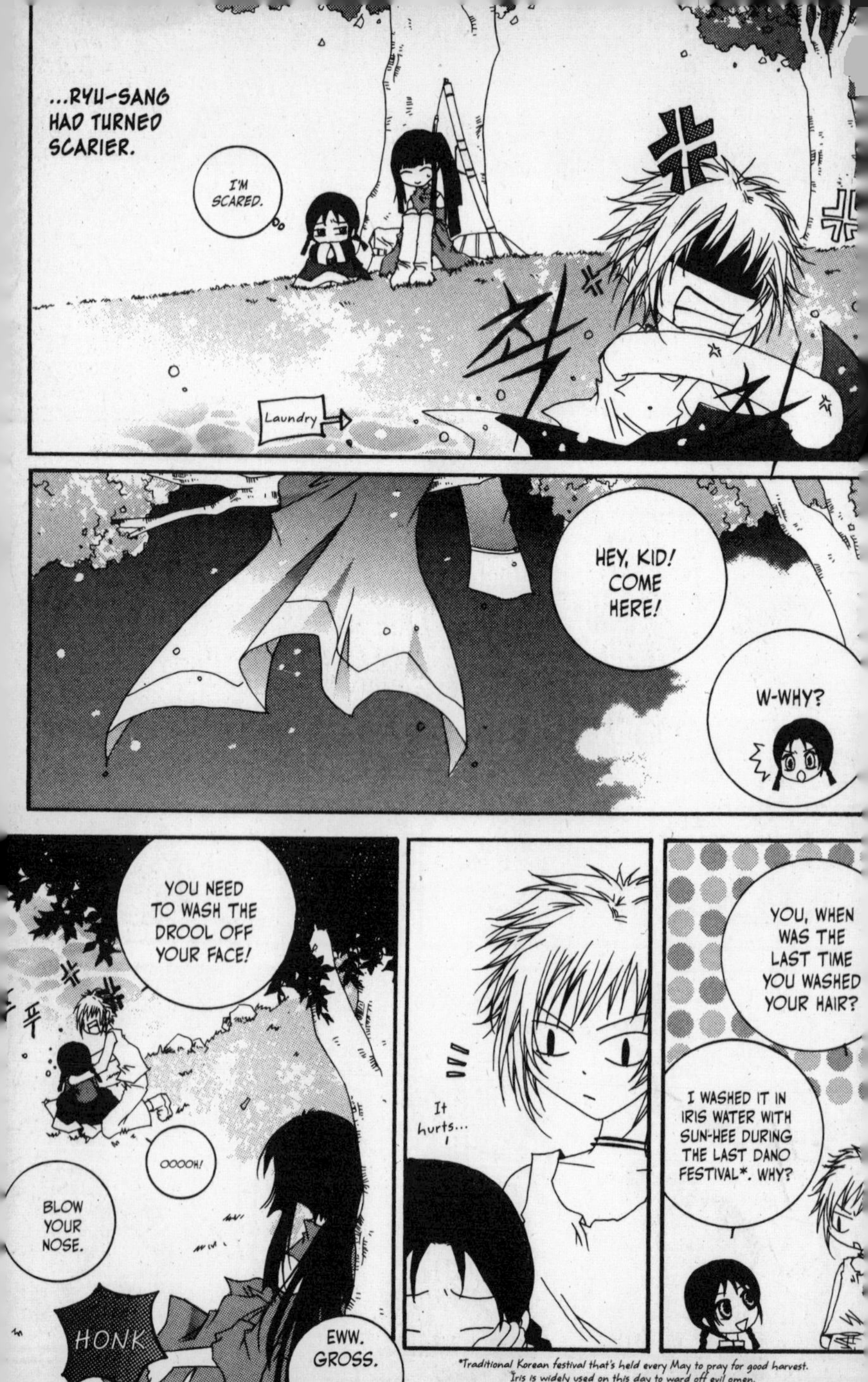
...RYU-SANG HAD TURNED SCARIER.
I'M SCARED.
Laundry
HEY, KID! COME HERE!
W-WHY?
YOU NEED TO WASH THE DROOL OFF YOUR FACE!
OOOOH!
BLOW YOUR NOSE.
HONK
EWW. GROSS.
It hurts...
YOU, WHEN WAS THE LAST TIME YOU WASHED YOUR HAIR?
I WASHED IT IN IRIS WATER WITH SUN-HEE DURING THE LAST DANO FESTIVAL*. WHY?

*Traditional Korean festival that's held every May to pray for good harvest. Iris is widely used on this day to ward off evil omen.

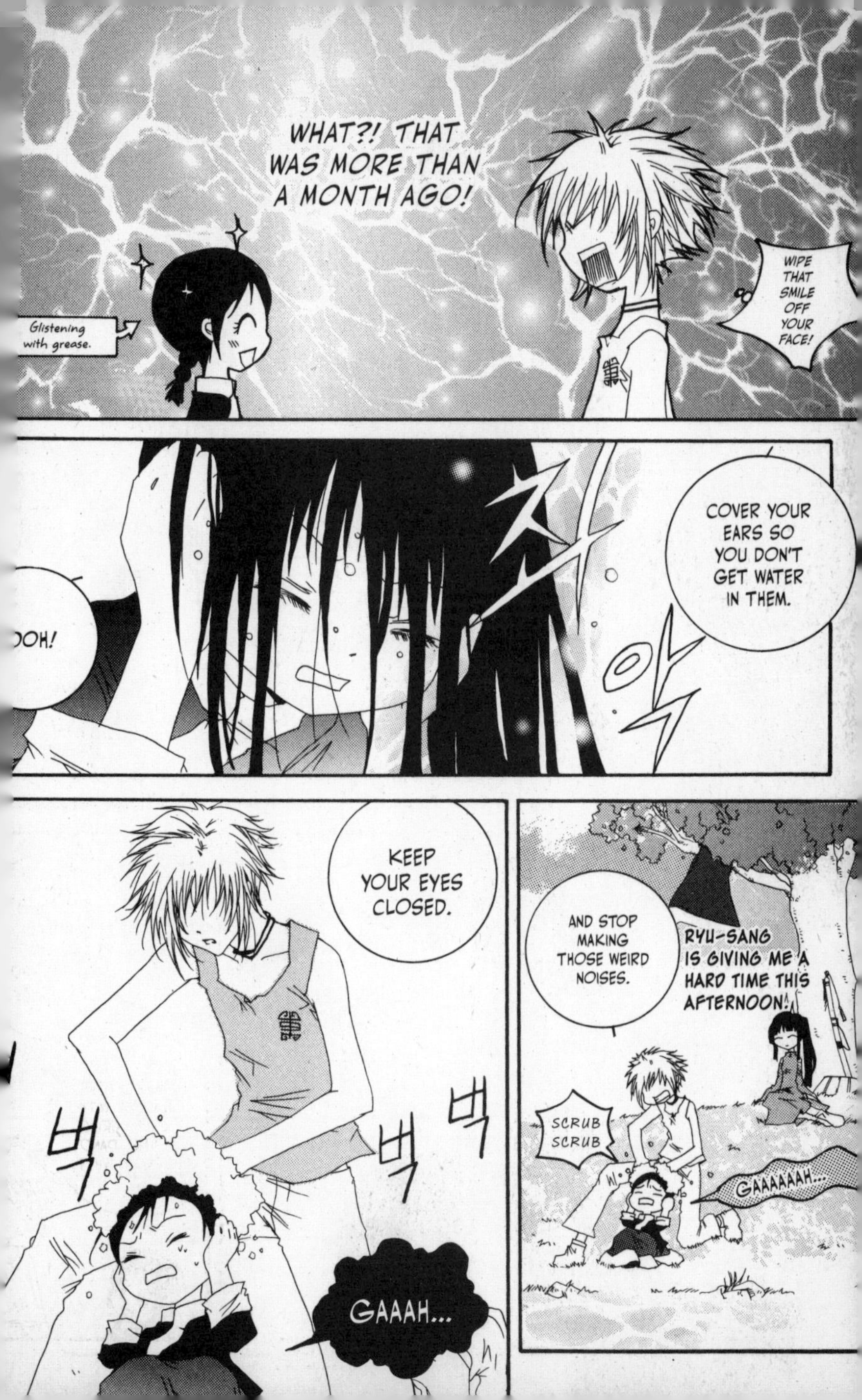
WHAT?! THAT WAS MORE THAN A MONTH AGO!
WIPE THAT SMILE OFF YOUR FACE!
Glistening with grease.
OOH!
COVER YOUR EARS SO YOU DON'T GET WATER IN THEM.
KEEP YOUR EYES CLOSED.
GAAAH...
AND STOP MAKING THOSE WEIRD NOISES.
RYU-SANG IS GIVING ME A HARD TIME THIS AFTERNOON!
SCRUB SCRUB
GAAAAAH...

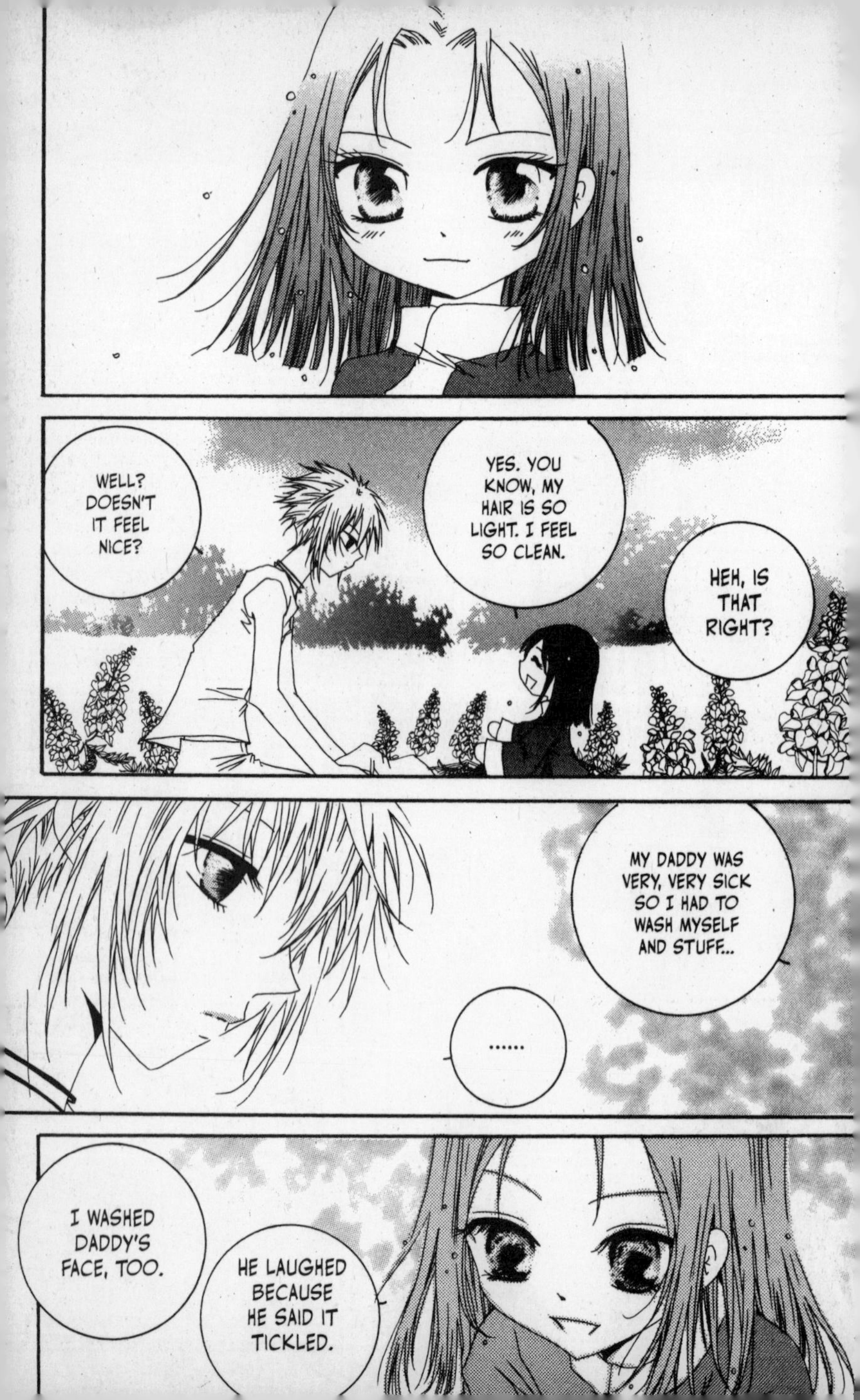
WELL? DOESN'T IT FEEL NICE?
YES. YOU KNOW, MY HAIR IS SO LIGHT. I FEEL SO CLEAN.
HEH, IS THAT RIGHT?
MY DADDY WAS VERY, VERY SICK SO I HAD TO WASH MYSELF AND STUFF...
......
I WASHED DADDY'S FACE, TOO.
HE LAUGHED BECAUSE HE SAID IT TICKLED.

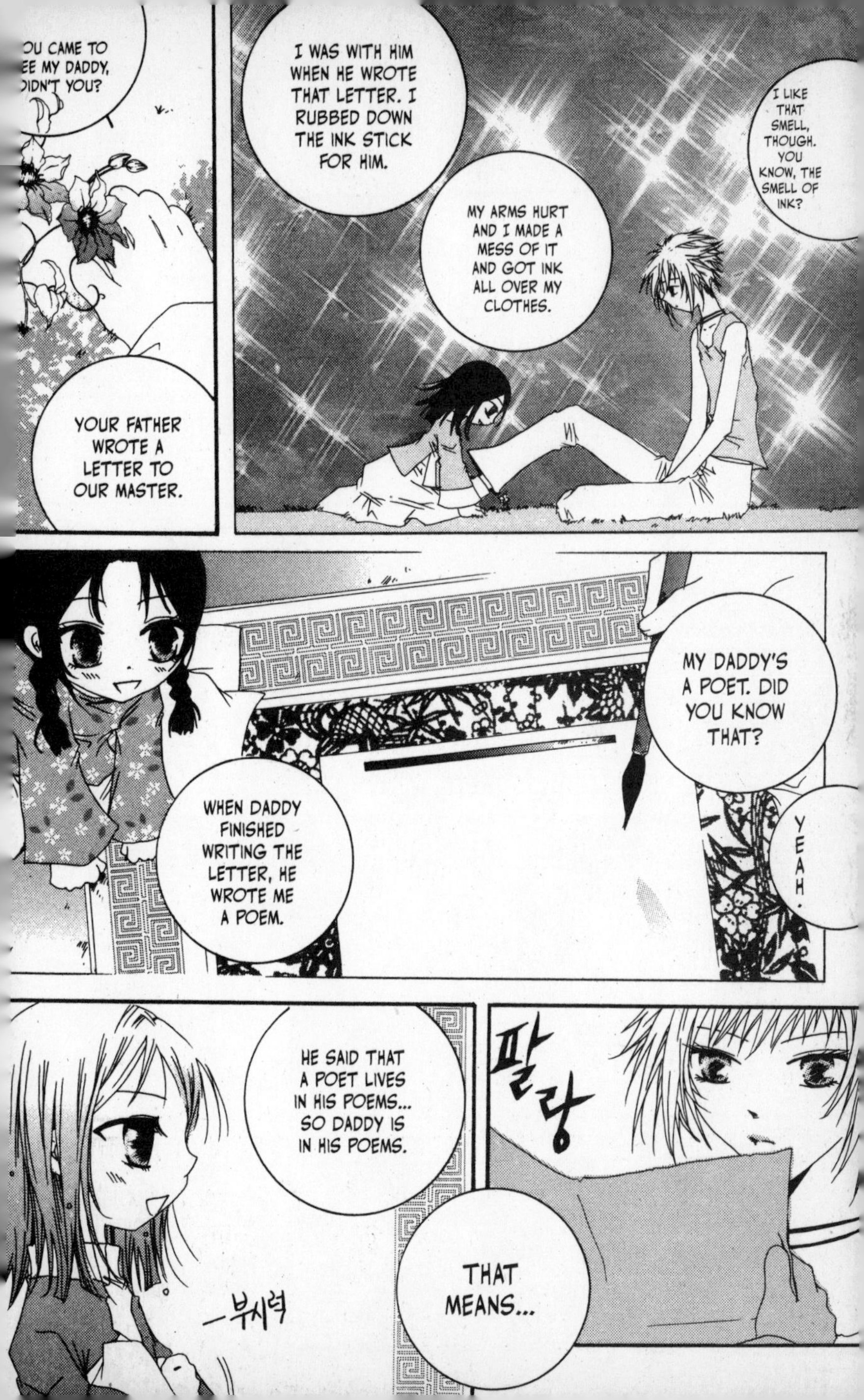

OU CAME TO EE MY DADDY, DIDN'T YOU?
YOUR FATHER WROTE A LETTER TO OUR MASTER.
I WAS WITH HIM WHEN HE WROTE THAT LETTER. I RUBBED DOWN THE INK STICK FOR HIM.
MY ARMS HURT AND I MADE A MESS OF IT AND GOT INK ALL OVER MY CLOTHES.
I LIKE THAT SMELL, THOUGH. YOU KNOW, THE SMELL OF INK?
WHEN DADDY FINISHED WRITING THE LETTER, HE WROTE ME A POEM.
MY DADDY'S A POET. DID YOU KNOW THAT?
YEAH.
HE SAID THAT A POET LIVES IN HIS POEMS... SO DADDY IS IN HIS POEMS.
―부시럭
팔랑
THAT MEANS...

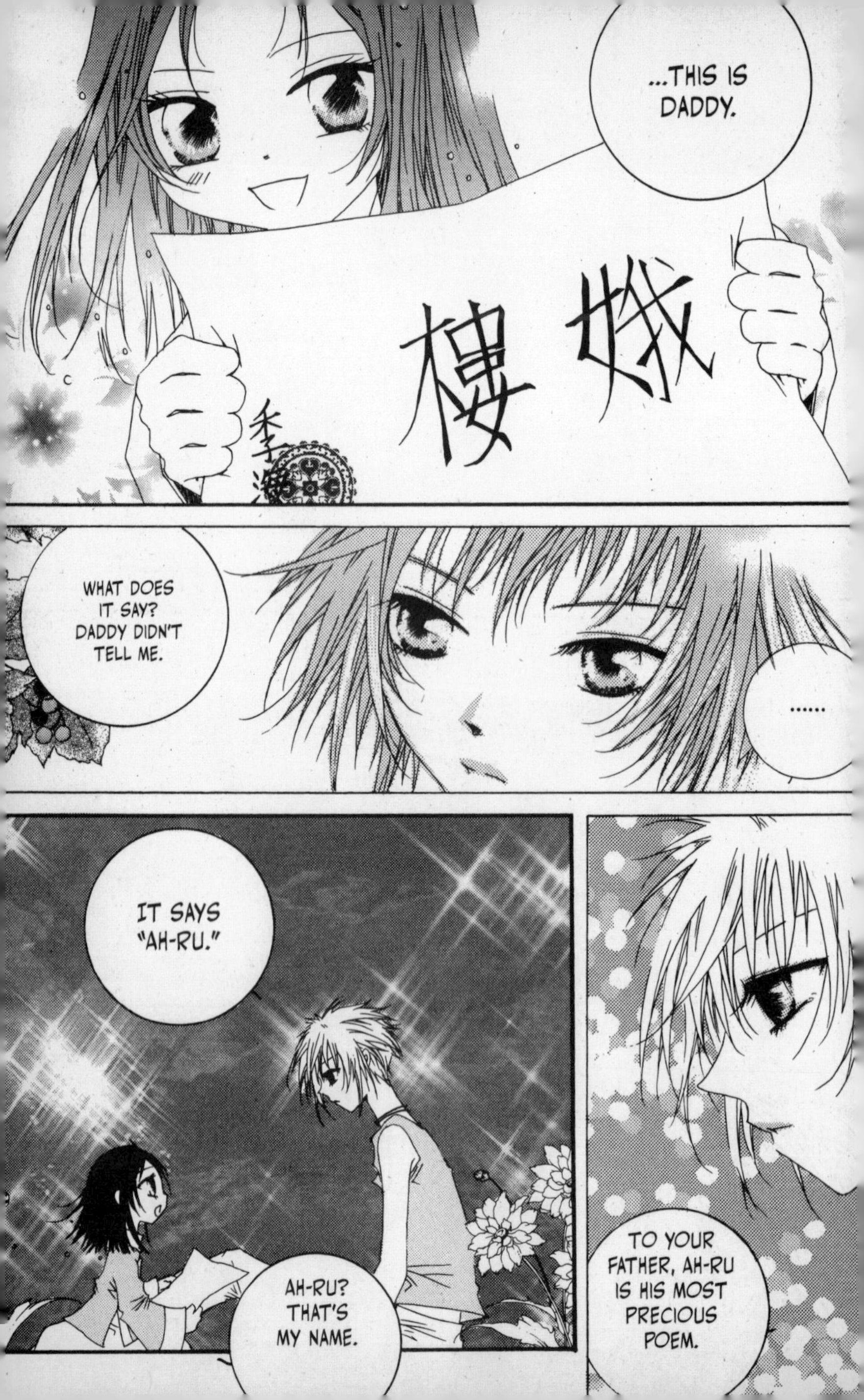
...THIS IS DADDY.
WHAT DOES IT SAY? DADDY DIDN'T TELL ME.
......
IT SAYS "AH-RU."
AH-RU? THAT'S MY NAME.
TO YOUR FATHER, AH-RU IS HIS MOST PRECIOUS POEM.

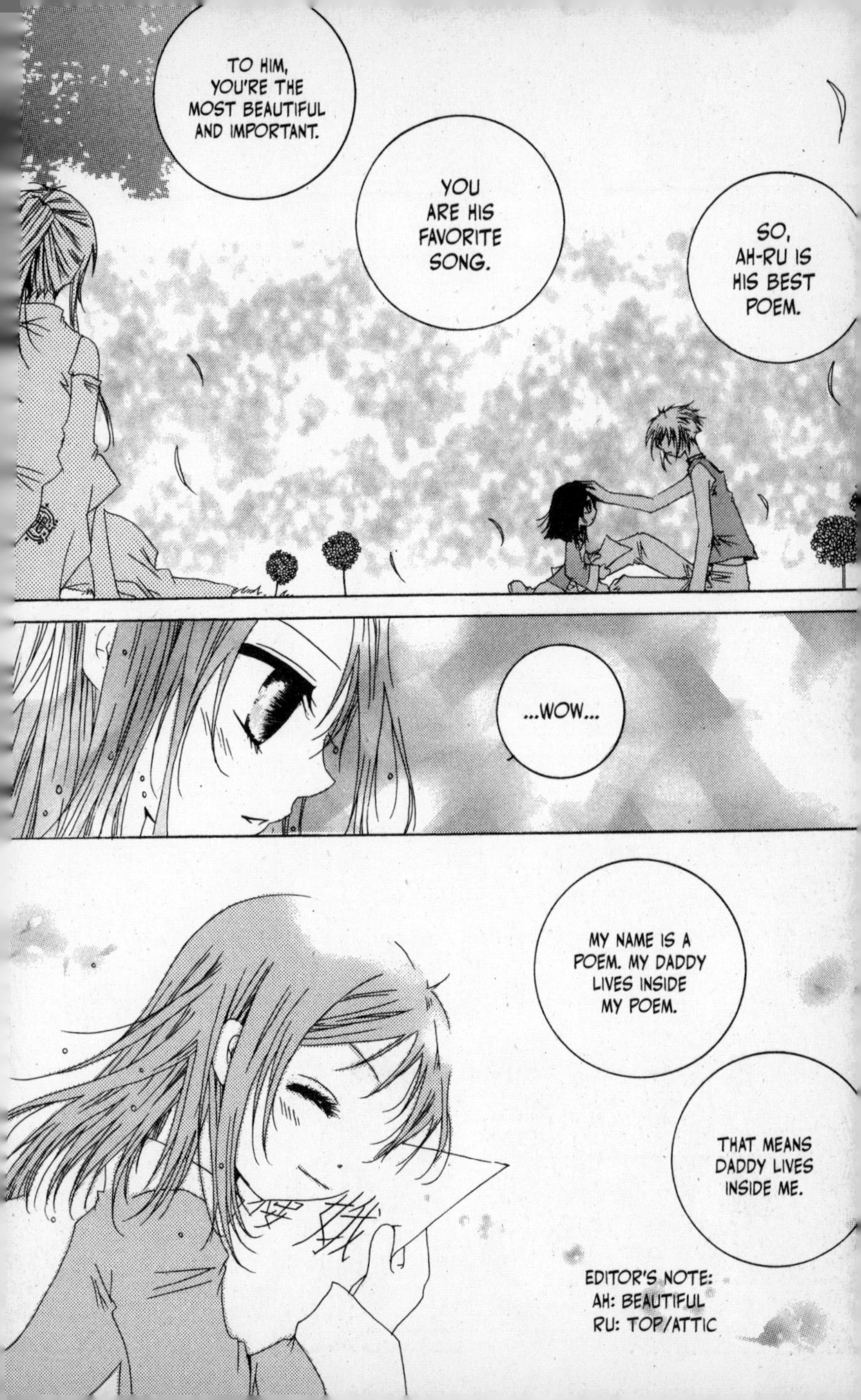
TO HIM, YOU'RE THE MOST BEAUTIFUL AND IMPORTANT.
YOU ARE HIS FAVORITE SONG.
SO, AH-RU IS HIS BEST POEM.
...WOW...
MY NAME IS A POEM. MY DADDY LIVES INSIDE MY POEM.
THAT MEANS DADDY LIVES INSIDE ME.
EDITOR'S NOTE: AH: BEAUTIFUL RU: TOP/ATTIC

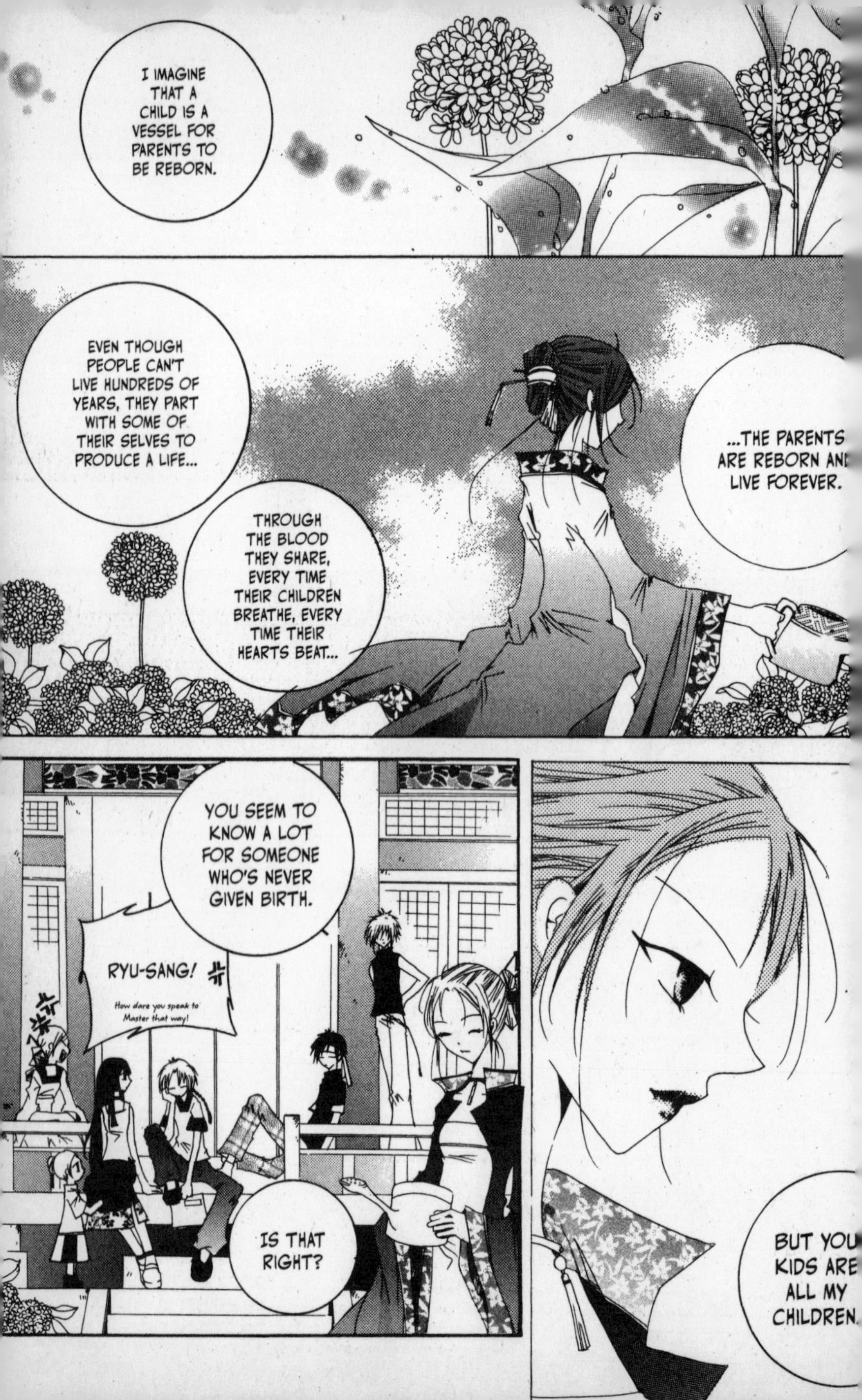
I IMAGINE THAT A CHILD IS A VESSEL FOR PARENTS TO BE REBORN.
EVEN THOUGH PEOPLE CAN'T LIVE HUNDREDS OF YEARS, THEY PART WITH SOME OF THEIR SELVES TO PRODUCE A LIFE...
THROUGH THE BLOOD THEY SHARE, EVERY TIME THEIR CHILDREN BREATHE, EVERY TIME THEIR HEARTS BEAT...
...THE PARENTS ARE REBORN AND LIVE FOREVER.
YOU SEEM TO KNOW A LOT FOR SOMEONE WHO'S NEVER GIVEN BIRTH.
RYU-SANG!
How dare you speak to Master that way!
IS THAT RIGHT?
BUT YOU KIDS ARE ALL MY CHILDREN.

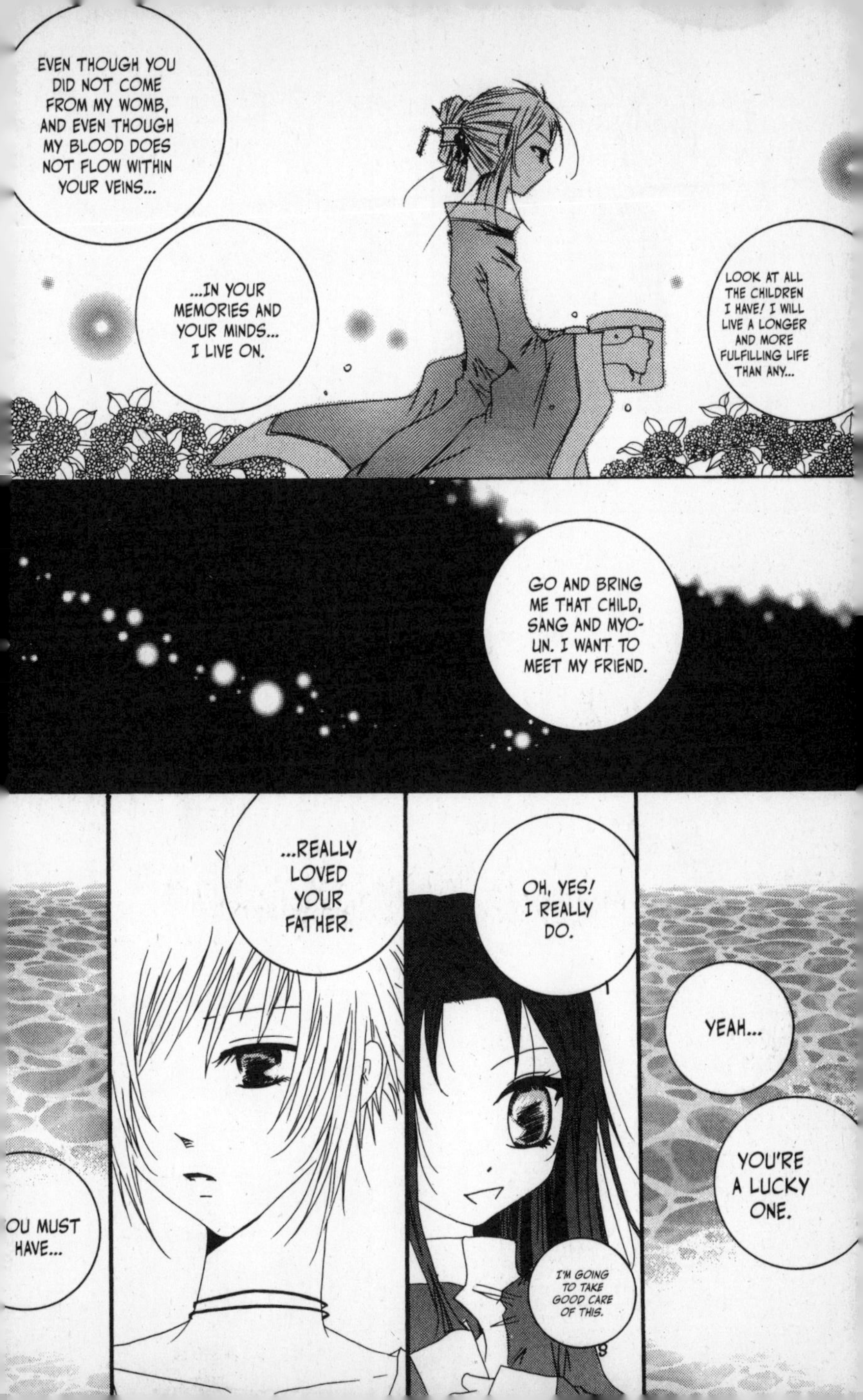

EVEN THOUGH YOU DID NOT COME FROM MY WOMB, AND EVEN THOUGH MY BLOOD DOES NOT FLOW WITHIN YOUR VEINS...
...IN YOUR MEMORIES AND YOUR MINDS... I LIVE ON.
LOOK AT ALL THE CHILDREN I HAVE! I WILL LIVE A LONGER AND MORE FULFILLING LIFE THAN ANY...
GO AND BRING ME THAT CHILD, SANG AND MYO-UN. I WANT TO MEET MY FRIEND.
OU MUST HAVE...
...REALLY LOVED YOUR FATHER.
OH, YES! I REALLY DO.
I'M GOING TO TAKE GOOD CARE OF THIS.
YEAH...
YOU'RE A LUCKY ONE.

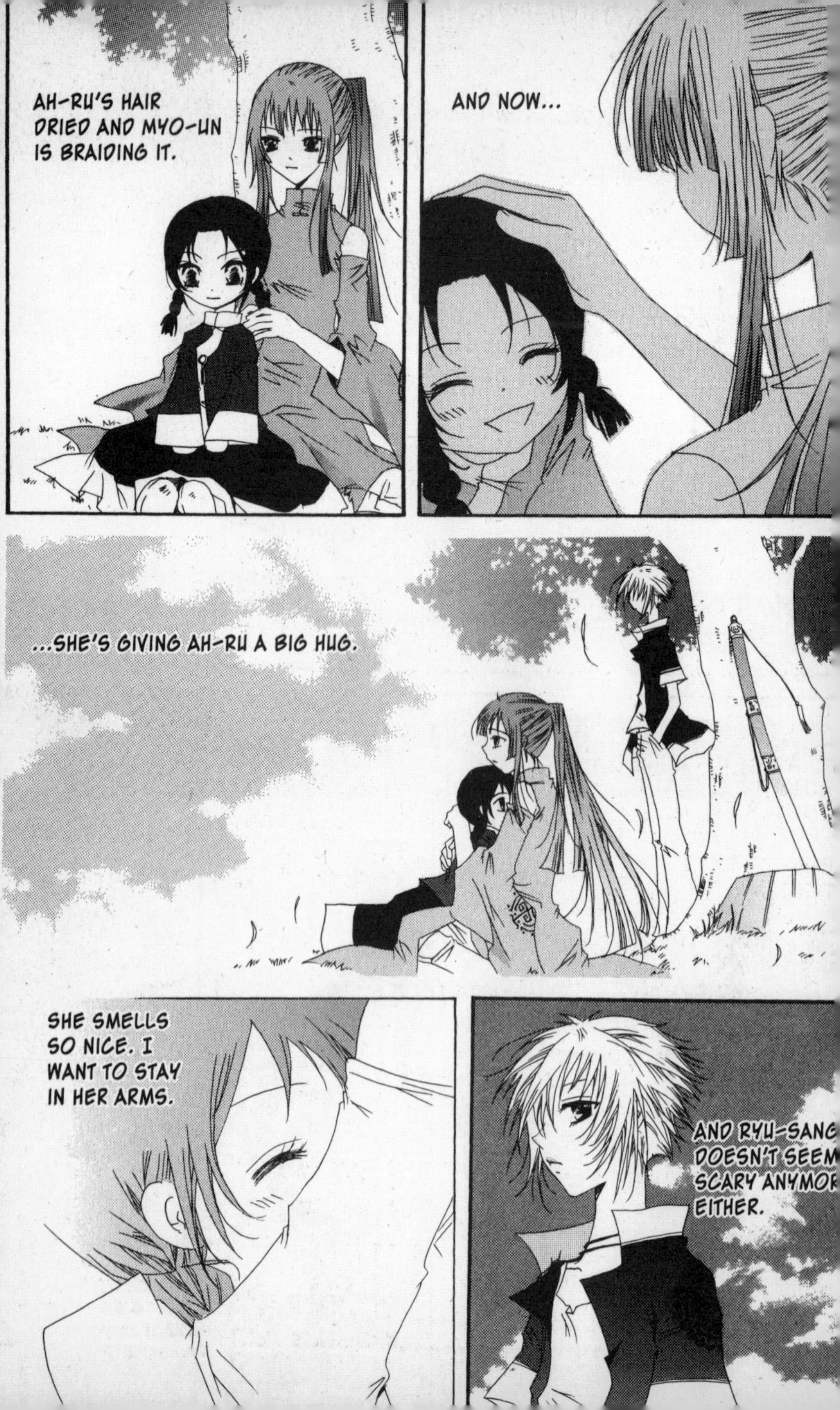
AH-RU'S HAIR DRIED AND MYO-UN IS BRAIDING IT.
AND NOW...
...SHE'S GIVING AH-RU A BIG HUG.
SHE SMELLS SO NICE. I WANT TO STAY IN HER ARMS.
AND RYU-SANG DOESN'T SEEM SCARY ANYMOR EITHER.

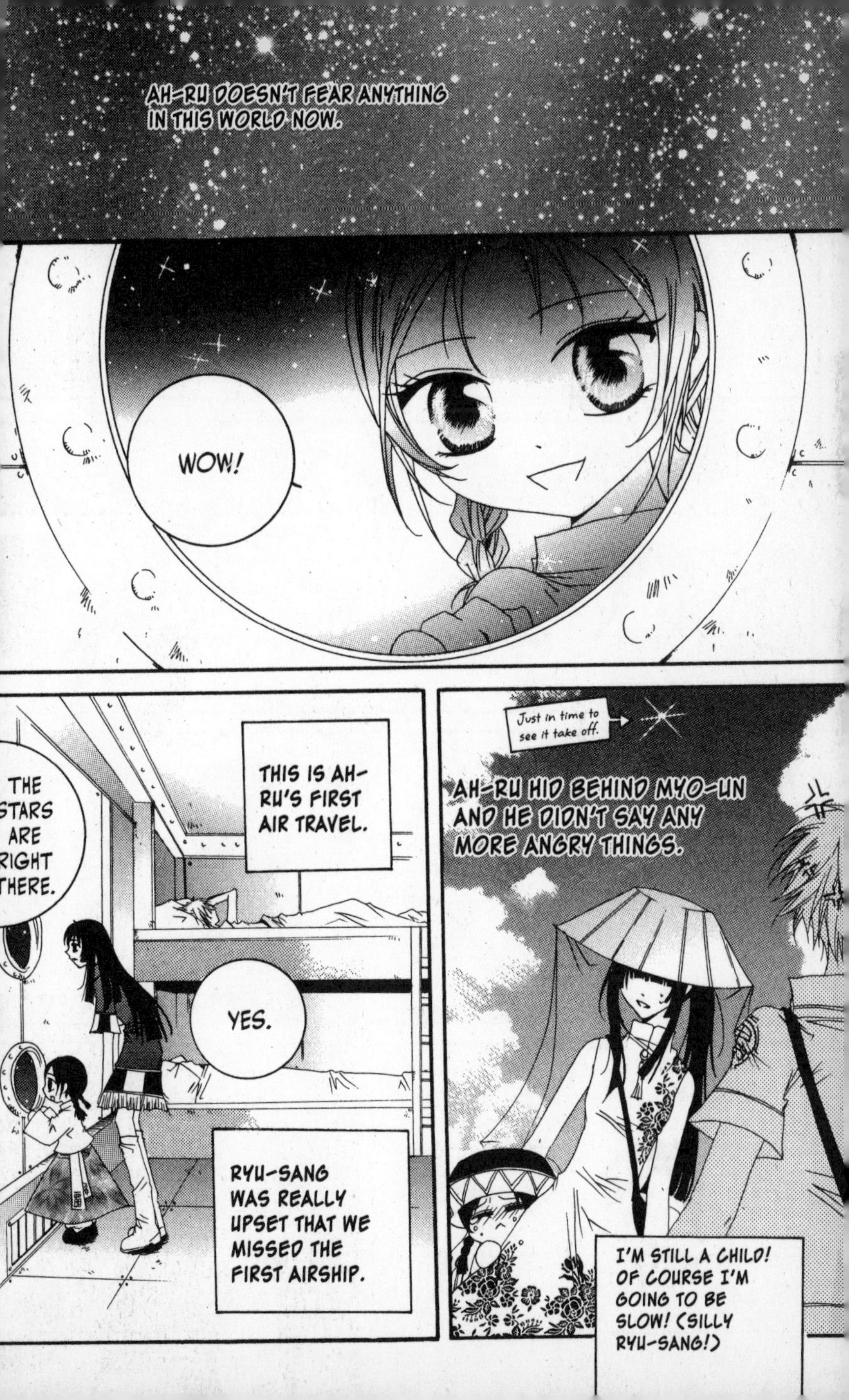

AH-RU DOESN'T FEAR ANYTHING IN THIS WORLD NOW.
WOW!
THE STARS ARE RIGHT THERE.
THIS IS AH-RU'S FIRST AIR TRAVEL.
YES.
RYU-SANG WAS REALLY UPSET THAT WE MISSED THE FIRST AIRSHIP.
Just in time to see it take off.
AH-RU HID BEHIND MYO-UN AND HE DIDN'T SAY ANY MORE ANGRY THINGS.
I'M STILL A CHILD! OF COURSE I'M GOING TO BE SLOW! (SILLY RYU-SANG!)

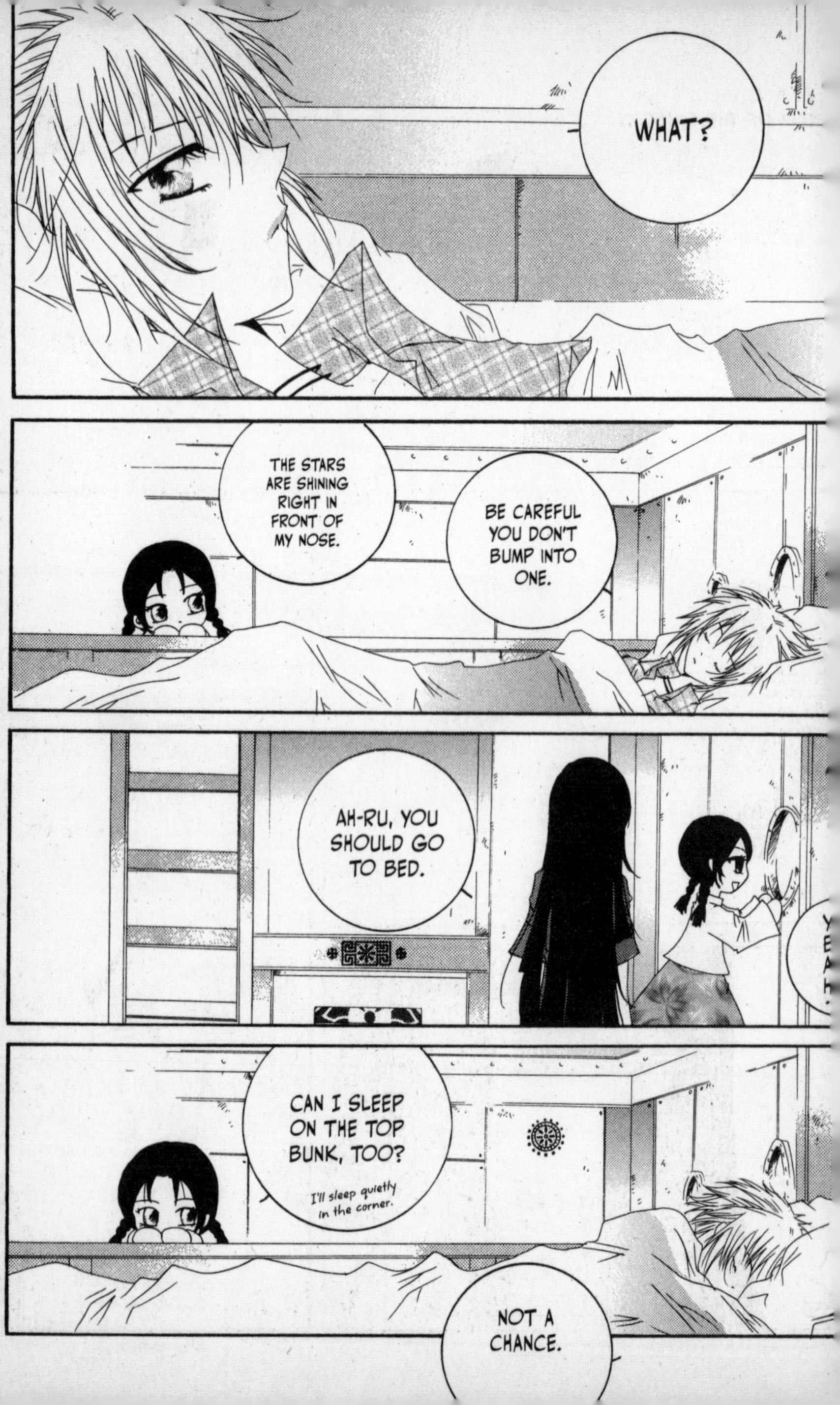
WHAT?
THE STARS ARE SHINING RIGHT IN FRONT OF MY NOSE.
BE CAREFUL YOU DON'T BUMP INTO ONE.
AH-RU, YOU SHOULD GO TO BED.
YEAH
CAN I SLEEP ON THE TOP BUNK, TOO?
I'll sleep quietly in the corner.
NOT A CHANCE.

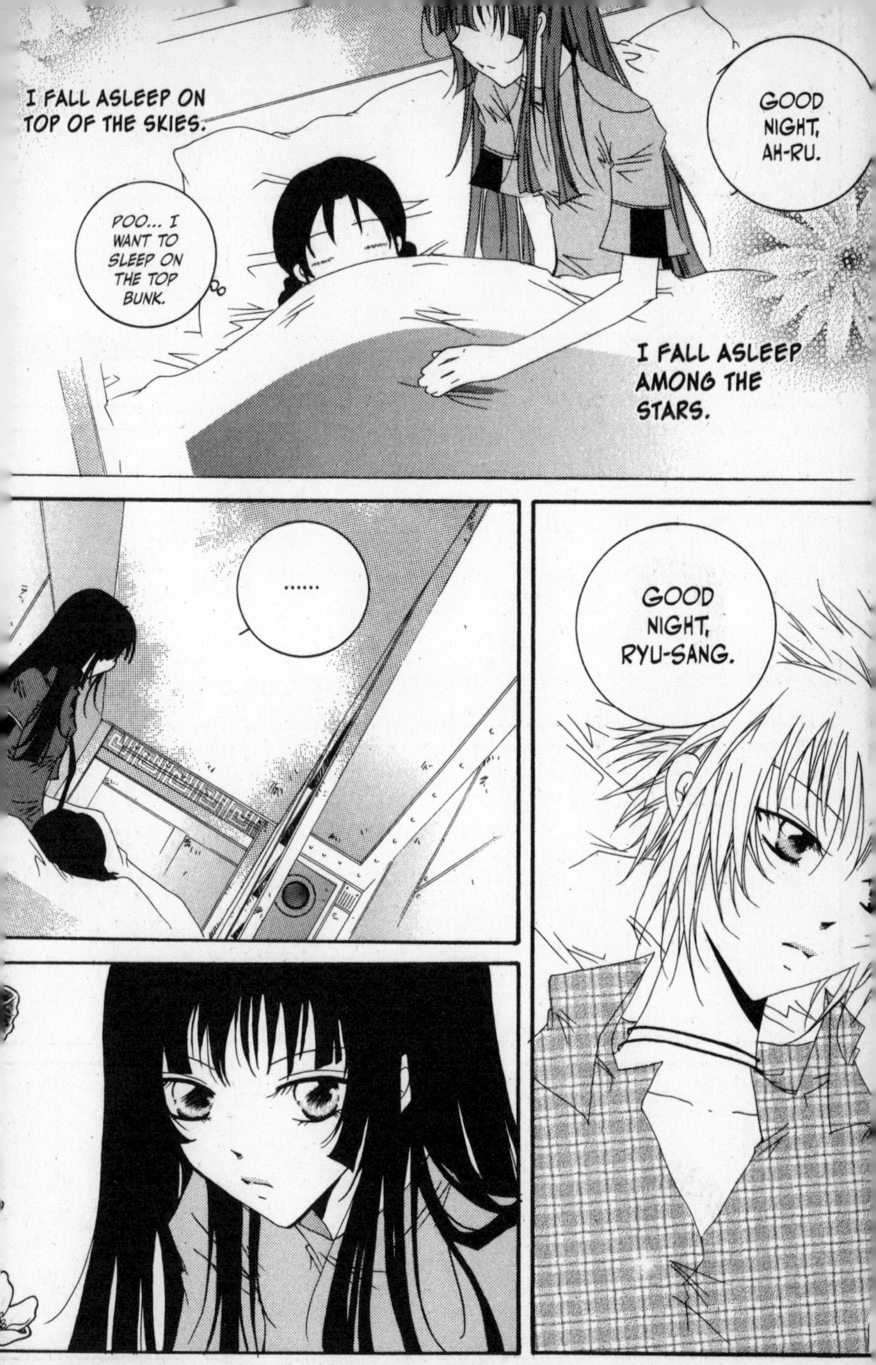
I FALL ASLEEP ON TOP OF THE SKIES.
GOOD NIGHT, AH-RU.
POO... I WANT TO SLEEP ON THE TOP BUNK.
I FALL ASLEEP AMONG THE STARS.
......
GOOD NIGHT, RYU-SANG.

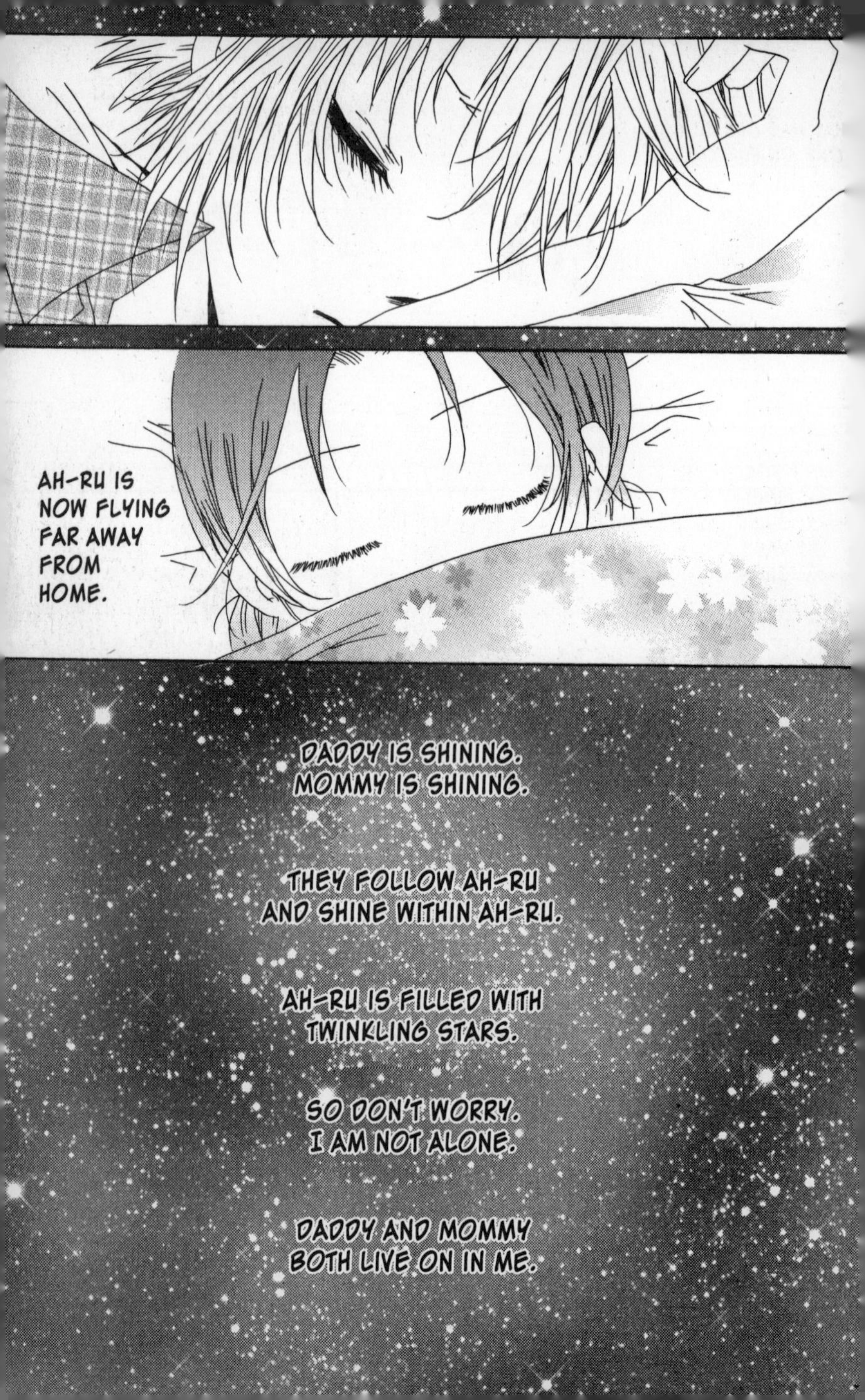
AH-RU IS NOW FLYING FAR AWAY FROM HOME.
DADDY IS SHINING. MOMMY IS SHINING.
THEY FOLLOW AH-RU AND SHINE WITHIN AH-RU.
AH-RU IS FILLED WITH TWINKLING STARS.
SO DON'T WORRY. I AM NOT ALONE.
DADDY AND MOMMY BOTH LIVE ON IN ME.

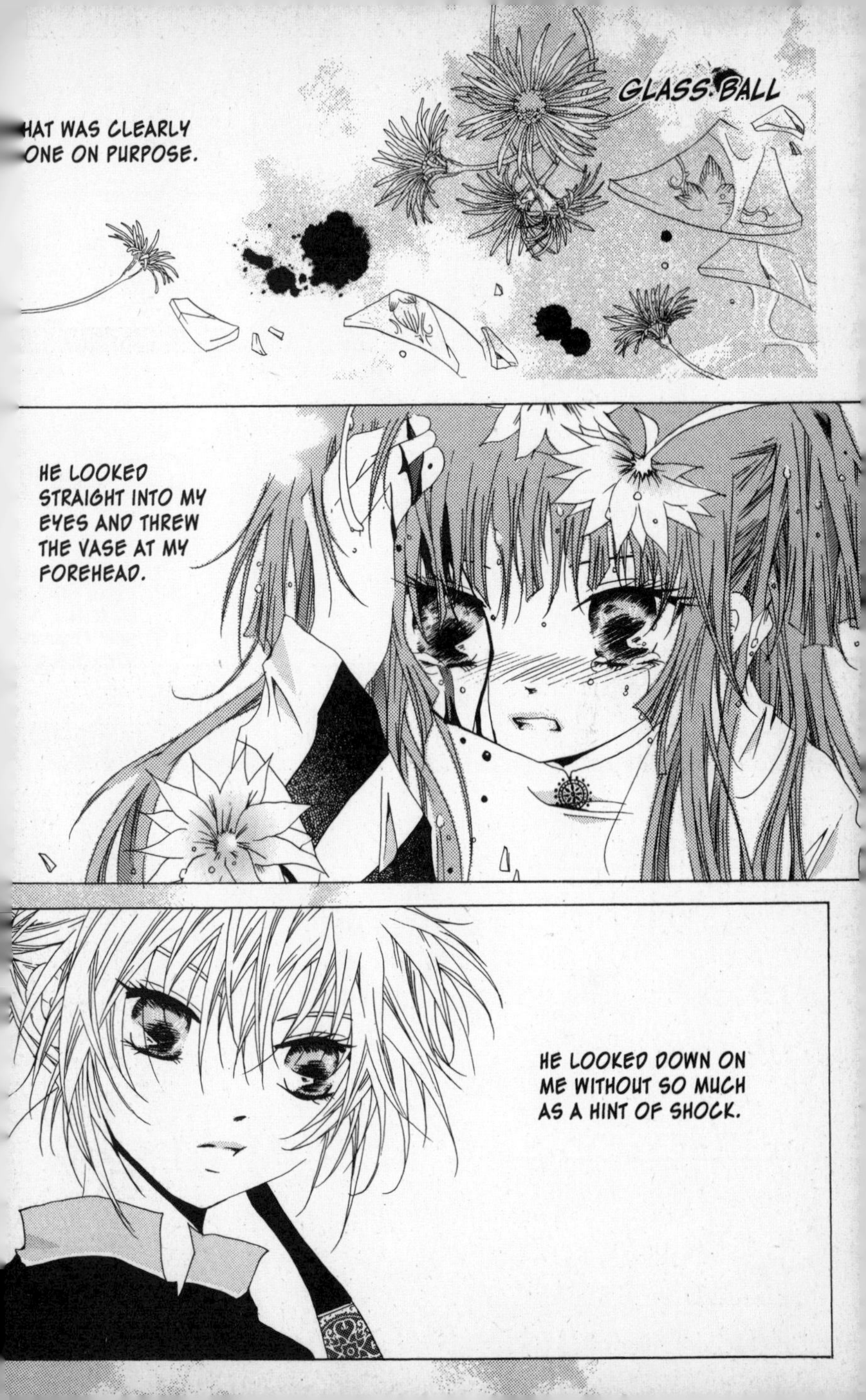
GLASS BALL
HAT WAS CLEARLY ONE ON PURPOSE.
HE LOOKED STRAIGHT INTO MY EYES AND THREW THE VASE AT MY FOREHEAD.
HE LOOKED DOWN ON ME WITHOUT SO MUCH AS A HINT OF SHOCK.

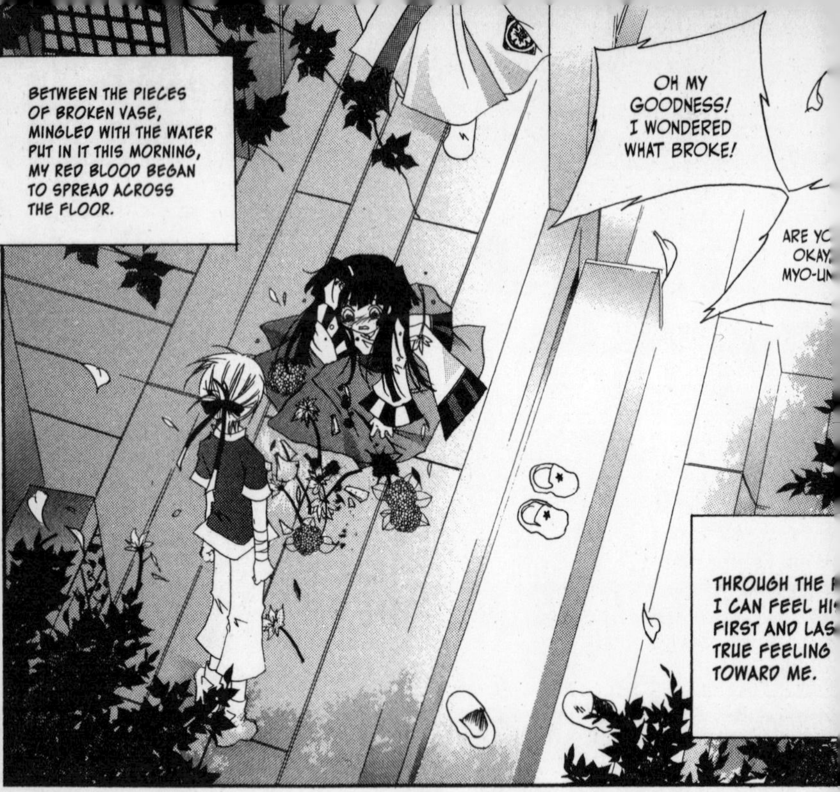
BETWEEN THE PIECES OF BROKEN VASE, MINGLED WITH THE WATER PUT IN IT THIS MORNING, MY RED BLOOD BEGAN TO SPREAD ACROSS THE FLOOR.
OH MY GOODNESS! I WONDERED WHAT BROKE!
ARE YO OKAY MYO-UN
THROUGH THE I CAN FEEL HI FIRST AND LAS TRUE FEELING TOWARD ME.

HE HATES ME.
HE HATES ME.

HE REALLY...

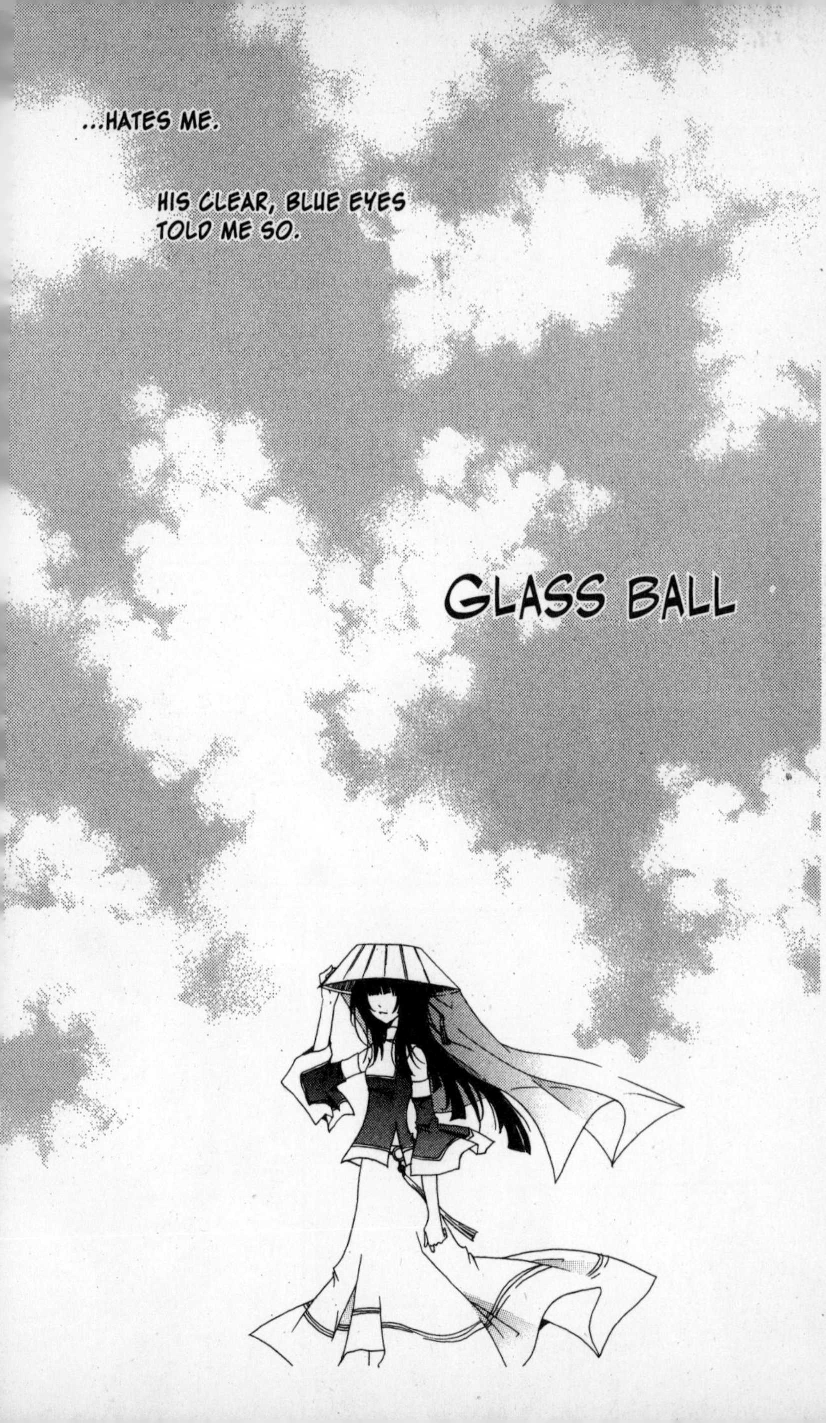
...HATES ME.
HIS CLEAR, BLUE EYES TOLD ME SO.
GLASS BALL

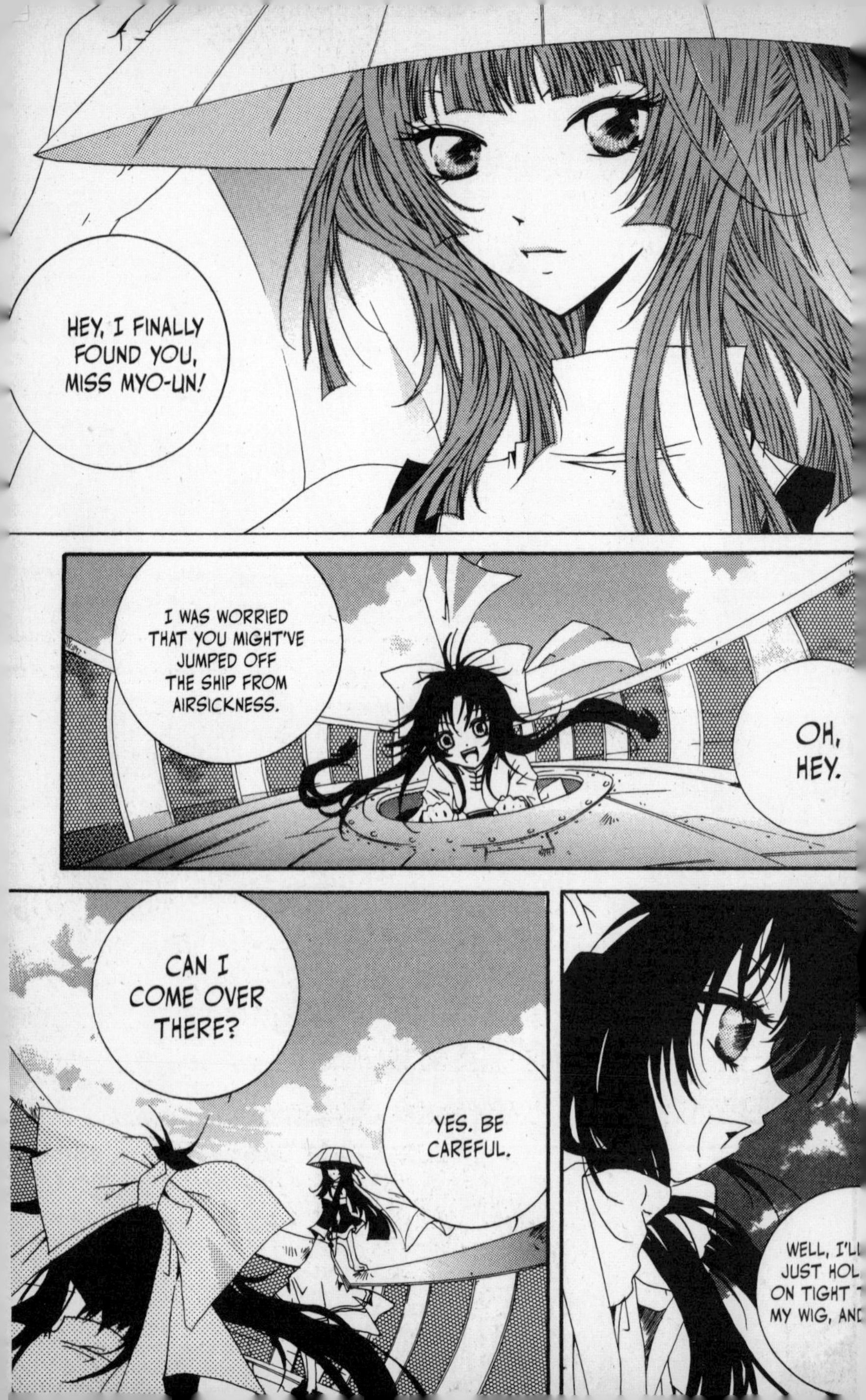
HEY, I FINALLY FOUND YOU, MISS MYO-UN!
I WAS WORRIED THAT YOU MIGHT'VE JUMPED OFF THE SHIP FROM AIRSICKNESS.
OH, HEY.
CAN I COME OVER THERE?
YES. BE CAREFUL.
WELL, I'LL JUST HOL ON TIGHT T MY WIG, AND

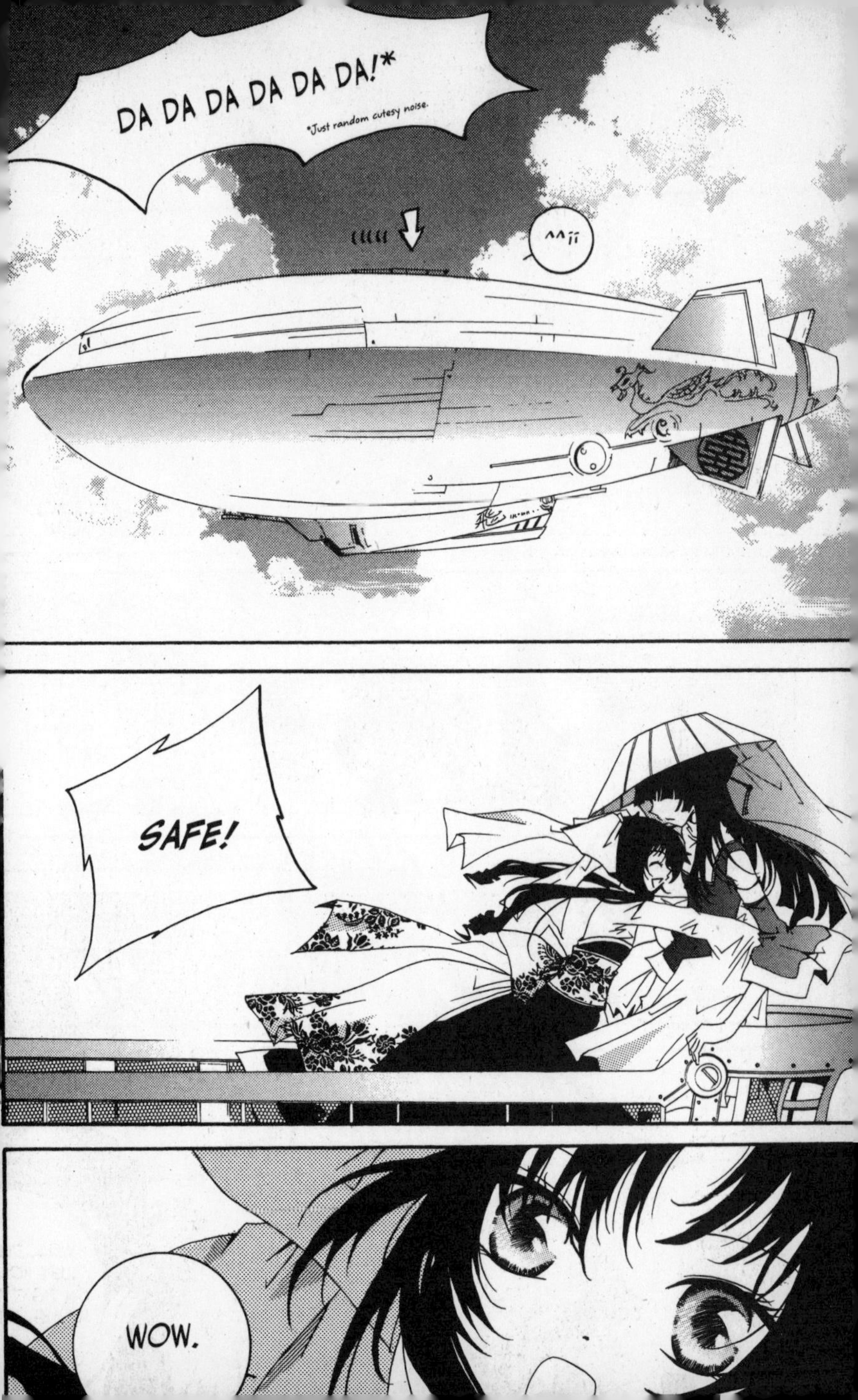
DA DA DA DA DA DA!*
*Just random cutesy noise.
^^;;
SAFE!
WOW.

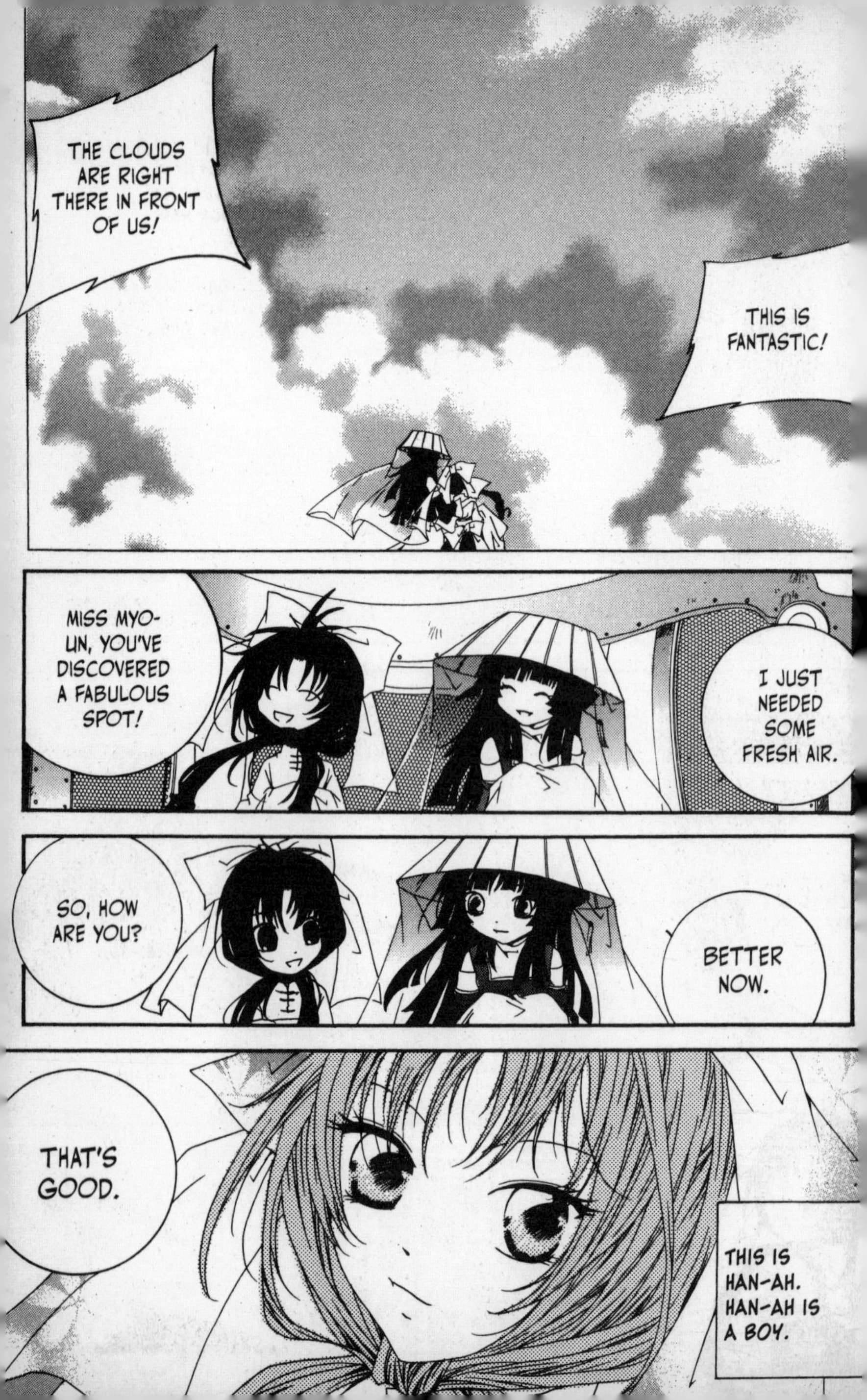
THE CLOUDS ARE RIGHT THERE IN FRONT OF US!
THIS IS FANTASTIC!
MISS MYO-UN, YOU'VE DISCOVERED A FABULOUS SPOT!
I JUST NEEDED SOME FRESH AIR.
SO, HOW ARE YOU?
BETTER NOW.
THAT'S GOOD.
THIS IS HAN-AH. HAN-AH IS A BOY.

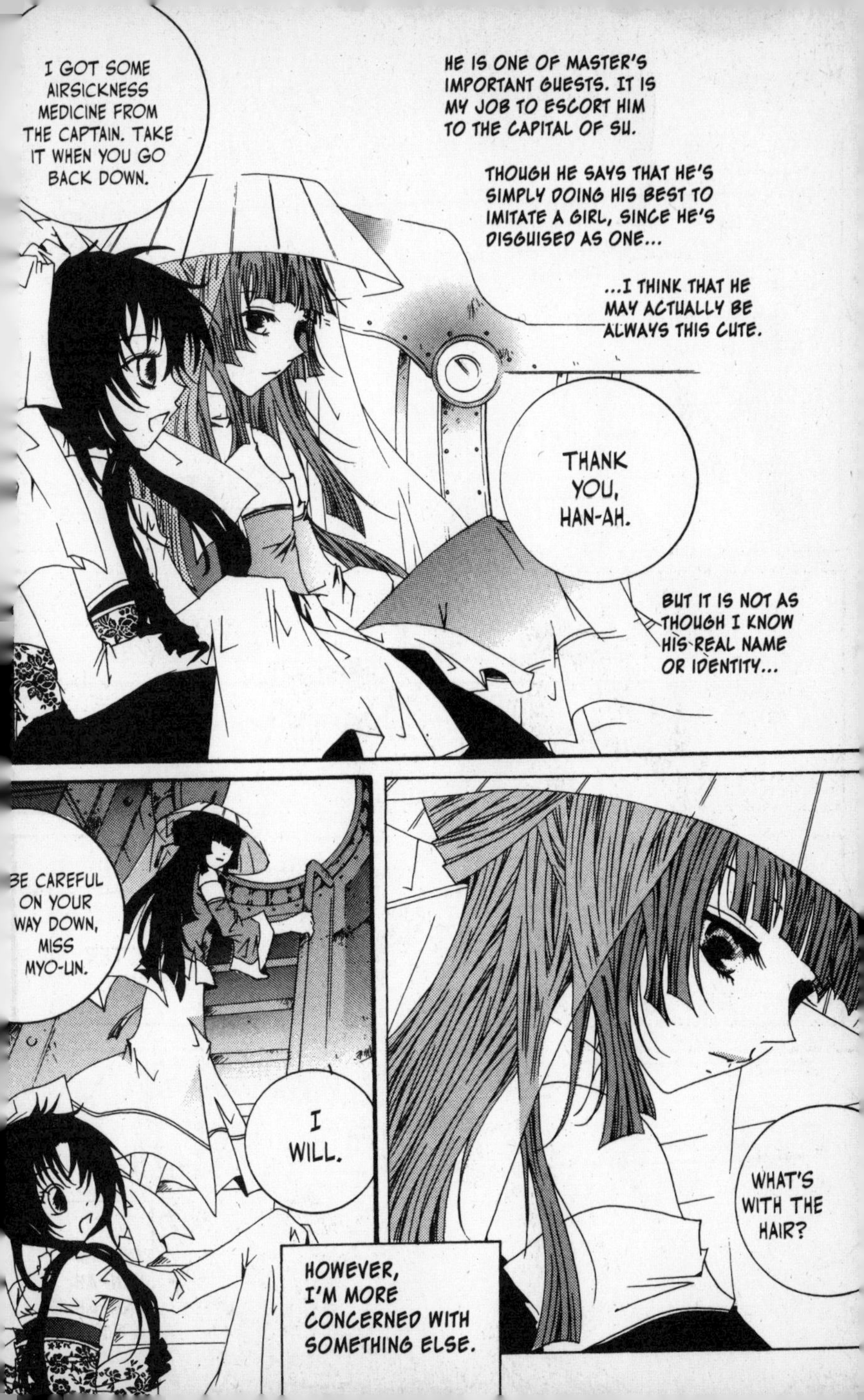
I GOT SOME AIRSICKNESS MEDICINE FROM THE CAPTAIN. TAKE IT WHEN YOU GO BACK DOWN.
HE IS ONE OF MASTER'S IMPORTANT GUESTS. IT IS MY JOB TO ESCORT HIM TO THE CAPITAL OF SU.
THOUGH HE SAYS THAT HE'S SIMPLY DOING HIS BEST TO IMITATE A GIRL, SINCE HE'S DISGUISED AS ONE...
...I THINK THAT HE MAY ACTUALLY BE ALWAYS THIS CUTE.
THANK YOU, HAN-AH.
BUT IT IS NOT AS THOUGH I KNOW HIS REAL NAME OR IDENTITY...
BE CAREFUL ON YOUR WAY DOWN, MISS MYO-UN.
I WILL.
HOWEVER, I'M MORE CONCERNED WITH SOMETHING ELSE.
WHAT'S WITH THE HAIR?

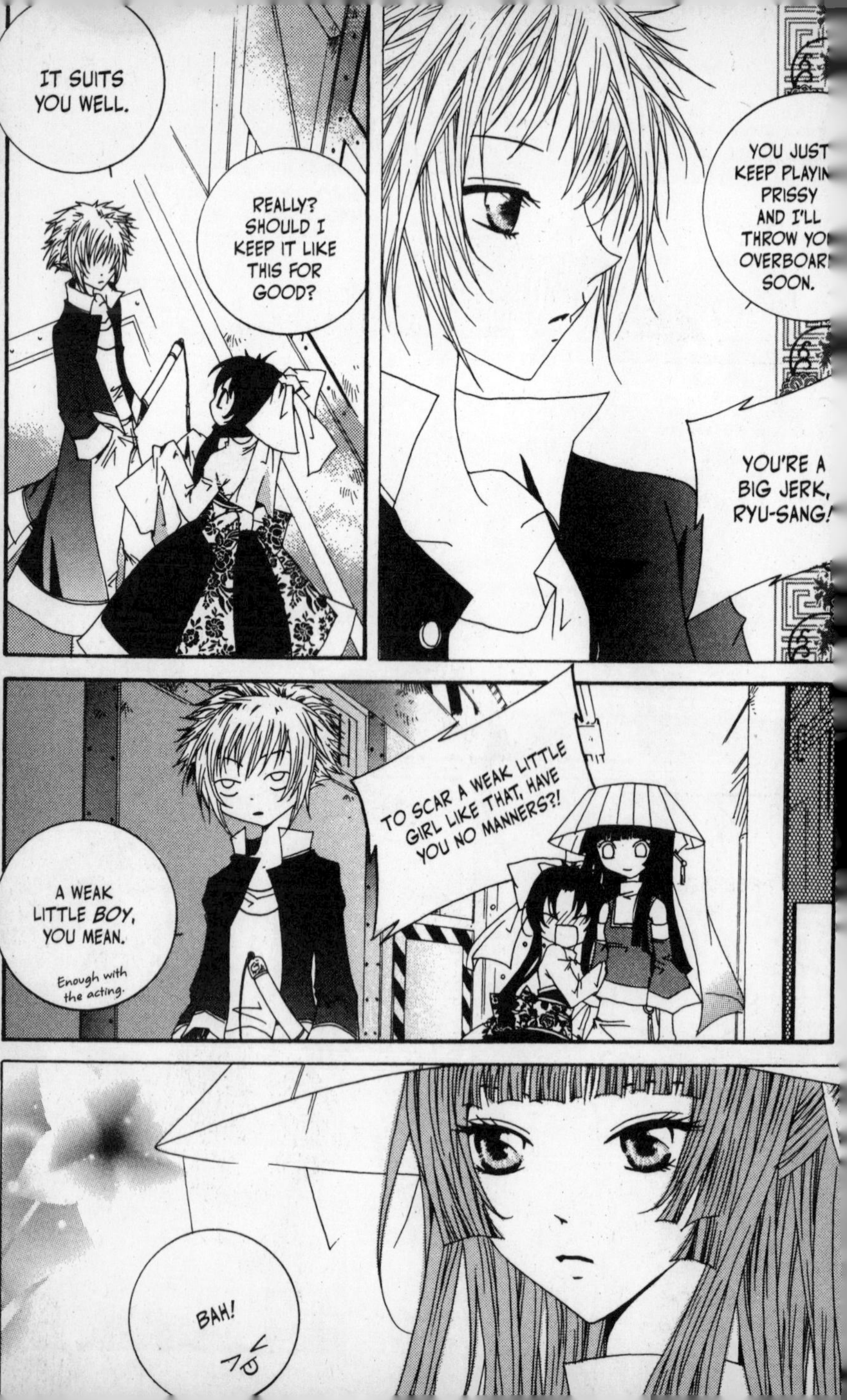
IT SUITS YOU WELL.
REALLY? SHOULD I KEEP IT LIKE THIS FOR GOOD?
YOU JUST KEEP PLAYIN PRISSY AND I'LL THROW YO OVERBOAR SOON.
YOU'RE A BIG JERK, RYU-SANG!
A WEAK LITTLE BOY, YOU MEAN.
Enough with the acting.
TO SCAR A WEAK LITTLE GIRL LIKE THAT, HAVE YOU NO MANNERS?!
BAH!

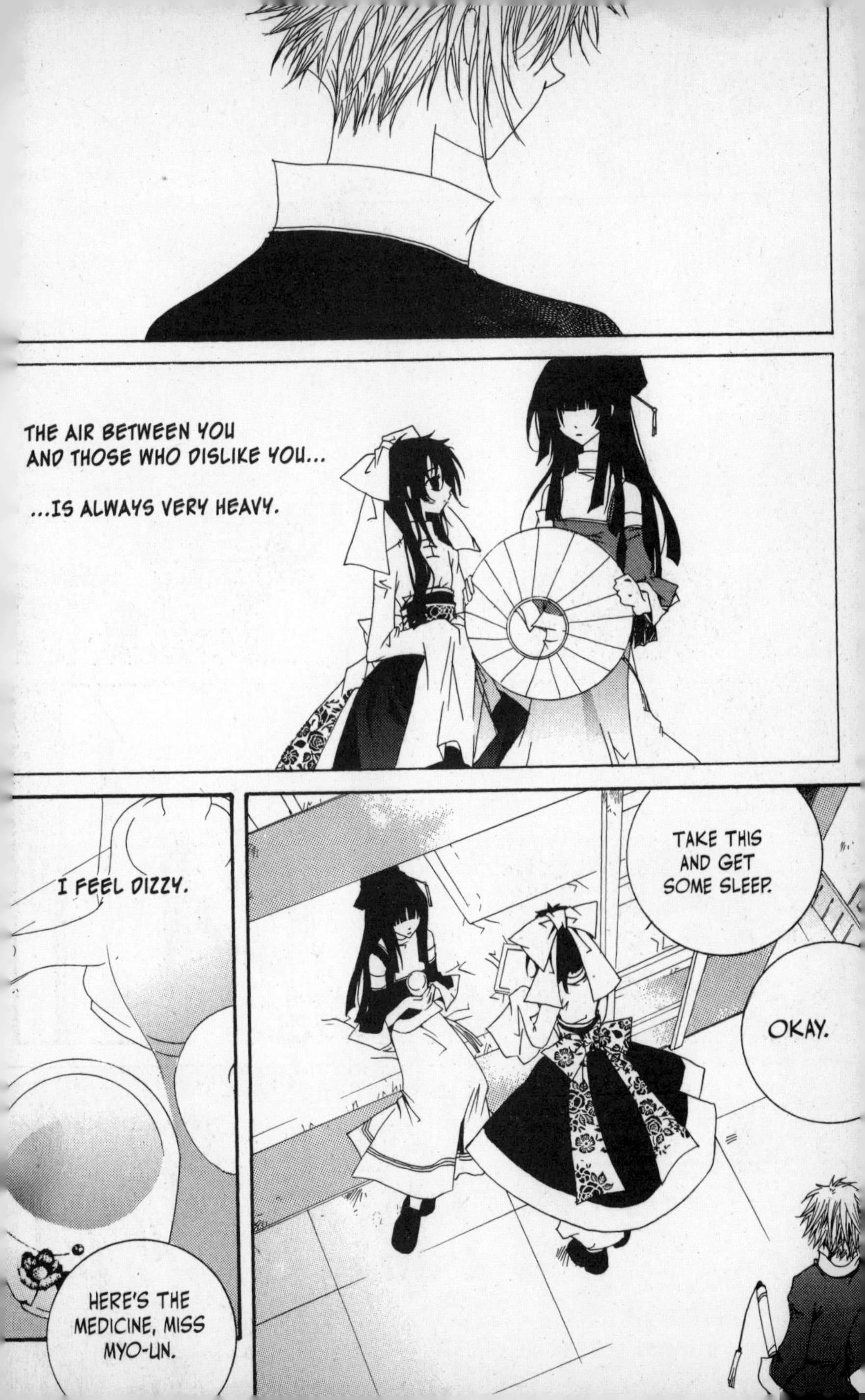
THE AIR BETWEEN YOU AND THOSE WHO DISLIKE YOU...
...IS ALWAYS VERY HEAVY.
I FEEL DIZZY.
HERE'S THE MEDICINE, MISS MYO-UN.
TAKE THIS AND GET SOME SLEEP.
OKAY.

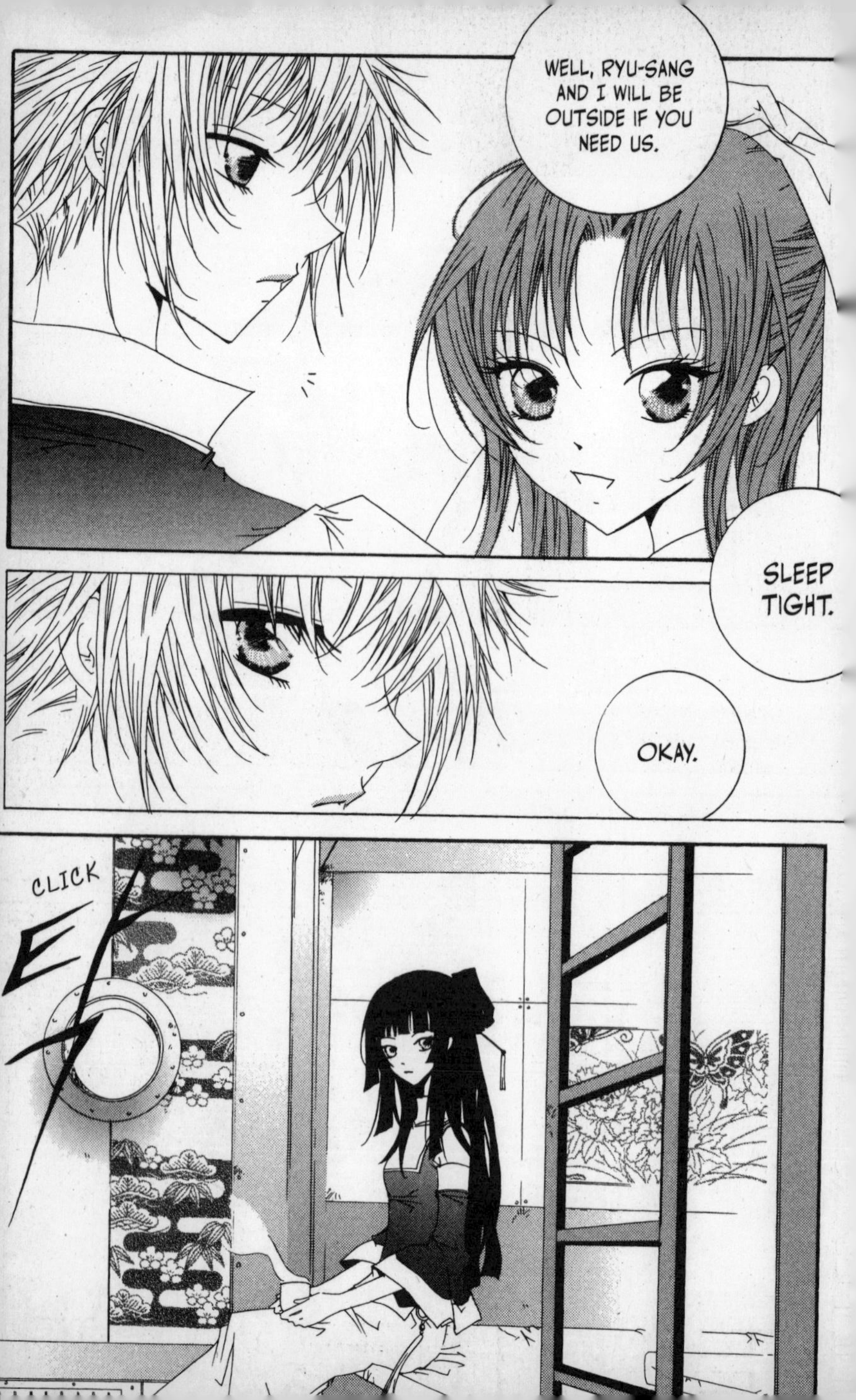
WELL, RYU-SANG AND I WILL BE OUTSIDE IF YOU NEED US.
SLEEP TIGHT.
OKAY.
CLICK

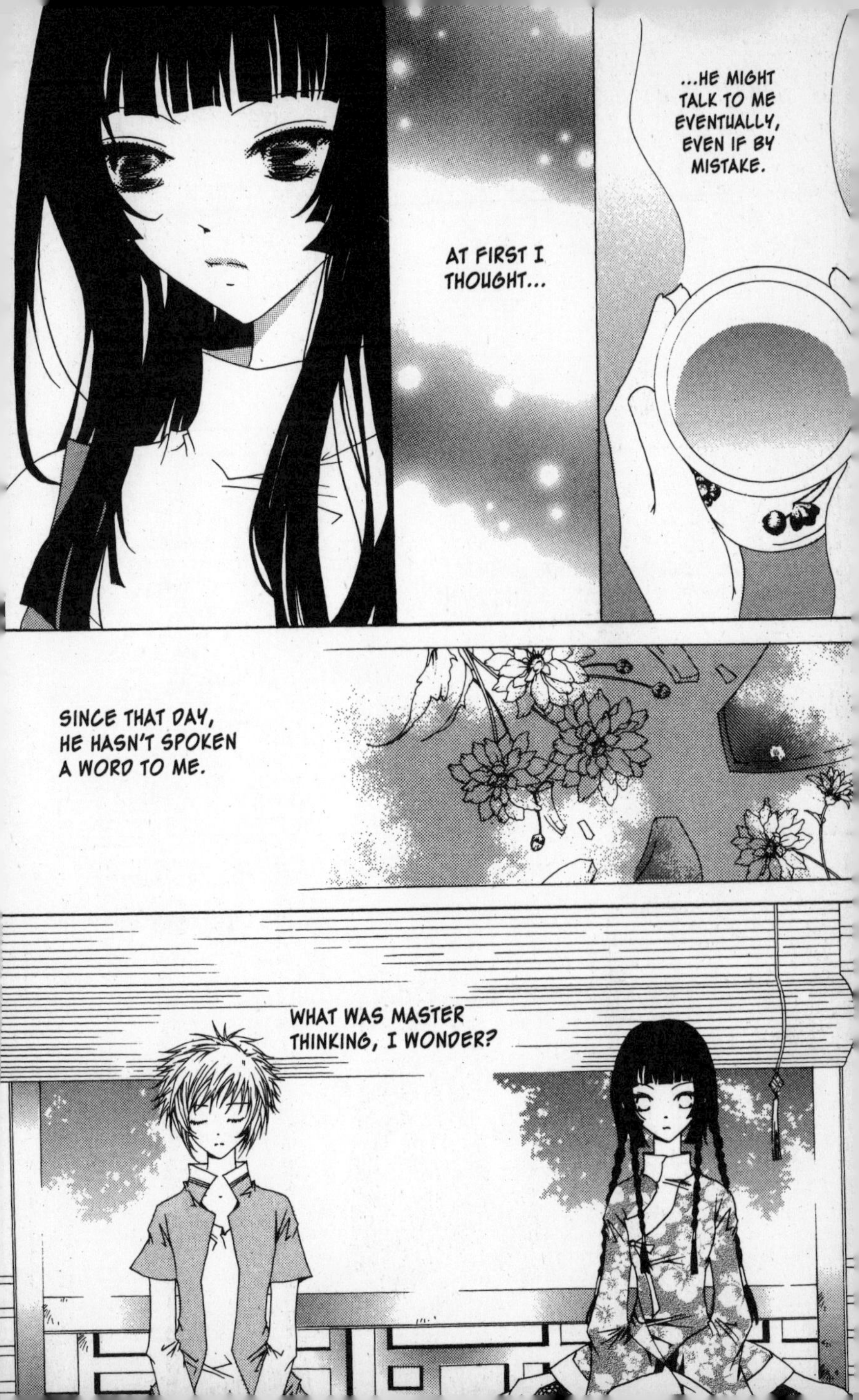
AT FIRST I THOUGHT...
...HE MIGHT TALK TO ME EVENTUALLY, EVEN IF BY MISTAKE.
SINCE THAT DAY, HE HASN'T SPOKEN A WORD TO ME.
WHAT WAS MASTER THINKING, I WONDER?

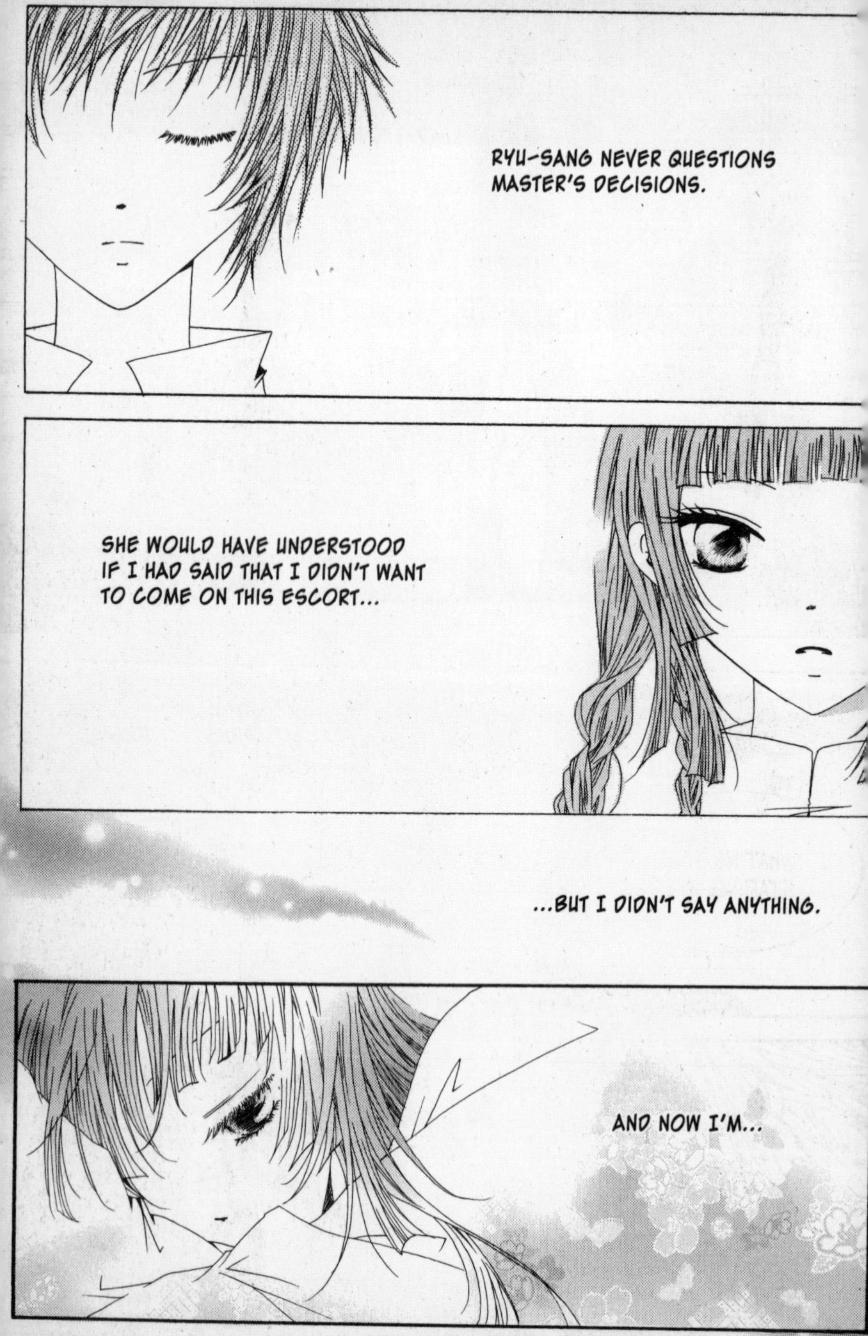
RYU-SANG NEVER QUESTIONS MASTER'S DECISIONS.
SHE WOULD HAVE UNDERSTOOD IF I HAD SAID THAT I DIDN'T WANT TO COME ON THIS ESCORT...
...BUT I DIDN'T SAY ANYTHING.
AND NOW I'M...

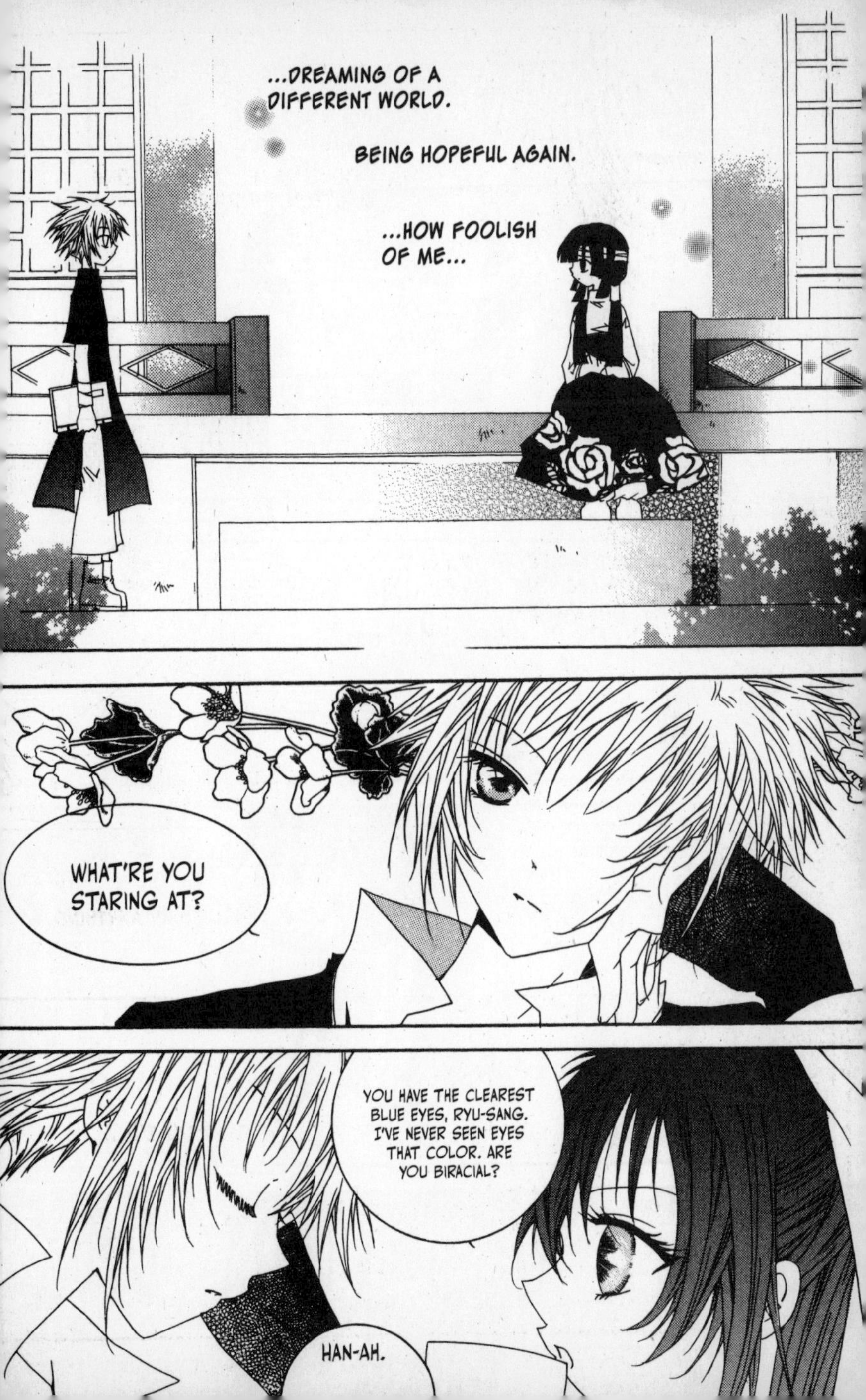
...DREAMING OF A DIFFERENT WORLD.
BEING HOPEFUL AGAIN.
...HOW FOOLISH OF ME...
WHAT'RE YOU STARING AT?
YOU HAVE THE CLEAREST BLUE EYES, RYU-SANG. I'VE NEVER SEEN EYES THAT COLOR. ARE YOU BIRACIAL?
HAN-AH.

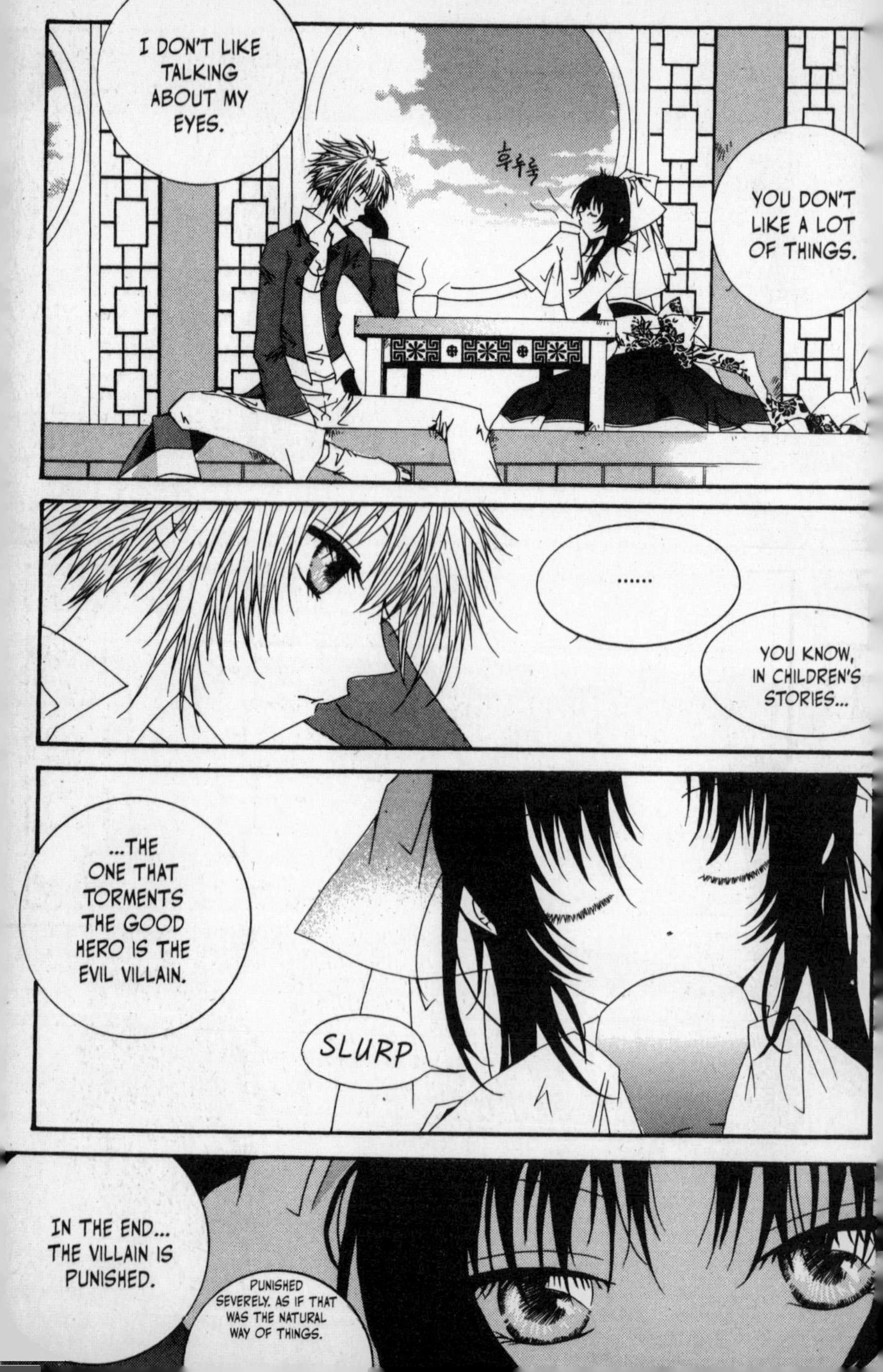
I DON'T LIKE TALKING ABOUT MY EYES.
후루룩
YOU DON'T LIKE A LOT OF THINGS.
......
YOU KNOW, IN CHILDREN'S STORIES...
...THE ONE THAT TORMENTS THE GOOD HERO IS THE EVIL VILLAIN.
SLURP
IN THE END... THE VILLAIN IS PUNISHED.
PUNISHED SEVERELY. AS IF THAT WAS THE NATURAL WAY OF THINGS.

THAT'S WHY I LIKE THE WORLD OF CHILDREN'S STORIES... IT DOESN'T MATTER HOW REALITY WORKS.

AND ONCE THE VILLAIN IS GONE, THE HERO LIVES HAPPILY EVER AFTER.

후루룩~

WHAT DO YOU THINK, RYU-SANG?

후루룩

DON'T SLURP YOUR TEA.

UM... RYU-SANG...

I, UH ...

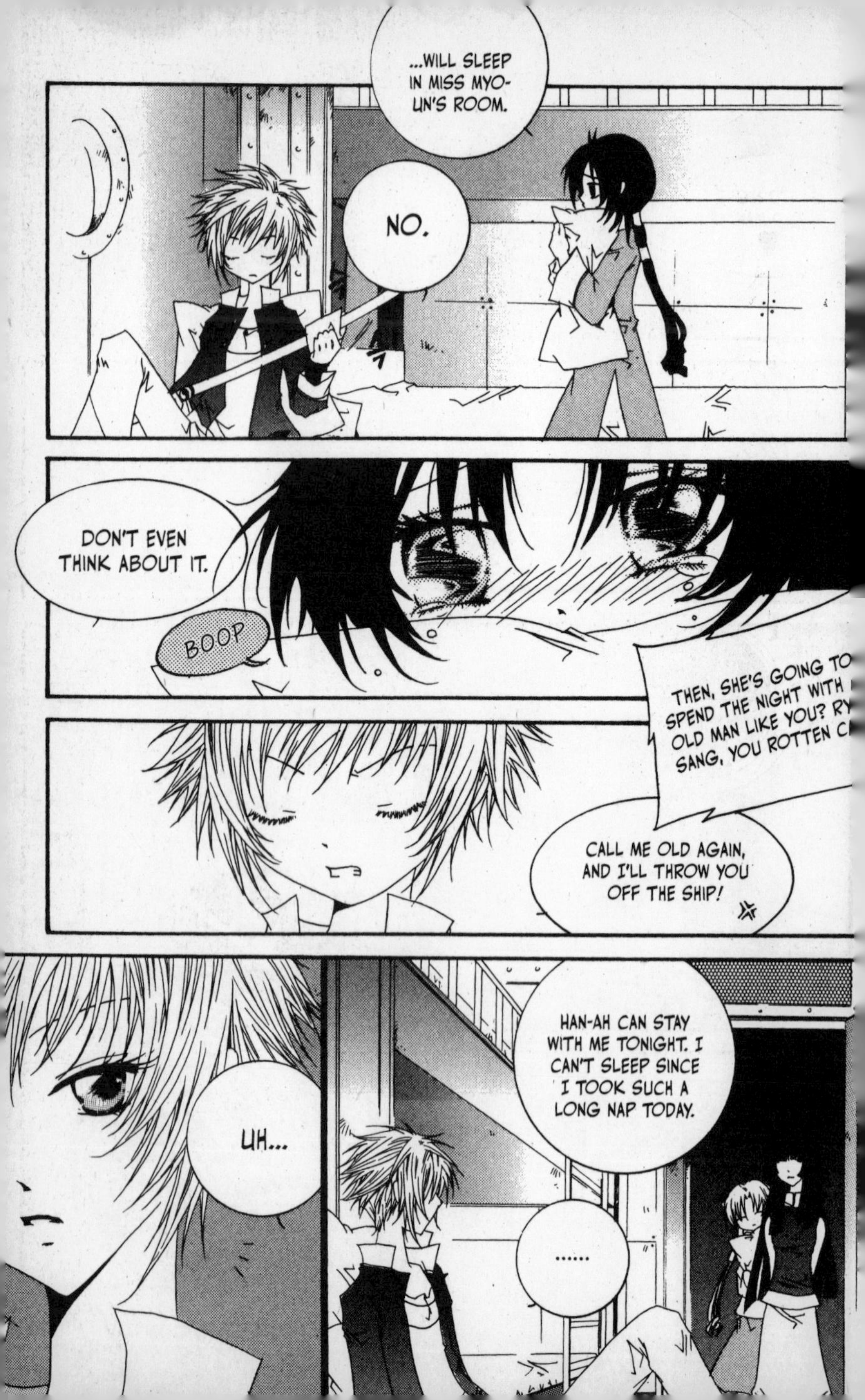
...WILL SLEEP IN MISS MYO-UN'S ROOM.
NO.
DON'T EVEN THINK ABOUT IT.
BOOP
THEN, SHE'S GOING TO SPEND THE NIGHT WITH OLD MAN LIKE YOU? RY SANG, YOU ROTTEN C
CALL ME OLD AGAIN, AND I'LL THROW YOU OFF THE SHIP!
UH...
HAN-AH CAN STAY WITH ME TONIGHT. I CAN'T SLEEP SINCE I TOOK SUCH A LONG NAP TODAY.
......

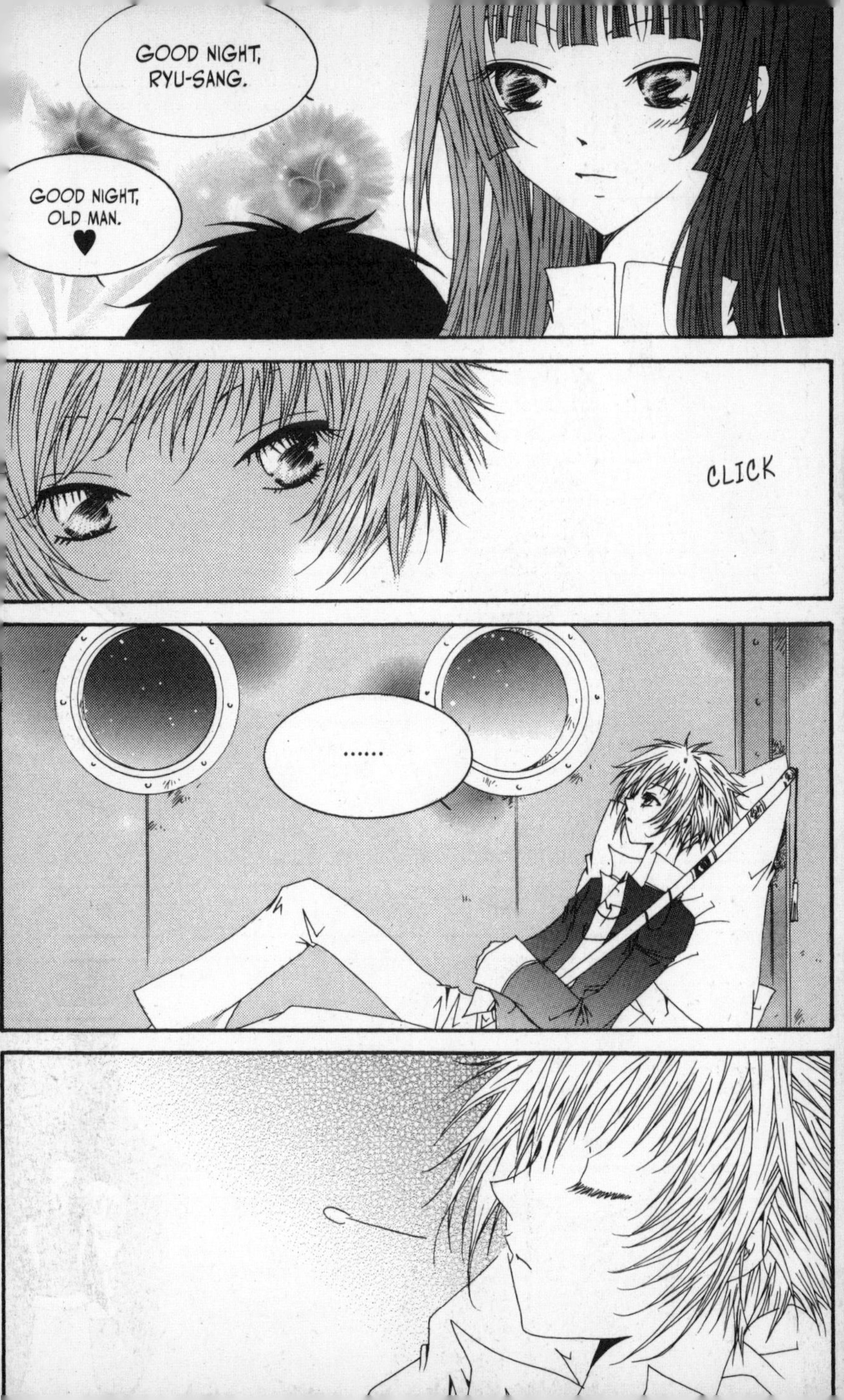
GOOD NIGHT, RYU-SANG.
GOOD NIGHT, OLD MAN. ♥
CLICK
......

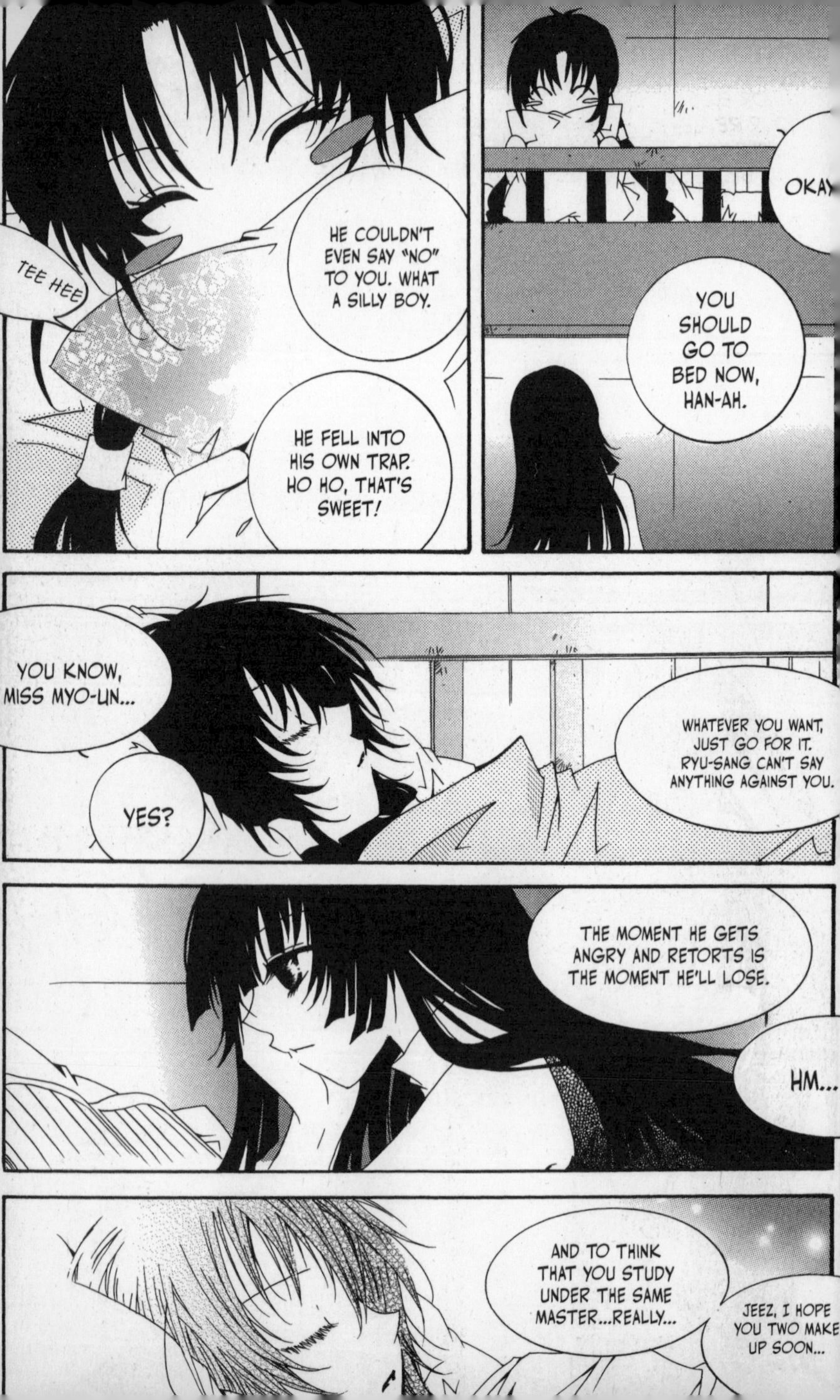
TEE HEE
HE COULDN'T EVEN SAY "NO" TO YOU. WHAT A SILLY BOY.
HE FELL INTO HIS OWN TRAP. HO HO, THAT'S SWEET!
OKAY
YOU SHOULD GO TO BED NOW, HAN-AH.
YOU KNOW, MISS MYO-UN...
YES?
WHATEVER YOU WANT, JUST GO FOR IT. RYU-SANG CAN'T SAY ANYTHING AGAINST YOU.
THE MOMENT HE GETS ANGRY AND RETORTS IS THE MOMENT HE'LL LOSE.
HM...
AND TO THINK THAT YOU STUDY UNDER THE SAME MASTER...REALLY...
JEEZ, I HOPE YOU TWO MAKE UP SOON...

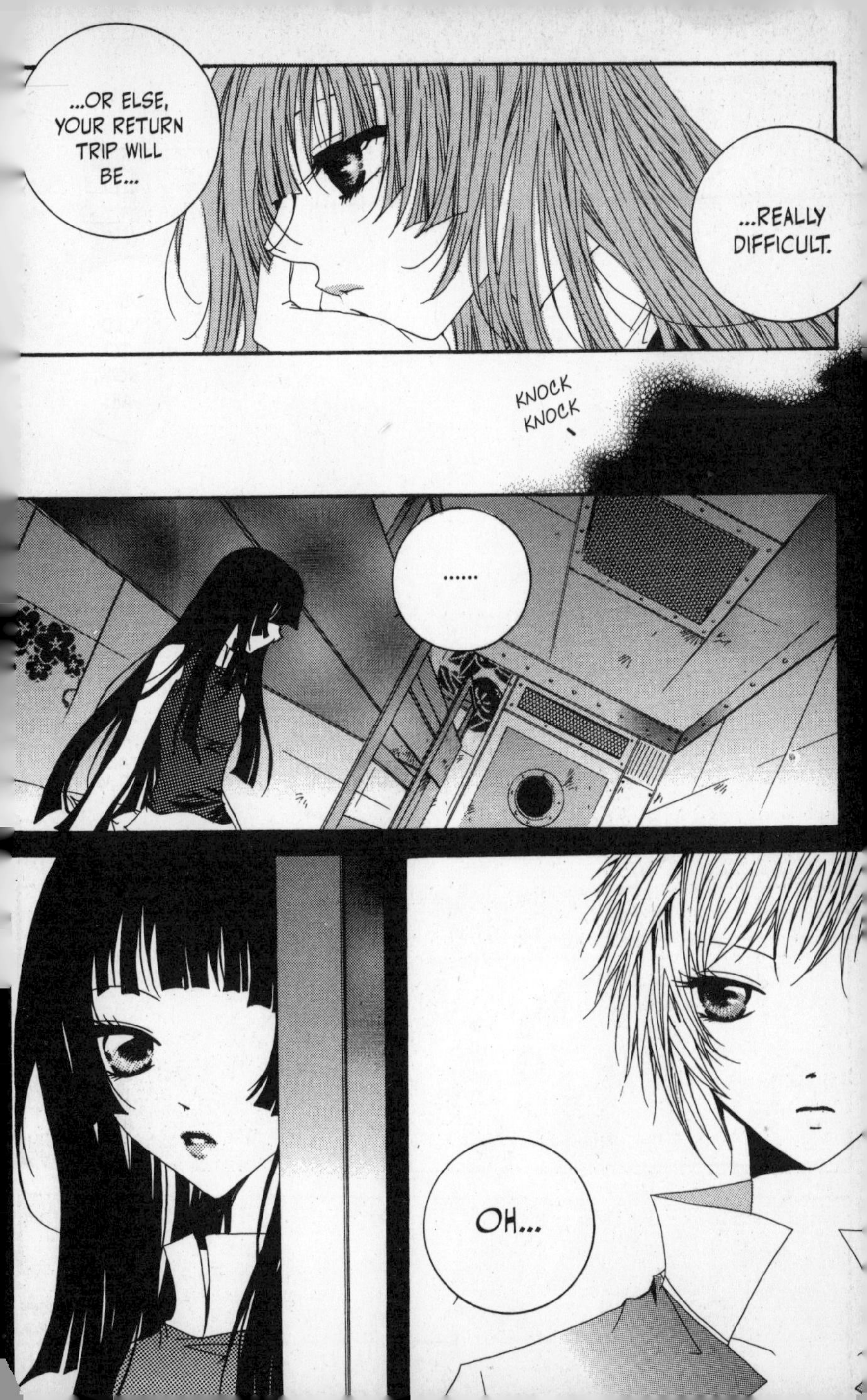

...OR ELSE, YOUR RETURN TRIP WILL BE...
...REALLY DIFFICULT.
KNOCK KNOCK
......
OH...

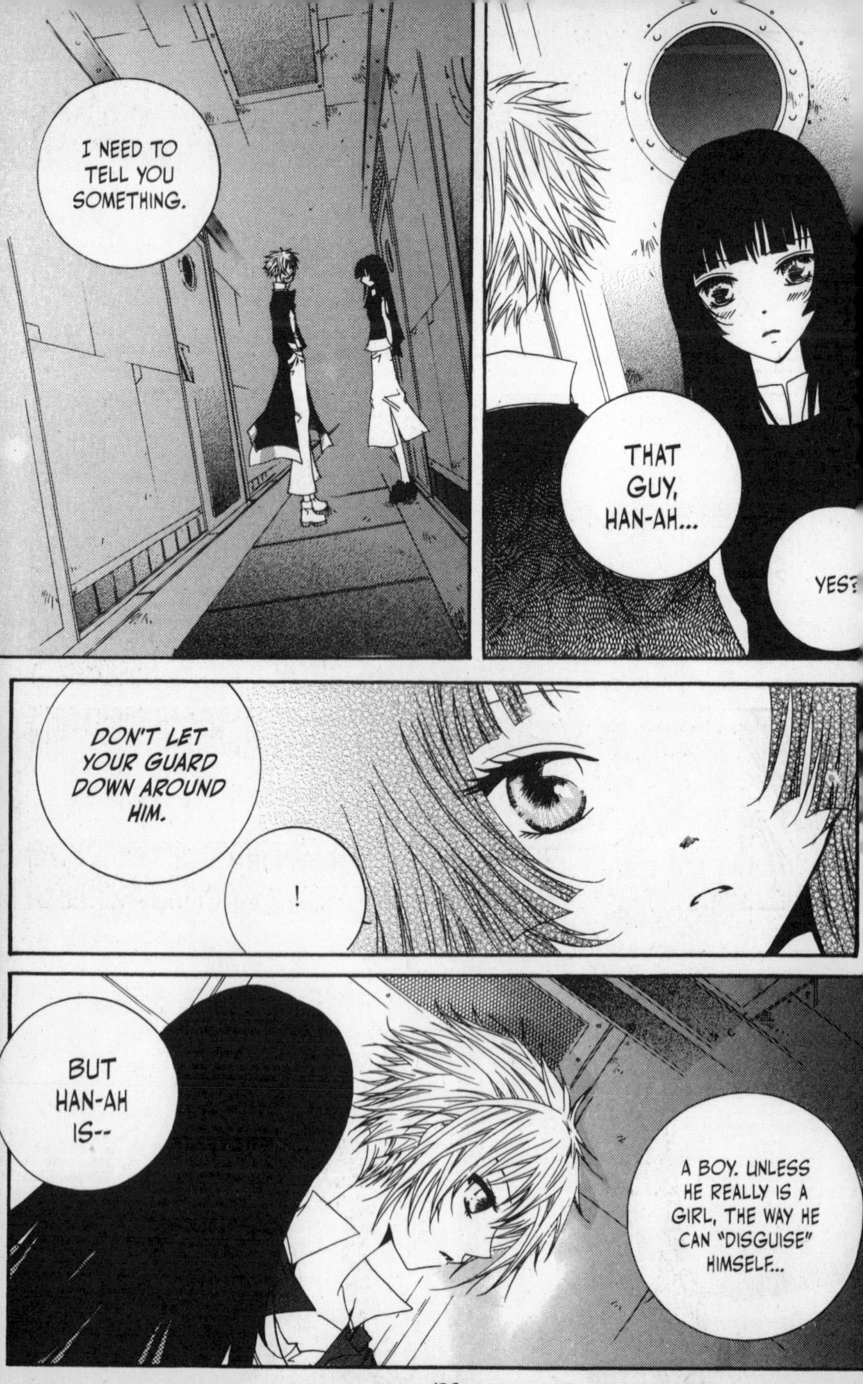
I NEED TO TELL YOU SOMETHING.
THAT GUY, HAN-AH...
YES?
DON'T LET YOUR GUARD DOWN AROUND HIM.
!
BUT HAN-AH IS--
A BOY. UNLESS HE REALLY IS A GIRL, THE WAY HE CAN "DISGUISE" HIMSELF...

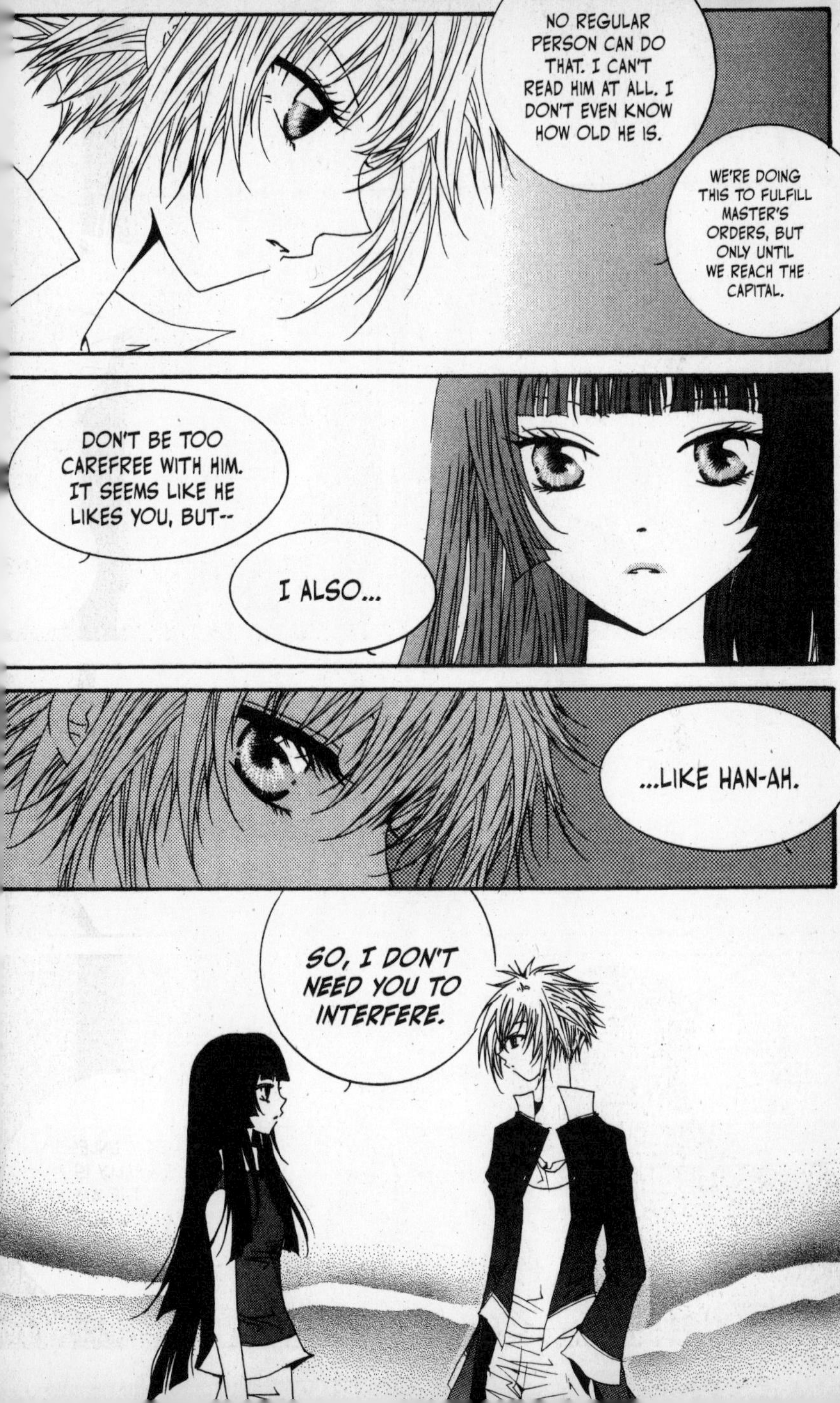
NO REGULAR PERSON CAN DO THAT. I CAN'T READ HIM AT ALL. I DON'T EVEN KNOW HOW OLD HE IS.
WE'RE DOING THIS TO FULFILL MASTER'S ORDERS, BUT ONLY UNTIL WE REACH THE CAPITAL.
DON'T BE TOO CAREFREE WITH HIM. IT SEEMS LIKE HE LIKES YOU, BUT--
I ALSO...
...LIKE HAN-AH.
SO, I DON'T NEED YOU TO INTERFERE.

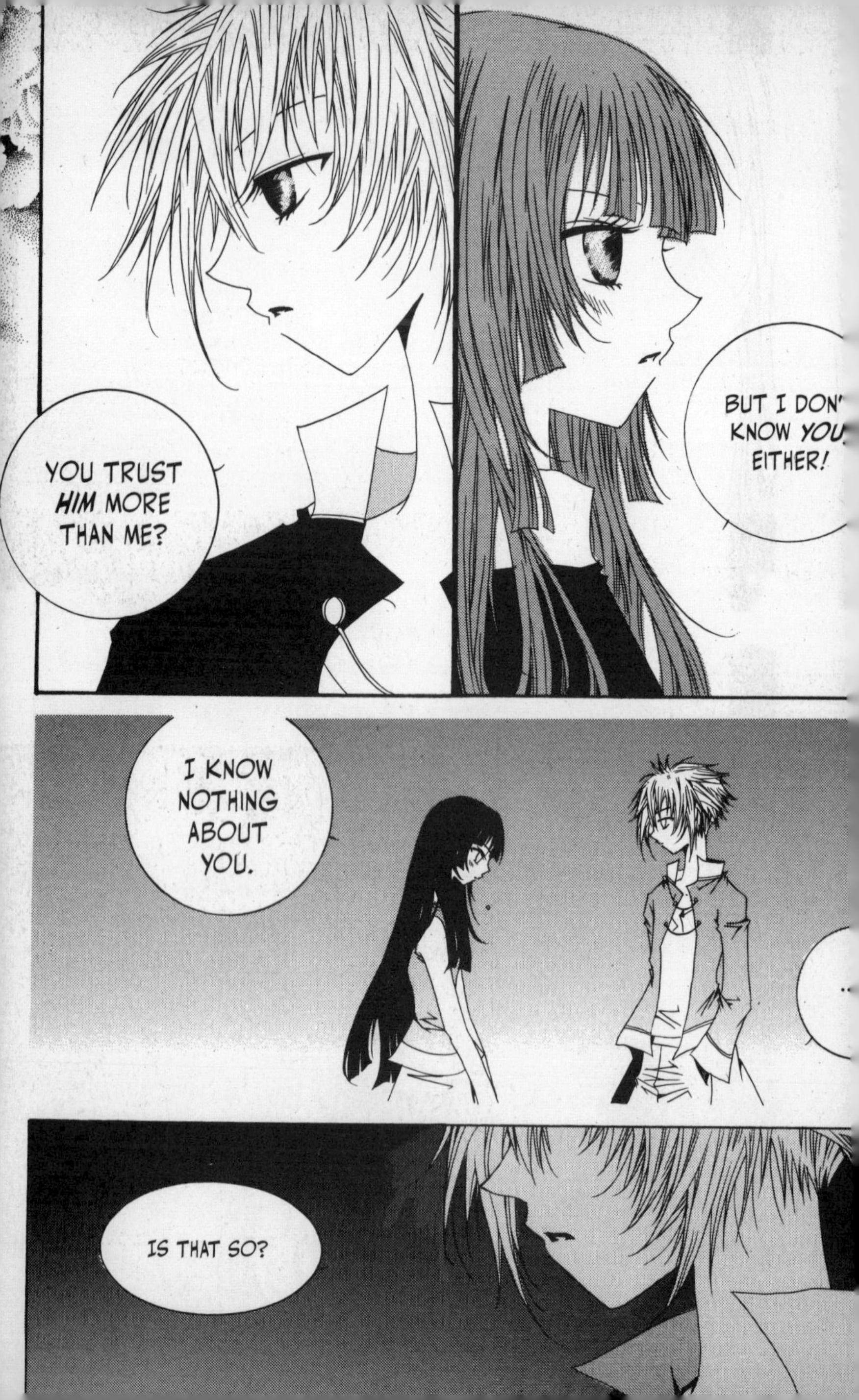
YOU TRUST *HIM* MORE THAN ME?
BUT I DON' KNOW *YOU* EITHER!
I KNOW NOTHING ABOUT YOU.
IS THAT SO?

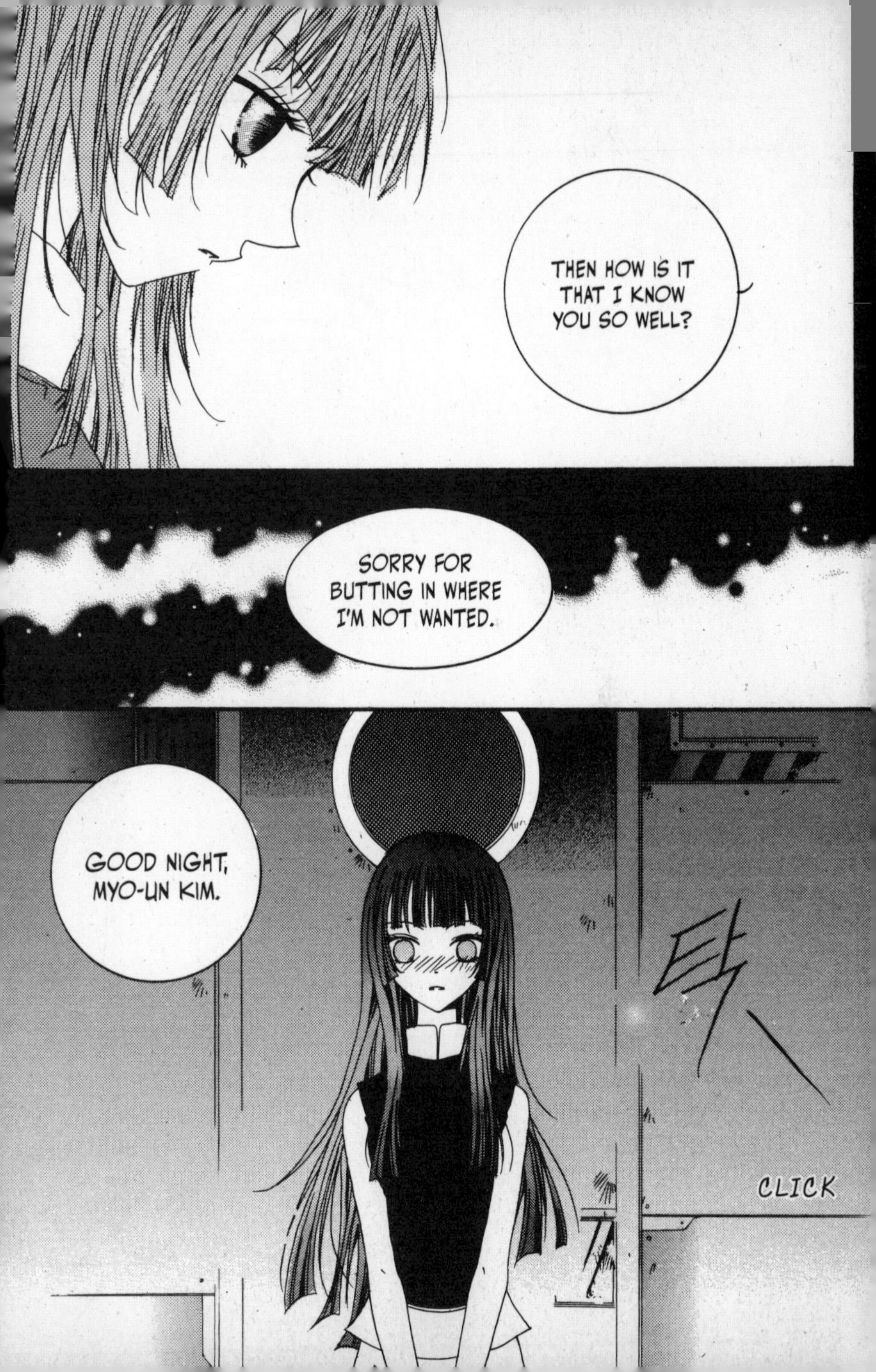

THEN HOW IS IT THAT I KNOW YOU SO WELL?
SORRY FOR BUTTING IN WHERE I'M NOT WANTED.
GOOD NIGHT, MYO-UN KIM.
CLICK

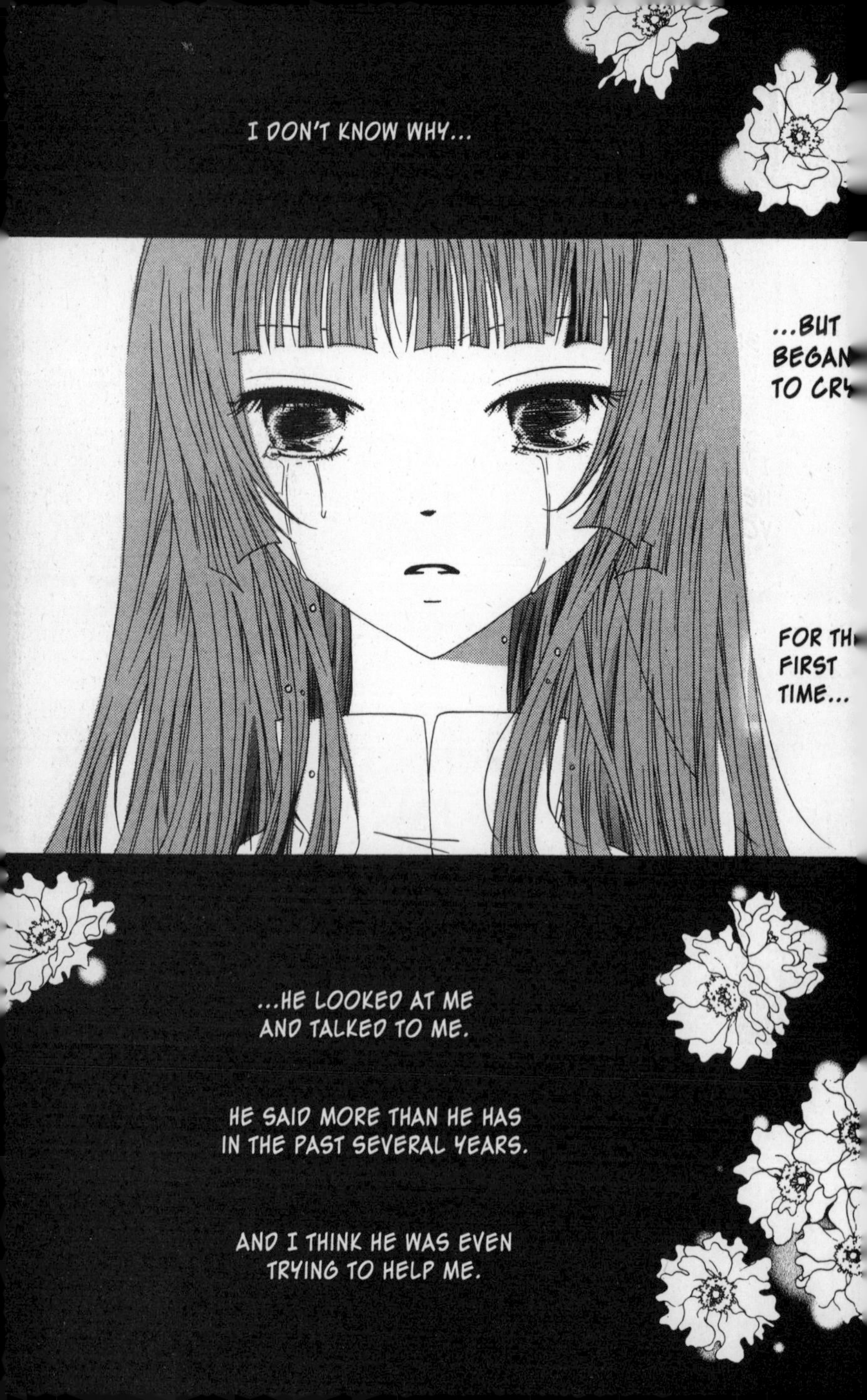
I DON'T KNOW WHY...
...BUT BEGAN TO CRY
FOR THE FIRST TIME...
...HE LOOKED AT ME AND TALKED TO ME.
HE SAID MORE THAN HE HAS IN THE PAST SEVERAL YEARS.
AND I THINK HE WAS EVEN TRYING TO HELP ME.

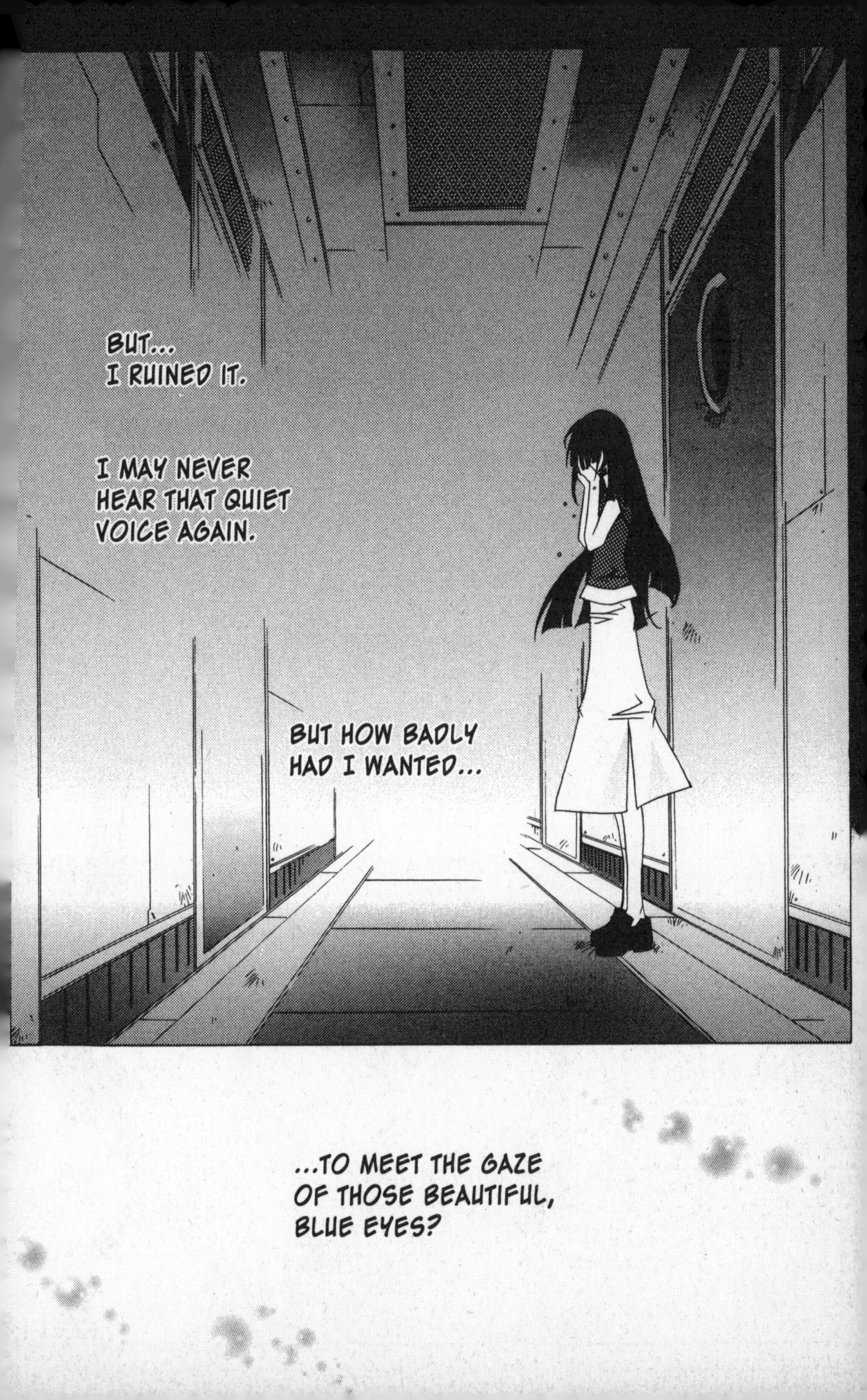
BUT... I RUINED IT.
I MAY NEVER HEAR THAT QUIET VOICE AGAIN.
BUT HOW BADLY HAD I WANTED...
...TO MEET THE GAZE OF THOSE BEAUTIFUL, BLUE EYES?

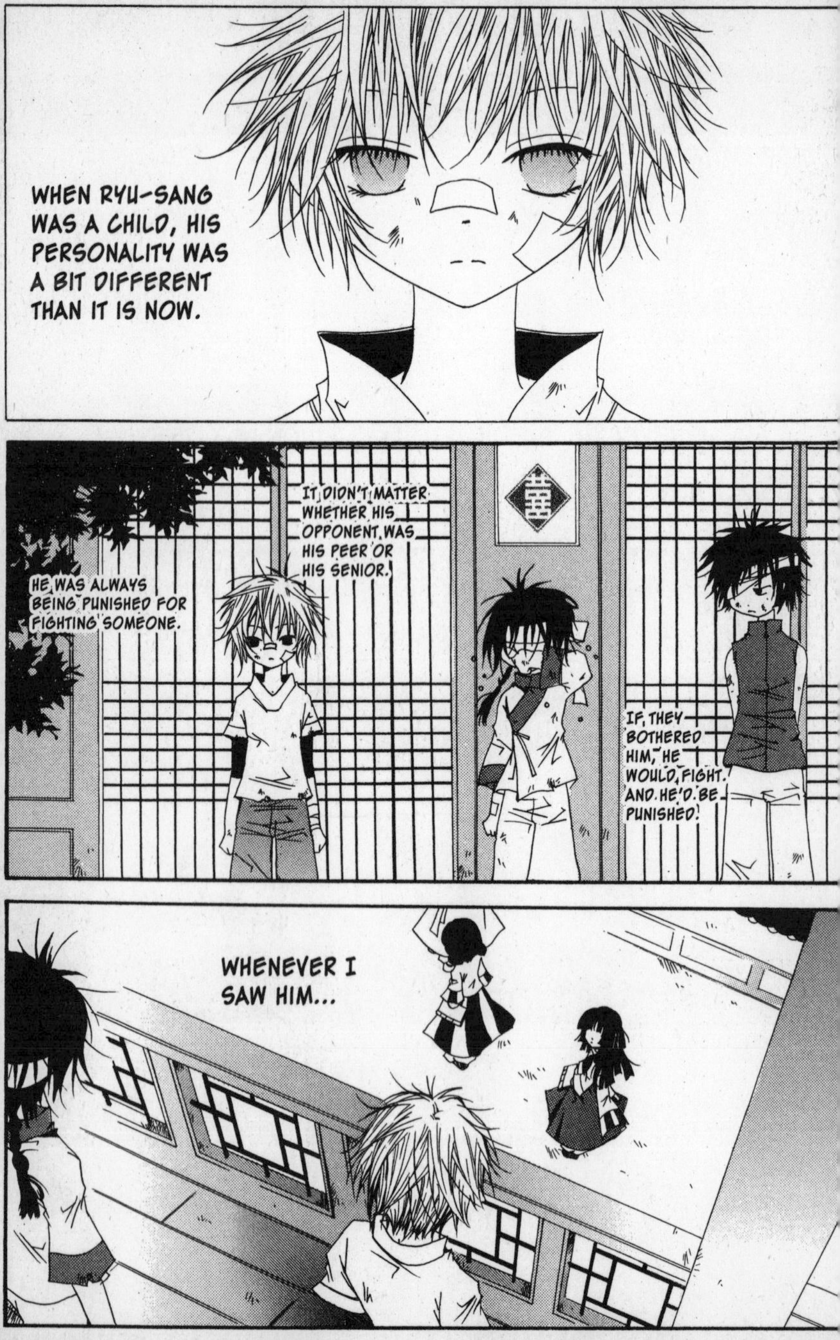
WHEN RYU-SANG WAS A CHILD, HIS PERSONALITY WAS A BIT DIFFERENT THAN IT IS NOW.
HE WAS ALWAYS BEING PUNISHED FOR FIGHTING SOMEONE.
IT DIDN'T MATTER WHETHER HIS OPPONENT WAS HIS PEER OR HIS SENIOR.
IF THEY BOTHERED HIM, HE WOULD FIGHT. AND HE'D BE PUNISHED.
WHENEVER I SAW HIM...

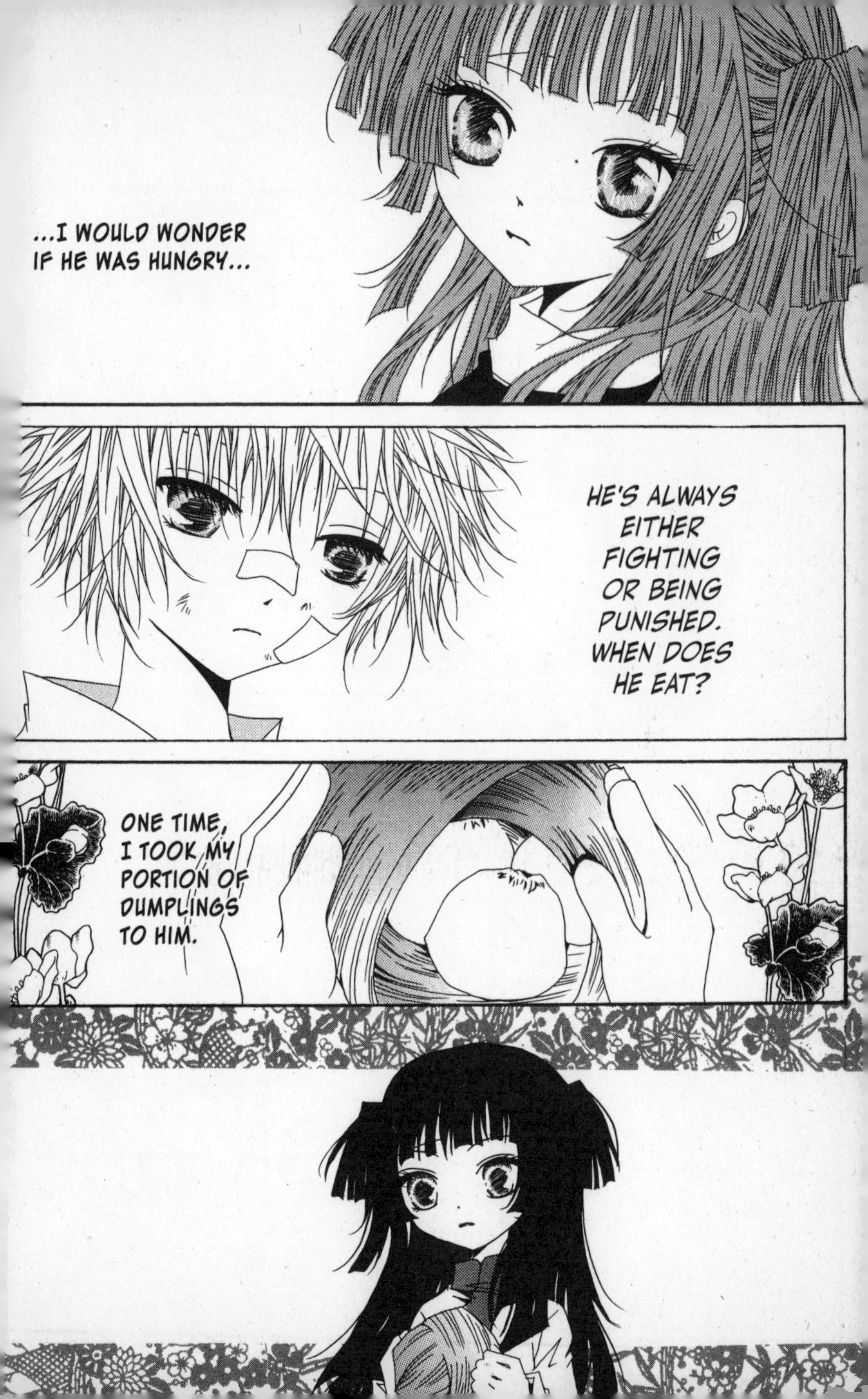
...I WOULD WONDER IF HE WAS HUNGRY...
HE'S ALWAYS EITHER FIGHTING OR BEING PUNISHED. WHEN DOES HE EAT?
ONE TIME, I TOOK MY PORTION OF DUMPLINGS TO HIM.

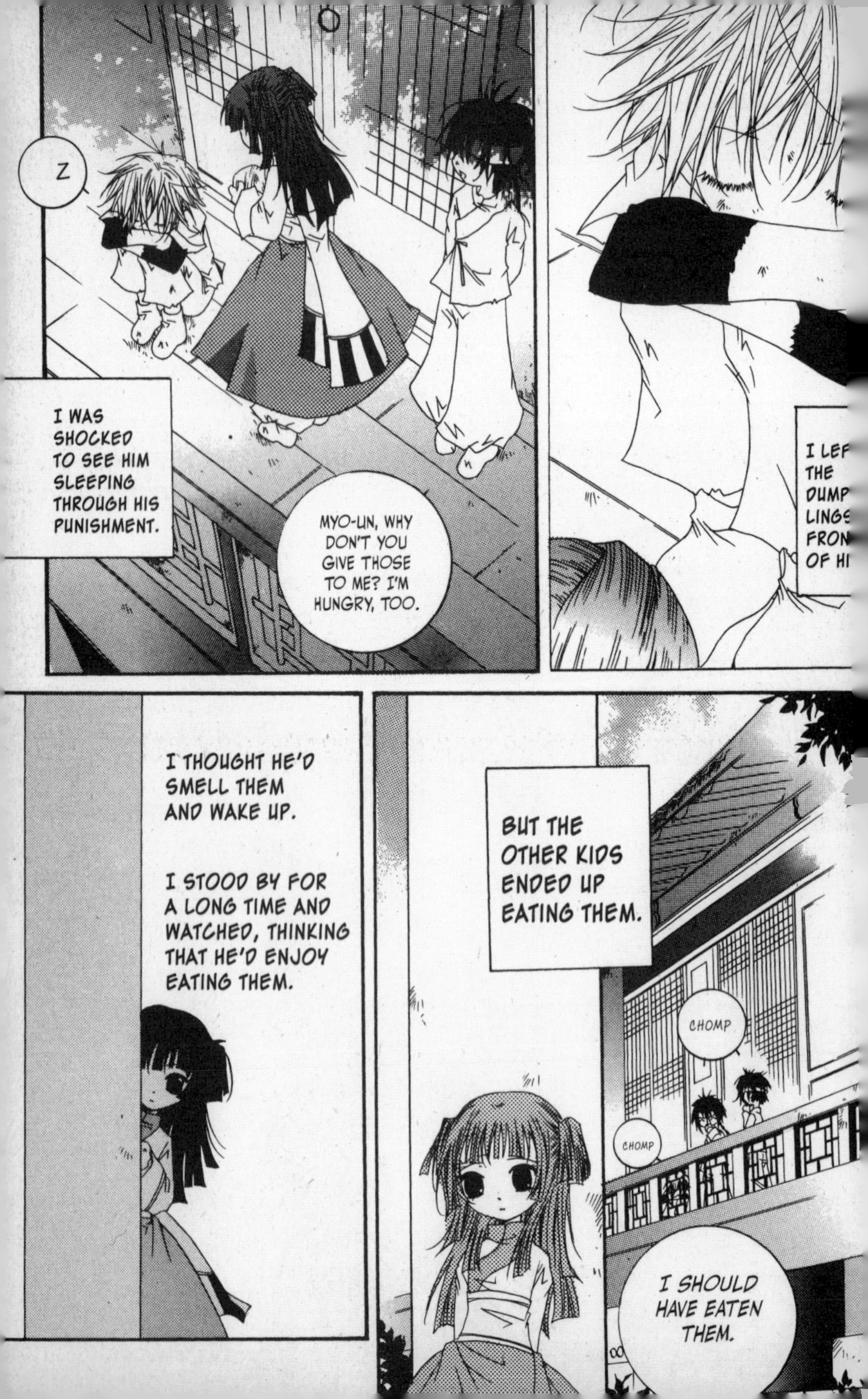
Z
I WAS SHOCKED TO SEE HIM SLEEPING THROUGH HIS PUNISHMENT.
MYO-UN, WHY DON'T YOU GIVE THOSE TO ME? I'M HUNGRY, TOO.
I LEF THE DUMP LINGS FRON OF HI
I THOUGHT HE'D SMELL THEM AND WAKE UP.
I STOOD BY FOR A LONG TIME AND WATCHED, THINKING THAT HE'D ENJOY EATING THEM.
BUT THE OTHER KIDS ENDED UP EATING THEM.
CHOMP
CHOMP
I SHOULD HAVE EATEN THEM.

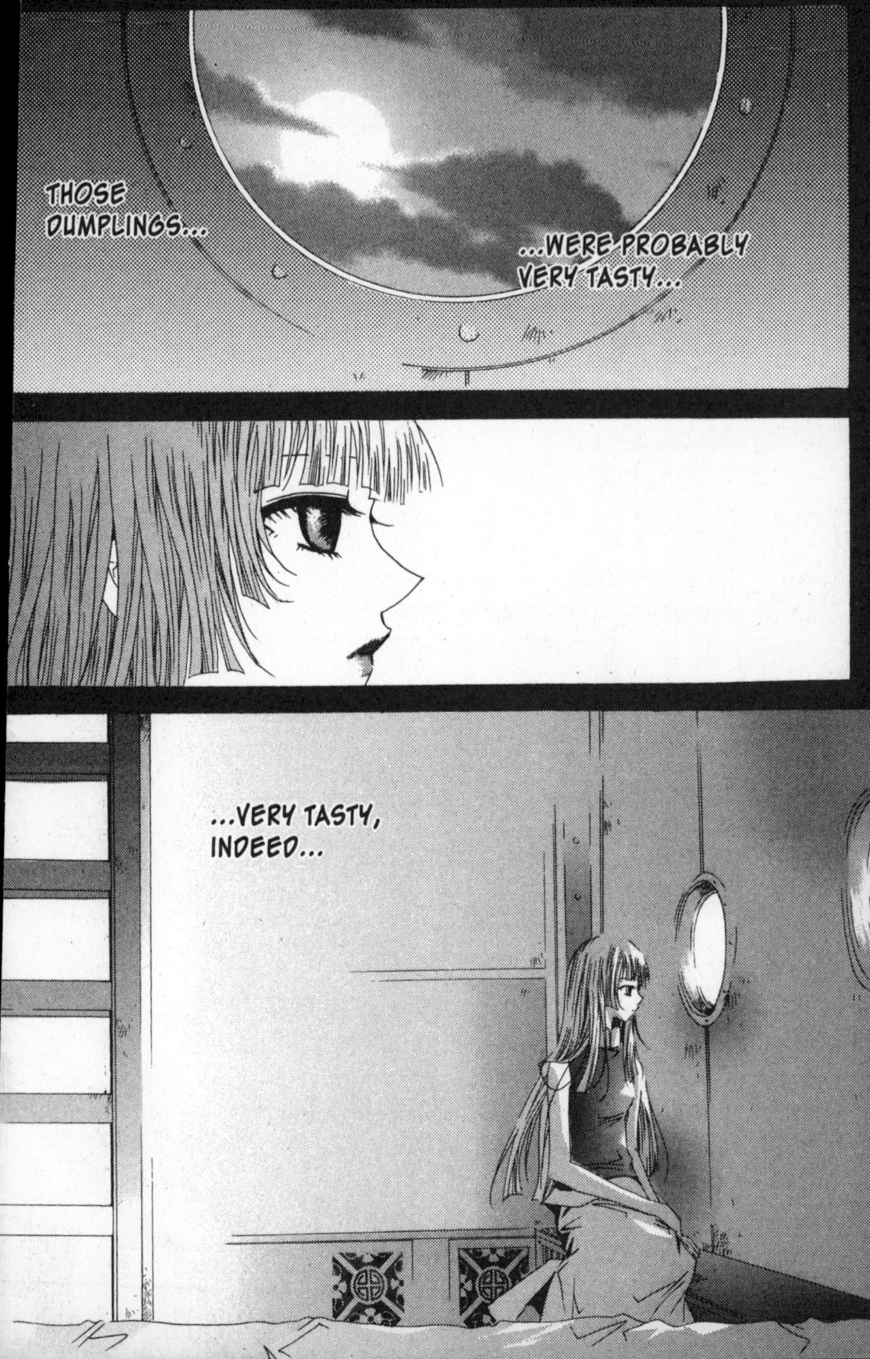
THOSE DUMPLINGS...
...WERE PROBABLY VERY TASTY...
...VERY TASTY, INDEED...

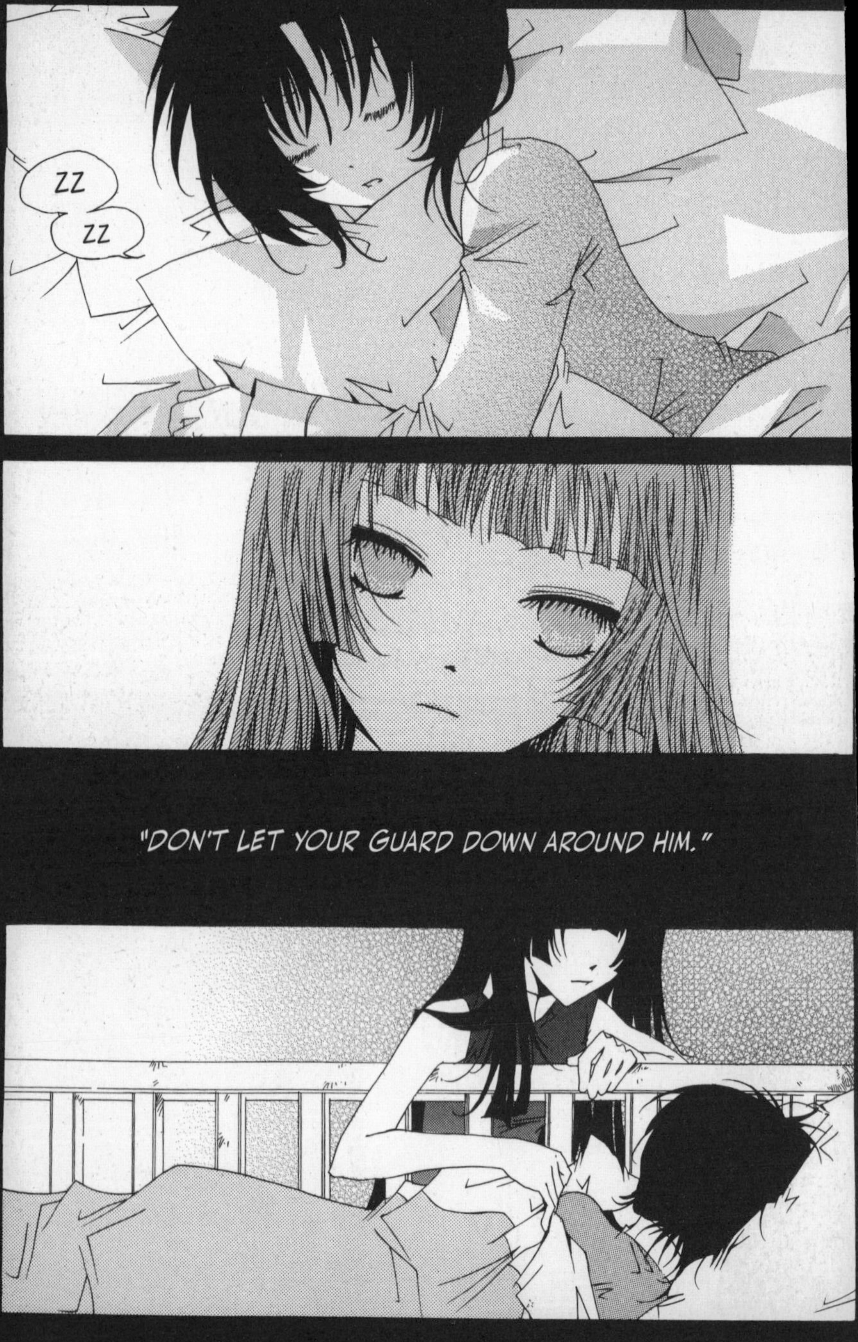
ZZ
ZZ
"DON'T LET YOUR GUARD DOWN AROUND HIM."

I WONDER WHY RYU-SANG WOULD SAY THAT...

TO BE HONEST, IT IS EASY TO FORGET THAT HAN-AH IS ACTUALLY A BOY... EVEN HIS SLEEPING FACE IS FEMININE...

NEVERTHELESS, PROTECTING HAN-AH IS OUR JOB.

BUT...KEEP MY GUARD UP AROUND HIM?

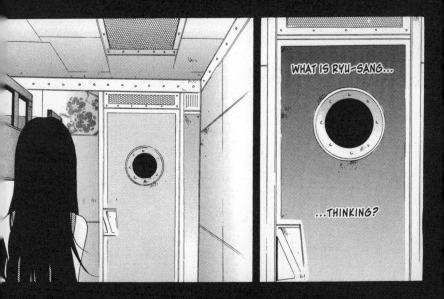

WHAT IS RYU-SANG...

...THINKING?

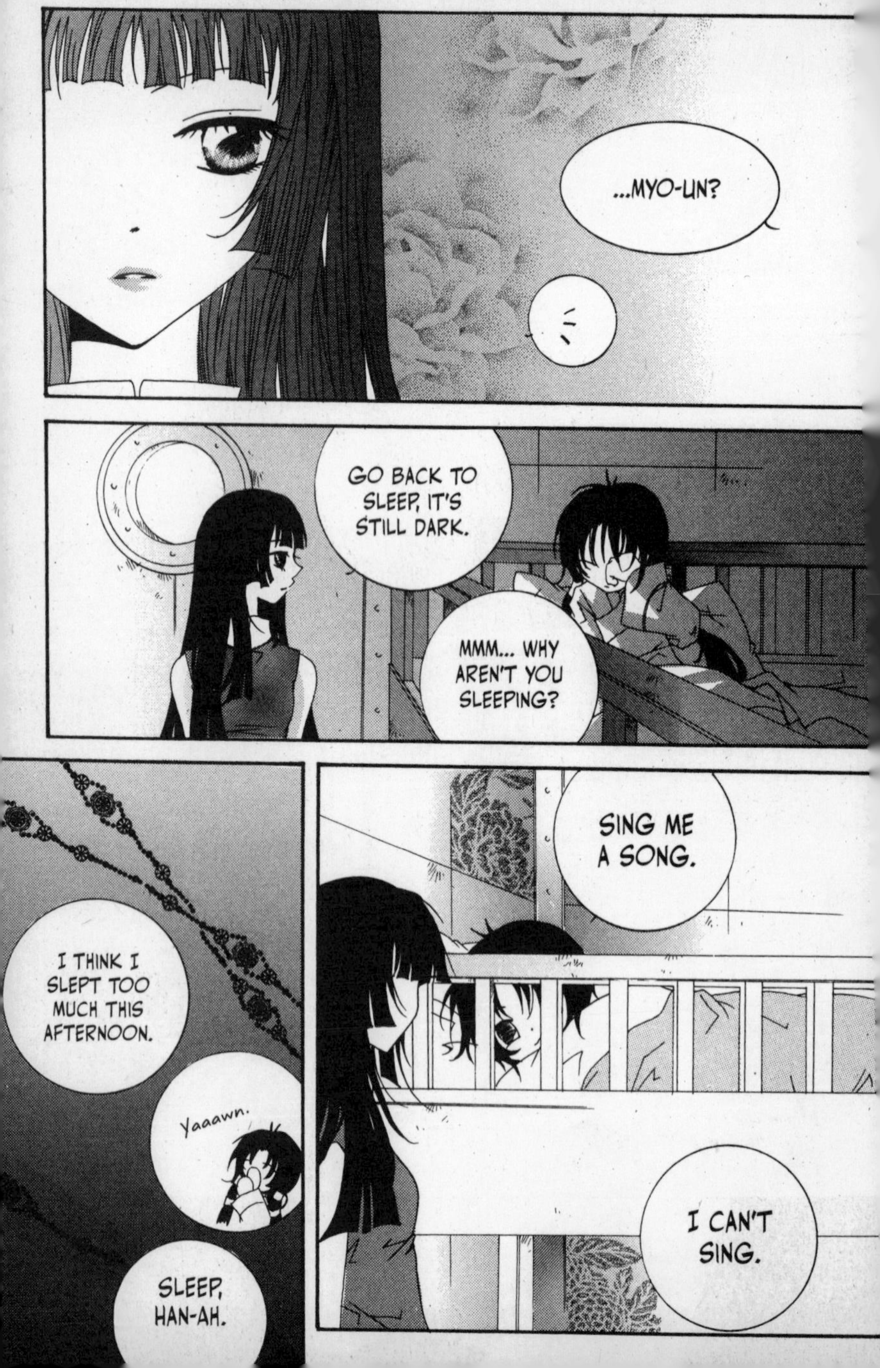
...MYO-UN?
GO BACK TO SLEEP, IT'S STILL DARK.
MMM... WHY AREN'T YOU SLEEPING?
I THINK I SLEPT TOO MUCH THIS AFTERNOON.
Yaaawn.
SLEEP, HAN-AH.
SING ME A SONG.
I CAN'T SING.

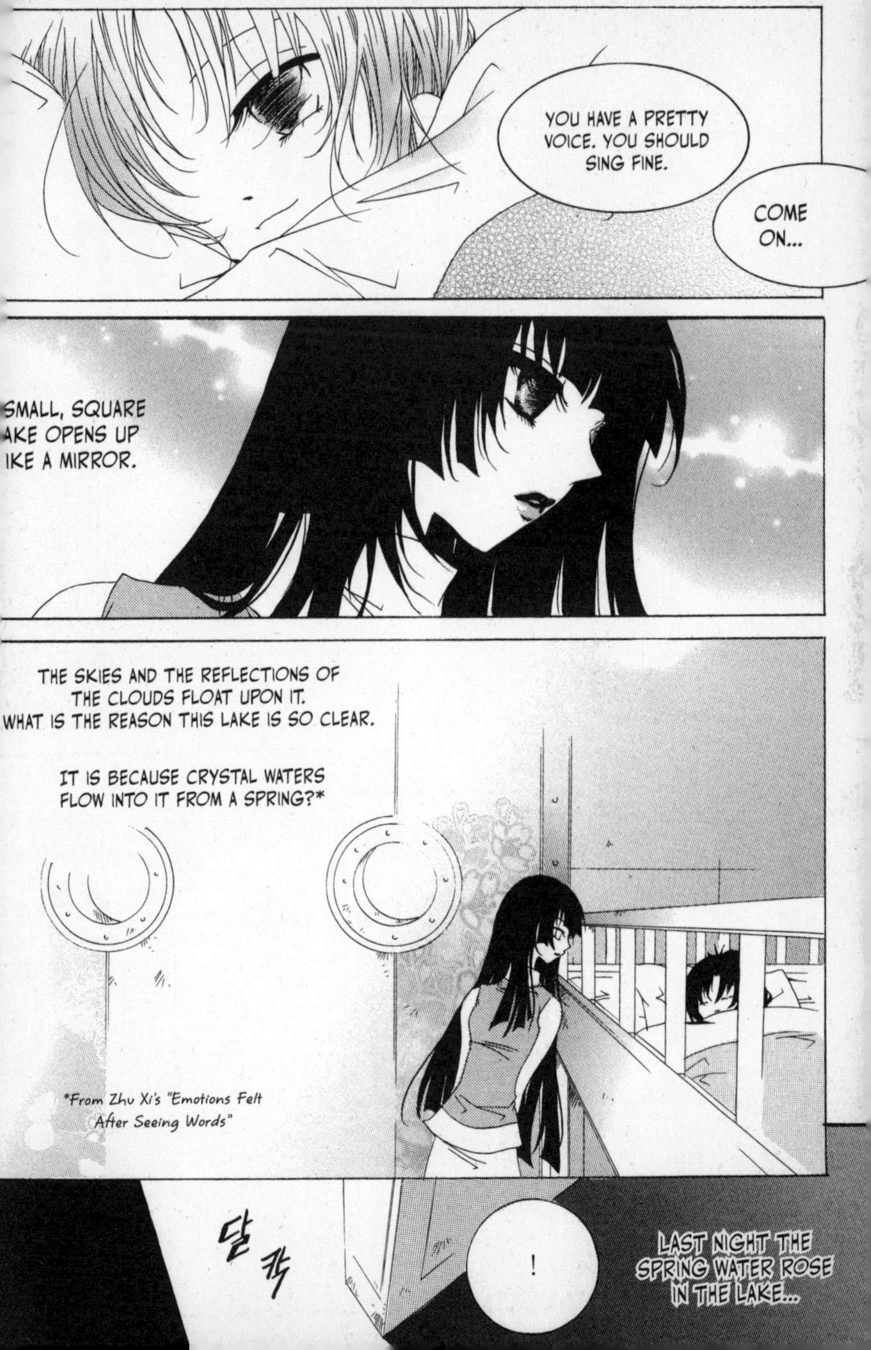
YOU HAVE A PRETTY VOICE. YOU SHOULD SING FINE.
COME ON...
SMALL, SQUARE
AKE OPENS UP
IKE A MIRROR.
THE SKIES AND THE REFLECTIONS OF THE CLOUDS FLOAT UPON IT.
WHAT IS THE REASON THIS LAKE IS SO CLEAR.
IT IS BECAUSE CRYSTAL WATERS FLOW INTO IT FROM A SPRING?*
달칵
!
LAST NIGHT THE SPRING WATER ROSE IN THE LAKE...

*From Zhu Xi's "Emotions Felt After Seeing Words"

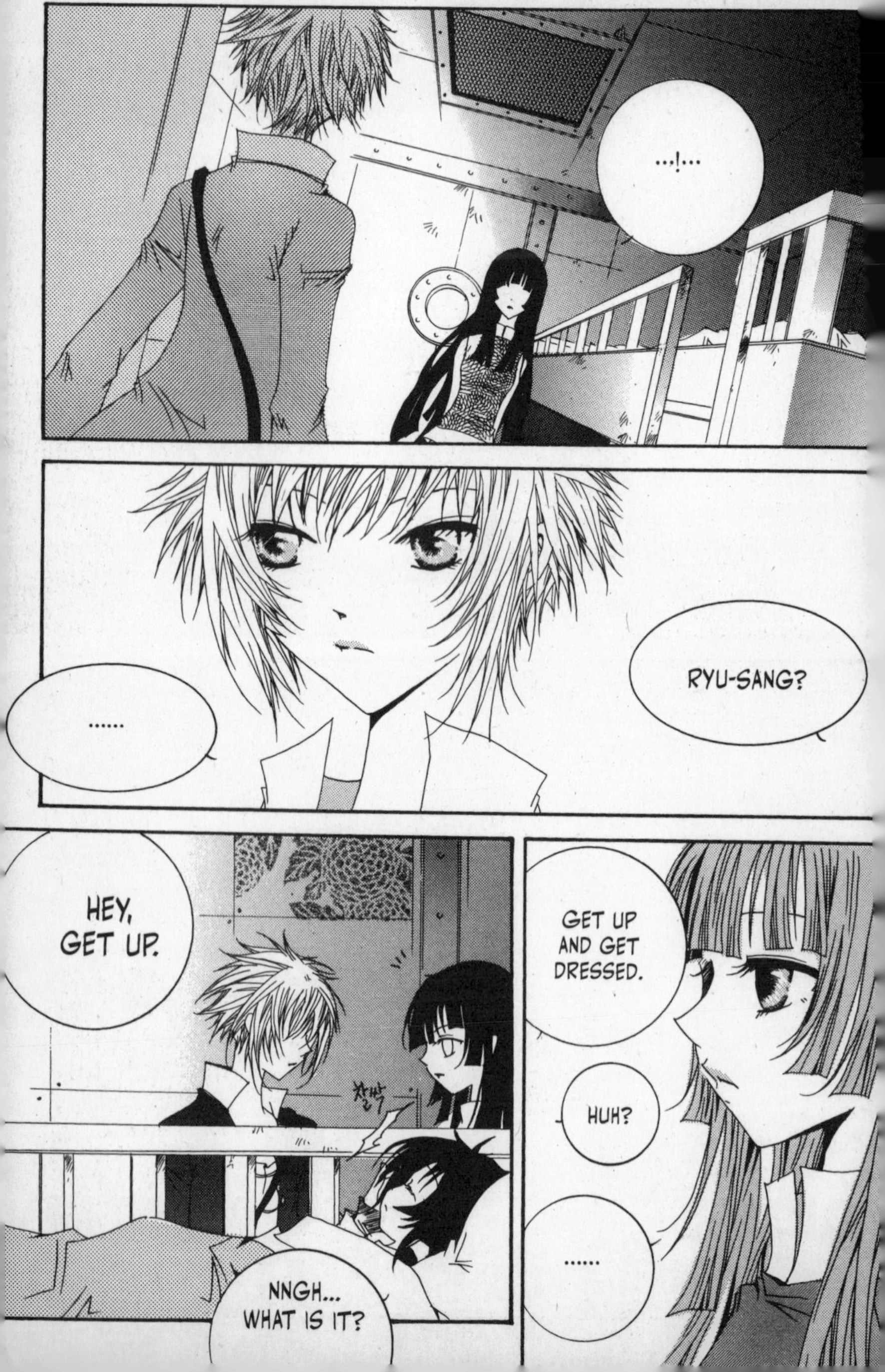
...!...
......
RYU-SANG?
HEY, GET UP.
NNGH... WHAT IS IT?
GET UP AND GET DRESSED.
HUH?
......

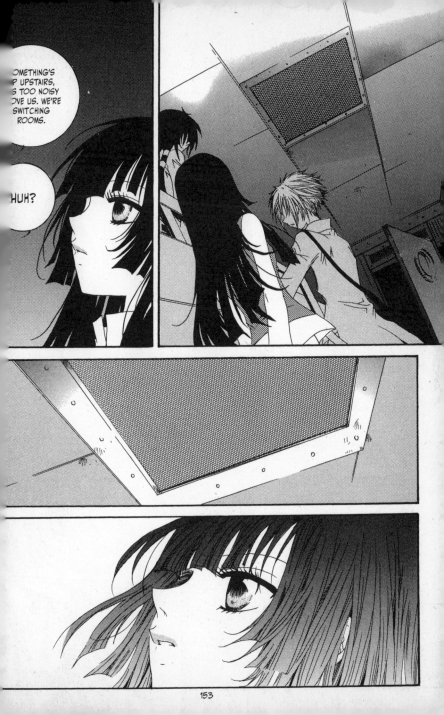

SOMETHING'S
UP UPSTAIRS,
IT'S TOO NOISY
ABOVE US. WE'RE
SWITCHING
ROOMS.

HUH?

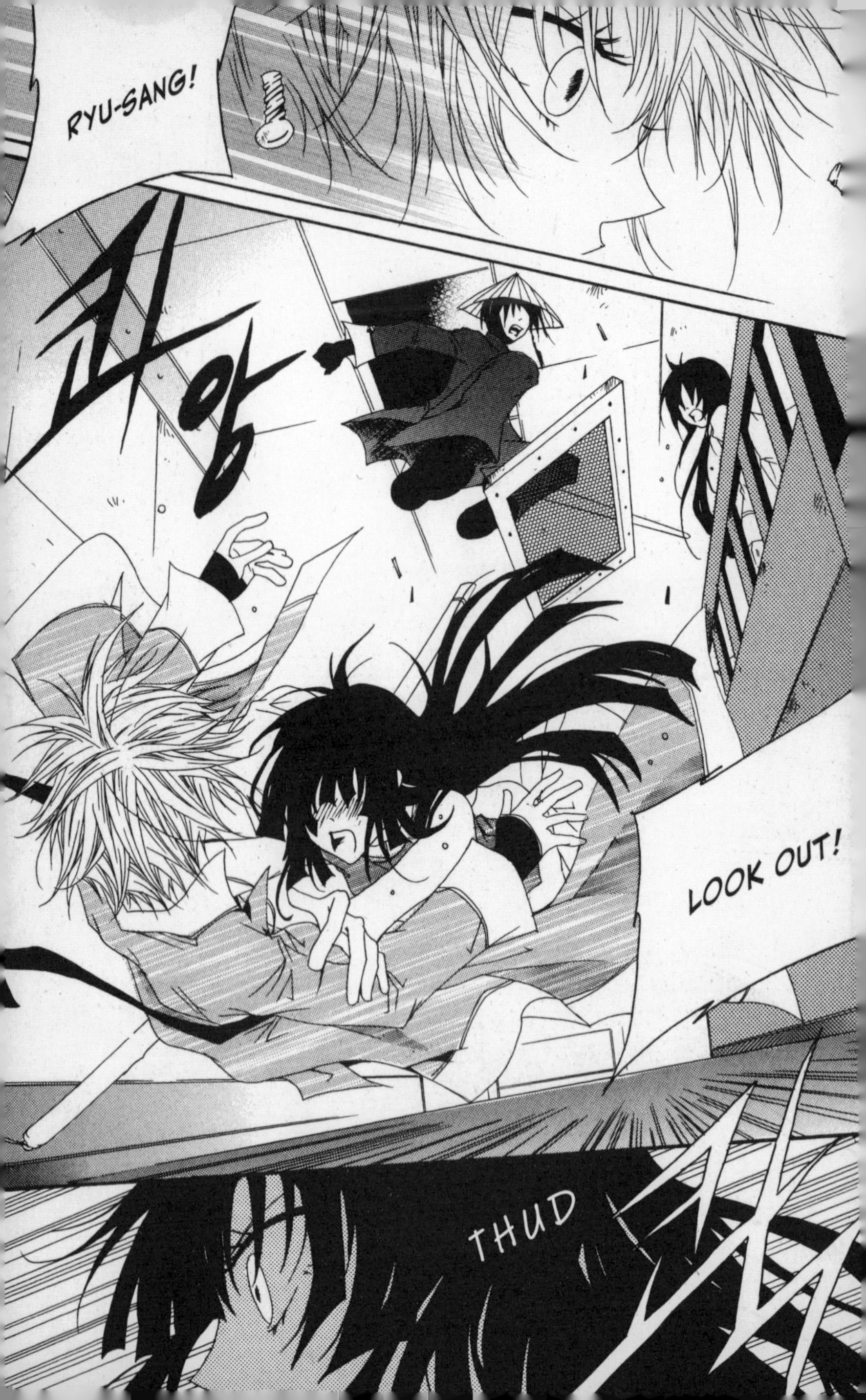
RYU-SANG!
콰앙
LOOK OUT!
THUD

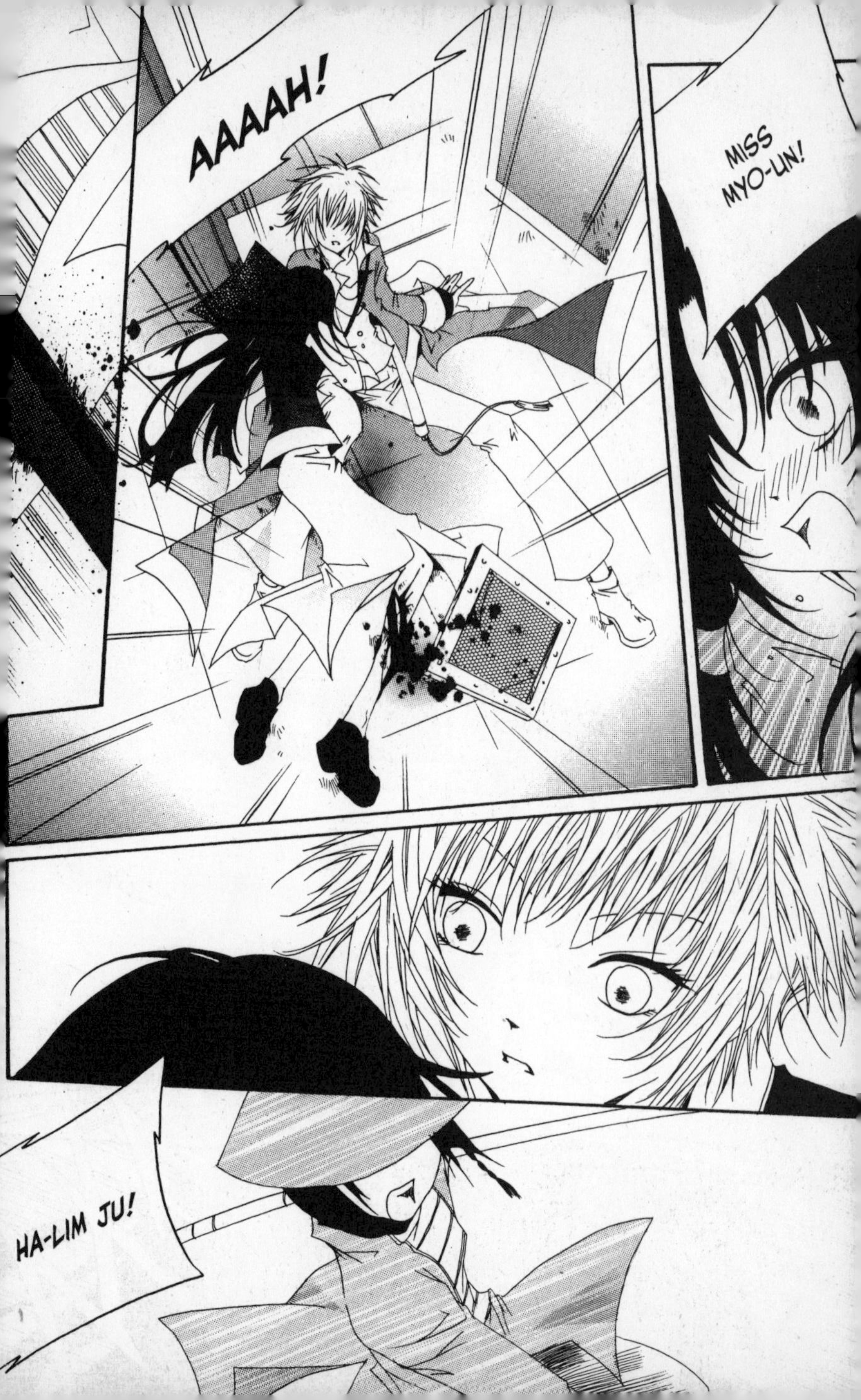
AAAAH!
MISS MYO-UN!
HA-LIM JU!

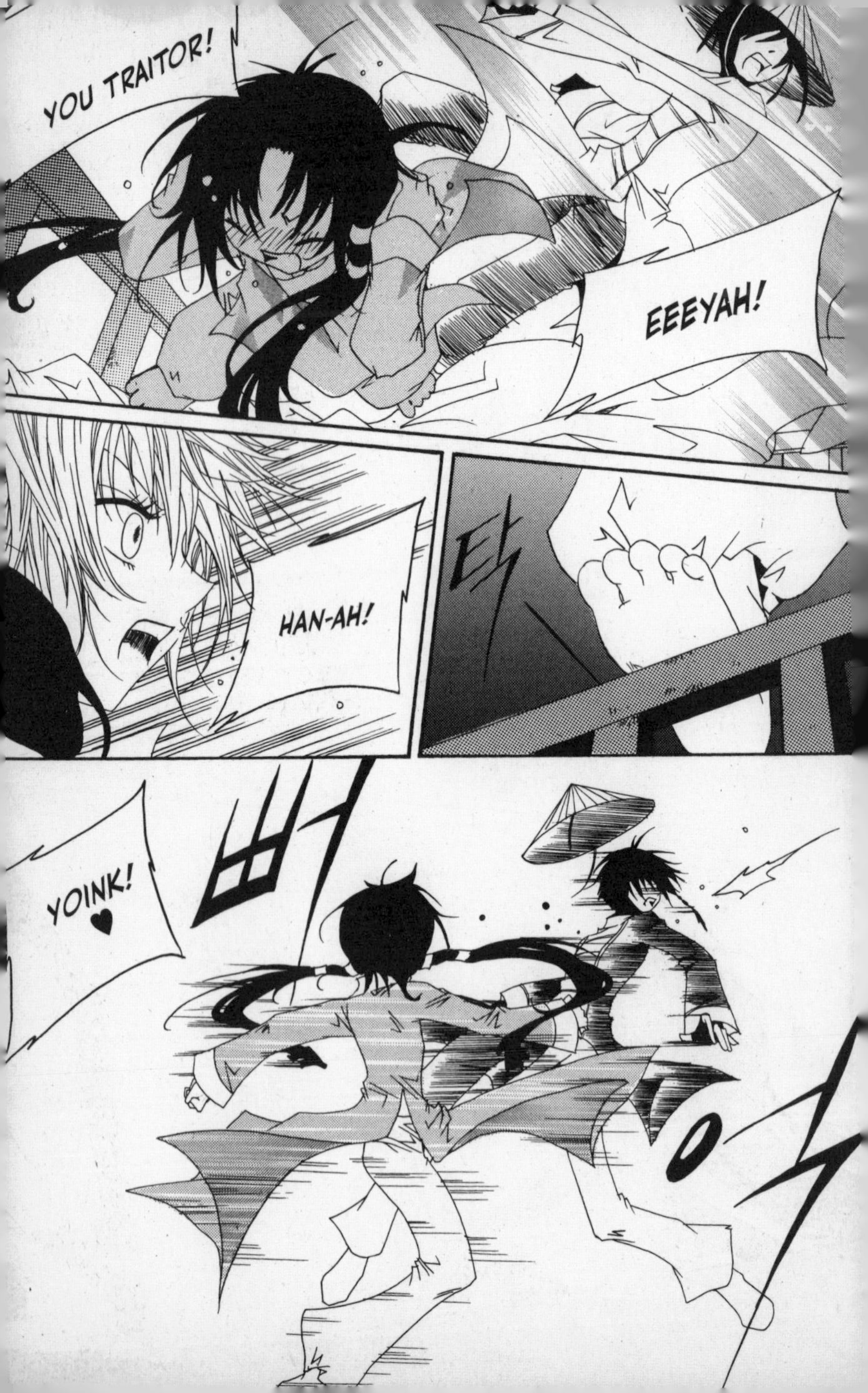
YOU TRAITOR!
EEEYAH!
HAN-AH!
YOINK! ♥

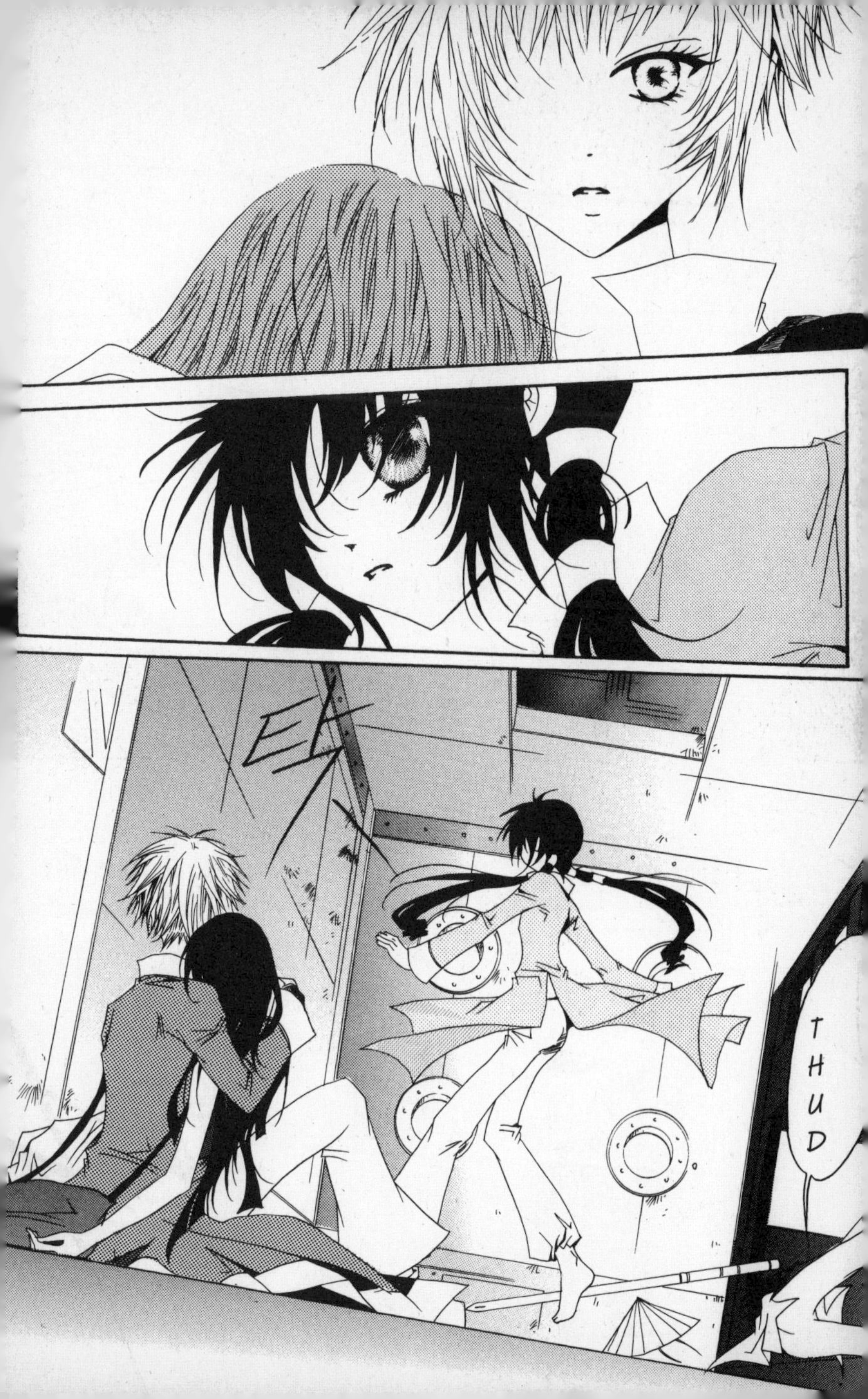
THUD

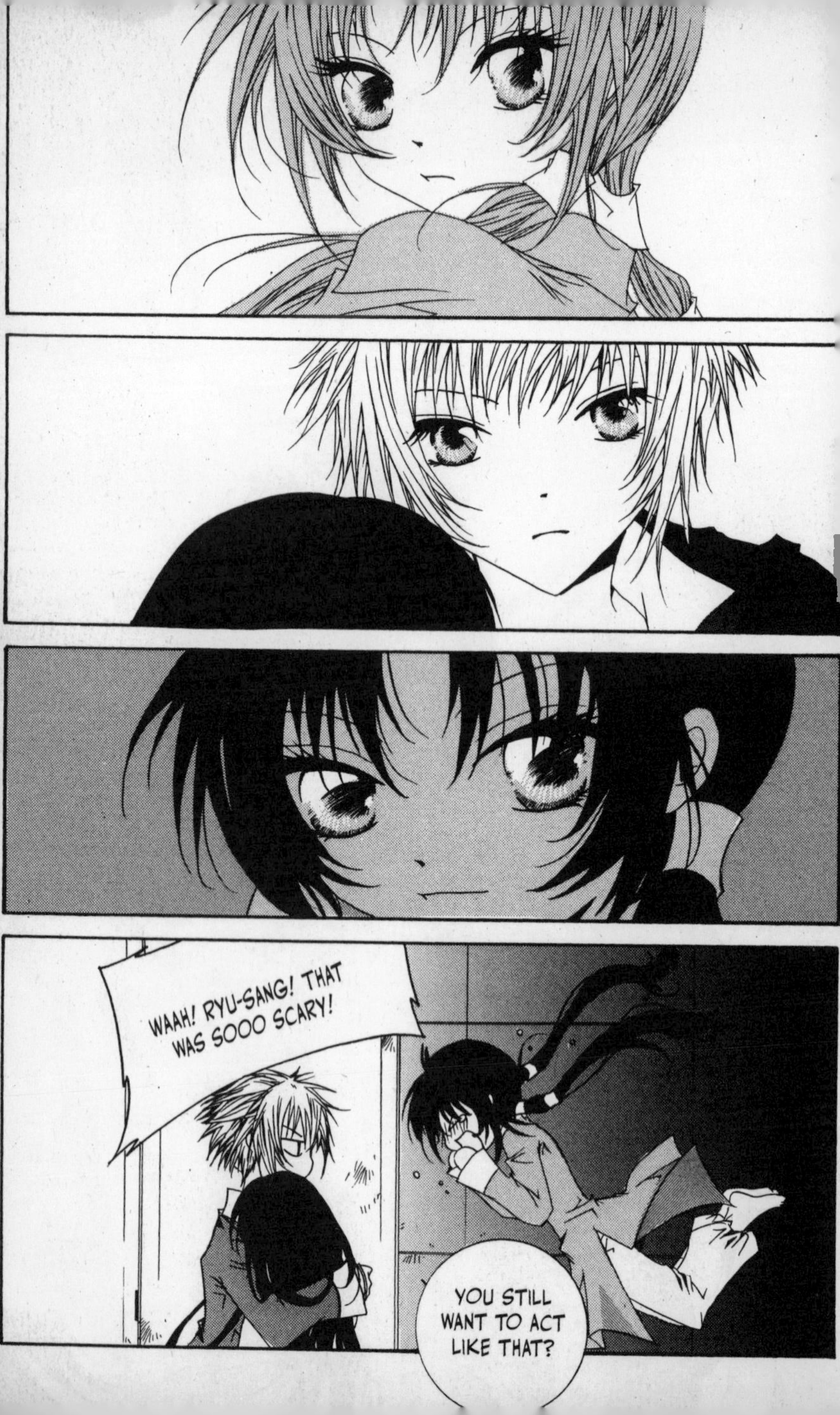
WAAH! RYU-SANG! THAT WAS SOOO SCARY!
YOU STILL WANT TO ACT LIKE THAT?

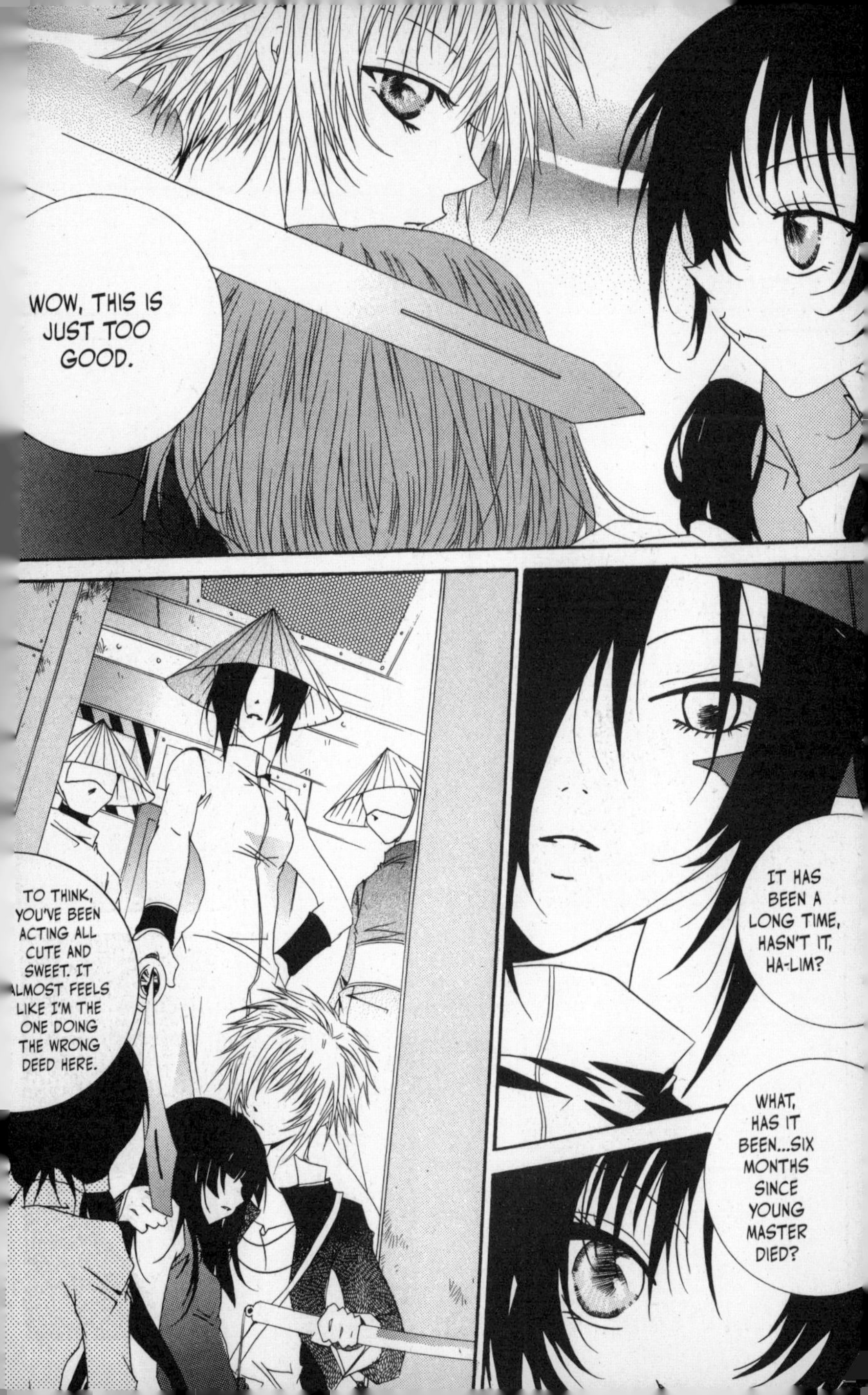
WOW, THIS IS JUST TOO GOOD.
TO THINK, YOU'VE BEEN ACTING ALL CUTE AND SWEET. IT ALMOST FEELS LIKE I'M THE ONE DOING THE WRONG DEED HERE.
IT HAS BEEN A LONG TIME, HASN'T IT, HA-LIM?
WHAT, HAS IT BEEN...SIX MONTHS SINCE YOUNG MASTER DIED?

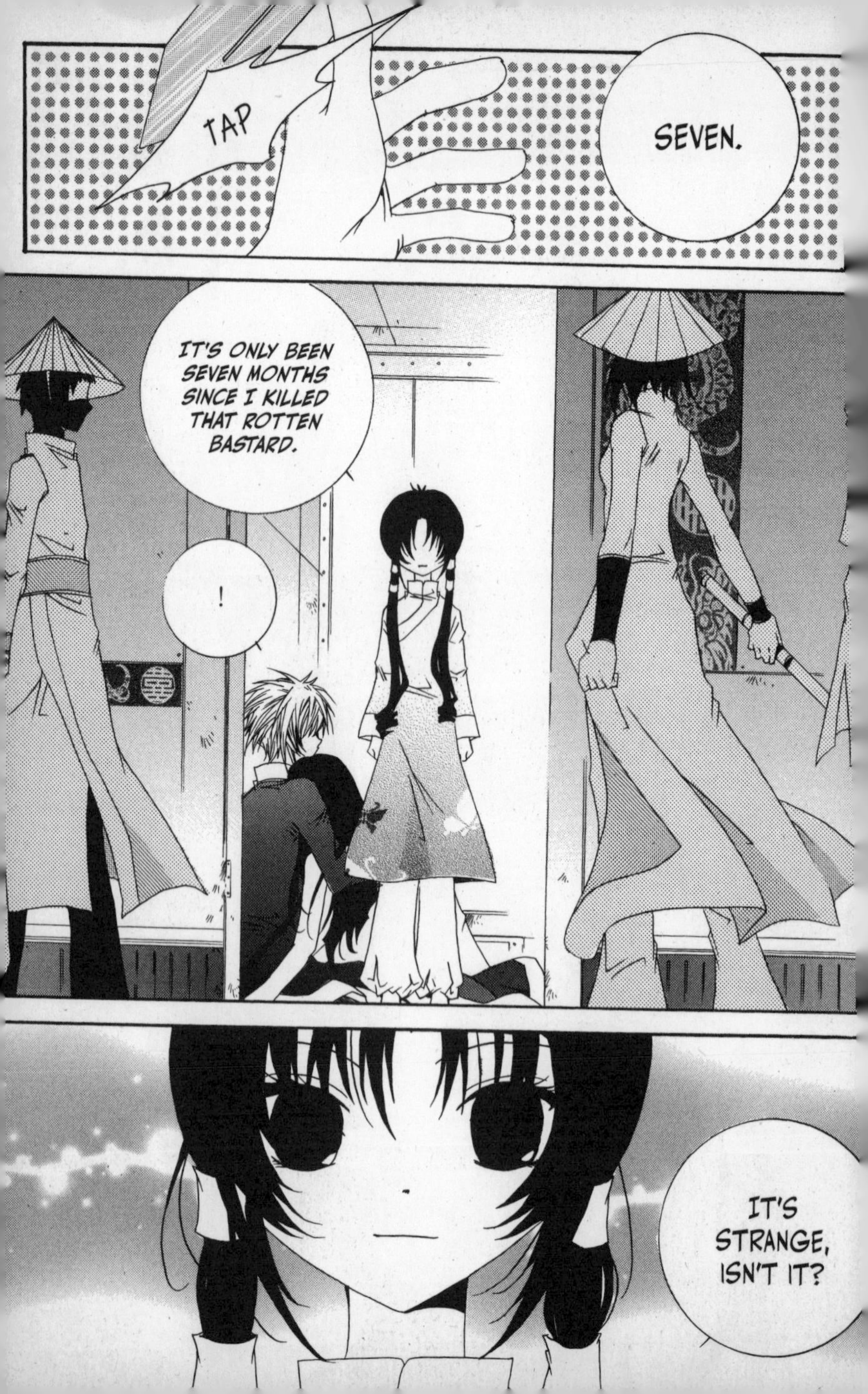
TAP
SEVEN.
IT'S ONLY BEEN SEVEN MONTHS SINCE I KILLED THAT ROTTEN BASTARD.
!
IT'S STRANGE, ISN'T IT?

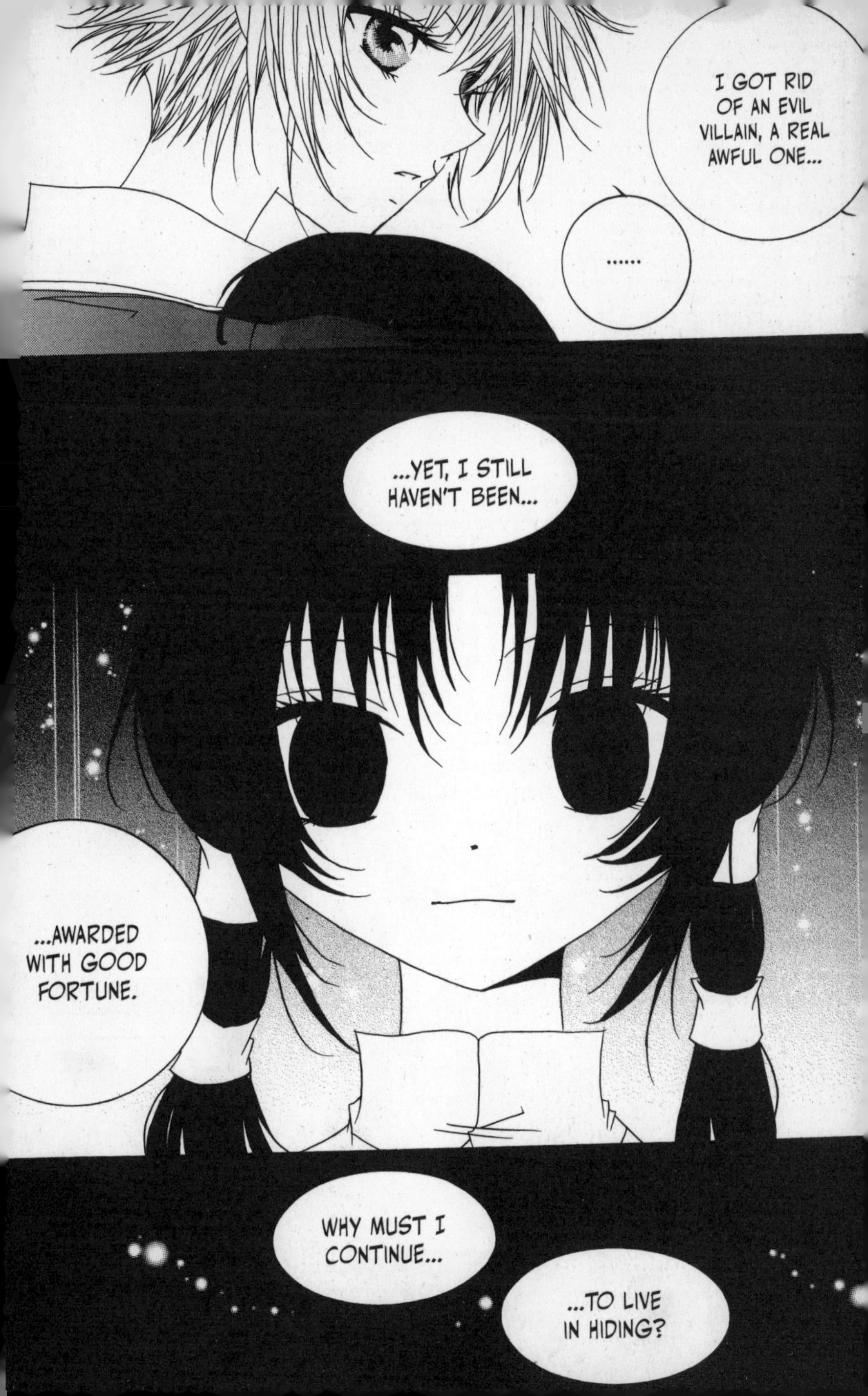
I GOT RID OF AN EVIL VILLAIN, A REAL AWFUL ONE...
......
...YET, I STILL HAVEN'T BEEN...
...AWARDED WITH GOOD FORTUNE.
WHY MUST I CONTINUE...
...TO LIVE IN HIDING?

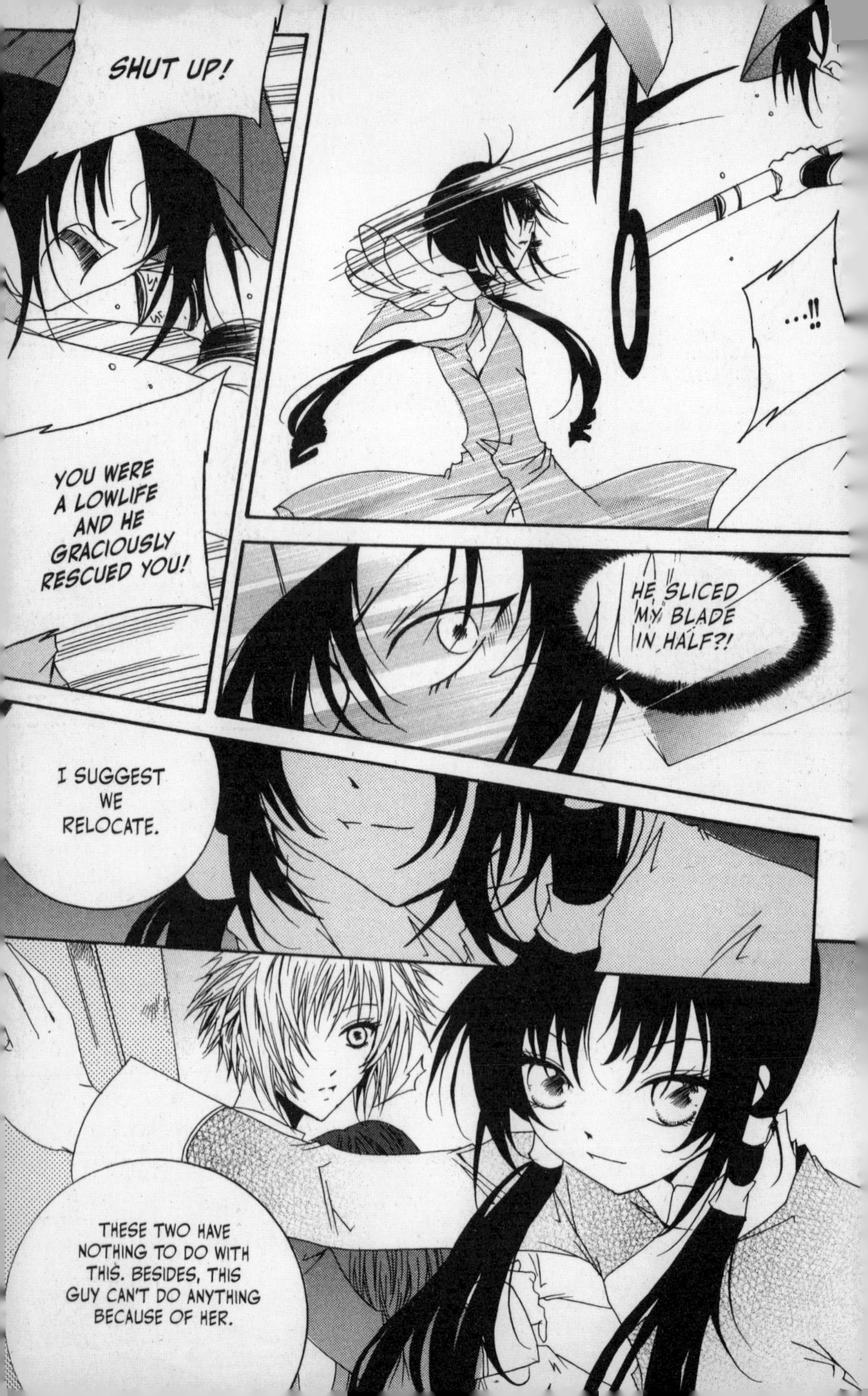
SHUT UP!
YOU WERE A LOWLIFE AND HE GRACIOUSLY RESCUED YOU!
...!!
HE SLICED MY BLADE IN HALF?!
I SUGGEST WE RELOCATE.
THESE TWO HAVE NOTHING TO DO WITH THIS. BESIDES, THIS GUY CAN'T DO ANYTHING BECAUSE OF HER.

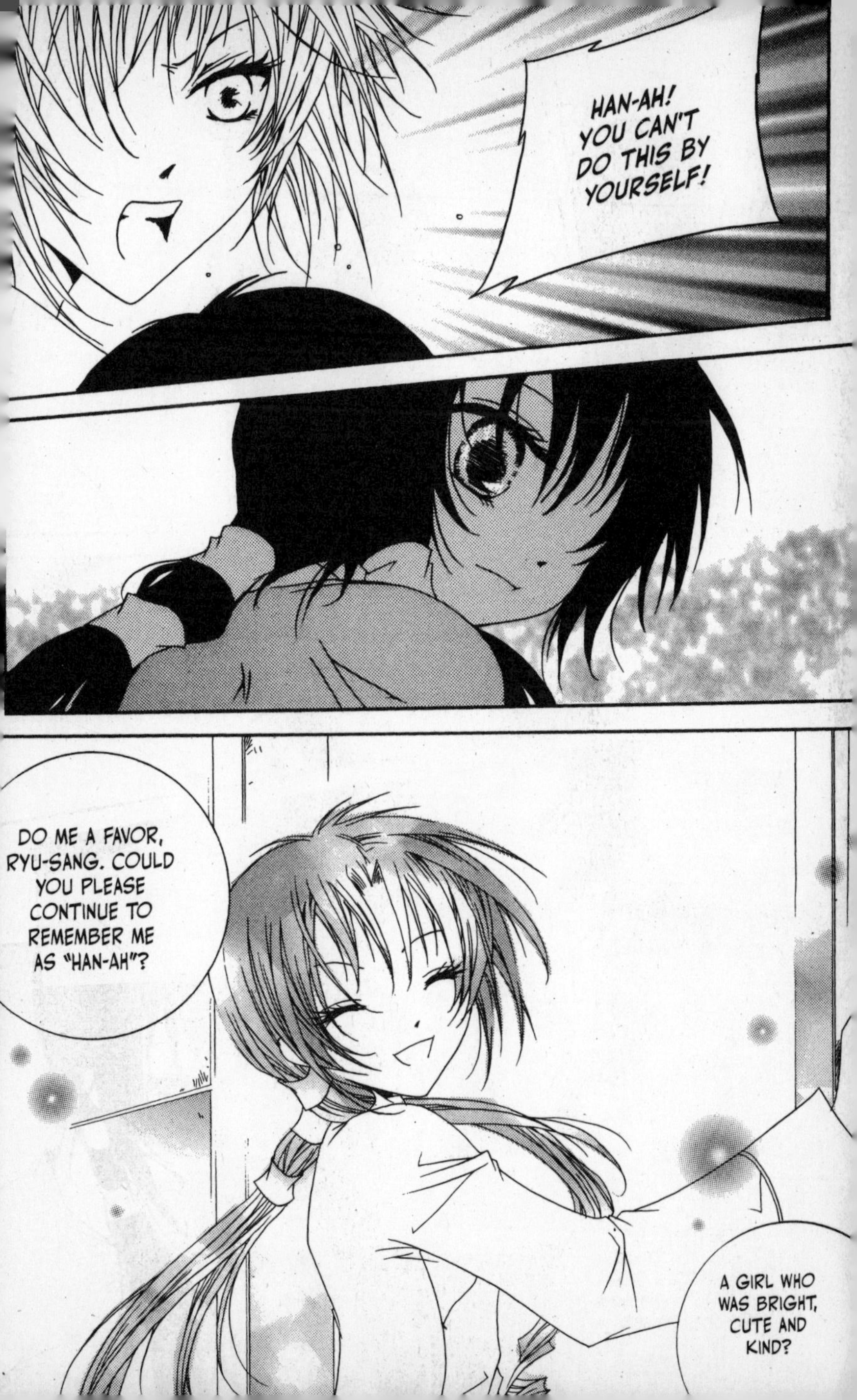
HAN-AH! YOU CAN'T DO THIS BY YOURSELF!
DO ME A FAVOR, RYU-SANG. COULD YOU PLEASE CONTINUE TO REMEMBER ME AS "HAN-AH"?
A GIRL WHO WAS BRIGHT, CUTE AND KIND?

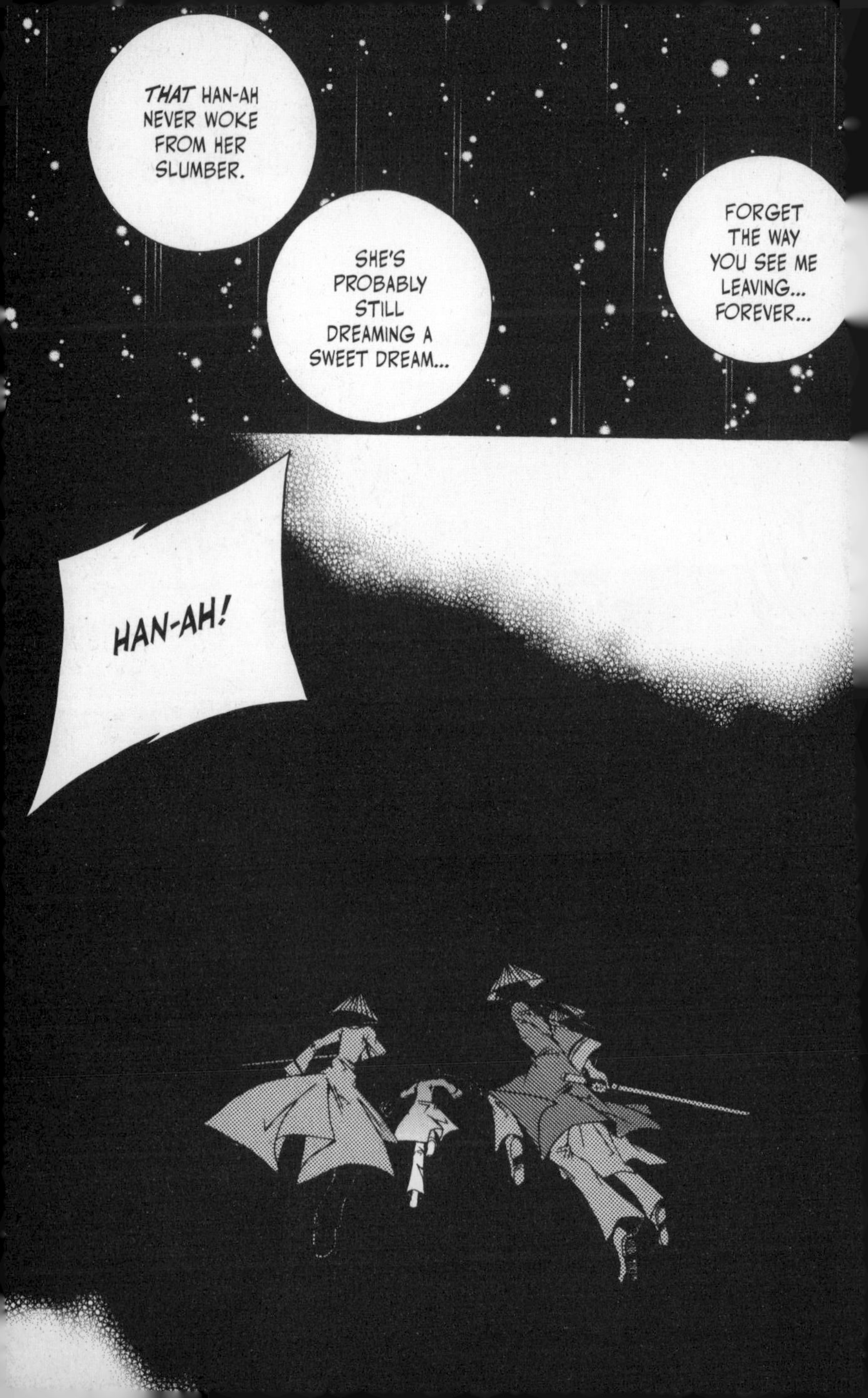
THAT HAN-AH NEVER WOKE FROM HER SLUMBER.
SHE'S PROBABLY STILL DREAMING A SWEET DREAM...
FORGET THE WAY YOU SEE ME LEAVING... FOREVER...
HAN-AH!

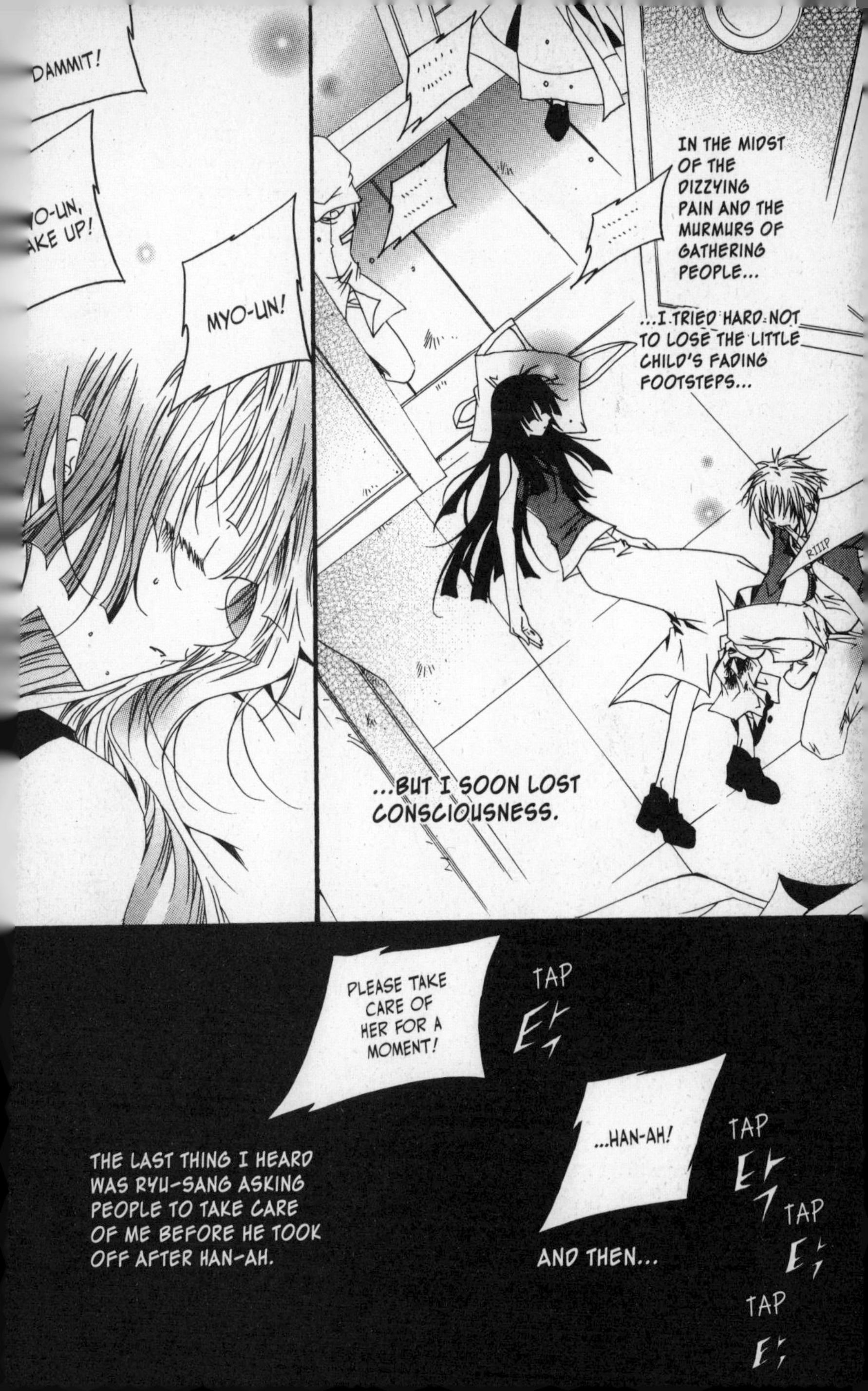
DAMMIT!
YO-UN, AKE UP!
MYO-UN!
IN THE MIDST OF THE DIZZYING PAIN AND THE MURMURS OF GATHERING PEOPLE...
...I TRIED HARD NOT TO LOSE THE LITTLE CHILD'S FADING FOOTSTEPS...
RIIIP
...BUT I SOON LOST CONSCIOUSNESS.
PLEASE TAKE CARE OF HER FOR A MOMENT!
TAP
...HAN-AH!
THE LAST THING I HEARD WAS RYU-SANG ASKING PEOPLE TO TAKE CARE OF ME BEFORE HE TOOK OFF AFTER HAN-AH.
TAP
AND THEN...
TAP
TAP

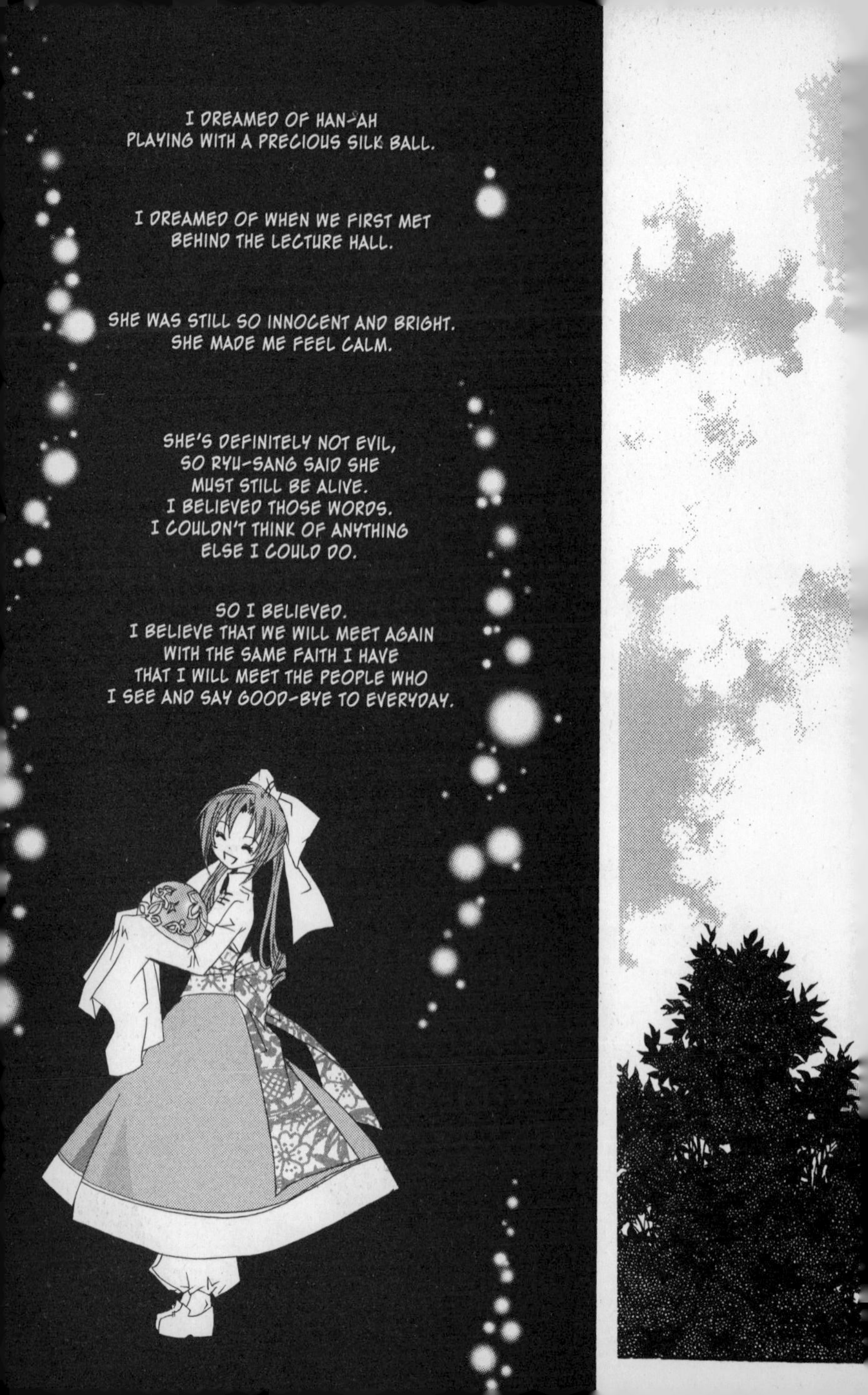
I DREAMED OF HAN-AH
PLAYING WITH A PRECIOUS SILK BALL.
I DREAMED OF WHEN WE FIRST MET
BEHIND THE LECTURE HALL.
SHE WAS STILL SO INNOCENT AND BRIGHT.
SHE MADE ME FEEL CALM.
SHE'S DEFINITELY NOT EVIL,
SO RYU-SANG SAID SHE
MUST STILL BE ALIVE.
I BELIEVED THOSE WORDS.
I COULDN'T THINK OF ANYTHING
ELSE I COULD DO.
SO I BELIEVED.
I BELIEVE THAT WE WILL MEET AGAIN
WITH THE SAME FAITH I HAVE
THAT I WILL MEET THE PEOPLE WHO
I SEE AND SAY GOOD-BYE TO EVERYDAY.

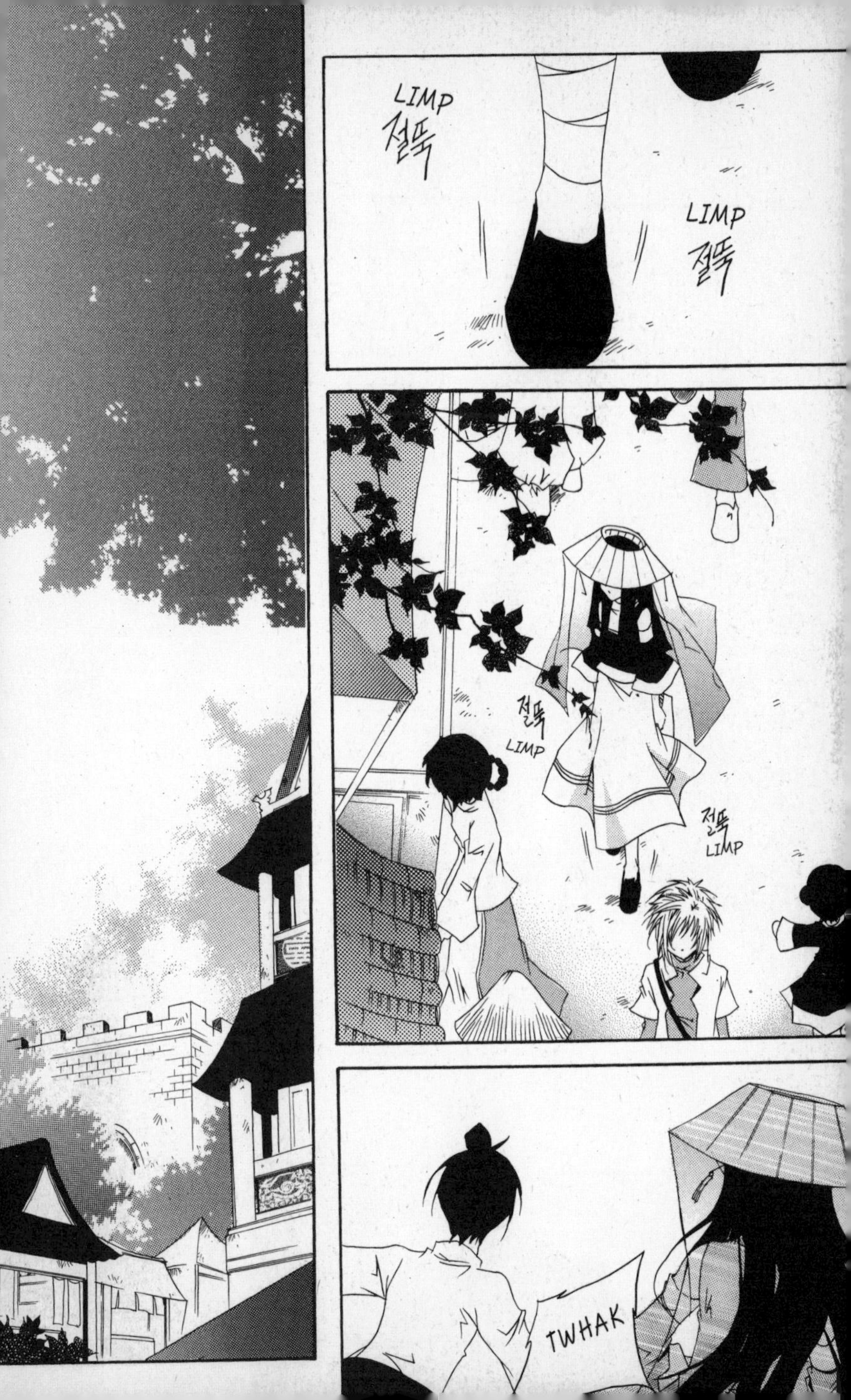
LIMP
절뚝
LIMP
절뚝
절뚝
LIMP
절뚝
LIMP
TWHAK

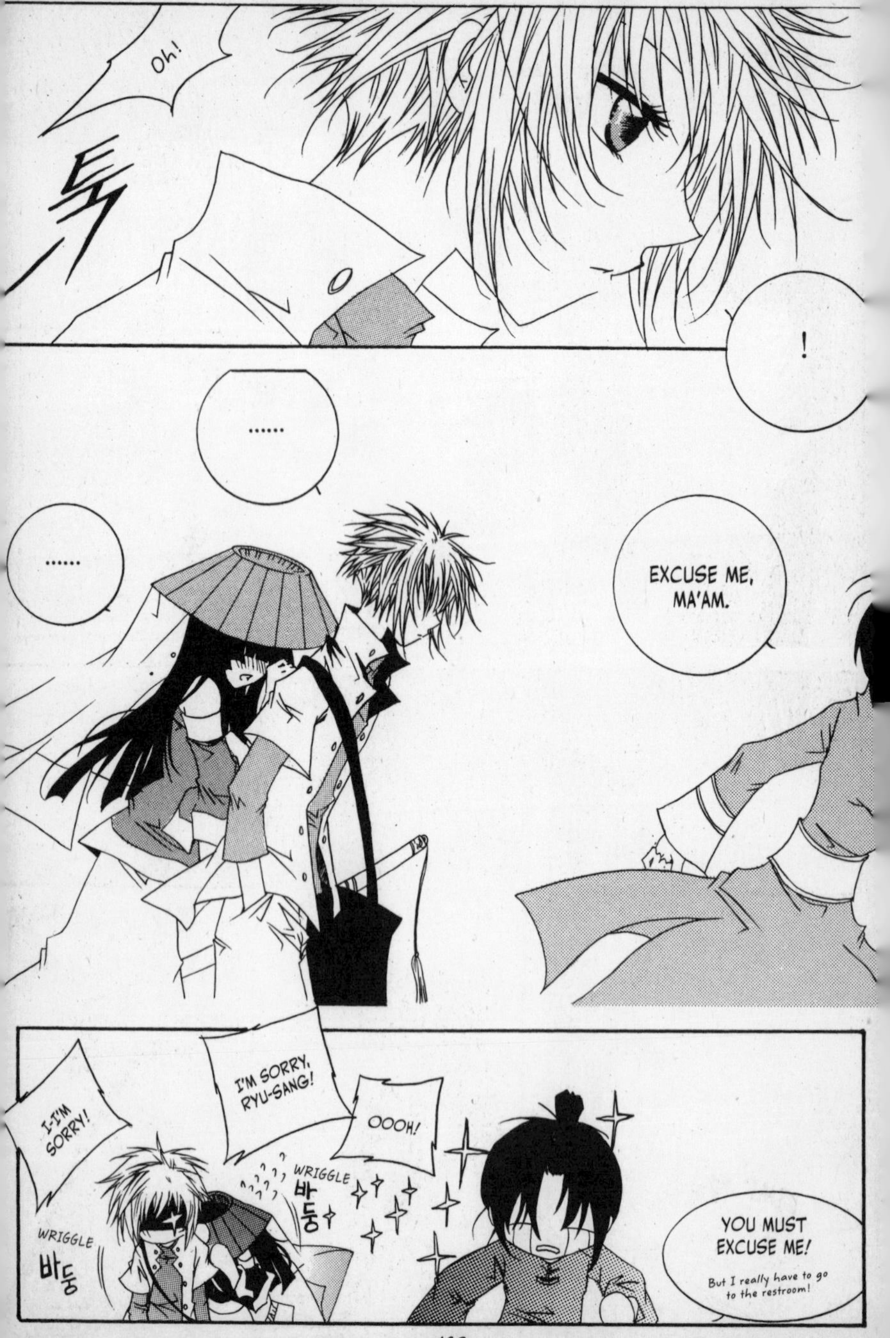
Oh!
!
......
......
EXCUSE ME, MA'AM.
I-I'M SORRY!
I'M SORRY, RYU-SANG!
OOOH!
WRIGGLE
바둥
WRIGGLE
바둥
YOU MUST EXCUSE ME!
But I really have to go to the restroom!

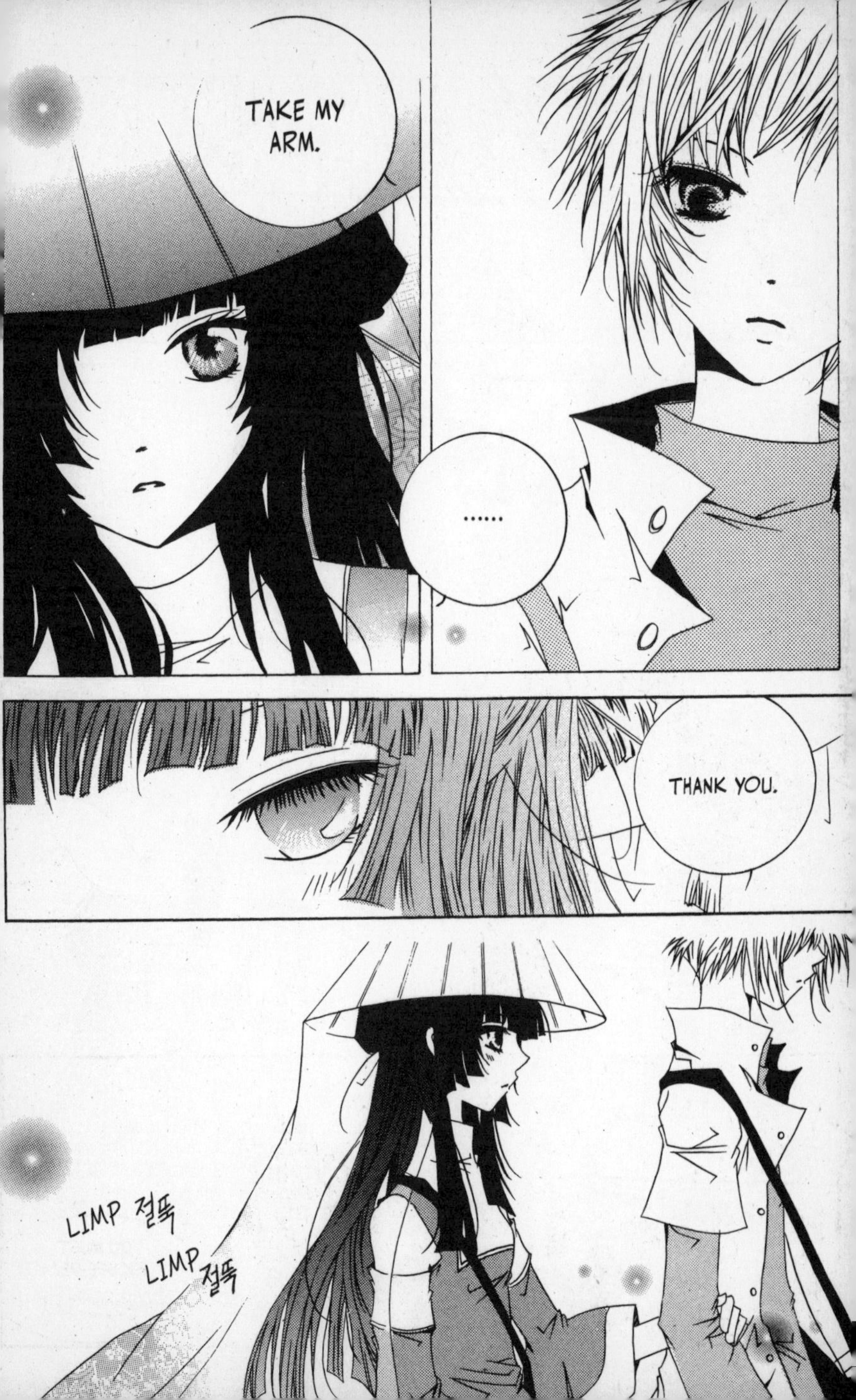
TAKE MY ARM.
......
THANK YOU.
LIMP 절뚝
LIMP 절뚝

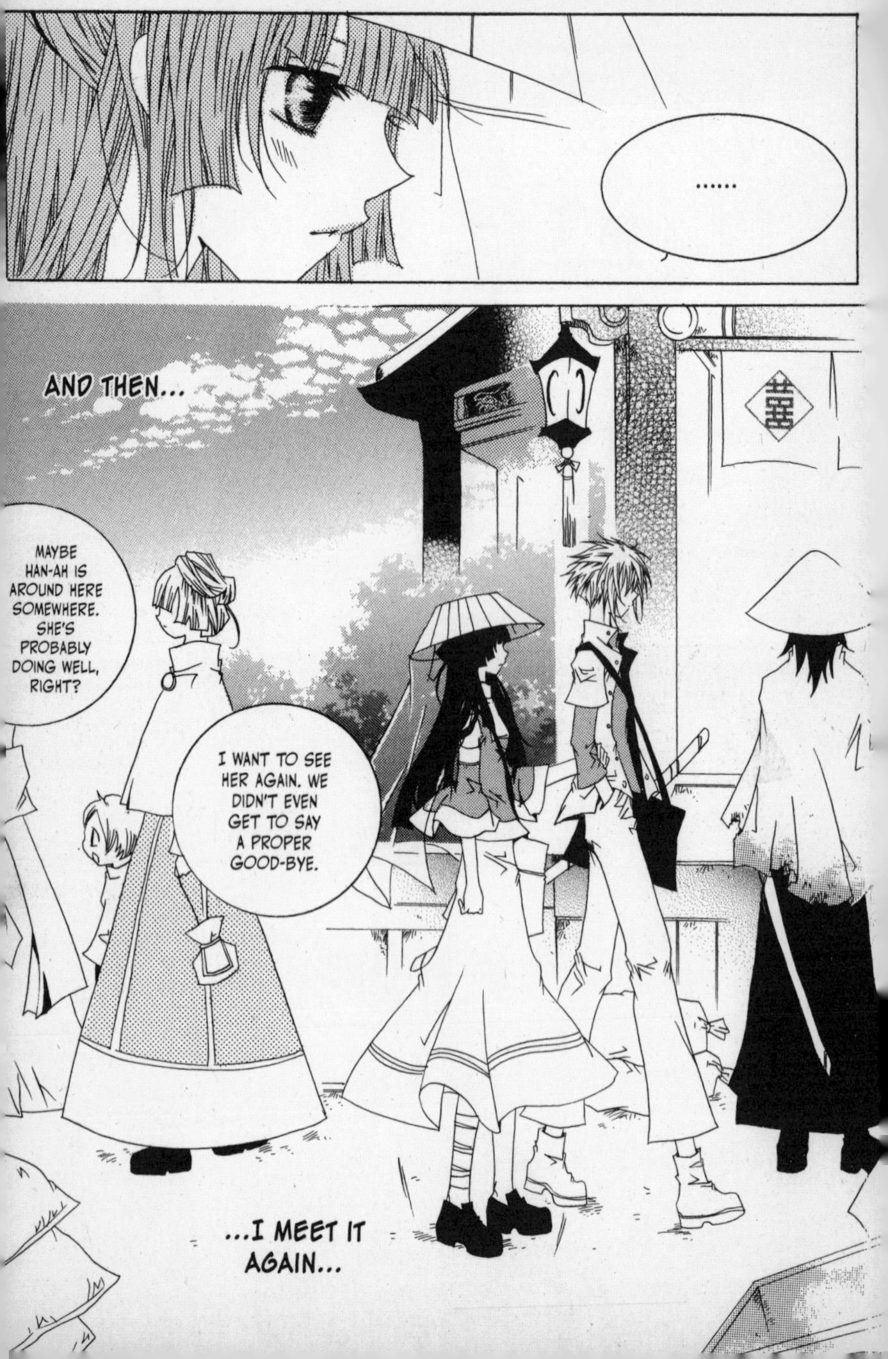
......
AND THEN...
MAYBE HAN-AH IS AROUND HERE SOMEWHERE. SHE'S PROBABLY DOING WELL, RIGHT?
I WANT TO SEE HER AGAIN. WE DIDN'T EVEN GET TO SAY A PROPER GOOD-BYE.
...I MEET IT AGAIN...

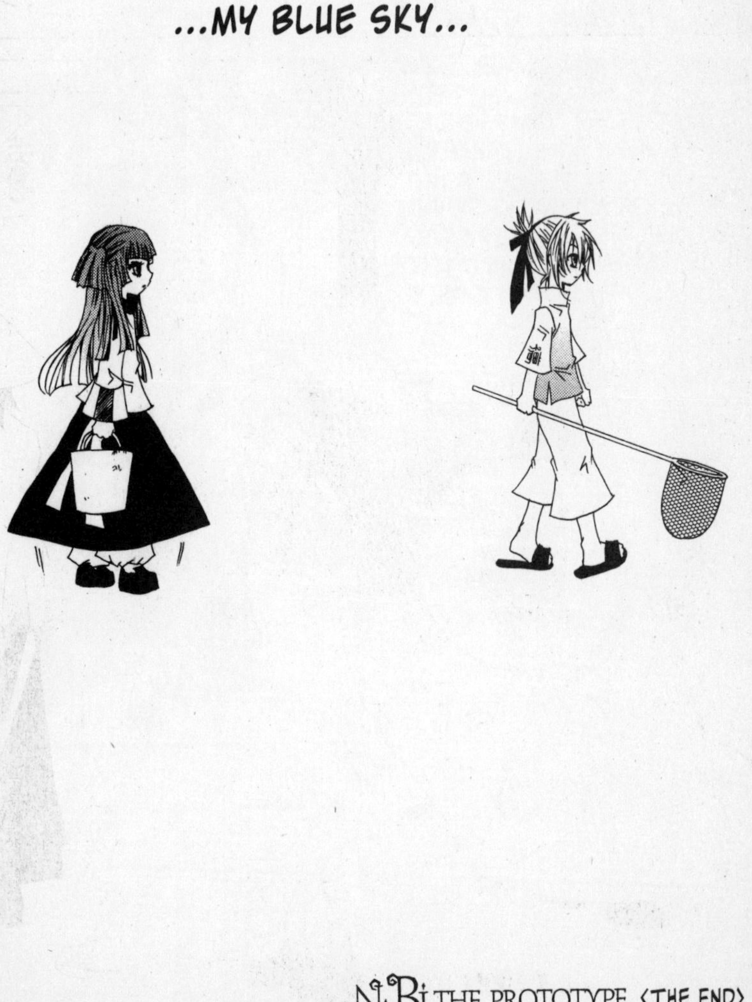
...MY BLUE SKY...
NABI THE PROTOTYPE ‹THE END›

THE FIRST STORY, "ASH TREE," IS FROM 2002, AND THE LAST STORY, "GLASS BALL," IS FROM 2005. (YIKES!)

SOME OF YOU MAY KNOW THAT THESE ARE SIDE STORIES TO AN UPCOMING SERIES CALLED *NABI*. WHEN I GET A CHANCE, I'D LIKE TO WORK ON THAT.

WHEN THE BOOK BY THE SAME TITLE COMES OUT IN THE FUTURE, PLEASE GIVE IT A READ. AND THEN FIND OUT HOW THE CHARACTERS IN THIS STORY INTERTWINE WITH EACH OTHER.

THANK YOU FOR READING.

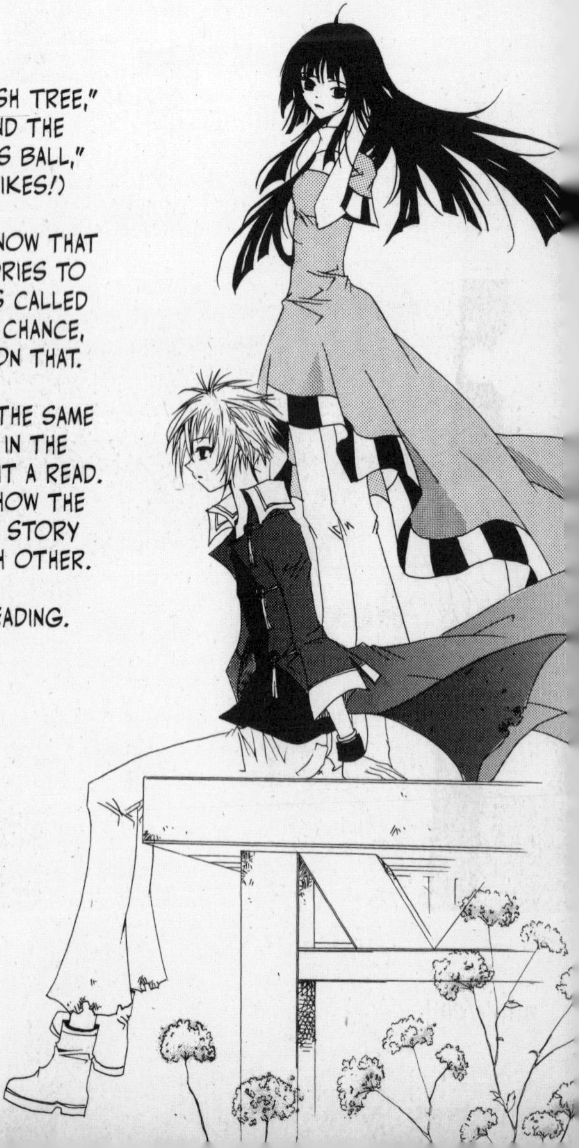

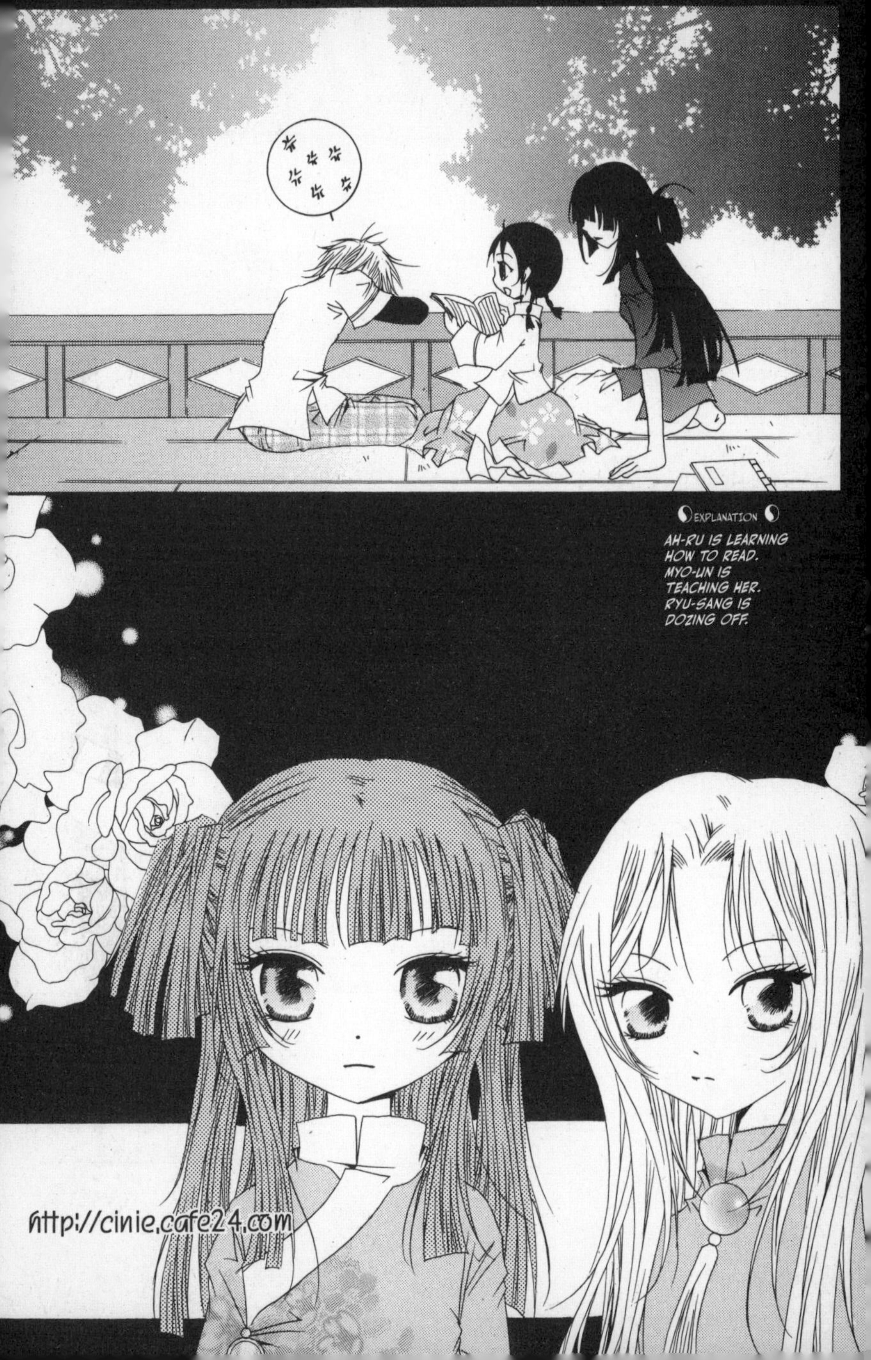
EXPLANATION
AH-RU IS LEARNING HOW TO READ. MYO-UN IS TEACHING HER. RYU-SANG IS DOZING OFF.
http://cinie.cafe24.com

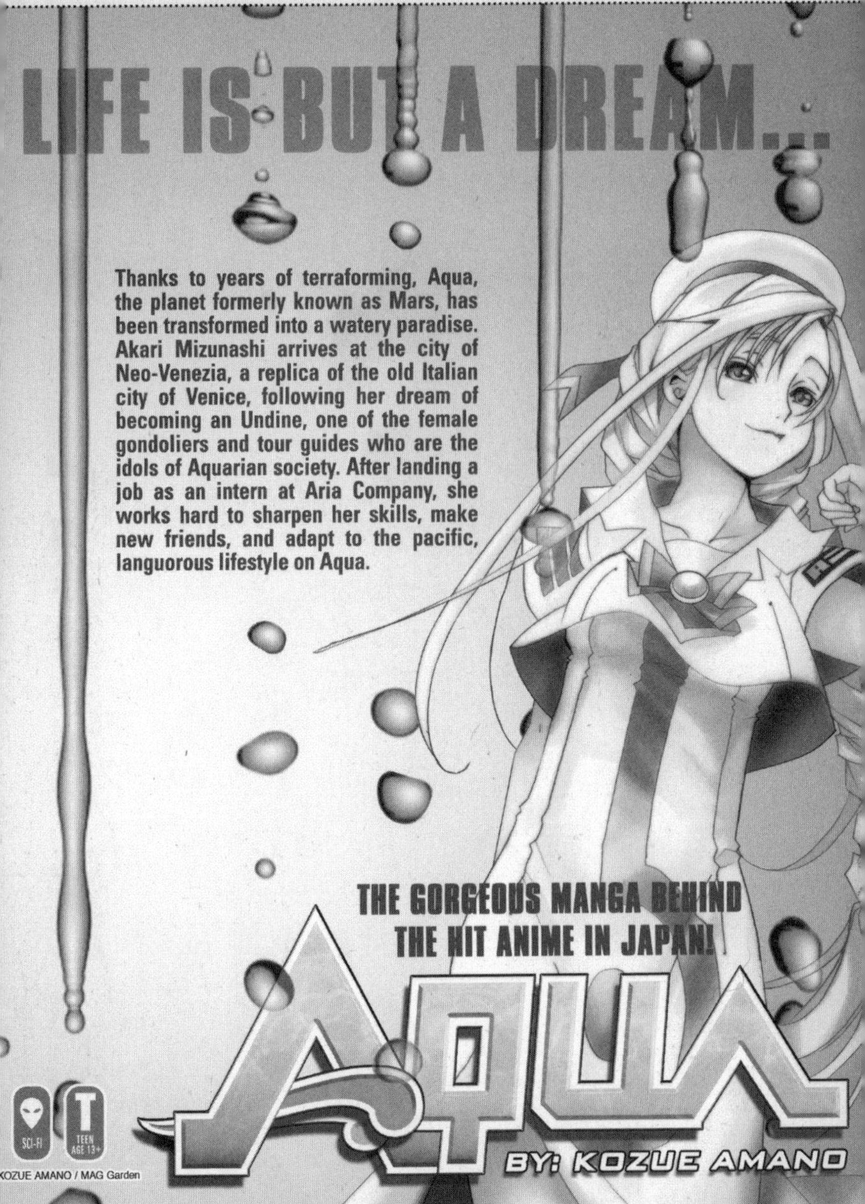
LIFE IS BUT A DREAM....
Thanks to years of terraforming, Aqua, the planet formerly known as Mars, has been transformed into a watery paradise. Akari Mizunashi arrives at the city of Neo-Venezia, a replica of the old Italian city of Venice, following her dream of becoming an Undine, one of the female gondoliers and tour guides who are the idols of Aquarian society. After landing a job as an intern at Aria Company, she works hard to sharpen her skills, make new friends, and adapt to the pacific, languorous lifestyle on Aqua.
THE GORGEOUS MANGA BEHIND THE HIT ANIME IN JAPAN!
AQUA
BY: KOZUE AMANO
SCI-FI
T
TEEN AGE 13+
© KOZUE AMANO / MAG Garden

A kiss sweeter than poison
SHINSHOKU KISS
From the creator of tactics!
An exciting new story filled with beautiful girls and boys, black magic and enchanted spirits by the co-creator of tactics! Aspiring teen doll maker Kotoko Kashiwagi always dreamt of meeting her idol, the famous doll maker "Fool." But when the two meet, Kotoko finds herself not just under Fool's spell, but cursed to be his servant--or else!
DRAMA
OT
OLDER TEEN AGE 16+
© 2004 KAZUKO HIGASHIYAMA.